The
NEW
MEDIA

The NEW MEDIA

FOREWORD BY ROBERT JOHANSEN

Communication, Research, and Technology

RONALD E. RICE

James H. Bair
Milton Chen
John Dimmick
David M. Dozier
Mary Ellen Jacob
Bonnie McDaniel Johnson

W. David Penniman
Lynne L. Svenning
Everett M. Rogers
Eric W. Rothenbuhler
John E. Ruchinskas
Frederick Williams

 SAGE PUBLICATIONS Beverly Hills London New Delhi

For information address:

SAGE Publications, Inc.
275 South Beverly Drive
Beverly Hills, California 90212

SAGE Publications India Pvt. Ltd.
C-236 Defence Colony
New Delhi 110 024, India

SAGE Publications Ltd
28 Banner Street
London EC1Y 8QE, England

Printed in the United States of America

Library of Congress Cataloging in Publication Data

Main entry under title:

The new media.

1. Mass media—Research. 2. Mass media—Technological innovations. I. Rice, Ronald E.
P91.3.N49   1984   001.51   84-3287
ISBN 0-8039-2271-X
ISBN 0-8039-2272-8 (pbk.)

FIRST PRINTING

Contents

Foreword

Robert Johansen
Institute for the Future

As new fields evolve, there are periodic attempts to take stock of what's happened so far, how things are going, and what still needs to be done. This book is one such attempt, and it is a good one.

Newcomers to the new media will find an overview, including a taste of many important concepts and results. Those from business settings will be introduced to well-trained academic researchers. Those from academic disciplines other than communications research will find a collection of views from specialists in the new media. And communications researchers will find Ron Rice's view of the uses and impacts of the new media, as well as a call to action. The book is patient and encouraging for newcomers; it is critical and a bit impatient with communications researchers for not acting more quickly in this new field.

There is a definite attempt in the book to do bridge building: between university and business, between research and policy, and between traditional and novel research approaches. This bridge building is successful, even though the book is more of a collection than an integrated plan. The choice here was diversity versus cohesiveness, and the lead author leaned toward diversity. Indeed, it can be argued that such a choice is reflective of the current state of the new media: They are not neatly organized and certainly not integrated.

Ron Rice points out an apparent lag in responses of academic researchers to the new media. He makes a plea for more active responses by those who should be best trained to study uses and impacts—particularly the discipline of communications research. It's a convincing argument. I certainly hope this book will be adopted for university courses and will stimulate new avenues of research. Beyond academia, I hope the book will stimulate business users and vendors of the new media to learn from the basic methodologies of communications research. Communications research can provide useful tools and results for business, but only if researchers recognize opportunities to apply their skills and business people express an openness to learn from the teachers.

This book should convince you of the importance of the new media. It should also convince you that there are competent people out there ready to tackle the challenge of understanding impacts. But there are still questions about whether communications research—or any other academic discipline—is ready to respond aggressively. This book issues a challenge, waiting to be answered.

The frequent excursions into communications theory remind us how much work is relevant, yet how little is known with certainty. Research to date provides no straightforward answers regarding uses and impacts of the new media. It does, however, provide valuable perspectives that can assist greatly as challenges of the new media are tackled. A careful reading of this book will certainly help avoid remaking old mistakes. For creative readers, it will also help in building new approaches to assessing uses and impacts of the new media.

The book will not be easy reading for everyone, however. The extensive citations, for example, provide useful follow-up sources, but they will also bog down the nonacademic reader. Such a reader may also be disappointed that more business conclusions are not drawn directly. It is not that there are no business lessons to learn. They are there and they are significant; but the business reader will need to do some work to pull them out. In short, the book will feel more comfortable to academics than business people. I recommend that the latter stay with the task, however, because there are useful conclusions to be gained. The new media will have major effects on business, and the early fruits will be seen in competitive advantages for the innovators. This book provides a source for many insights, even though some of them are not yet translated into business applications or terminology.

The table of contents reveals the diverse range of topics to be covered: new media research, theories, evaluation methods, electronic news reading, mediated group communication, word processing, productivity, teleconferencing, libraries, computers and children, and media displacement. Certainly this list reflects the broad range of areas affected by the new media. But there is also potential confusion for a reader here, particularly one who ventures a cover-to-cover excursion. I'd recommend a cafeteria approach—starting with the early chapters as appetizers and sampling those topics that are most interesting to you. Later passes through the book can then provide additional perspectives in topic areas that did not catch your fancy on the first pass. In short, it will be an excellent reference work for many people; I expect to refer to it frequently.

One thing that will become clear to readers is that the new media are shaking the foundations of how communications can occur. Designations such as "mass media," "interactive," "broadcast," and even "communications" are being redefined on-the-fly. The scale of impacts is staggering. The potential uses are intriguing. The impacts are puzzling.

I finished the book longing for a conclusion. On second thought, perhaps the neat wrap-up I craved would have been inappropriate: a freezing of what is obviously fluid as we read this book today. No, the conclusions are up to each of us as readers. Rice and his collaborators have given us a valuable resource with insights about where the new media are now and what needs to be done. But the way is not clear and the conclusion cannot be written—at least not yet. And that's one big reason why the new media are so exciting.

Preface

There can be no doubt that new communication media pervade our homes, offices, institutions, and, in some countries, our societies. Popular, trade, and academic journals cover developments weekly, and new publications appear to explain or predict the latest trends. It is my hope that this book makes a contribution to the recent and growing literature on new communication media.

The *communication* in "communication media" is emphasized here, because this book is intended to fill a noticeable communication gap. There are actually three gaps. One is between policy and current academic research. There have been numerous noteworthy works concerning issues of telecommunications and social policy (some more anecdotal, some more theoretical; others more economic or legal in orientation), and there have been conference proceedings of research results. The research results have generally been too inaccessible or too diffuse to be of much use to policymakers. The second is between lay-oriented, management texts on how actually to use new media in the organization, and very abstract or propositional statements about the future of the office (though there are two or three notable exceptions). The third is disciplinary in nature. There are as yet only a few books on new media that take a communication perspective.

The New Media: Communication, Research, and Technology is intended to fill the first gap by providing state-of-the-art summaries of recent research in one, integrated source. It approaches the second gap by linking this research to applied situations, and by extending current theoretical concerns to these situations. The third gap is considered by taking a predominantly communication perspective in organizing and interpreting research results.

In particular, then, this book fits between futures-oriented technology or policy readings and the array of specific research articles and technical reports that one now has available. It provides a central starting point for becoming familiar with communication and related research on the use and impacts of new media. The scope of this book and the research it reviews is generally bounded by intrapersonal and international levels of analysis. On the micro-level, it does not much consider cognitive psychology and matters of step-by-step processes in perceiving, coordinating, and interpreting information. For example, there is no chapter on the psychological processes involved in the human-computer interface, although there is some discussion of satisfaction toward and use of different software retrieval approaches in Chapter 6. There is much active research in this area, but it seems a year or two away from being presentable in a cohesive, integrated summary to nonspecialists.

At the other end of the boundary, this book does not much consider questions of ideology and politics. This is not because we do not value these perspectives—along with linguistics, historical analysis, or systems engineering—but simply because they are not our (at least my) areas of expertise. Chapter 3 summarizes some of the theoretical positions about theories of the social impacts of telecommunications; Chapter 10 and 12 do consider some economic and political aspects of institutional information systems and media industries. In general, however, these more global analyses are well presented in other books.

William Blake (1946: 77) wrote, as the conclusion to "There is No Natural Religion," that

> If it were not for the Poetic or Prophetic character the
> Philosophic & Experimental would soon be at the ratio of all
> things, and stand still, unable to do other than repeat the same
> dull round over again.

In this book, we do not claim to be either poetic or prophetic; rather, we would like to describe and use the philosophic and experimental to transcend the current ratio of all things. As McLuhan wrote, "Any understanding of social and cultural change is impossible without a knowledge of the way media work as environments" (McLuhan and Fiore, 1967: 26). We choose to report and inspect the philosophical and experimental—primarily empirical investigations into behaviors and attitudes, uses and impacts, of new media—not out of an ignorance of these other perspectives, nor out of a misplaced sense of priority of our approaches, but generally because this is what we are interested in, and in some cases because knowledge at this level is helpful to people. But we at the same time insist that this approach be used to transcend simple technological determinism or presumptuous systems and organizational design, in order to achieve the poetic and prophetic. It is becoming quite clear that new media are forcing us to look at issues such as organization work and ergonomics, which perhaps have been overlooked until now. Social context, media use, and communication content create meaning, form, and consequences of the new media, while new media constrain and shape context, use, and content. The awareness of empirical and micro-level knowledge can inform theory, research, policy, implementation, design, use, social structure, and culture.

The introductions to the four sections of this book provide an overview of the chapters and summarize each with an eye to the issues represented by these gaps. Most chapters discuss a specific new medium (such as videotext or personal computers), but only as an example of theoretic (diffusion of innovations or media competition) or applied (organizational productivity or organizational teleconferencing), concerns of the author or with respect to a particular locus of activity (groups or organizations).

There is at least one major theme running throughout the chapters of this book. Its general emphasis and goal is to integrate the study of new media into the field of communication research. Other writers are arguing for the same process in information science, cognitive psychology, organizational behavior, and education as well as human factors, engineering, and other disciplines. The theme has two arguments. The first is that researchers in subfields such as interpersonal, intercultural, instructional, health, political, organizational, and philosophical communication have considerable theoretical foundations and analytical approaches to apply to situations in which the new media play a role in specific kinds of communication. That is, traditional communication research should not avoid the new media just because they are "new" or because they are technologies; current communication theories have much to offer in the way of understanding the impacts and uses of new media. At the same time, the different situations and capabilities of the new media will likely force researchers to respecify some of their theories, to make them more widely applicable or include new media as contingent conditions. The second argument is that there will be situations, uses, and impacts involving the new media that require *new* theories, *new* analytical methods, and *new* data. Thus we have opportunities to apply and improve our concepts and methods; but we also have challenges to develop additional concepts and methods.

There is a growing awareness in universities and institutions of the importance of this challenge. Many schools are establishing new faculty positions in telecommunications impacts, communications technology, office automation, and the information society, or revamping entire programs to focus on these issues where such positions or directions have not already been developed. And these trends are not limited to communication schools. Computer science and social science schools at University of California, Irvine, and at Carnegie-Mellon University in Pittsburgh have such faculty positions and are developing joint research projects. Schools of Library and Information Science at Berkeley, UCLA, Pittsburgh, and Rutgers are hiring communication Ph.D.s to teach such content. Conferences by the American Society for Information Science, Institute of Electrical and Electronics Engineers (IEEE), Association for Computing Machinery, International Communication Association, Academy of Management, Office Systems Research Association, Speech Communication Association, Telecommunications Policy and Research Committee, Western Social Sciences Association, Public Administration Association, International Policy Affairs Association, and many others are including panels and paper presentations on these issues, and in some cases establishing interest groups or full divisions.

The New Media is intended for this wide variety of disciplines, all with a need for a firm foundation in the research to date, relevant theoretical developments, and helpful guides to appropriate uses of new media in the future. But those managers, researchers, vendors, and designers interested in communications are the primary audience of this book. We have a great opportunity to increase understanding of a major change in our lives, and to orient ourselves in ways that might have more influence on those who make policy and technological decisions. As William Paisley (1984) concludes in his analysis of the communication sciences,

> The information society will require thousands of professional personnel to design, implement, and evaluate new communication systems. The communication megacorporations will endow programs at communication schools in which social

researchers, engineers, management specialists, economists, etc. will want to participate. Some communication programs will welcome this path of development and become more like social-research-oriented business programs. Other programs will follow a basic-research path, tying themselves more closely to social science departments where intersections of interests occur. Against these bright prospects for the development of the field, communication programs that try to remain unchanged will be snatching defeat from the jaws of victory.

Theoretic, administrative, practical, financial and social support for my interests in the social impacts of telecommunications have come from many people. Particularly helpful have been Roxanne Hiltz, Bonnie Johnson, Everett Rogers, Edwin Parker, and William Paisley. Others who have provided sympathetic conversation, insightful criticism, dinner parties, and access to materials include Don Case, Chris Borgman, Jerome Johnston, Mary Culnan, Jim Danowski, John Ruchinskas, Lynne Svenning, Charles Steinfield, Fred Williams, Peter Monge, and Rolf Wigand.

Patricia Johnson has shown tremendous patience, inexorable good humor, and superb text management skills throughout the preparation and text management of this book. Diane Woods, Agnes Uy, and Jean Campbell also helped in getting the text to the publisher on time. Bill Darst helped in preparing the figures. The Annenberg Learning Center, directed by Carolyn Spicer, has been invaluable in its ability to track down the most obscure document. Special thanks go to Zhila Sadri, Ron Moseley, Richard Connor, and Roger Felder for continuing to suffer my requests for materials. I thank the Annenberg School of Communications and Dean Peter Clarke for generally supporting my efforts.

Mel Voigt was very kind in responding to my early proposals concerning this book. The good people at Sage provided sound advice, timely encouragement, and strong publishing support.

Finally, I thank those friends who still have faith that I will return their calls and actually join them for dinner or basketball rather than spend another evening with my computer terminal.

This book is dedicated to Ellen Sleeter,

who makes it all worthwhile.

R.E.R.

Part I: New Media Technology and Research

Research can never be an isolated, purely "scientific" event. Research always occurs within the context of prior and emerging research, theories, methodologies, objects of analysis and paradigms. Additional context stems from ideological, economic, and social trends. Part I considers some aspects of the context in which the study of new media is developing.

Chapter 1 makes several contextual arguments. First, "new" media are only relatively so, as all communication media were considered new at one time and generated research interest, whether slowly or quickly. There was, in fact, considerable empirical and theoretical activity over mainframe computers in the early 1960s and 1970s, although only some of this work looked at computers as facilitators of communication. Early television research rose to meet the challenge of that new medium, and instructional television research was prolific through the mid-1970s.

Second, analysis of several bibliographic data bases shows that the social sciences are lagging far behind business and popular writers in their interest in what we would now accept as "new media." This noticeable lack of research interest in topics deemed important by other significant segments of society indicates a great need and opportunity for communication and related research. An analysis of past conference programs of the International Communication Association shows that the percentage of conference papers devoted to the new media has not only been growing rapidly, but is much greater than the percentage coverage in the social sciences as a whole.

Third, the chapter ends with a call to communication, information science, and related fields to take the lead in the social sciences in increasing our understanding of the new media.

Chapter 2 introduces the concept of interactivity as central to an appreciation of new media. The fundamental reason for the interactivity of these media is the development and miniaturization of the microprocessor. Its history is briefly discussed. Other technological components of communication media are briefly surveyed, including transmission channels, an important new storage medium, and an intriguing example of the convergence and integration of these components: videotex. The theme of this chapter is that because some new media (e.g., videotex) are "medium-independent," research is forced to focus on the functions, uses, and impacts of the technology rather than on the technology itself. However, to understand this integration requires some familiarity with technical aspects of new media.

Chapter 3 essentially argues that we need not consider new media as foreign research topics requiring all new theories and, as such, limiting the interest and contributions of researchers in other aspects of communication, information science, and sociology. Indeed, many of the more traditional communication theories have much to offer by providing insight into the ways new media are perceived and used, and how and to what extent they have consequences for our attitudes, behaviors, and society. On the other hand, many of these extant theories need to be respecified to consider the contingencies presented by new media. So there are opportunities to apply and refine theories; simultaneously there is a clear need to develop concepts, theories, and hypotheses that focus on the unique aspects of new media.

The chapter discusses a variety of theories more or less familiar to communication and information science research, such as diffusion of innovations, uses and gratifications, organizational contingency theory, interpersonal communication, and social presence. It ends by considering what theories of communication technology impacts have to tell us about the hidden assumptions of media designers, implementors, users, and analysts.

The final chapter in Part I considers methodological and empirical aspects of new media research. There seem to be several constraints on such research due to limitations in traditional analytical designs and methods, to the natural settings of most new media, to the nature of the media themselves, and to the evolving character of these media within their settings. These limitations are identified, such as the insufficient application of process research, assumptions as to the stability of users' perceptions, and the difficulty in making reliable generalizations. The chapter suggests several design and analytical alternatives, including the use of data collected by the servicing computer. These data have considerable advantages, particularly with respect to relational (network) and longitudinal analyses. There are, of course, attendant disadvantages, such as complex data management, computer expense, and threats to privacy.

RONALD E. RICE

1 Development of New Media Research

As we become aware of the technological developments and wide-spread uses of the new communication media, one might expect that social scientists in general, and those specializing in communication behavior in particular, would play an important role in conducting policy-relevant investigations and in establishing research agendas. But this has not yet occurred to a great extent. As an eminent Finnish scholar recently stated,

> Communication scholars could have been in the forefront of not only studies of new communication technologies but also in planning its applications. However, research has been both late and inadequate; many fine research opportunities have been lost forever. Research data have been replaced with personal opinions and normative value judgments [Wiio, 1981].

Newness, of course, is in the eye of the cohort. At this time, we might consider "new media" to include personal computers, videotext and teletext, interactive cable, videodiscs, electronic mail and computer conferencing, communication satellites, office information systems, and the like. But when television was first publicly demonstrated in England in 1927, or the first time radio was commercially broadcast—from Pittsburgh in 1920 to cover the presidential election results—these were new communication technologies (see Dordick and Rice, 1984). Conversely, the idea of geosychronous communication satellites was first proposed by Arthur C. Clarke in 1945. Or consider the so-called revolutionary office technologies such as the typewriter and vertical files discussed in Chapter 7.

It is not misleading, however, to talk about the new media of the last decade or so. One indication of their expansion consists of the frequent advertisements for video games and personal computers on television. More emphatic are the actual dollar amounts being spent. The percentage of consumer media spending allocated to cable and pay TV, videocassette recorders, video games, and home computers rose from 7.5% in 1978 to 30.8% in 1982. Total new consumer media revenues rose 573% in 1978-1981. Spending for new media by 1987 is expected to rise 411% for home computers, 104% for videocassette recorders, 85% for cable and pay TV, but only 5% for videogames. Spending on more traditional media will rise considerably more slowly (20-50%) (Knowledge Industry Publications, 1983).

Another indication is the frequency of mentions of such media in the literature. The DIALOG information service contains over 200 data bases consisting of bibliographic, abstract, and time-series information. Searching the computerized DIALOG information service or references to new media,[1] and noting the occurrence of these references by year, we can gain insight into the growing interest in new media over the years—from 1974 through early 1982—and across three categories of literature—the *Magazine Index, Management Contents,* and *Sociological Abstracts.*

Figure 1.1 shows the rise in the number of articles over time in new media topics. The greatest rise by far is in the so-called popular magazine literature, from 39 in 1974 to 1326 in 1982. The second greatest rise is in the management/business literature, starting from 2 and growing to 503 in the nine-year period. The social science literature—or the subset included in *Sociological Abstracts*—shows a near-conscious avoidance of the subject, with 17 articles in 1974 and only 1 in 1981. (Frequencies for 1981 and 1982 in *Sociological Abstracts* are not representative because that data base is updated more slowly than the business and popular data bases.) The 17 articles in 1974 come primarily from a special issue of the journal *Communications* (1974: Vol. 21) concerned with cable studies.

Of course portrayals of frequencies from data bases with constantly growing and differing populations of literature can be misleading. Figure 1.2 shows the trend over time in the three data bases for the ratio of new media articles to total articles in each data base each year. Because of the much larger base in the magazine data base (over 800,000 in the nine

FIGURE 1.1 Number of New Media Articles Contained in 3 Data Bases, by Year

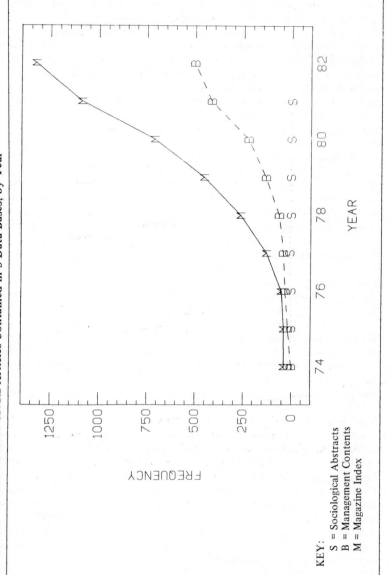

KEY:
S = Sociological Abstracts
B = Management Contents
M = Magazine Index

years) than in the management contents data base (over 120,000 articles), the actual greater importance to the business and management communities of new media is masked by the raw frequencies.

Figure 1.2 shows a much larger rise in the percentage of business articles concerning new media than the rise in the popular literature. So, although there is absolute exposure in the popular literature, there is greater density of coverage in the business literature. Again, however, we see that the sociological literature, even relative only to social science, seems unconcerned about a topic that is growing in absolute and relative importance for the majority of serials readers. Table 1.1 especially indicates the relative emphasis on new media in four data bases. Academic researchers may dismiss this lack of emphasis as the rightful adherence of social science activities to nonconsumer issues; but this approach, as reflected in the low (or, we might hope, only delayed) concern with new media, assumes no sociologically relevant impacts or contingencies of a major variable in the communication process. That variable is the communication channel, and the general and business publics seem to judge that new channels of communication are indeed important.

The then-new media of radio and television spawned tremendous social science research into their organization, uses, content, and effects. (An example is the early radio studies by Lazarsfeld and Stanton, [1942].) Some communication research on the current new media fits easily into those paradigms, research approaches, and hypotheses (see Chapter 3). But the bulk of this research tradition did not consider the medium itself as a variable. This is moderately surprising, because the Shannon and Weaver information-theoretic model became, along with revisions by communication scholars, the basis of the linear model of communication (see Shannon and Weaver, 1949; DeFleur and Ball-Rokeach, 1975: 126-127). This linear model clearly includes "channel" as a necessary component of the process of communicating.

The importance of the channel with such a wider definition is particularly salient when the linear model is rejected for a model of convergence (see Rogers and Kincaid, 1981: Chap. 2). The particular medium would be especially crucial (for example) if, because of its attributes, it prevented interaction or rapid feedback, or if it tended to centralize content and switching functions (such as network television). Conversely, if a medium (such as computer conferencing) facilitated the convergence process, then again the medium would be a critical variable in the process. Even models of the persuasion process explicitly show the role of the channel (see McGuire, 1981: 45), although the medium has rarely been manipulated by persuasion researchers, except for social psychologists and sociologists such as Short, Williams, and Christie (1976), Johansen (1977), or Hiltz and Turoff (1978), and a specialized group of psychologists (see Taylor and Thompson, 1982; Williams, Paul, and Ogilvie, 1957).

The notion that the channel of communication might be as important a variable in the communication process as source, message, receiver, and feedback, may have been overlooked (or at least underemphasized) in the

FIGURE 1.2 Percentage of New Media Articles Contained in 3 Data Bases, by Year

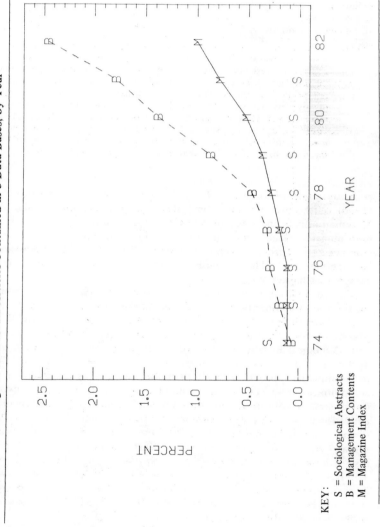

KEY:
S = Sociological Abstracts
B = Management Contents
M = Magazine Index

TABLE 1.1 Relative Frequency of Articles Mentioning
New Media in Three Dialog Data Bases, 1974-1982

Data Base	Number of Articles on New Media	Percentage of Total Articles
Sociological Abstracts	47	0.09
Magazine Index	4098	0.50
Management Contents	1438	1.12

NOTE: A "mention" is the occurrence of a new-media term in title, keyword, or abstract; 1974 was chosen as the baseline year because it
was the earliest year that all three data bases include. *Social Science
Citation Index* does not include a publication year index, so it could
not be used in the longitudinal comparison; nor does it include text
of abstracts, so it would naturally include fewer mentions of new-
media terms. However, a very rough percentage—involving 1,126
"hits" on a base of over 1,177,000 records from 1972—of new-
media articles is 0.10%, equal to the percentage for *Sociological Abstracts*, in spite of its far greater diversity of journals indexed.

communication research literature, although it had been argued by Innis
(1950) quite early on and then taken further (and farther afield) by
McLuhan (1964) and Carpenter (1973). One need not be a technological
determinist to agree that the medium may be a fundamental variable in the
communication process even if a "medium" may be media-independent,
such as videotex. (This example of medium-independent media is discussed in Chapter 2.)

This recognition of the influence of media was behind the high hopes
for the use of communication (and concommitant media) in the development process in the 1950s and 1960s (Lerner, 1958; Schramm, 1964). The
passing of this intellectual paradigm was due largely to failures of political
and ideological insight and lack of economic change rather than to an
irrelevance of media to development efforts (see Rogers, 1976). A
programmatic approach to including the medium as a variable in the
communication process, from a communication perspective, awaited the
intersection of educational and development research. Although media for
educational purposes were compared in a typological sense early on
(Bretz, 1971), Chu and Schramm (1967) are the primary communication
researchers to investigate the relative effects of the medium itself in the
instructional process. However, research concerning educational television has been quite frequent since the early 1960s. Figure 1.3 shows a rise
in such studies ("transmission of educational or informational programs
or mentioned by television," as defined in DIALOG'S ERIC data base) to a
peak of nearly 400 a year, and then a decline after 1974.[2]

It is informative to note the bimodal rise in studies of computer-
oriented programs ("the application of computer technology to such tasks
as instruction, documentation, research, administration, etc.") to nearly

FIGURE 1.3   Number of Articles on Educational Television in ERIC Data Base, 1966-1982

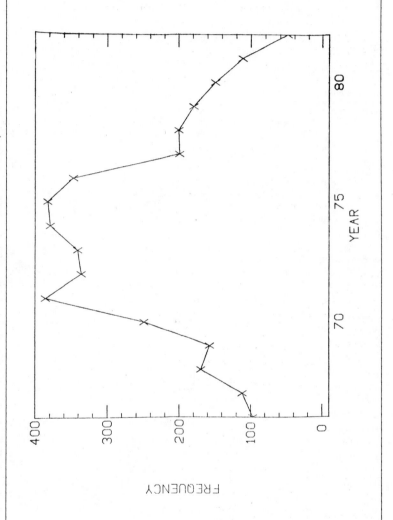

FIGURE 1.4 Number of Articles on Computer-Oriented Educational Programs in ERIC Data Base, 1966-1982

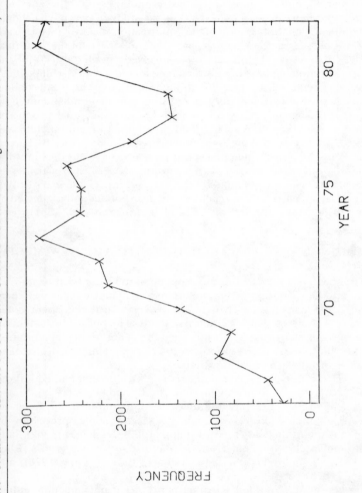

300 in 1973, and then a second rise in 1980, as shown in Figure 1.4. Studies specifically involving microcomputers (not included in Figure 1.3) rose from 0 before 1976, to less than 40 in 1979, to over 320 in 1982. Here, certainly the rise in the number of research studies parallels the rate of acceptance, and the impacts, of the technology.

One other more general precedent for the study of new media should be mentioned; that is the notion of the "information society." (See Dizzard [1982] for technological, economic, and political aspects of the "information age".) Initial works on this topic involved specific aspects of the creation, diffusion, and use of information in an economy (Machlup, 1962) and more general social trends due to the transition of the U.S. economy from an industrial base to a service and then information-handling base (Bell, 1976). Approximately half of the U.S. gross national product is devoted to the creation, handling, and distribution of information, and this fact is one measure of our transition to an information society (Parker, 1978a; Porat, 1977). A wider concept of such a society considers how the transition from manufacturing and agriculture as principal activities in society affects business, community, and personal life. Japan, in particular, places great emphasis on how quality of life incorporates and is affected by the increasing influence and diversity of information (Ito, 1981).

COMMUNICATION RESEARCH TURNS TO THE NEW MEDIA

Before a short discussion of how communication has been turning its attention to new media, it is very important to emphasize that researchers *outside* of the communication field have been concerned about some aspects of the new media since the early 1960s. The bulk of this attention has been focused, of course, on the computer—not as a communication medium, but as an information processor, computational device, and simulator of human mental functions.

The relationships between computers and society, thought, education, and work were major concerns in books by Greenberger (1962), Simon (1960), and Wiener (1961). Even studies of "office automation" appeared early on, although the term was applied to electronic data processing by authors including Diebold (1964), Dunlop (1962), Englebart (1962), Jaffe and Froomkin (1968), Mann (1962), Mumford and Banks (1967), Rhee (1968), Shultz and Whisler (1960), Stewart (1971), Taviss (1970), and Whisler (1970).

The notion of a knowledge worker is no recent phenomenon, either; Bush set out the issues in 1945; Paisley (1980) ended his review and analysis of the concepts involved in information work with a reconsideration of Bush's propositions. The early work by Englebart (1962) on the "knowledge workshop" is seeing light, more than ten years later, in the design of Apple's Lisa computer. Negroponte's work on videodiscs at MIT's Architectural Machine Group led the way toward interactive learning and mass-storage information retrieval systems. Ithiel de Sola Pool, a political scientist at MIT with strong interests in communication research, started the Center for Policy Alternatives, which has conducted research on the information economy and on telecommunications policy. Anthony Oettinger formed the Harvard Program on Information Technologies and Public Policy, and created the word "compunications" to emphasize the convergence between computers and communications.

The evaluation of the social and philosophical benefits and dangers in computing continues by scientists in various disciplines, such as Gotlieb and Borodin (1973), Moshowitz (1976), Weizenbaum (1976), Wessell (1976), Winner (1977), and many others. Many of these authors are computer scientists particularly concerned with the effects on human values and thought processes and are involved in the debate as to how "human" computers can become. This tradition is maintained to this day (see Dertouzos and Moses, 1980; Forester, 1981). Clearly, communication researchers were not the first or foremost in considering the origins, uses, impacts, and policies of computers in social and organizational life. However, except for some of those authors involved in office automation (such as Don Tapscott, Dave Conrath, James Bair, and Murray Turoff) or those of Simon's and Wiener's ilk, aware of the role of information in managerial behavior, few were concerned specifically with computers as communication *media* or with new telecommunications media outside of data networks.

As discussed in the prior section, currents in the study of new media by communication researchers had been swirling in the late 1960s and early 1970s, but most remained, with respect to communication research, offshore or isolated in tidal eddies. Perhaps the first concerted effort to include the new media in communication research was by Dr. Edwin Parker. He was a student of Wilbur Schramm's—as a Canadian, aware of Innis and McLuhan's writings—and a coauthor of one of the first books on television and children (Schramm, Lyle, and Parker, 1961).

Yet, while television effects were being studied in the early 1960s, the policy decisions had already been made ten years earlier. Parker thus became convinced that we should look forward, instead of backward, to shape and determine possible (and desired) effects of new media; the medium he was using as a *tool* for research—the computer—was going to have much more social impact and be a factor in social change, than the medium he was then studying—television. Parker started graduate school in fall, 1957—when Sputnik was launched—and new communication media were becoming part of the culture.

Stanford University itself was noted for its achievements in new technologies, and the Silicon Valley was just developing nearby (see Rogers and Larsen, 1984). An Information Systems Program at Stanford was funded by the National Science Foundation, involving Professors Bruce Owen, Donald Dunn, and others in economics and engineering. The National Science Foundation funded Dr. Parker and others in 1967 to develop a multiindexing information retrieval language (eventually named SPIRES), initially to facilitate research efforts at the Stanford Linear Accelerator Center.

Readings in the history of technology, and the industrial revolution, along with the research activities in information systems, led to a series of articles on new media (Parker and Dunn, 1972; Parker, 1970a,b,c, 1973a,b,c,d, 1976).[3] A National Institute of Health biomedical training grant to the Stanford Institute helped produce communication researchers particularly attuned to computers as information and communication media, such as Thomas Martin (Syracuse University), Heather Hudson (University of Texas, Austin), Ray Panko (University of Hawaii), William Richards (Simon Fraser University), and Mark Porat (formerly with the U.S. Department of Commerce and the Aspen Institute.)[4]

This research on communication technology fit well with the strong interest at Stanford in the 1970's on development communication problems in the Third World. It was reflected in a variety of writings (Parker, 1978a,b, 1979; Parker and Hudson, 1973, 1975; Parker and Lusignan, 1977; Parker and Mohammadi, 1977; Rice and Parker, 1979), coming out of research and experience in Alaska, Iran, Indonesia, and other developing nations. Parker himself applied communication theory and his awareness of new media to launch Equatorial Communications, a highly successful telecommunications company in Mountain View, California.

Another, related, thrust to the study of new media was set by Dr. Frederick Williams, the founding Dean of the Annenberg School of Communications at the University of Southern California. In 1969, while at the University of Texas at Austin, he had the opportunity to start a new television project, involving the use of television in bilingual language training. He saw this as an opportunity to use the *medium* rather than the *content* to affect language. In 1972 Dr. Percy Tannenbaum invited him to attend a seminar on the Future of Communications at the Center for Advanced Studies in the Behavioral Sciences (at Stanford), where he heard Parker's comments on the impacts of communication technology. The Annenberg School was founded on the principle of the importance of the new media, with the first courses based upon such core concepts as communication technology, practices, and theories. The early faculty included communication technology researchers and consultants such as Thomas Martin, James Carlisle, Dave Holzman, Gerald Hanneman,[5] Herbert Dordick, and James Danowski. Several grants at the University of Southern California at this time helped develop the research focus on new media: (a) one with Jack Nilles, that led to the first comprehensive study of transportation/telecommunications trade-offs (Nilles, Carlson, Gray, and Hanneman, 1976), and (b) another leading to a study of the network marketplace (Dordick, Bradley, and Nanus, 1981). Williams (e.g., 1983) continues to be a commentator on the "communications revolution."

Other influences were the early cable studies by Greenberg and colleagues at Michigan State University (Baldwin, Greenberg, Block, and Stoyanoff, 1978), Rand (see a Rand reprint by Goldhamer, 1971) and Clarke and colleagues at the University of Michigan (Clarke, Kline, Schumacher, and Evans, 1978). Smith (1972) and Maddox (1972) were early on interested in cable and electronic media; see also Pool (1973).

In England the Communication Studies Group established some of the basic principles and results in comparing alternative conferencing media (see Short, Williams, and Christie, 1976). Other members of the group included Champness, Reid, Pye, Elton, Wilson, and Young, all active in telecommunications research and policy. This work was parallelled by the Institute for the Future in California (see Johansen, Vallee, and Spangler, 1979).

It might be of interest to look at how the field of communication research has included the new media on its agenda over time. The International Communication Association (ICA) is the umbrella organization for communication research in the United States, and does hold its meetings in other countries every four or five years. By assuming that the papers and session topics that are presented at the annual conference represent current and acceptable interests, the number of papers involving new media each year is one measure of the importance of the subject to the communication field.[6] Briefly, ICA programs from 1973 through 1983 indicated how many total content units there were and how many of those were concerned with some aspects of the new media. The total number of new papers and the percentage of new media papers relative to the total number of all content units were then calculated.

As Figure 1.5 shows, there was interest in the new media from a research perspective from the 1973 program on. Although one or two were interpreted loosely as new media papers ("Telephone Communication for the Handicapped" and "Some Principles of Information Storage and Retrieval in Society"), most were explicit ("Computer Credibility for French and English Canadians" and "An Intelsat Dilemma"). However, the bulk came from a four-paper panel on "Man-Computer Interactive Systems" sponsored by the American Society for Information Science. Thus the main thrust in 1973 comes from another association. The ten papers in 1974, however, were scattered over seven sessions and typically focused on information system design, teleconferencing, and man-machine interaction. Three papers in the 1975 conference came from a panel on teleconferencing, while the other six were spread over five sessions. Both papers in 1976 were concerned with computer-based communication, while Berlin in 1977 saw the first great increase in communication interest in new media. The 21 papers appeared in ten sessions, also indicating increased "specialization" of interest, or a community awareness leading to organization of panels of more homogeneous concerns. Both because of the number and the clustering of new media topics in 1977, we can say that this was the year that new media became an accepted content area in ICA. Perhaps this was because there were European researchers at this conference who were concerned about direct broadcast satellites.

The next year saw a drop in the number of new media papers (seven) and a return to scattered papers (except for a three-paper panel on "Telecommunications Policy and Human Communications Research"); the following year again indicated growing interest groups, with fourteen papers in only five sessions. Three of these panels were interested in "The

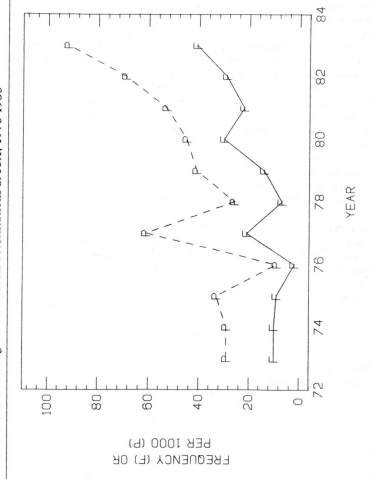

FIGURE 1.5 Number and Percentage of New Media Presentations at ICA, 1973-1983

Impact of New Electronic Media in the Home," "Communication Technology, Culture and Human Communication," and "Interactive Telecommunication for Civic Participation." International conferences seem to draw more people, so there were more than double the number of new media papers (30), distributed over 121 sessions; seven of these were specifically new media panels. The following two years showed continued growth and continued support by panels and groups interested in new media. Indeed, the Human Communication Technology (HCT) Interest Group was started at the 1980 Acapulco conference, and went on to establish continued emphasis on communication research in the new media. In 1983 and 1982, many of the media papers appeared in HCT sessions, although increasingly in conjunction with the other ICA divisions. However, new media papers are beginning to appear regularly in divisional sessions, and 1983 marked a high-water mark in interest, with 41 papers.

As with the other analyses, we need to scale these frequencies by the total number of content units (mostly papers) at each conference, because of the fluctuating number of presentations (from a low of 232 in 1976 to a high of 660 in 1980). The *percentage* of new media papers, also shown in Figure 1.5, clearly indicates a growing trend. The last two years have shown particularly large increases: in 1983, 9.2% of all content units at the annual ICA Conference involved some aspect of the new media. These percentages, right from the start, are greater than that of the magazine and business index rate (see Figure 1.2). This recent high, and growing, level of interest at the communication conference paper level is not mirrored in the published social literature, as also shown in Figures 1.1 and 1.2.

SUMMARY

Three implications follow from this discussion of the sources and development of communication research involving new media:

(1)   Communication research conference papers, which may be more informal but are more current than published works, seem to reflect the large and growing social interest in the new media—as reflected in popular trade and business publications—more than the rest of the social sciences.

(2)   The established social science journals still consider research concerning the new media inappropriate and insufficiently rigorous, and/or are ignoring an area of great social interest.

(3)   It seems that communication research has an opportunity to *lead*, with increased rigor and a growing body of prior research, the social sciences in understanding the nature of the new media, their use, and their impacts. Popular and business segments of society would welcome the useful insights and practical implications; the academic community needs to become more aware of research opportunities and needs generated by the new media.

This is not simply a call for more research. It is part of a growing awareness of the increasing insularity of communication research on one hand, and the opportunity for interdisciplinary growth on the other. The depth and extent of this situation has been analyzed by Paisley (1984). Along with other authors, he points out that the primary norms of science are (a) public disclosure, (b) stimulation and cross-fertilization (implying support for exploration in new areas), (c) feedback and evaluation, and (d) peer rewards. Yet the growing isolationism of disciplines (and even of subdisciplines among the communication sciences) thwarts these norms through xenophobia, ethnocentrism, and dogmatism. This situation is a paradoxical result of the natural development of a new discipline. During the 1930s to the 1950s

> communication was a confluence of interest for leading social scientists in the United States . . . [but with a rise of communication as a discipline] . . . research was published not in the journals of the other social sciences but in new journals of communication . . . indicators of independence may also be indicators of isolation.

Through citation analysis and content analyses documents, Paisley shows that (a) communication science is not cited by other disciplines, except in a lagged fashion that concentrates only in recent materials from a few leading figures, (b) the communication subdisciplines are often segmented from each other, and (c) there is *decreasing* attention paid to "mass communication/mass media" in the disciplines of education, sociology, and psychology.

The topics that have drawn attention from diverse sources are the uses and gratifications approach, the knowledge gap, and the information society. This latter topic has drawn the most diverse attention. Paisley turns this and related evidence into his concluding theme:

> The communication sciences are entering a period of ferment that has already begun at the technological level. Epistemological ferment will follow. . . . No group of social researchers could wish for more than to find their variable (communication) at the center of transformations of work, learning, political participation, play, and other functions of society.

NOTES

1. DIALOG files 47, 37, and 75 were searched for the combined terms cable, cable (w) television, cable (w) TV, CATV, subscription (w) television, videotex?, teletext?, electronic (w) mail, electronic (w) messag?,, computer (w) conferenc?, communication? (w) satellite, microcomputer?, videodis?, fiber (w) optic?, communication? (w) satellite, office (w) automation, word (w) process? office (1w) future, office (2w) future, and viewdata. Then this combined search was sequentially "anded" by year of publication from 1974 through 1982.

The DIALOG Database Catalog provides the following descriptions of the three files. "Magazine Index covers over 370 popular magazines and provides extensive coverage of current affairs, leisure time activities, home-centered arts, sports, recreation and travel, the performing arts, business, science and technology, consumer product evaluations, and other areas. . . . [Management Contents includes] articles from over 400 U.S. and international journals, proceedings, and transactions . . . fully indexed and abstracted to provide up-to-date information in the areas of accounting, decision sciences, finance, industrial relations, managerial economics, marketing, operations research, organization behavior, and public administration. . . . *Sociological Abstracts* covers the world's literature in sociology and behavioral sciences. Over 1200 journals and other serial publications are scanned."

2. Figures 1.3 and 1.4 are courtesy of Dr. Milton Chen at Stanford University's Institute for Communication Research.

3. One example of Parker's position in the information science and library field is indicated in a recent conomination/cocitation analysis by Lenk (1983). By means of factor analyses and hierarchical clusterings of conomination data within seven scientific specialty fields, researchers central to and within these fields were mapped into multidimensional space. Parker is the lone representative of communication research, and is located in the direct center of information science, occupying a liaison position between algorithmic researchers on one side and information retrieval specialties on the other.

4. The author of this chapter was the last student funded by Dr. Parker.

5. Hanneman, Dr. Williams says, was the first to use the term "new media," and developed the first communication textbook involving the topic (Hanneman and McEwen, 1975: Chapters 15, 16, 19).

6. (My thanks go to Jan Goldman and Bob Cox of ICA for their generosity in supplying the needed conference programs.) The intent of this analysis was to describe the relative attention paid by ICA conferences (1973-1983) to research involving the new media, as reflected in the final ICA programs. Thus the focus was on substantive *content*, and not simply on items on the conference agenda. What was counted included identifiable paper titles, topics of panels, and the topic of a special address. A very rough weighting scheme was used to reflect differential agenda-setting or attention-getting effects of addresses versus panels versus papers. Each identifiable paper title was one unit, so that a typical paper panel totaled around four to six units; a panel with several members but no specific paper titles was three units, representing somewhat less than a typical paper panel; a special address or plenary session with one guest or keynote speaker was one unit. A rough copy of all the enumeration of such papers or content units is available from the author.

Other program sessions that were not counted because they did not represent research content per se included action caucuses, business meetings, no-host bars, poolside parties, workshops, tutorials, curriculum-building seminars, and skill-building sessions.

The total number of units for a given conference represented the total number of research/content items that ICA deemed important enough to include in its program, and, because they were so identified, were in some ways accessible and perhaps even attractive to a conference attender. The total number of new-media papers included all those units identifiably concerned with uses, impacts, regulatory issues and other communication research interests involving new media. Thus a paper on standard cable delivery or use would not be included, while a philosophical paper on telecommunication technology in the information society would. Finally, a title including "computer" because a computer was used to calculate or simulate a communication measure or activity of interest was not included, while a paper about communication data *collected by* a computer (as a communication medium) was included.

Needless to say, there is an ad hoc atmosphere in this coding scheme, but I was sufficiently familiar with the papers to apply it. As with all content-coding schemes, the relative weighting has nothing to do with actual exposure, evaluation, or use of the research and the conference papers themselves. Another difficulty was the changing nature of the ICA conference program itself. There seemed to be more diverse forms of sessions in the earlier programs, making it difficult to be consistent in categorization over time. (For example, in 1977 there were a few tutorials that looked suspiciously like paper panels, with paper titles and authors. These were counted.) Also, until 1978, there were "contributed papers" sessions that did little more than list 25 paper titles. This was changed in 1978 to a "poster session" that in some years listed the titles, and in others did not. This of course will bias the denominator in the percentage of media papers, unless the "contributed papers" included a proportional selection of new-media papers. Because most such poster or contributed paper sessions are in interpersonal or instructional communication, this is not a safe assumption.

RONALD E. RICE

2 New Media Technology: *Growth and Integration*

Near the end of the 18th century, William Blake (1946: 150) wrote

> To see a World in a Grain of Sand,
> And heaven in a Wild Flower
> Hold Infinity in the palm of your hand
> And Eternity in an hour

Prophet and visionary, Blake was affirming the omnipresence and holiness of life. Yet we are approaching the time when we can achieve these goals through our communication media. Optical fibers of spun glass, made from the silicon in sand, bring worlds of sound and sight into our lives; the same laser beam used in optical fiber transmission, when used in holograms, contains enough information in any part of its message to recreate the entire original three-dimensional image; a single strand of spun glass can contain nearly infinite bandwidth; and an hour's worth of information transmitted by these fibers would take nearly an eternity with most other media.

New ways of encoding, transmitting, distributing, and displaying information appear most overtly in the form of new communication technologies. For example, digital, as compared to analog, encoding dramatically increases the speed, accuracy, and volume of information that can be exchanged. It efficiently integrates voice, data, and video. It facilitates signal processing and coding techniques. It offers greater privacy and security. But more important, humans are beginning to communicate in new ways as well. New media—from videotex to personal computer networks, from communication satellites to fiber optics—are blurring distinctions that seemed so clear and useful a generation ago:

(1) Technician versus artist. Computer graphics is a new art form that challenges technical expertise as well as creative genius.

(2) General versus limited access. The telephone currently provides near-universal access to people in the United States; with regulatory and commercial developments, local telephone usage may in fact become less accessible.

(3) Regulated versus unregulated media. Commercial network television is heavily regulated: yet the new Federal Communications Commission (FCC) policies for direct broadcast satellites are so unrestricted that potential service providers are asking for more guidelines.

(4) Communication versus processing. This is what the divestiture of AT&T was all about; computerization and communication have nearly completely converged, and both AT&T and IBM are in the "information business." These distinctions are useful at the gross level: local distribution and long-haul transmission are officially communications but not processing; value-added carriers provide both; while service bureaus provide processing but not communication. AT&T's Teleterminal does it all.

(5) Time and space. A public speech delivers a common content to a common set of people at a common time at a common location. Network television delivers a generally common content to a generally common mass. Cable television delivers a (debatably) more diverse content to a generally more diverse set of people. Videotex delivers customized content across varying sets of people, at undetermined times to places potentially unreached by politicians or television. (See Williams, Rice, and Dordick [1984,] for further discussion of these factors.)

(6) Active versus passive control. Early computer-assisted instruction was heralded for letting the student take an active role in learning, but the early systems required nearly mindless passivity from its users, compared to the newest video games.

(7) Transmission versus reception. A mediated communication exchange now may involve so many transmission transformations that any given medium can be both a transmitter and receiver, both medium and

content. For example, filmed content may be transmitted by satellite, delivered by cable and shown on television.

The last two of these blurred distinctions lead to a concept crucial to the purpose of this book: interactivity. We generally define new media as those communication technologies, typically involving computer capabilities (microprocessor or mainframe), that allow or facilitate interactivity among users or between users and information. Because of developments in technology and applications, even this definition is not without blurred distinctions. Bretz (1971, 1983) distinguishes between "quasi-interaction" and "interaction": Fully interactive media imply that the sender and receiver roles are interchangeable; they imply that there be a response from A to B based on B's response to A's first initiation (though A or B may be nonhuman). So, teletext systems would not be considered interactive. He does not include videogames either, because there is no cognitive message between interactants; but that is a matter of debate. The distinction is helpful, though, in that our definition as yet provides little lower boundary: choosing among three network stations does, after all, provide some interactivity.

However, this distinction is too fine for the purposes of considering the social and organizational uses and consequences of new media. Perhaps the social distinction lies between interactivity that still operates at the "mass" level and interactivity that makes it very difficult to define a particular mass using a specified content of a given medium. Under this refinement, teletext *is* interactive because it would be quite difficult to argue that a given mass was using the same specific information at the same time. The technical distinction of this definition typically requires a two-way link, within the same transmission channel (as, networked microcomputers) or using different paths each way (as, one-way cable content chosen by a one-way telephone link). This distinguishes between telephone and radio, which are otherwise quite similar technically, in that they use similar components and are transmitted over similar media (wires, microwave, satellites); but radio involves only a one-way link.

We also extend the notion of interactivity to include the expansion of the utility and capabilities of media by means of a computer. Joining a computer (whether mainframe, personal, or microprocessor) to a telecommunications medium or transmission system enables interactivity among the system components, as well as human control over the pace, structure, and content of the communication. So, for instance, computer conferencing is not only interactive in the sense that participants may exchange comments with other participants in real or delayed time, but the system as used is a product of interactions with the system designers, programmers, and conference moderators as they create a communication environment.

SOME COMPONENTS OF THE NEW MEDIA

This book is not about technology. There are fine texts on all manner of communications technology. We might suggest Dordick, Bradley, and Nanus (1981), Martin (1978), Meadow and Tedesco (1984), Pool (1983), or Robinson (1978, particularly the chapter by Walter Bear) as readable places to start. However, subsequent chapters will have occasion to mention certain communication technologies or components of new media. This section very briefly describes processing, transmission, and recording media, and then more fully describes videotex as an example of how various media are redesigned and combined to create new media. As an aid to the reader, Figure 2.1 relates the frequency spectrum to frequency allocations of particular transmission systems.

A Crucial Part Of New Media—The Microprocessor[1]

Some observers claim that the transistor represents the most important single invention of this century. Its discovery occurred in 1947 at Bell Telephone Laboratories in New Jersey. The transistor is so important because it makes possible the miniaturization of electronic equipment such as the computer. Until the transistor, the heart of electronics was the vacuum tube, which had the undesirable characteristics of producing heat, burning out, and taking up quite a bit of space. With transistors replacing vacuum tubes, electronic devices became much smaller and cheaper. Thus the invention of the transistor set off a revolution in miniaturization.

One of the three coinventors of the transistor was Dr. William Shockley. In 1955 he left Bell Labs and moved back to his hometown of Palo Alto, California, to launch Shockley Semiconductor Laboratory. Shockley was very effective in attracting talented young scientists, but they were not happy working under his supervision. In 1957 eight of these brilliant young men left to form Fairchild Semiconductor. Their entrepreneurial fever was copied by other electrical engineers in what soon came to be known as Silicon Valley. Fairchild was the ancestral firm from which about 80 other semiconductor companies have spun off. All but three of the large U.S. semiconductor firms are located in Silicon Valley (a 10-by-30-mile area between Palo Alto and San Jose, California), laying the foundation for the computer firms that were to spring up a few years later. Today there are about 3100 electronics manufacturing firms in Silicon Valley, with about half having fewer than 10 employees. In contrast, 54 firms have 1000 employees or more (Rogers and Larsen, 1984). The dominant themes of Silicon Valley culture are entrepreneurship, high technology, competition in technological innovation, and free market forces (rather than public policies) as a basis for important decisions.

A *microprocessor* is a semiconductor chip (or a set of two or more chips) that contains the logic circuitry or "brains" of the computer. A microprocessor (together with memory chips) forms the essential part of a computer. The microprocessor was invented by Dr. Ted Hoff at Intel

FIGURE 2.1   Frequency, Bandwidth and
Categories of Transmission Media

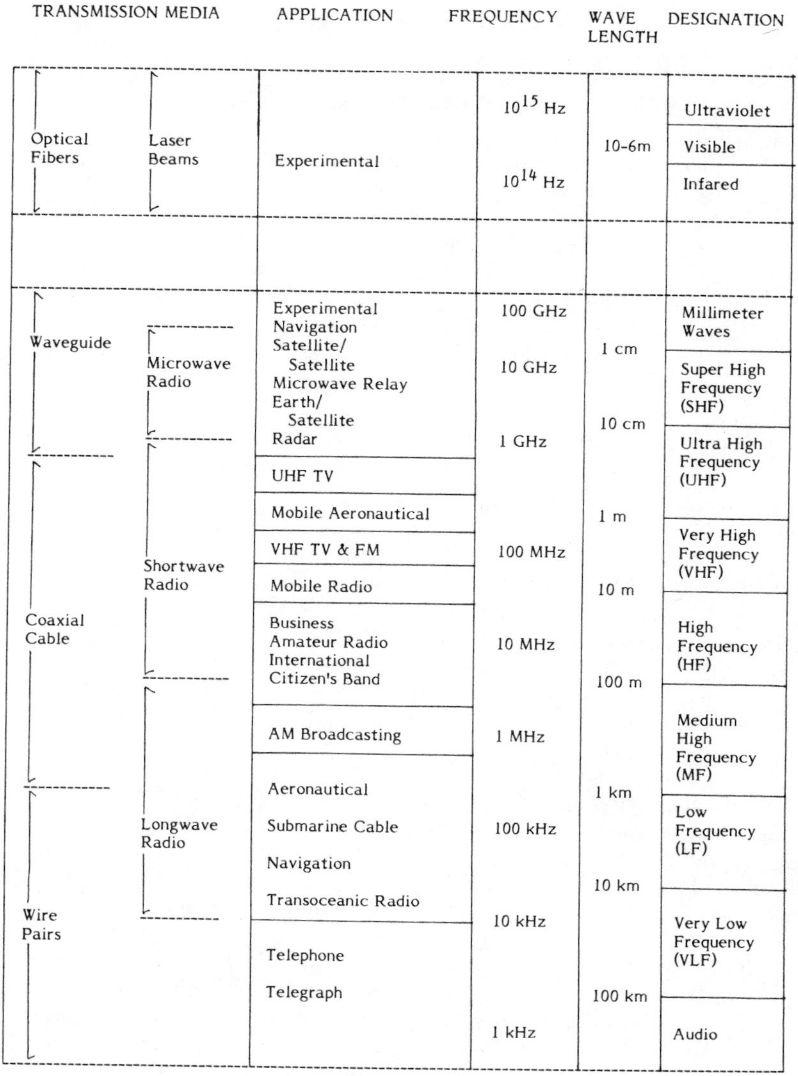

TRANSMISSION MEDIA		APPLICATION	FREQUENCY	WAVE LENGTH	DESIGNATION
Optical Fibers	Laser Beams	Experimental	10^{15} Hz 10^{14} Hz	10-6m	Ultraviolet Visible Infared
Waveguide	Microwave Radio	Experimental Navigation Satellite/ Satellite Microwave Relay Earth/ Satellite Radar	100 GHz 10 GHz 1 GHz	1 cm 10 cm	Millimeter Waves Super High Frequency (SHF) Ultra High Frequency (UHF)
		UHF TV			
	Shortwave Radio	Mobile Aeronautical		1 m	
		VHF TV & FM	100 MHz		Very High Frequency (VHF)
		Mobile Radio		10 m	
Coaxial Cable		Business Amateur Radio International Citizen's Band	10 MHz	100 m	High Frequency (HF)
		AM Broadcasting	1 MHz		Medium High Frequency (MF)
	Longwave Radio	Aeronautical		1 km	Low Frequency (LF)
		Submarine Cable	100 kHz		
		Navigation		10 km	
		Transoceanic Radio	10 kHz		Very Low Frequency (VLF)
Wire Pairs		Telephone		100 km	
		Telegraph			
			1 kHz		Audio

Corporation in Santa Clara, California, in 1971, thus opening the way for the continued miniaturization of computers. Hoff's invention was a key event setting off the Information Revolution; it made possible the microcomputer. The first "real" personal computer was devised in late 1974, and combined the Intel 8080A microprocessor, Altair hardware, and Bill Gates's (founder of Microsoft) Basic software. Two thousand kits were shipped in 1975. The second breakthrough came that fall when M05 Technology demonstrated the 6502 microprocessor for $25.00 ($154 less than the 8080 or Motorola's 68000). This made it easier for hobbyists to design their own kits.

The microprocessor amounted to putting computing functions on a tiny semiconductor chip. In the past decade or so, the most widely sold microprocessor (the Intel 8080) has decreased in cost from $360 in 1974 to $2.50 (if purchased in bulk today), and has been used as a component in over 100,000 new products. Such low-priced computing power has facilitated the development of new media in general, and has led to possibilities for increased decentralization and democratization with new media. Such tendencies are, of course, greatly debated. See Danzinger, Dutton, Kling, and Kraemer (1982), Slack and Fejes, (1984), Schiller (1982), and Wicklein (1981) for a skepticism based upon past patterns of multinational and governmental control of information and technologies.

Microcomputers are smaller than either mainframe computers or mini-computers, usually costing from $50 to $10,000. A microcomputer (also called a "personal computer" or a "home computer") sits easily on a desk top, and some are smaller than a briefcase. A typical microcomputer system comprises (a) input devices (such as a keypad, joysticks or keyboard); (b) magnetic storage devices (cassette tape recorder, disk drives for "floppy" diskettes, or large-storage "hard" disks); (c) the central processing unit consisting of the microprocessor, working memory, and connections for the various components; (d) output devices (a TV set or a monitor or a hard-copy printer); and (e) communication to the outside world (modems to connect to telephone lines). Perhaps the most crucial component is the software—disk operating system software for running the central processing unit, and task software for word processing, file management, calculations, custom programming, and the like. Future developments will include light pens, "mouse" or "cat" cursors (such as Apple's Macintosh, Tymshare's Augment, and Xerox's 860 office systems now offer), graphics tablets, voice recognition, and voice synthesis.

Leading manufacturers of microcomputers in the United States are Apple, Tandy/Radio Shack (TRS), IBM, and Commodore. The once clearcut distinction between microcomputers and minicomputers is becoming less important as microcomputers gain more computing capacity. Archetypical of the microcomputer industry is Apple, founded by Steve Jobs and Steve Wozniak—two college dropouts—in 1976, to manufacture microcomputers; today Apple and IBM have a dominant market share (20%-25% each) followed by Tandy/Radio Shack, Timex, and Commodore in the low-cost bracket; producers of larger PCs are being threatened by IBM. See Blundell (1982), Byte (1983), Electronic Business (1982),

Home Video and Cable Yearbook (1982), and Libs (1982) for market share and units shipped for each major vendor. Today there are an estimated 167 firms producing microcomputers in the United States. Before 1975 there were none. During 1982, from 621,000 to 2.8 million microcomputers were sold in the United States for $4.9 to $6.1 billion (depending upon the source and definition). From 7 to 10 million personal computers are expected to be shipped in 1990 (Blundell, 1982; Byte, 1983). About 5%-8% of United States households today have a microcomputer, and an estimated 20% of companies (Time, 1983a).

Currently, based upon a January 1983 Gallup poll[2] the uses mentioned by most PC owners are videogames (51%), business/office homework (46%), children's learning (46%), adults' learning (42%), checkbook budget balancing (37%), home business work (27%), and word processing (18%). Consumer Reports (1983) summarizes how over 2800 of their readers use a PC: games (69%), learning about computers (63%), learning to program (61%), word processing (59%), home accounting (45%), and so on. The primary uses stated in a Yankelovich survey[3] were business (33%), games (25%), learning about computers (15%-20%), and household record-keeping (10%-15%).

Personal computer users are better educated, younger, more affluent, predominantly male, and racially white according to several research organizations specializing in defining the market. Users watch less television, listen to average amounts of radio, and read more magazines than the norms. Primary consumers of PCs are innovators, self-achievers, inner-directeds, and forerunners in the population. That is, they are psychographically predisposed toward adopting new products and services before the rest of the consumer universe (such as cable and pay TV). Two-thirds live in metropolitan areas of 250,000 or more persons. Three-quarters live in central city and urban areas. They are more likely to have had some college or graduated. They are heads of households (with 3-5 persons) and/or are professional/technical workers or lower-middle managers to directors. Their salaries range from $20,000 on up to $90,000, and they are aggressive and goal-oriented (IDC, 1983; Naisbitt, 1980; Simmons Market Research Bureau, 1983; SRI, 1982; Yankelovich, Skelly and White, 1979).

Transmission Channels

This section briefly describes some common means for transmitting communication content.

Twisted pair. Local exchange telephone lines consist of a pair of twisted copper wires. These are quite versatile, but a major problem until recently is what is known as the skin effect: At higher frequency transmission, electrons tend to gather on the surface of the wire. Due to system congestion, the skin effect and other problems, high speed data or wideband video just cannot be pushed through twisted pair; even at low speeds the error rate of telephone line transmission is too high for satisfactory computer communication, which is not nearly as redundant (and thus tolerant) as human voice communication. New transmission techniques and termination equipment are making phone lines capable of handling increasingly greater analog and even digital transmission. In fact, the public switched telecommunications network as we now know it is being dramatically changed due to its conversion to digital transmission. Already value-added services like packet-switched networks (such as Telenet) use high-speed long-haul telephone lines (not twisted copper, but a combination of microwave, satellite, and cable) to connect computers with computers and people with computers. Other processing/transmission services are described by Dorros (1982). They include automatic call billing, whereby a caller can enter a personal identification number to which the call will be billed; localized answering of 800-number requests, by means of a data base of zip codes and phone numbers that will reroute 800 requests to the most appropriate location or service representative; and a personal locator number, whereby you would inform a local service where you will be, again by means of a dialed identification number, and all calls would be routed to that number.

Coaxial cable places insulated multiple conductors inside each other in one cable; the increased wire surface reduces the skin effect. Use of coax for telephone transmission began in 1936, and is used for long-haul phone (carrying as many as 13,000 simultaneous voice channels) and cable TV (a 450-Mhz(Megahertz) system provides 60 TV channels). Cable delivery of television was originated for areas that could not receive broadcast TV, but of course now has begun to compete with network and local TV by providing tremendous diversity. See Figure 2.2 for the increase since 1976 in basic and pay cable TV; see Chapter 12 for a discussion of media competition. As of July 1983, 35% of U.S. TV households have cable service and 50% are passed by cable services. Currently 6200 cable systems serve 10,500 communities; another 1,500 systems are under construction. There are 65 satellite-delivered cable services (35 nationwide, 30 regional). Concentration is increasing here as with newspapers: 10 companies or multiple system operators have 50% of all subscribers. The most popular basic service is Spanish International Network, with 3.2 Spanish subscribers alone; the most popular pay service is Home Box Office, with 12 million. However, pay cable demand has dropped off in 1982-1983.

Interactive cable involves either one bidirectional or two coaxial channels, and a microprocessor at the head end (or both ends) to control the flow of information and use the TV as a distribution system. The first two-way cable experiments were in 1971 (see Veith, 1976). They were (a) Rediffusion, Inc.'s pilot system, in which 200 participants were able to view and order a delicatessen's offerings; (b) Sterling Communications' TV polling system, involving 10 terminals in four buildings (they were bought out by Time, which invested in HBO); and (c) Telecable Corp, which provided educational applications with audio and visual communication for some institutional users. Later the National Science Foundation

FIGURE 2.2 Penetration of Basic TV Cable in the United States

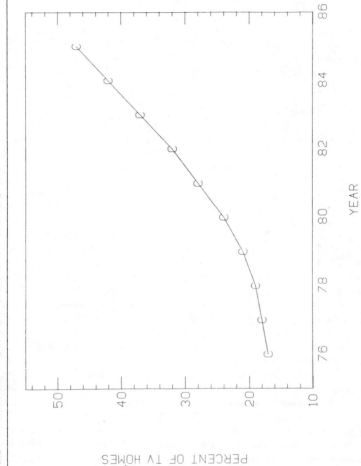

SOURCE: Cablevision (1983a).

sponsored two-way cable experiments (see Journal of Communication, 1978).

Optical fibers are finely spun silicon (in some cases, "plastic") threads (from 5 micrometers for "monomode" fibers to 100 micrometers for some "multimode" fibers). Monochromatic light from a laser (or light-emitting diode) is encoded with information and entered into the fiber at a critical angle to ensure total internal reflection, and received at a photoelectric receptor. Advantages of fiber optics include the abundance of cheap silicon, freedom from interference, weather-resistance, small size, massive bandwidth, and transmission security. At the Olympics, fiber optics carried 1342 simultaneous voice channels at 90 Mbps (megabits per second); some pilot cable TV fibers transmit 35-Ghz (gigahertz) TV signals. The transatlantic cable TAT8 will use optical fiber. However, repeaters are necessary (now, only every 26 km), fibers are quite fragile, so splicing techniques are expensive and touchy; and laser performance is not universally acceptable.

Microwave transmission is high-frequency radio transmission, and is used extensively for long-haul telephone transmission. Line-of-sight signals from towers within 30 km are amplified and retransmitted. AT&T has utilized analog microwave data links to provide digital service, called Data Under Voice (DUV). Short, high-traffic routes are fairly inexpensive, although a complete network link is dependent on each tower; additional nodes or routes are quite expensive. A related service is Multipoint Distribution Service (MDS), a microwave common carrier service. Until 1982 each city was assigned one 6 Mhz channel for use in redistribution of video signals. Each MDS tower is limited to 100 watts. Now, the FCC will shortly allocate about 10 channels per city (taking spectrum from Instructional Televison Fixed Service). The first commercial MDS service began in late 1973; future systems will likely be used to deliver commercial movie channels, but could be used for hybrid interactive communications such as delivery of software. There are currently about 750,000 subscribers to MDS services.

Cellular radio. Mobile telephone systems until recently were limited to a very few users who typically experienced busy signals. (See Bowers [1982] for an excellent review of mobile communications.) This was because only a few frequencies were available, they had to be separated by 75 miles before being reused, and they were assigned so they could not be shared.

Cellular radio involves a microwave link to a computer switch in the small geographical area (cell) where the user is currently located, and a retransmission to an unused frequency in the cell. Therefore a large area can provide many users with service because any one set of frequencies is unlikely to interfere with another set in another cell. (Digital packet radio uses bursts of digital pulses on the entire mobile frequency.) The 40 Mhz-bandwidth around the 900-Mhz frequency to be allocated by the FCC translates into about 222 simultaneous channels for each of three cells. As more users subscribe, the cell size can be reduced, freeing up more channels overall. (A controversial aspect of the allocation is that one license per city goes to the local telephone company, and one to a competitive provider who has made the best deal in terms of reducing FCC hearing paperwork.) Eventually this will be accomplished by satellite service, so there will be no connection to local telephone switching or retransmission. Telephone calls using cellular radio will have almost nothing in common with the invention by Bell! AT&T currently has a 2,000-user mobile phone pilot in Chicago. Telocator Network of America estimates there are now 180,000 mobile phone users but will be as many as 3 million by 1990. Arthur D. Little estimates 2.5 million beepers (small mobile phones in the form of pagers) now and 7 million by 1990 (Time, 1983a). The most advanced beepers display written text via LEDs; one model can store 9,100 characters (Dizzard, 1983).

Communication satellites are based upon the fact that an object orbiting at 35,680 km above the earth revolves around it at the same rate the earth rotates; hanging above the equator, it appears stationary over the earth. Thus, only three satellites are needed to cover most of the earth. Communication satellites are microwave relays, receiving and retransmitting frequencies in the C-band (6/4 Ghz), Ku-band (14/12 Ghz) and soon in the Ka-band (30/20 Ghz). (Japan already has a Ka-band satellite for data, facsimile, and video.) The satellite's transponders provide the communication relays; typically there are 24 per satellite, each with a bandwidth of 36 Mhz. For example, one of Westar's transponders provides one color TV channel, 1,200 voice channels, 16 1.544-Mbps channels, 400 64-Kbps (kilobits per second) channels, 600 40-Kbps channels, and some 50-Mbps channels used in the remaining 2 Mhz. At higher satellite frequencies and power, smaller ground antenna satellites can provide thin-route point-to-point networks, multipoint specialized networks (such as business data or teleconferencing), or point-to-multipoint networks (for audio, video, data broadcasts). They provide low-cost, low-error data communications, theoretically distance-insensitive pricing, and great flexibility for adding or changing network configuration. However, transmission security is still a problem, there is a half-second delay from the ground-satellite-ground "hop" that is a difficulty for data transmission, and inexpensive ground antennae require higher-frequency and more powerful satellites. The issue of satellite design, particularly for inexpensive international development purposes, is discussed by Rice and Parker (1979). With powerful-enough satellites combined with innovative transmission techniques, 2-foot receiver-only dishes are now being sold for $2,500 (Parker, 1982, 1983; Markoff, 1983). There are about 55,000 (of all sizes) in use now, up from 25,000 in 1981. These small antennae are already in use by information providers—such as Equatorial's "Spacetext," which will update online personal computer data bases, from satellites in the C-band. Continuing developments to conserve spectrum includes reducing the orbital spacing from 3 degrees to 2, reusing frequencies (polarizing, time division multiple access) and switching between satellites.

The next step, of course, is *direct broadcast satellites* (DBS; see Wigand, 1980, 1982). The FCC has given DBS "regulatory carte blanche," requiring no limits on the number of channels an operator may provide, no programming or access requirements, no ownership restrictions, and allowing either common-carrier or broadcast status. Service has been allocated to 50 Mhz in the 12-Ghz range. DBS services will broadcast commercial video directly to home receivers, as well as provide teletext capability. This will force local TV stations to localize and advertise, will stimulate more program production, extend coverage past cable limits, and will compete with theaters (although it may provide content to theaters). International DBS issues are very controversial (see the Wigand articles), insofar as national sovereignty (cultural and political) as well as economic exploitation and data security are concerned.

A variety of these separate transmission technologies may be combined into a transmission *network*. The motivation for the development of data networks came from an effort in the late 1960s by the Advanced Research Projects Agency (ARPA) to connect computer terminals over long distances, so that research institutions could use other institutions' computers. The first contact civilians had with such a network came in the form of the now-famous ARPANET, which also stimulated much of the early electronic messaging activity (see Rice and Case, 1983).

The ARPANET project director, Larry Roberts, was persuaded in 1972 to join some staff in forming Telenet, which was the first, and is still the most successful, public data network. Acquired by General Telephone (GTE) in 1979, Telenet corners 40% of the network market, serves about 250 cities, and in over 20 provides a 56 Kbps transmission channel by means of "backbone switches," which concentrate the data flow. Tymshare's Tymnet has nearly 40% of the market as well, and serves a similar number of cities with 4.8 or 6.9 Kbps lines. Following in revenue shares are United Telecommunications' Uninet, RCA's Cylix Corporation, Control Data's Cybernet, and Compuserve's Comlink. Several of these are or will soon begin using satellite distribution, to avoid long-distance carrier rates. A recent entry, Satellite Business Systems, is founded on the concept of satellite transmission to rooftop antennas belonging to large corporations with extensive data communication needs. AT&T's Net 1000 offers data storage, remote data processing, and data communications services.

Telecommunications networks represent the convergence and integration of many developments in communication technology. As such, they are the focus of intense engineering, marketing, and competitive efforts. They are also becoming the lightning rod for critical analyses of telecommunications infrastructures. Networks are seen to facilitate better control and coordination by transnational corporations of their activities in less developed countries; thus perpetuating the stratified world system (Mosco, 1982: Chap. 6). To provide their own national networks, or to compete with government-supported transnationals, developing countries have to avoid entering into dependent economic and technological relations. Yet it is very difficult to achieve the necessary technical expertise and financial resources without being drawn into such relations. Further, networks encourage unbalanced flows of information between the developed and developing nations, by storing and processing data outside of the country where they originated or are applied (Schiller, 1982: Chap. 2).

These issues are beyond the scope of this discussion, although alternative perspectives on telecommunications impacts are considered in the next chapter. The social and economic structures generating and maintaining telecommunications networks are appropriate and, some argue, the most fundamental elements of understanding media systems and technologies (Murdock and Golding, 1977).

A Storage Medium: Videodisc

Videodisc is a medium struggling for consumer acceptance, yet with vast potential for interactive education as well as for straightforward random-access storage. The earliest instructional projects were designed by Negroponte at MIT. These involved a simulated "tour" around Aspen, an interactive instructional program showing how to assemble and repair a bicycle, and an online visual catalogue of the Boston Museum of Fine Arts. Other applications include the entire slide collection of cell cultures for a biomedical specialty. A single optical videodisc can contain up to 54,000 visual frames on each side with a bandwidth of 14.7 Mhz. Sony (1982) considers videodisc part of a continuum of interactive video, from basic videotape recording (VTR), remote controlled VTR, "Responder" VTR, consumer laser videodisc, industrial laser videodisc, microcomputer-driven VTR, and microcomputer-driven videodisc. Each of these systems combines various attributes, such as fast duplication, compatibility with standard VTRs, media wear and recyclability, recording "in the field," system monitoring of user performance, frame-accurate access, flow-charting of the progress through content, branching capabilities, user-control of data encoding, and types of responses accepted. Videodiscs themselves have reached .3% to .7% penetration in the United States (Media Science, 1983; Nielsen, 1982a).

The videodisc process in general involves frequency modulation of a video and audio signal into one signal; the frequency spacing is then converted into spacings between, and lengths of, micropits in the disc. A read device reconverts signals from these pits into the intended image with sound. (The November 1983 issue of the Journal of the American Society for Information Science is devoted almost entirely to articles on videodiscs; also see Heath [1981] for an excellent introduction to videodisc technology and vendors; and Lerner, Metaxas, Scott, Adams, and Judd [1983,] for detailed tables on technical and storage characteristics.)

There are two general categories of videodisc technologies: stylus/capacitance/constant linear velocity and laser/optical/constant angular velocity. Within the two categories are two more distinctions.

Stylus/capacitance systems include *grooved* and *grooveless* systems. Both use a stylus, but the first involves a diamond-tipped stylus that tracks very thin grooves (38 grooves in the same width as a phonograph groove) to pick up electrical information instead of undulations. The grooveless system involves a flat stylus that does not read grooves but micropits, which convey information to an electrode in the sapphire stylus tip.

Laser/optical systems include *transparent* discs and *reflective* discs. The first type uses a flat, very flexible transparent disc through which light passes to project the micropit information into a laser decoder. The second type uses a stiff opaque disc, and light is reflected off the disc to a small mirror, which reflects the light into a laser decoder. Case (1981) compares the videodisc approaches in Table 2.1.

One of the implications of videodiscs is rapid access to massive storage for office information. Toshiba has released a system called DF-2000, which copies documents with a laser, stores them on a disc, and retrieves them in seconds. A videodisc can hold the equivalent of 2500 double-density floppy diskettes, or 2 gigabytes of data. The error rate is still too high at this time and system interfaces are basically still in development. However, an integrated information system using videodiscs, fiber optics, and simulated touch-sensitive TV screens has been installed at Disney's EPCOT Center in Florida (Guterl and Truxal, 1982). The system mixes still frames and motion video, even with real-time video contact with

TABLE 2.1 Videodisc Designs Compared

| | *TYPE OF SYSTEM* | | | |
| | *Capitance* | | *Optical* | |
Feature	*Groove*	*Grooveless*	*Reflective*	*Transparent*
Lower price:				
player	X	X		
disc				X
Playback (per side)				
60 min	X	X		
30 min			X	X
Still frame	(some)	(some)	X	X
Random access		X	X	X
Programmable		X	X	X
Microprocessor		(optional)	X	X
Slow motion forward/reverse		X	X	X
No disc/stylus wear			X	X
Local production/reproduction				X
Stereo/two-track sound		X	X	X
Software variety	X		X	
Life	shortest	short	long	long
Developer (Example)	RCA	JVC	Philips	Thompson ARDEV

SOURCE: Case (1981).

reservation clerks at restaurants. The rapid growth of videodiscs in education and training is described by Kearsley (1981).

AN EXAMPLE OF MEDIA COMBINED: VIDEOTEX

Tyler's (1979) definition of *videotex* seems the most serviceable: Videotex is a

> system for the widespread dissemination of textual and graphic information by wholly electronic means for display on low-cost terminals (often suitably equipped television receivers) under the selective control of the recipient, using control procedures easily understood by untrained users.

There are two general kinds of videotex: broadcast videotex, often called teletext, and interactive videotex, often called videotext.

In the most common form, teletext consists of one-way transmission over video broadcast frequencies, using several lines of the vertical blanking interval (VBI). The VBI contains video control lines pertaining to the picture, the audio, line synchronization, framing, testing, and technical codes; and are the (typically unseen) lines during which the picture cursor returns from the bottom of the video screen to the upper left. Some of the VBI lines are empty, so information can be encoded in them. Each time the cursor is returned, one or more pages of information are delivered. A set of "pages" or screens constitutes a cycle of information and is broadcast continuously. The more pages in a cycle, the longer it takes to retrieve a given page, because more pages have to pass through the cycle until the desired page is broadcast again. Using two VBIs, a reasonable access time of ten seconds limits the data base to about 100-200 pages. A teletext user can press a button on the teletext keypad that selects certain pages of information; they are "stripped" from the VBI as they pass by in broadcast stream, decoded, stored, and displayed, either replacing the video or overlaying it (as in captioning for the deaf). A TV set must be connected to a keypad and decoder (which includes memory, a display generator, and processing capabilities) and switched to teletext mode, to provide information service. Further teletext distinctions are between *narrowband* (using the VBI or a FM radio station signal) and *broadband* (using a full video channel, cable, or MDS).

Videotext generally involves two-way (interactive) communication by means of a telephone link between a modem, a processor-enhanced TV screen (possibly even a special, expensive terminal) and a local or distant computer data base via some network. Here the user selects specific pages from a large computer data base. Limits on pages are based upon computer response time and available computer ports. Videotext distinctions are between narrowband (telephone links) and broadband (cable, optical fibers); and further, between *intermittent* interactivity (where the information is downloaded and stored in the processor, freeing up the phone line) and *continuous* (involving a connection during the entire session). Some continuous systems are so-called hybrids in which the downlink uses a different medium than the uplink. Further technical considerations relate to how the data and graphics are transmitted and displayed at the terminal. See Tydeman, Lipinski, Adler, Nyhan, and Zwimpfer (1982) for the most comprehensive discussion of technical, policy, and market aspects of videotex.

There are clear benefits and disadvantages with the teletext and videotext approaches: trade-offs of content limits, access time, interactivity, expense, utilization of networks, and charging mechanisms.

As of March 1983 the FCC has ruled that VBI lines 14-18, 20, and 21 are available for teletext, that individual operators can decide to carry the signals or not, that they are not subject to the fairness doctrine or equal-time rules, and that teletext service providers can decide if they are common or private carriers. Such policy decisions affect the many actors in videotex delivery: the information providers, advertisers, the data-base operators (local and remote), the service center, communication networks, terminal and monitor vendors, billing arrangements, and the users. Tydeman et al. define five kinds of service: information retrieval, transactions (such as home shopping), messaging, computing (including video-games and user storage), and telemonitoring (e.g., home security).

Videotext originated at the British Post Office in the late 1960s, as Sam Fedida figured a way to increase utilization of the phone service. The TV screen was first used only as a display device; Prestel service began in 1970-1971. General U.S. consumer videotext service began in 1979 with THE SOURCE, followed by H&R Block's COMPUSERVE and the Dow Jones News/Retrieval. Other systems—mostly pilots—are shown in Table 2.2.

Videotex is taking all forms and shapes. Cable or satellite can deliver full channels of information and, thus, access to much larger teletext data bases; the channel can be broken into multiple teletext services, or diverse content can be made available at different times of the day or in different proportions (by altering the times it is broadcast within any cycle) or to different subaudiences (as in Reuter's monitor service delivered by satellite and cable). For example, KSL-TV in Salt Lake augments teletext with touchtone teletext; users request additional menus and information pages by phone, which are broadcast once, and that user receives the desired information without delaying others' access time. Videodisc storage is already increasing system capacity and decreasing access time in some videotex projects. Distribution by cellular radio would allow portable terminals. Speech and data can be multiplexed on the telephone network so that videotex use would not obstruct voice use. Video compression would allow delivery of two video channels to be reconstructed in the receiving TV. CBS's REACH service, a joint test with American Bell in Ridgewood, New Jersey, included 100 information sources, a personal electronic clipping service, messaging, a personal calendar with a tickler file, personal files to save pages, financial transaction, and a way to search across all data bases at once. Both the Hi-Ovus interactive community information system in Japan and the Elie/St. Eustache project

TABLE 2.2 List of Videotext Trails and Services

System	Sponsor	Location	Start Date	User[a]	First Status	Number[b]
UK						
Prestel	British Telecom	UK	1978[c]	R	C	25K
Prestel International	British Telecom	Nine countries	1981	B	C	—
France						
Teletel	PTT	Velizy	1981[c]	R	T	10K
Directory	PTT	Ille-et-Vilaine	1981	R	T	250K
Germany						
Bildschirmtext	Deutsche Bundespost	Dusseldorf	1980[c]	R	T	6000
Netherlands						
Viditel	PTT	Netherlands	1980[c]	B	T	6800
Italy						
Videotel	PTT	Rome	1981	—	—	1000
Norway						
Teledata	PTT	—	—	—	—	60
Finland						
Telset	Helsingin Telset Oy	Helsinki	1978	B	C	260
Telset	Teletieto Oy	Finland, six cities	1981	—	T	—
Spain	PTT	—	—	—	—	200
Sweden						
Datavision	Swedish PTT	Stockholm	1979	—	T	100
Switzerland						
Videotex	PTT	Berne	1979	R	T	150

(Continued)

Table 2.2 Continued

System	Sponsor	Location	Start Date	User[a]	First Status[b]	Number[b]
Austria						
Bildschirmtext	PTT	Austria	1981	R	T	300
Denmark						
Teledata	PTT	Denmark	1981	R	T	200
South Africa						
Beltel	PTT	—	1982	—	—	300
Japan						
Hi-Ovis	MITI/VISDA	Higashi Ikoma	1978	R	T	156
CCIS	MPT	Japan	1976	R	C	500
Captain	MPT and Nippon	Tokyo	1979	—	T	2000
Hong Kong						
Viewdata	Tel Co	Hong Kong	1981	R	T	500
Venezuela						
SOI Project	Office of Information & Statistics	Caracas	1980	R	T	30
Brazil						
Videotex	Telsep	Sao Paulo	1982	R	T	—
Venezuela	—	Caracas	1981	—	—	25
Australia						
Myer Emporium	Myer Emporium	—	1982	—	—	12
Canada[d]						
Vista	Bell Canada & Canadian DOC	Toronto & Montreal	1981	R	T	491
Telidon Project	OECA	Ontario	1980	E	T	55
Project Vidon	Alberta Tel Co	Calgary	1980	—	T	150
Grass Roots	Manitoba Tel Co	Manitoba	1981	F	C	700
Mercury	New Brunswick Tel Co	St Johns	1981	R	T	50
Elie	Manitoba Tel Co	Elie	1981	F	T	145
Videotron	Telecable Videotron	Montreal	1981	R	T	250

Name	Owner/Provider	Location	Year			
Ida	Manitoba Tel Co	Winnipeg	1980	R	T	100
CANTEL	Canadian Govt.	National	1981	R	C	100
INET	Transcanada Tel Co	National	1982	B	T	400
Marketfax	Faxtel	National	1982	B	C	30
BC Tel	British Columbia Tel Co	B.C.	1981	B	T	50
—	Alberta Tel Co	Alberta	1981	E	T	30
Pathfinder	Sastzatchewan Tel Co	Sask.	1982	R	T	25+
Teleguide	Infomart	Ontario	1982	R	C	1000
TVOntario	TVOntario, others	Ontario	1979	E	T	—
Vidacom	Communications Dept., Telecable Videotron, others	Montreal	1983	R	T	250
—	Martime Tel Co	New Brunswick	1982	R	T	—
Cabot	Memorial University	New Foundland	1981	R	T	tourists
Novatex	Teleglobe Canada	National	1981	B	T	325
United States						
GTE's 'Infovision'	GTE	US	1982	B	C	—
Green Thumb	USDA	Kentucky	1980	F	T	200
Viewtel/Channel 2000	OCLC	Columbus Ohio	1980	R	T	200
Viewtron	AT&T and Knight-Ridder	Coral Gables	1980	B	T	260
Dow Jones News Retrieval Service	Dow Jones	Princeton	1977	B	C	70K+
The Source	STC/Readers Digest/CDC	US	1979	B	C	75K
CompuServe	CompuServe	US	1979	R	C	100K

(Continued)

Table 2.2 Continued

System	Sponsor	Location	Start Date	User[a]	First Status	Number[b]
Express Information	Un.Am.Bank/Compuserve	Knoxville	1980	R	T	400
AT&T EIS	Radio Shack	Albany	1979	R	T	75
Instant Update	AT&T	US	1981	F	C	—
Cox Cable/Indax	Profarmer	San Diego	1981	R	T	300
Dow Jones Cable	Cox Cable/KPBS	Park Cities, TX	1980	R	T	35
Project Pronto	Dow Jones/Sammons	New York	1981	R	T	200
Qube	Chemical Bank	Columbus	1981	R	T	100
Times Mirror Gateway	Warner-Amex	Los Angeles	1982	R	T	350
ContelVision	Times Mirror	Atlanta, Manassas	1982	R	T	100
PLATO	Continental Tel Co	US	1961	E,B	C	1000's
	CDC		PLATO IV:1974			
Reach	CBS/AT&T Info. Sys.	Ridgewood, NJ	1982	R	T	200
CompUStar	Comp-U-Card	—	—	R	C	—
Firsthand	J.C. Penney	Minneapolis	1982	F	T	188
Bison	A. H. Belo	Dallas	1981	B	C	80
Knowledge Index	Dialog	Palo Alto, CA	—	B	C	19K
Newsnet (Newsletters)		—	1982	B	C	1000
AgVision	Elanco	Indianapolis	1981	F	C	850
Keyfax	Nat'l Teletext Machine	—	—	R	C	350
Electronic News	Harris	Kansas	—	R	C	58
A-T Videotext	Tiffin Advertiser Tribune	Tiffin, Ohio	—	R	C	30
Agristar	Des Moines Register/	Des Moines	New	F	C	—
	Agridata Resources					
—	Agribusiness	Bakersfield,CA	1982	F	C	500
Learn Alaska Network	University of Alaska	Alaska	1982	E	T	20

				R	T	100
Homebase	Citibank	New York	—	R	T	140
Viewcom Electronic Editions	Cowles	Spokane	—	R	T	45
Louisville Courier Journal		Louisville	—	R	C	—
Game Line	Control Video Corp	Vienna, VA	New	R	C	—
Shuttle	Microperipheral	Regional: Seattle 1st	New			

SOURCES: Arlen (1983) Butler Cox and Partners, (1980), Canadian Ministry of Supply and Services (1983), Rice and Paisley, (1982), Tydeman et al. (1982), trade literature.

NOTE: Most of these trials have ended or have developed into commercial services. For example, the Cox Index trial is the first phase of developing commercial services for the 200,000 on the cable system. Most services use specific videotex technology such as Prestel, Telidon, or Antiope, though some (and soon more) offer services via home computers. Most financial transaction services are not included; neither are closed user group/private systems (such as England's SONY which offers 5,000 pages and plans to connect its 4,000 dealers; there are more than 200 private systems each in England and the rest of Europe (CSP International, 1982).

a. Many services actually treat multiple groups, such as residential use of banking transactions, or general/public use. General and public uses are included under residential. B=Business; E=Educational; F=Farming; R=Residential.
b. Number of terminals, trial participants, or subscribers.
c. Experiments were begun in mid-1970s.
d. For an overview of the more than 30 Telidon trials and services, see Feeley (1983).

in Canada use optical fibers—in the former case, to facilitate TV retransmission, TV studio broadcasting, video request services, still pictures, and videotex services; in the latter case, to transmit digital telephone, cable TV, FM radio, and Grassroots (agricultural) videotex simultaneously. It's clear that videotex is a wide-ranging "medium" that is medium-independent!

SUMMARY

The point here is that we must understand technological developments and implications of regulatory policies concerning specific technologies; but it is most important to understand what kinds of communication functions they provide. In the videotex example, nearly any portion of the system may be facilitated by a wide range of media technologies. In one sense this means we have more to learn about the technological aspects of various media; in another it means that the uses and impacts of the medium are the enduring research issues. The next chapter couches both new media and their research issues in the context of traditional and developing communication theories.

NOTES

1. Parts of this section were written by Everett Rogers, and appeared first in earlier versions of Chapter 4.
2. This survey is reported in the *San Francisco Chronicle* (1983).
3. This survey is also reported in the *San Francisco Chronicle* (1983).

RONALD E. RICE and
FREDERICK WILLIAMS

3 Theories Old and New: *The Study of New Media*

"New media" is used in this book to refer to a broad class of recently available communication technologies. However, as Chapter 1 emphasized, these media are new only to the generation first experiencing them, and indeed they may be viewed in light of theoretic and empirical work associated with more "traditional" media. That is one of the main points of this chapter: We need not jettison useful communication theories when we wish to understand the new media. Indeed, the new media provide fertile test beds for many of our theories and models.

However, we also argue that we should take advantage of the communication behaviors and social contexts associated with the new media to further specify and modify those theories. Several sections pointedly review theories developed during the rise of the mass media, by questioning their complete applicability to new uses and users. Finally, we argue that we may have to not only rethink current communication theories but, indeed, borrow from other disciplines and even construct new concepts and theories. This process is one area in which communication researchers may take the lead, as suggested at the end of Chapter 1. On the other hand, we cannot ignore the new questions and challenges the new media put to old theories.

The chapter considers such issues at three levels of analysis: the interpersonal, the organizational, and the institutional. Some of the topics introduced here are discussed more fully in separate chapters. Finally, the assumptions *behind* such theorizing—theories *about* theories of use and impacts—are briefly summarized. That section is intended to raise questions about the biases, ideological concepts, and analytical constraints that are associated with specific theoretical perspectives.

ON THE PERSONAL QUALITIES OF NEW MEDIA

The new media loosen the constraints of traditional media, yet allow the use of combinations of attributes of each of those media. Indeed, we are able to talk about certain functional characteristics of new media with which communication research is already familiar. New media, like previous media, are basically extensions of human senses and effectors. In fact, some of the distinctions between the new media and traditional media are not as discontinuous as are the distinctions between traditional media and natural media such as hearing, seeing, and speaking.

The fundamental interactivity of new media was discussed in Chapter Two. Because the new media are interactive and may be used in a variety of new situations—flexible interpersonal communication (for example, through electronic mail), group communication (through video conferencing), and private use of public information (through videotex)—the discrete distinction between interpersonal communication and mass-mediated communication is giving way to a continuum of communication behaviors. Figure 3.1 shows this continuum.

With traditional communication media, there was often a visible distinction between sources of personalized communication and impersonalized information. If individuals wanted to learn more from one another or to affect one another's behaviors, they engaged in an unmediated interactive situation, where nuances and responses would arise quickly, based upon questions or statements as well as the nonverbal channel. That sort of personalized instruction or information is not fully possible from traditional television or newspapers. However, it is no longer available only from unmediated conversation. Sources of satisfaction for personal communication needs are no longer limited to face-to-face contexts, traditional mail, or the telephone. Perhaps the new media highlight the fact that although satisfaction of individual needs was inherently *possible* through most traditional media, as long as media were marketed to mass audiences, interactivity was typically *unlikely*. One implication is that theories involving media uses and needs satisfactions

FIGURE 3.1   New Media Create a Continuum Between
Formerly Discrete Categories of Interpersonal
and Mass-Mediated Communication

Interpersonal	Group or Organizational	Mass-Mediated
Communication	Communication	Communication

←-------------------------------------New Media------------------------------------→

should be expanded to accommodate the ability of certain new media to satisfy different as well as more traditional interpersonal needs.

One of the issues on the personal level of communication is that the new media are often claimed to be impersonal or to depersonalize relationships among users. Yet, research into the subjective qualities of media and of their uses and gratifications indicates that these effects may be as much a consequence of our restricted use of a medium as of the physical restrictions a given technology may impose. In this section we first survey some of the concepts advanced by Short, Williams, and Christie (1976) in their monograph, *The Social Psychology of Telecommunications*, then add a few notes about the interaction of media "personalness" and uses and gratifications.

The Social Presence of a Communication Medium

How does one sense that an act of communication is "person oriented" or that the message conveys some of the person's "presence"? This personal or social differentiating quality of communication acts is what Short et al. have stressed in the study of the psychological aspects of using telecommunications media. They call it *social presence*. It is reflected in how a participant in a communication exchange would fill in such semantic differential scales as "unsociable-sociable," "insensitive-sensitive," "cold-warm," and "impersonal-personal" when evaluating the medium used. The mean score of the summed scales represents to what extent the medium is considered to convey social presence. Short et al. and Albertson (1980) provide more details on these scales.

You might expect that a business letter would typically have less social presence than a face-to-face conversation. Indeed, studies have shown this. Table 3.1 provides one such set of ratings of perceived social presence.

Chief among the reasons given for the differentiation among media in social presence are the stimulus-conveying restrictions of some media compared with others. The most salient restrictions are those related to the conveyance of the *nonverbal* aspects of communication. For example, the telephone cannot convey the proxemic (physical distance and placement) and kinesic (gestures and facial expressions) dimensions of a personal conversation.

Precisely because the telephone is lower in social presence than face-to-face communication, people are less easily deceived by other communicants and are able to make more accurate evaluations of others' information via the telephone. This decrease in visual cues and physical proximity may lessen negative feelings in negotiating over the phone. People seem to feel more effective in their dealing with others, and participation is more equal. Muson (1982) argues that most speaker cues are verbal anyway, so the phone increases their effect. But a combined audio and television link can allow the exchange of many nonverbal cues (see Chapter 9).

Short et al. (1976) and Johansen (1977) exhaustively review the research on comparisons among communication channels such as face-to-face, telephone, and audio/computer/video conferencing. (See also Dutton, Fulk, and Steinfield, 1982; Fowler and Wackerbarth, 1980; Johansen, 1977; Johansen, Vallee, and Spangler, 1979; Krueger and Chapanis, 1980; Muson, 1982; Reid, 1977; Strickland, Guild, Barefoot, and Patterson, 1978; and Williams, 1978.) Generally, these studies indicated that teleconferencing, for example, was accepted and effective for tasks involving information exchange, routine decision making, or cooperative problem solving (low social presence tasks); but it is not as good for getting to know people, bargaining and negotiation, and tasks involving serious conflict (high social presence tasks) (Champness, 1973: Noll 1977; Thorngren, 1977; Tyler, Katsoulis, and Cook, 1976; Williams, 1978).

TABLE 3.1 Social Presence Ratings of Five Media

Communication Mode	Social Presence[a]
Face-to-Face	0.81
Television	0.24
Multispeaker audio	-0.18
Telephone audio	-0.52
Business letter	-0.85

SOURCE: Short, et al. (1976:71).
a. Social presence index ranges between +0.9 and –0.9.

Table 3.2 shows how organizational members rated the appropriateness of electronic mail for a variety of tasks typically performed in business activities (Rice and Case, 1983). These tasks and the questions were the same as those developed and used by Short et al.

In general, respondents felt that electronic mail was most appropriate for the kinds of tasks requiring less social interaction and less social intimacy. Note, however, that some tasks (generating ideas, decision making, resolving disagreements, and bargaining) do not seem inappropriate to experienced computer users as they do to the casual, novice, or nontechnical user. Thus, one's social or organizational role and task context affect the perceived social presence or appropriateness of the medium used.

We also suggest that the amount and type of channel *redundancy* may affect the appropriateness and effectiveness of a medium. That is, highly interpersonal relationships entail kinds of uncertainty that can be reduced only by sufficient amounts of redundancy provided by nonverbal (proxemic and kinesic) information, or simply more redundancy within a single channel. For example, the spoken language provides more ongoing redundancy and contextualization than textual language, so the telephone is perceived as more appropriate than a letter, for many social activities.

Two further qualities of a medium are also particularly relevant to social presence—the potential for interactivity and the privacy-versus-public quality of the medium. The former is simply the potential for immediate, two-way exchanges. Feedback facilitates an ongoing regulation

TABLE 3.2 Appropriateness of Electronic Mail for Various Tasks

	Percentage Responding *"Appropriate"*[a]	
Task	*Manager*[b]	*Computer Personnel*
Exchanging Information	100.0%	97.0%
Asking Questions	95.0	100.0
Exchanging Opinions	81.0	95.5
Staying in Touch	84.1	89.1
Generating Ideas	73.0	89.1
Decision-Making	46.7	64.5
Exchanging Confidential Information	30.0	39.4
Resolving Disagreements	15.3	35.6
Bargaining/Negotiating	18.0	32.3

a. Bipolar scale. Average $N = 62$; range $N = 55$ to 66. The most conservative and global 95% confidence interval for between-task and across-personnel comparisons is equal to 1.96 times the square root of $(.5x.5)/62$. Thus, percentages differing by more than 12.4% are significant.

b. Measured at two to five months after first usage of electronic mail. By t-tests, there were no significant differences in managers' responses between this time 2 period and time 1, shortly after first use. Computer personnel responses were collected only at time 2.

and cueing of a communication interaction. The privacy or public aspect of a medium refers to the individual's consciousness of whether "outside" individuals may be able to monitor an exchange. The less privacy, the less potential for communication to become personalized and, hence, the lower the social presence.

One additional consideration is that the *context* in which we choose a medium may itself affect attitudes about social presence. For example, a written note between two individuals might be taken as low in social presence if one had rejected the opportunity to speak to the other personally, but may be rated high if it is a love letter mailed across the country.

Several media-related factors are critical for interpersonal communication. For example, the nonverbal code weighs heavily in this process and any restrictions upon its exchange, when such codes provide information important to, or about, the communication, are apt to make communication more impersonal. Also, the movement of communicative interactions from impersonal to personal levels benefits according to the potential for interaction. Further, if others are eavesdropping on a conversation, it is likely to be less personal. Finally, movement to a personal level of exchange is not likely to be encouraged if it begins with the other person's intentionally choosing a less personal medium of communication.

This reasoning is consonant with contemporary theory in interpersonal communication (e.g., Miller, 1976, 1978; Miller and Steinberg, 1975). In general, interpersonal communication evolves from communication based upon cultural or social stereotypes to a mutual focus upon individuals. This necessitates a gathering of "personal information" in the context.

The importance of social presence may be heightened when other media are competing for the user's attentions, or when a specific individual is being singled out from a group for communication (Williams, Paul, and Ogilvie, 1957). Conversely, decreased social presence may facilitate the learning of novel tasks, as there would be less interference due to heightened arousal (Goleman, 1983). This again reinforces both the contextual and interpersonal aspects of social presence.

The point of all this is that in choosing our alternatives among the new technologies—e.g., electronic messaging over voice telephone, teleconferencing over face-to-face meeting—there is a dual consideration of both technical and contextual restrictions of a medium (reflected in its ability to convey social presence) as well as our willingness to overcome those restrictions by persuasive and stylistic strategies. Indeed, Hiemstra (1982), by analyzing the interaction sequences and content of a computer conference, found that most of the forms of the very interpersonal process of "saving face" were maintained even in this text-based communication medium.

We must also take into account the perceptual sets that others may have when they are invited to communicate using a particular medium. An individual may have received so many impersonal telex messages that even if a sender employed a variety of personal stylistic devices, they might be overlooked because no personal communication is expected. (This is akin to parents' complaining about the use of instructional television in schools on the belief that nothing serious can be learned from a "light entertainment" medium.)

In all, if we are to consider the personalness (or potential "depersonalization") of alternative technologies of communication, we might consider more specifically the concept of social presence. If we require that mediated communication be able to operate at the interpersonal level for motivation or conflict resolution, we will want to select a medium with high social presence and capitalize on it in our message formulations. If we are technically restricted—as when a teleconference is audio only—then we may want to put a special emphasis upon stylistic and persuasive strategies that increase social presence. At the other extreme, if our communication does not particularly require social presence, as in a purely informational exchange or simple direction-giving, there may be no need to invest in expensive technologies for purposes of obtaining it. For example, if the members of an organization have a need to coordinate their calendars, a modest shared computer file (as a "computer conference") might be far superior to face-to-face meetings (see Hiltz and Turoff, 1978; Rice, 1980b; Short et al., 1976). These considerations are just a few components of a more complete understanding of how people seek, need, use, and exchange information (Dervin, 1981; Taylor, 1982).

The social presence theory is not without difficulties, however. First, in an effort to isolate any medium effects, some social presence research was conducted in laboratory settings, using simulated tasks and "unrepresentative" ad hoc groups. This limits the research's generalizability to actual "business conditions" where other factors associated with the medium may be far more instrumental in determining acceptance and use. Steinfield (1983), for example, shows that many uses of organizational electronic mail are for routine and highly social activities that fall outside those functional, business meeting tasks identified by Short et al.

Second, social presence is at best a vague concept, never clearly defined by its proponents. Social presence is typically marked by such adjectives as "sociable, sensitive, warm, and personal," yet is never explicitly operationalized.

Third, some research results question the influence of "social presence" in specific situations. Although Irving (1981) found greater use of oral channels for activities rated "intermediate" on social presence, telephone was ranked higher than was face-to-face (p. 96). Irving also found that distance effects seemed to override social presence influences in his study (p. 104). Other activity/media relations also appear unrelated or contrary to the social presence notion. Rosenbloom and Wolek (1970) demonstrated that researchers typically used oral channels for acquiring research information and written means for assessing and evaluating results (p. 49) a finding that seems more related to the permanence of written communications than to any variation in social presence. Goddard's (1973) results go directly against the social presence model, showing the high social presence activity of bargaining was accompanied by substantial use of the telephone. Dormois, Fioux, and Gensollen (1978) demonstrated that written communication was often a follow-up to prior oral exchange, such that high social presence activities (e.g., negotiating) can and often did result in a heavy paper flow. Ruchinskas (1982) also showed a positive relationship between negotiation and use of the telephone. The most comprehensive review of media comparisons involving the telephone (Reid, 1977), concluded that the very small incremental effect of the visual channel (face-to-face or video) over the audio channel (telephone) indicated that there actually may be little effect of social presence at all.

Thus, we must reserve judgment upon the adequacy or universality of this theory until we can develop an explicit operationalization and an understanding of the social, organizational and task attributes specifying the nature of social presence.

Personalness, Uses and Gratifications, and Other Attitudinal Dimensions

Looking at attitudes toward and use of media from a wider perspective than social presence theory further illuminates the contextual nature of media. Two reports of ongoing studies in the attitudinal correlates of communications technologies offer evidence of the distinction of personalness as well as other attitudinal dimensions. In one study (Williams, Phillips, and Lum, 1982), twelve different media were rated by 68 university students according to their importance for fulfilling 35 of the "media-related needs" as defined in an earlier study by Katz and his colleagues (Blumler and Katz, 1974; Katz, Gurevitch, and Hass, 1973) of uses and gratifications. As would be expected, very self-oriented or personal needs that were rated to be important to the student (e.g., "to know myself," "to participate in discussions with my friends," "to participate in the experience of other people") were all highly associated with face-to-face communication. Items that would less likely require a quality of social presence in communication ("to understand what goes on in the United States," "to get to know the true quality of our leaders," "to know what the world thinks about the United States") were associated much more with mass media (newspapers, broadcast television) than with more intimate forms of communication. The respondents related videotape and cable television to such needs as "to be entertained" or "to escape from the reality of everyday life."

Although these findings can be considered commonplace, it was of interest to the researchers to see how certain other media would be differentiated according to these needs. Particularly visible in the results was how the telephone elicited responses markedly in accordance with most person-centered needs that might benefit from a medium high in social presence. For example, use of the telephone was most highly related to the need "to spend time with friends." This is in contrast to the generalizations of Short et al., who saw the telephone as a somewhat impersonal medium when used in business communication (as it often is).

We mention this finding not so much as evidence of attitudes of certain groups, but as evidence that we can probably assume that social presence as associated with the telephone is probably far more a function of context and needs gratifications than it is a quality of the medium. (It is ironic, we think, that although the telephone has now been with us for a century, with the exception of the research referenced in Pool's work [1977, 1982a] and that by Short and colleagues, the serious study of the telephone has been largely overlooked in communication or social psychological circles.)

Although Williams et al. acknowledge theoretical shortcomings of the uses and gratifications categories, the results of this study do point out considerable emphasis upon personalness in rating the importance of needs.

The second study (Phillips, 1982) also provided evidence of the importance of personalness in differentiating among media or communication technologies but also suggested the relevance of certain other attitudinal dimensions. In this research 60 university students' discussions of media were content-analyzed for adjectives that were subsequently the basis for a 37-scale 7-point semantic differential instrument. Then 128 students evaluated 7 media on these scales: radio, broadcasting television, cable television, newspapers, video cassette recorders, the telephone, and home computers.

A subsequent multiple discriminant analysis yielded three main functions that were subjectively labeled as (a) familiarity, (b) importance, and (c) personalness. The discrimination of those media on each of the three functions can be seen in the centroid values given in Table 3.3.

The first point to note is that unlike the findings by Short et al., subjective qualities of familiarity and importance preceded personalness as discriminating attitudinal dimensions among the different media. Although these results, due to methodological and respondent differences,

TABLE 3.3 Media Functions as Portrayed by Multiple Discriminant Analysis

Medium	Familiarity[a]	Importance	Personalness
Radio	1.33[b]	-.34	-.07
Broadcast Television	.57	-.55	-.47
Cable Television	-1.09	-.12	.07
Newspaper	1.98	.42	-.90
Video Cassette Recorder	-1.66	-1.05	.27
Telephone	.97	.84	1.64
Computers	-2.08	1.92	-.49

SOURCE: Phillips (1983).
a. "Familiarity" comprised inexpensive, old, and common. "Importance" comprised important, time-saving, and necessary. "Personalness" comprised personal and private.
b. Centroids; positive values are in the direction of the function labels. Wilks's stepwise selection method used. Three functions accounted for 88% of variance.

are not directly comparable with the preceding study, we suggest that the subjective correlates of media have more of a multidimensional quality than was stressed in the earlier research. Distinctions in terms of familiarity were what most researchers would expect; for example, newspapers are maximally distinguished from computers. Yet despite their unfamiliarity, computers, as shown in terms of Function 2 are rated as more *important* than newspapers. Further, on this function newer media such as video cassette or cable TV are relatively unimportant. Finally, in terms of personalness, the telephone again is highly rated, with newspapers rated impersonal. Plotting the centroids with respect to the orthogonal functions shows the telephone and newspapers to be perceived as inexpensive, common, and serious; or television radio and newspapers as familiar, impersonal, and public.

As a summary, we might point to the analysis of eight media from the uses and gratifications perspective by Lometti, Reeves, and Bybee (1977). This is one of the most straightforward and explicit analyses of media functions from the "uses and grats" literature. The primary theme of their research was, what exactly are the dimensions of gratification? Naturally, the authors could not answer whether the dimensions related to the *content* typically associated with a given channel or to specific *attributes* of that channel. This is a critical topic for communication research.

From their review of gratification dimensions suggested or tested by previous researchers, and from a thoughtful discussion of the drawbacks in that research, Lometti et al. scaled nine potentially salient gratifications with respect to eight communication sources (books, family, film, friends, magazines, newspapers, radio, and television). The questionnaire included a variety of univariate measures for each medium, to further identify the resultant dimensions. Subjects were 117 middle school, 135 high school, and 200 college students, probabilistically sampled. Three-way multidimensional scaling (INDSCAL) revealed three dimensions, which explained 95% of the variance. In order of decreasing variance, they were (a) surveillance/entertainment, (b) affective guidance, and (c) behavioral guidance. The behavioral guidance dimension primarily comprised the specific behavioral guidance variable as well as "companionship" and "factual information." Interpersonal sources were located high on this dimension; radio and television were located low. The surveillance dimension comprised factual information (very strongly), and (negatively) "excitement," companionship, and "substitute companionship." Print media were located high on this dimension; interpersonal and electronic media were located low. In general, interpersonal, electronic, and print communication sources tended to cluster in similar locations across the three dimensions.

Although all three subject subgroups produced the same three dimensions and discriminated equally well among them, they attributed changing salience to the three dimensions. The first dimension decreased in salience as age increased; the third increased; and the second showed little change. For the purposes of the discussion in this section, we might argue that our preliminary results can be accommodated within Lometti et al.'s framework. Personalness can be interpreted as affective as well as behavioral guidance. While the typically one-way mass media of radio and TV are negatively, if at all, related to the more personal dimensions, electronic (but mass) media co-locate with interpersonal sources on the entertainment end of the surveillance dimension, as opposed to the print media. We would hypothesize that were the telephone and the more interactive new media included in Lometti et al.'s study, they would cross some of the dimensional poles, and co-locate with the interpersonal sources on one or both of the personal dimensions.

Communicating Through or With New Media?

Hewes (1983) wonders whether some new media, such as computers, are indeed media, in that we do not really communicate with another person when using them. This demurral would apply to programming, videotex, online delphi analysis, interactive cable, and the like. Specifically, his comments imply that we communicate with the original system designers, programmers, and data-base indexers when we use such new media. This is, of course, a crucial and raging controversy in the fields of information processing, learning theory, artificial intelligence, cognitive psychology, and computer science. The question is, do we actually "communicate" with computers? This topic is a bit of a red herring for our purposes: Insofar as we view new media as facilitating interactive (but mediated) communication for instrumental as well as entertainment purposes, this very important philosophical question may be kept in the wings. We mention here only a few aspects of the question, which may provide opportunities for communication researchers to contribute to the debate.

The co-orientation model of communication posits that we build models of another person, and of ourselves, as we exchange information and evaluate each other's responses (McLeod and Chaffee, 1973). This approach is quite similar to the results of an analysis by McGuire and Stanley (1972), which found the same communication patterns in person-to-person interactions as in person-to-computer interactions. In general, commercial computers do not build up a model of the user, although operational artificial intelligence systems are able to parse the logic in users' interactions with the system, "learn" about users' knowledge and experience with the system, and provide guidance for further use. But this co-orientation modeling is similar to the "mental model" theory of human-technology interaction. This theory posits that humans, no matter their level of experience, develop images that lead to a "conceptual representation of a device which is used in interacting with that device" (Borgman, 1982). This mental model may be at the heart of actual use of information systems, particularly retrieval systems. The "conversation" that a user has in such interactions may be analyzed in ways quite similar to how interpersonal conversations develop, change, and are maintained. Indeed, one of the very first evaluations of information retrieval behavior

(Penniman, 1975) was heavily based upon conversational sequencing research by Jaffe and Feldstein (1970) and continued by Cappella (1980). The data for both studies are conceptually similar and may be provided and analyzed automatically (see Chapter 4 and Rice and Borgman, 1983). An integrated theory of communicative interaction may profit by research at the interface of these various disciplines.

Videogames: Entertainment, Interaction, and Computer Literacy

Another opportunity to consider social dimensions of new media is in the area of entertainment. Except for a few authors, this topic has generally been ignored by communication researchers (Mendelsohn, 1966; Stephenson, 1967; Tannenbaum, 1980; see also Chapter 5 of this volume). This oversight is particularly glaring given that "most people use most media most of the time for entertainment" (Comstock, Chaffee, Katzman, McCombs, and Roberts, 1978; Roberts and Bachen, 1981). Videogames offer an opportunity to study significant cultural aspects of communication as they involve symbolic, mythic, social, and entertainment elements. Videogame arcade users spent $5 billion in 1981, equal to the Las Vegas take combined with the gross of the U.S. film industry, or equal to three times the combined TV revenues and gate receipts of major league baseball, basketball, and football. This figure rose to $7 billion in 1982, or greater than the combined revenues of the movie and record industries. Videogame parlors reached a peak of 10,000 in the United States in 1982, but 2,000 closed in 1983 due to slackening demand (Time, 1983b). The installed base of home videogames, in millions, has risen during 1977 through 1982 from .35, .80, 1.63, 2.95, 7.45, to 14 million (Yankee Group figures). Home penetration percentages range from 9% (Nielsen, 1982a) to 14.8% (Media Science, 1983). Compared to 51 hours, 37 minutes per week of TV viewing, Nielsen's July 1982 NTI sample report playing videogames 24 minutes per week.

Videogames not only provide instant public status (for a select subculture) but offer very public, interactive experiences. Observers wait in line, kibbitz, offer support, and feel intimately part of the experience of the performer-of-the-moment. This is more intimate than hockey fans shouting at players, and more active than a family watching television. Videogames offer public communication situations that are participatory.

The few available studies of videogame use indicate a number of themes that are familiar to researchers in interpersonal and televised communication. The first is that by far the primary reason for playing videogames is fun and entertainment (57% of all responses from a nonprobability sample of 200 arcade players, normalizing for multiple responses, reported by Schwartz, 1982). The second and third reasons— for the challenge, and to relieve boredom—are more instrumental motives in the uses and gratifications tradition, but their percentages (14% and 11%, respectively) indicated far less importance.

The second theme is that the public, yet interpersonal, communication surrounding videogame play is important and obvious to videogame players. Asking nearly 1000 players between the ages of 10 and 18 what they did while not actually playing, Brooks reported these top four percentages (allowing for multiple responses): watching others (83%), waiting for a turn (82%), talking with friends (66%), and trying to learn a new game by watching others (33%; Brooks, 1983; Carlson, 1982). Brooks emphasized the considerable interaction among young and adult players. The primary competition seems to be between the player and the machine, not between players, so there is frequent commentary and communication among observers and with skilled players.

Third, this interaction helps explain why the majority in one study found arcades more enjoyable than playing with home videogames: Not only were the games better, but the ambience of public excitement while watching and interacting with an unfamiliar but similarly motivated public was an experience not possible at home (Schwartz, 1982).

Fourth, the same study indicated that media substitution of use for social activity does occur within the videogame context—further, that substitution shifted with players' ages, consonant with research on the relationship between children's cognitive development and use of the media (Lyle and Hoffman, 1972). In particular, younger players felt that they watched TV or movies less, or did not "just sit around," while older players felt that it was an additional social activity, part of a widening social arena.

Fifth, the role of videogames in facilitating learning is quite controversial. A symposium at Harvard concluded that such games are intrinsically motivating because they are highly interactive, involve quick reactions, provide continuous feedback, and motivate improvement. They foster inductive reasoning and parallel processing, i.e., the evaluation of many variables simultaneously (Time, 1983c). However, high school educators do not see the "sense of mastery" or the "introduction to computing," which are attributed to videogame playing, having any effect on mathematical or programming skills in school (Needham, 1983).

Sixth, many social activists as well as researchers are curious about if not critical of the content of videogames—largely violent action, designed by males for males. Indeed, Kiesler, Sproull, and Eccles (1983) argue that computing cultures in general, and video arcades in particular, place obstacles to girls' gaining computer literacy. Typically, girls do not play alone in arcades, and the spatial abilities needed for such playing are generally less pronounced in females. They argue, however, that there is "no evidence that girls are deficient" in the procedural thinking needed to program and analyze computers and videogames, but that the surrounding culture and socialization reduces female attraction to such activities. Indeed, when videogames mediate the face-to-face interaction involved in such stereotypically male activities such as poker playing—such as by video poker games—then females are attracted to and enjoy playing gambling games.

Seventh, a radical communication-theory perspective would view video-games as simply another aspect of an information society, which produces not only commodities but consciousness too (see Dupuy, 1980: 7). Indeed, Mosco and Herman (1982) argue that such "leisure" activities help train people in the theory and practice of ownership: "leisure is work, the process of building the audience commodity" (see also Mosco, 1982: Chap. 4).

ORGANIZATIONAL CONSIDERATIONS

The widespread implementation of organizational communication systems is creating innumerable field experiments in the adoption, use, and impacts of new media. As research findings are reviewed in detail elsewhere (Keen, 1981; Kerr and Hiltz, 1982; Rice, 1980a; Rice and Case, 1983; Rice, Johnson, and Rogers, 1982; Tapscott, 1982; Uhlig, Farber, and Bair, 1979; Chaps. 8 and 9) we will consider several nonobvious theoretical implications in this section.

Information System as Symbol

One problem with many current adoption and impact studies is an unbalanced emphasis on the amount and functionality of information. Yet consider the observations of Feldman and March (1981: 174), as they argue that organizational "use of information is embedded in social norms that make it highly symbolic."

(1)   Much of the information that is gathered and communicated by individuals and organizations has little decision relevance.

(2)   Much of the information that is used to justify a decision is collected and interpreted after the decision has been made, or substantially made.

(3)   Much of the information gathered in response to requests for information is not considered in the making of decisions for which it was requested.

(4)   Regardless of the information available at the time a decision is first considered, more information is requested.

(5)   Organizational members complain that an organization does not have enough information to make a decision, while they ignore available information.

(6)   The relevance of the information provided in the decision-making process to the decision being made is less conspicuous than is the insistence on information.

From this perspective, a paradoxical implication of organizational communication systems is that they may *increase* the extent to which members use information for symbolic, rather than functional purposes, because of the higher visibility and political consequences of more complex systems. Thus, theories of information system adoption need to consider how the *meaning* of the information provided and of the system itself are negotiated in organizations (Putnam and Pacanowsky, 1983).

Communication System as Contingency

If actual communication changes when new communication systems are adopted, then perhaps the relationships that organizational communication research has uncovered between communication and other organizational variables will also change. That is, new media impacts may condition or falsify hypothesized relationships developed by past research.

Currently, computer conferencing and the more sophisticated electronic mail systems are particularly important for this discussion, because they are preeminently *group* media (Hiltz and Turoff, 1978). Designers, managers, or users can call upon the processing capabilities of the computer to *structure* communications. Chapter 6 specifically reviews research on mediated group communication.

The results in that chapter could be interpreted within the framework of Wiio, Goldhaber, and Yates's (1980) contingency approach to organizational communication research. We suggest that new organizational media, because of the kinds of impacts reviewed there, are a new contingency. For example,

(1)   Electronic messaging can increase cross-organizational communication, even over diagonal, divisional relations. Will such messaging weaken the relevance of organizational level to information and communication patterns?

(2)   Will early access by new members to other organizational members through electronic mail weaken the relationship between tenure, communication, and satisfaction?

(3)   Will the increased span of control by managers, made possible by office automation, lead to decreased superior-subordinate relationships and a shift to less interpersonal performance evaluation methods?

(4)   Will the expansion in the number of messages sent to and received from new members lead to "better relationships" and more satisfaction with organizational outcomes, or will managerial attention become even a scarcer resource?

The implication here is that new media should not be forced on organizational groups simply on the basis of the generalized benefits we know are possible from such technology. Rather, we need to match media usage to organizational tasks, group roles and norms, and individuals' personalities and preferences. Further, we need to specify our theories and concepts of organizational communication to include contingencies related to new media.

Communicating with the Organization

Typically, organizational communication research considers communication within organizations (as, between superiors and subordinates, or within functions, or across boundaries) or across organizations (such as organizational action sets and networks, interlocking directorates, and environmental interfaces). Rarely do we consider communication between an individual (say a customer) and an organization. In the past this was probably because the customer always dealt with a specific individual (say at the customer service desk, or with a salesperson). Now, however, with at-home videotex transactional services, automatic tellers, electronic funds transfer, and "smart cards," an increasing amount of communication involves an individual (or group) actually communicating (or attempting to communicate) with an electronic interface of an organization.

A new kind of communication frustration and interaction is developing that communication researchers have not investigated. We might call this "parried" organizational communication. The early empirical studies (Sterling, 1979) and theoretical analyses (Singer, 1977, 1980) have uncovered an array of ways in which organizations parry, confuse, and divert attempts at communication by persons external to the organization. These authors would argue that internal organizational emphases on efficiency and rationality necessarily create external inefficiencies and irrationality. Singer describes several of these processes:

(a)   hiding out (by using unlisted phone numbers),

(b)   making communications with the appropriate person expensive and time consuming for the individual,

(c)   responding with form letters,

(d)   using corporate advertising and communications as a one-way advantage relative to an individual's communication capabilities,

(d)   immediately enmeshing inquiring individuals in *error, work,* and *delay* circuits (both technical circuits such as insufficient telephone lines and organizational circuits such as routing the person to the wrong location),

(e)   forcing individuals to write or appear in person,

(f)   responding to requests with suspicion and secrecy, and

(g)   enforcing rules and regulations that do not help the individual but do routinize the organizational inputs.

Typically, people respond with apathy, explosive behavior, subservience, or, in some cases, with "counterbureaucratic coping," such as billing for time wasted.

The more economic or radical interpretation is that information organizations use these techniques to buffer the system from exceptional transaction costs; individuals must bear the externalities of a rationalized, technological system that is built to handle the bulk of repetitive transactions, but not errors or personalized interactions. Of particular interest to communication researchers would be questions such as the following: Do managers receive feedback from the environment (in the form of irate individuals) in ways that generate altered communication policies or system design? How do office communication structures respond to these signals, if signals in fact permeate the organizational boundaries? How are the messages interpreted upon reception, and what difficulties does the internal person dealing with the issue have in forwarding or distributing the information within extant organizational networks? In particular, if internal communication systems are routinized, these messages will appear as deviant and will be charged against the customer service office's political and operational capital. On the other hand, such communication problems may forge informal links between staff personnel and technical specialists (see Meyer, 1968).

THE PUBLIC DIMENSION

The Information Society and Media Organizations

As noted in Chapter 1, a growing number and variety of scholars and researchers are claiming that we are becoming an information society (Bell, 1976; Drucker, 1969; Ito, 1981; Machlup, 1962; Porat, 1978; Williams, 1983). By this is meant that the majority of economic activities in the United States is involved with creating, handling, processing, maintaining, and distributing information. Information has become a prime component of work, which in turn may have profound effects upon the structure and operation of our society.

The change to an information society will also require new media organizations such as data-base brokers (see, for example, Chapters 5 and 10). It is already reflected in the complex interconnections among media and other institutions (consider the growing interaction between television, cinema, video music, radio, book, and videogame corporations). Fombrun and Astley (1982) discuss the development of such separate industries into a "telecommunications community." This convergence of media institutions and technology is seen by critical media theorists as a sign of (1) impending corporate power struggles, as heretofore unrelated industries begin to compete, and (2) growing integration of information and media into a corporate infrastructure—"a new phase of capital accumulation" (Webster and Robins, 1979).

From a theoretical perspective on media organizations, the new media are also affecting the production, delivery, organization, and survival of traditional media (see Hirsch, 1977 and Chapter 12). The old categories of media organizations are changing as new media are used, for example in electronic publishing, out-of-school education, and at-home library services (Cherry, 1980; Paisley and Chen, 1982; Smith, 1980; Turoff and Hiltz, 1982a,b; Williams and Williams, 1984). Newsgathering, editing, distribution, advertising, and telecommunications may converge under the control of a few large organizations. Consider the fact that Warner Communications, Times-Mirror, or Time, Inc. have, through vertical integration, control over cable, broadcast media, books, magazines, newspapers, telecommunications (satellite transponders and private wire services), video, and facsimile. Or consider that extensive videotex penetration could lead to major realignments in sources and distribution of advertising revenues.

If researchers continue using traditional categories of information and media producers and distributors, they will increasingly overlook new concepts in the public media. Consider the concepts of gatekeeping and agenda-setting (McCombs and Shaw, 1977). The argument goes that due to professional norms, editorial philosophy, technological considerations, and the sheer volume of content, extensive gatekeeping is performed by editors, disk jockeys, and television broadcasters. The content that is chosen for further distribution tends to tell audiences "what to think about" if not what to think. A tiny proportion of content sets the agenda.

Overlooked in current research is the effect of home-based electronic newspapers already available (see also Chapter 5). When individuals can use indices based on their personal interests to search through the entire AP, UPI, and Reuters newswire, then who is doing the gatekeeping? How will agendas be fragmented or segmented? Will this segment of the audience develop pictures of social reality at odds with their less sophisticated neighbors who use traditional media? Will they lose sight of other agendas entirely? Communication researchers should test current models for contingent conditions and further subgroup effects.

The fundamental issue here is choice and diversity. With satellite distribution, even a national medium such as *Time* can produce issues for different regions and even demographically segmented audiences within a region. Gannett's satellite-transmitted *USA Today* newspaper provides truly national news as well as locally inserted news and advertisements. While the early criticism of traditional media was that they were creating a mass, homogenized culture, now we hear criticism that the new public media will fragment and isolate us.

As new media organizations begin to reach audiences that before could be tapped only, by, say, the three television networks, then the economics change in ways that may lead to audience segmentation similar to the format and audience changes earlier seen in magazines and radio. This segmentation may, however, at first come along previous lines of social stratification. Further, from the extra-organizational perspective, the major corporations may attempt to develop and control new media and their content, leading perhaps to the corporate "privatism" of information (Schiller, 1982). Or certain status groups in society may become information elites due to their higher access to new media. More important, insofar as new media allow greater message flow among their users, the high-status elites could increasingly coordinate their power over others.

The segmentation of markets can also take the form of social stratification and create "knowledge gaps" (Ettema and Kline, 1977; see also Chapter 4). The gap could even take the form of cultural preferences for different media. The youth in one neighborhood achieves status from, and becomes addicted to, the large cassette radio, while a youth in another neighborhood invites the gang over to play on the home computer. These differences may accentuate socioeconomic and cultural differences.

Further, the inroads new media are making on our national television networks, along with the access of certain socioeconomic and cultural groups to home information services, could result in reducing "free" commercial television to a very low quality level. In the past, the knowledge gap hypothesis posited that, with new means for communication, groups of users might increase their knowledge, but the information elite will rise to an even higher relative level. Now we must also consider whether some groups may even *decline* in knowledge levels or access to cultural diversity. This is a clearly testable hypothesis as the media environment of different social groups changes due to interactions between new and traditional media organizations and their markets.

We may now be in an era in which we have more and more organizations creating new markets rather than just satisfying perceived needs. It is possible that humankind is malleable enough in communication behaviors and needs that new media may be creating *new* needs— needs that have not been satisfied before, or that are externally created. Indeed, it is a testable question whether humans have still-unsurfaced communication needs.

Social Diffusion of New Technologies

In this section we consider personal computers and medical information systems as topics of diffusion research. The first is diffusing quite rapidly, while the last seems stymied by factors often overlooked by diffusion research.

Diffusion of most new media in general seem to confirm Olshavasky's (1980) analysis of the change over time in the general rate of innovation adoption. Looking at 25 household innovations, and measuring the time to adoption as the number of months between 5% and 95% adoption, he found a significant coefficient for the successive year each innovation was introduced. More recent innovations seem to diffuse more rapidly. Individual and organizational decision processes may well be overwhelmed, to be replaced by conformity, imitation, and recommendations. Diffusion research needs to consider this abrupt transition in adoption behavior.

Personal computers are being taken home and to the office in increasing numbers. Over 400,000 were sold in 1980, yet they were first sold only in the mid-1970s. Ten million households are expected to have personal computers by 1985 (Rogers, Daley, and Wu, 1982). In the university organization, educators and support personnel are being introduced to personal computers as well as electronic mail and other systems supporting researchers and invisible colleges (Hiltz, 1983; Rice and Case, 1983).

Case and Daley (1983) report that of 832 respondents to a university faculty/staff questionnaire (a 41% response rate; 366 of the respondents were faculty), 135 already owned personal computers and 331 planned to buy one in the next five years. However, 60% reported already using a terminal or word processor at work, although most (70%) used it no more than two hours daily. The most salient finding of the study was that, contrary to expectations that financial management and data-base access would be the primary reasons respondents bought small computers, text processing was by far the most common application, with more than three times (mean of eight hours per week) the number of hours used for the next most popular function, entertainment. This predominance held across a variety of subgroups. Projected uses by 324 potential adopters put word processing first in number of mentions (29% of all responses, 53% of cases) and entertainment fourth.

An in-depth diffusion study of the adoption of personal computers found similar results (Rogers et al., 1982). The top two reasons for purchase of a personal computer were "convenience of working at home" and "word processing," although those authors found the machines used most for games, and next most for work processing.

Other relevant results from the this study include (a) the entertainment functions lead to greater observability of the innovation, particularly in owners' communicating evaluations to potential adopters; (b) potential adoption was associated with considerable pre- and post-implementation communication networking; (c) in line with Olshavasky's proposition, there appeared to be a rapid rise in the rate at which certain variables influenced adoption over time; and (d) 40% of the owners reported decreases (averaging 1.5 hours per day) in their television viewing.

Clearly, university faculty are early adopters (as only 2% of all U.S. households are estimated to own personal computers now). Most universities, as organizations, appear totally unprepared for this rapid invasion of personal word processing and computing. Without adequate planning, and with continued ignorance of such diffusion, these organizations will be unable to cope with multiple incompatible systems. More important, their organizational culture, information flows, status relationships, and support personnel will be challenged to change and accept this particular communication medium.

Medical information systems appear to be an anomaly in the context of new media adoption (Gordon and Fisher, 1975). On the one hand, there are new approaches to the provision of information services to the medical profession, such as the joint venture by the American Medical Association (AMA) and General Telephone (GTE) to offer an online access system for medical information, via institutional and individual nodes in a nationwide network (Roberts and Crawford, 1982). The AMA will represent the quality control of content—a crucial medical concern—and GTE will represent the control of transmission technology. The system will even offer electronic mail, perhaps leading to more rapid diffusion of research and practice knowledge.

However, in-house medical information systems seem to be meeting stiff resistance. In spite of the heavy costs of patient-related data communications (nearly 40% of hospital cost per patient data—Ricord

[1982]), most studies show a lack of acceptance of computerized patient and medical records systems (Brenner and Logan, 1980). Their "nondiffusion" review shows that medical information systems generally have favorable innovation attributes (except perhaps for complexity, compatibility, and reversability; see Rogers [1983] and Chapter 7), but that organizational and environmental elements prevent their diffusion. In particular, physician professional values, government intervention, and the public's image of physicians all ran contrary to how the system seemed to interact with the personal, organizational, and public aspects of adoption. For example, most physicians have a sense of professional autonomy; they feel that individualism rules in the profession, as most knowledge is unstandardized and obtained by experience; and there is a fundamental humanism involved in the public perception of medicine. Use of a standardizing, "expert" system would threaten both. Additionally, the traditional hierarchical control and political structures in hospitals would be threatened by a computerized information system. Finally, echoing our suggestion that new media organizations are blurring boundaries between kinds and owners of information, the rights to publicly generated medical information are being strongly disputed (Cummings, 1982).

Diffusion studies, in particular, indicate how adoption of new media technologies may become inextricably caught up in social and institutional structures. Public education is another example.

Diffusion and Adoption in Education

How much can be the public benefit from new media as implemented by public institutions? In this section, we look briefly at television as a lost opportunity and small computers as a new one for our public schools.

The well-known Chu and Schramm (1967) reviews of the educational uses of television provide the best background for the present brief discussion. We know from many studies that television can be an effective instructional tool. One problem, until the application of formative research techniques in the development of *Sesame Street,* was that educational programming was often just an attempt to replicate a live instructional situation (see also Chapter 11).

The contributions of studies involving formative research of children's television span many theoretical areas—for example, attention qualities (Lesser, 1974; Palmer, 1981) as in *Sesame Street*; sex-role stereotyping (Johnson and Ettema, 1982; Williams, LaRose and Frost, 1981) in *Freestyle*; and organizational behavior involved in television production (Ettema and Whitney, 1982). All such studies go markedly beyond the earlier—yet valuable in their time—studies of educational uses of television.

Now another technology is pressing for implementation. It is the personal computer and its rapid and highly visible use by certain segments of society may force adoption by schools whether they like it or not. Since the early 1960s, the computer has been an intriguing topic for educational research and demonstration projects (see Figure 1.4). Yet the high initial costs of mainframe systems along with the problems of adoption have prevented traditional computing from gaining a foothold in the schools. By contrast, the low initial costs and the widespread public acceptance of microcomputers as well as software designed for children (Papert, 1980) imply significant diffusion of this educational technology.

Yet all is not going entirely smoothly in the institutional implementation of microcomputing. In a recent review of the literature on the topic supplemented by site visits, Williams and Williams (1984) suggested that microcomputer implementation has many of the characteristics of traditional adoption situations, and similar theoretical implications. For example, many implementation outcomes are tied to opinion leaders. However, the diffusion is often horizontal rather than vertical. There is also the typical technology-implementation problem of materials (software). Moreover, the teacher—the ultimate gatekeeper—seems to receive the least attention of all. Rogers (1984), commenting upon this research, sees microcomputer adoption as very interpretable according to the implementation paradigm. One contrast, however, is that the adoption of this newest technology seems to be proceeding at a very rapid rate—especially considering that the microchip itself is a relatively recent invention. In a similar vein, Paisley and Chen (1982) emphasize that the implementation of computers is taking place in the midst of a rapidly unfolding new media environment for children, including videotext, telext, and videogames.

THEORIES ABOUT THEORIES OF NEW MEDIA IMPACTS

This chapter has considered some theories at several levels of analysis—individual and group, organizational, and institutional—in order to suggest how the study of new media may profit from applying extant communication theories, and to suggest how those theories might need to be respecified in order to apply to new media. This section quickly surveys two frameworks for considering theories about technological impacts themselves. The very assumptions behind any particular approach to analyzing impacts—even assuming that the *are* impacts—naturally color and influence subsequent conclusions that researchers, implementors, managers, and users might have.

Technology as Central

Kling (1980) provides the most comprehensive and explicit analysis of the perspectives taken in analyzing computing; one task for communication theorists would be to refine Kling's model specifically with respect to new media. For example, it may well be the case that the more decentralized and personal use of new media (including even the telephone, but also the personal computer) may not only shift the balance between the location and extent of organizational conflicts, but may introduce a different way of conceptualizing decentralization.

Social analyses of computing may be categorized into two broad theoretical perspectives. The *systems rationalism* perspective takes technology as its starting point, and assumes that rational design and use of the system is possible, although different brands of systems rationalism emphasize technical experts, managers, or users. Further, it assumes that consensus is possible, and that hierarchical authority accepted by organizational members is one form of consensus. Technology is managed for efficiency and satisfaction by individuals, groups, and organizations. The wider environment and social forces are rarely considered. Varieties of this perspective include (a) technical rationalism, with an emphasis on procedures, efficiency, productivity, users, tasks, and goals; (b) structural analysis, with an emphasis on organizations and formal units, information flow, uncertainty and structural attributes; and (c) human relations, with an emphasis on small groups, organizational resources and rewards, motivation, leadership, and participation. For example, analyses of the adoption of word processing in organizations from the three perspectives would focus on, respectively, (a) economic motivations and technical designs, (b) attributes of word processing as a concept and a technology, of the organization, and of its environment; and (c) acceptance of word processing through user participation in sociotechnical systems design (e.g., Chapter 7).

Another way to view the systems rationalism perspectives is to concentrate on the guiding principle that technology is "autonomous" and central to subsequent activities. Slack (1984) divides analyses that take this position into those which posit direct impacts of technologies on a defined object (such as a group) under a mechanical, Cartesian notion of determinism, and those that posit that although technology is still externally imposed, it may be redesigned (through engineering, policy, or application) to avoid negative impacts. She calls the latter approach the "symptomatic" perspective.

Social Context as Central

Opposed to those perspectives are, in Kling's analysis, *segmented institutionalists.* For such analysts, relationships between technology and the social order are crucial. Indeed, the creation, design, and use of computing are inextricably wound up in the form and direction of the social order (such as an organization or public municipalities). Crucial issues here are control of the technology for maintenance of meaning, power, or social stratification. This perspective assumes that there will be social conflict, and that crucial values include individual and group sovereignty, equity, and the roles of stakeholders. Three perspectives within this category include (a) interactionism, with emphasis on computing as a package within a milieu, differentially situated social actors, and the negotiation and construction of meaning and identity; (b) organizational politics, with emphasis on the interests of social positions, opportunities and constraints, and bargaining; and (c) class politics, with emphasis on stratified social relations, control over production and distribution, and struggles for power. These three perspectives might focus on different aspects of the adoption of word processing, respectively: (a) the preservation of important social meanings in the midst of work restructuring; (b) how specific departments use control over the technology for their interests; and (c) whether word processing "deskills" workers and rationalizes their work.

Again, Slack provides a different view of this distinction, labeling the opposing perspective "effectivity." Technology emerges from a social order and a context of effectivity, and is not independent of the totality of that order (see, for example, Noble, 1977; Webster and Robins, 1979). So analysts need to understand the larger social context, and need to jettison any assumptions that technology is externally generated and imposed, leading to impacts separate from the totality. She subdivides this category differently than does Kling: into perspectives concerning the "essence" and those considering "structural relations." The first considers technology as expressions of some social essence, which may be some ideal (such as the "mechanical age," "technique," or the "information age") or may be materialistic (the perspective taken by Marxists), generally meaning capitalistic (Mosco, 1982; Schiller, 1982). For example, Mosco and Herman (1982: 59) have written

> The communications revolution is shaped by regional and class struggles, by powerful capitalist forces molding that revolution to meet accumulation and legitimacy needs, and noncapitalist forces resisting hegemony and using information resources to build a new social order.

This position is applied forcefully to the information society by Dupuy (1980: 4) who, indeed, sees such a society not as a revolutionary transition from material production but as "a phase in the history of capitalism coping with its contradictions," and thus leading to increased alienation. The structuralism approach rejects a totality constituted as one essence, but considers totality as fully interrelated levels of instances—economic, political, ideological, and theoretical. Contradiction, conflict, and influence occur among the levels, manifesting an effectivity in which technology occurs—how it comes about, its form, it uses. Further, relationships among levels may change as new communication media become part of the totality.

Theory as Central

There are several points to note about these models of perspectives (outlined in Table 3.4) taken about impacts of new media. First, Kling insightfully argues that the perspectives may be considered tools for

TABLE 3.4   Perspectives on Communication Technology Impacts

	Assumption: Technology as Central			Assumption: Technology as Part of Totality		
Modeled by Kling (1980)	Systems Rationalism			Segmented Institutionalism		
	Rational	Structural	Human Relations	Interactionist	Organization Politics	Class Politics
Modeled by Slack (1984)	Mechanistic			Effectivity		
	Direct Impacts		Symptomatic	Ideal or Materialist Essence		Structuralism

analysis: Using complementary or appropriate perspectives to analyze certain kinds of computing instances may lead to insights specific to that instance; another instance may call for a different analytical perspective. For example, systems rationalism may be more useful as a perspective in stable settings where consensual values are supported; the segmented institutionalist perspective may be a better tool in complex and dynamic instances where diversity of interests will likely lead to conflict. This leads to the second point: Whichever perspective is taken, if unswervingly held and indiscriminately applied, it will constrain understanding. Third, there are methodological constraints associated with particular perspectives that either may make evidence less persuasive or require the acceptance of new methods. Slack, for example, analyzes patent law to uncover interactions among levels in the development of communication technologies; interactionism may call for participant observation and qualitative analysis; technical rationalism may require a familiarity with cost-benefit analysis. Fourth, there are, as always, practical constraints to applying various theories: A manager in an organization may not be able to investigate, much less change, the social order; a symptomatic approach may not only be the only one possible, but may be quite fruitful.

Finally, it is perhaps misleading to categorize many analyses at all, and certainly to do so in simplistic ways. There are few evaluations of new media by social scientists that do not call attention to the social context. As Kling concludes (1980: 104), "the ecology of interests in any social setting must be a starting point for understanding computer use." Kerr and Hiltz similarly conclude (1982: 177) that "we believe that the challenge is not primarily in further perfecting the computer and telecommunication technology . . . but in the social engineering problem of fitting the technological possibilities within particular social contexts." This chapter has attempted to consider some of those theoretical and social contexts, with specific emphasis on communication theories.

SUMMARY

There is a need to rethink the contexts or paradigms by which we often organize our research focus. At the outset, we mentioned the blurring lines between interpersonal and mass-mediated contexts. We must increasingly account for the coalescence of personal, organizational, and public contexts of human communication. We may need entirely new paradigms.

For example, research aimed at understanding human benefits from new media should focus on the unique strengths of each medium rather than only on how they compensate or substitute for more natural media linkages. This requires research-based insights into these unique strengths and the broader subjective question of user satisfaction as well as media styles.

We need also to inspect our assumptions, or theoretical perspectives underlying theories, implementation, and analyses of new media. Without an awareness of other perspectives, we may fail to understand the contexts in which technology itself appears and functions, and in which people attempt to use, control, or evaluate new media.

Our argument, then, is simple. The new media need to be included in traditional communication research, but we need to look at those traditional theories untraditionally. The new media are providing new arenas for communication research, new perspectives in traditional areas of communication research, and new questions for analysis and theory. New media may, in fact, necessitate a considerable reassessment of communication research. Intellectual changes must occur to match the growing changes in communication behavior.

NOTE

This chapter significantly revises and extends some ideas first presented by Williams and Rice (1983).

RONALD E. RICE and
EVERETT M. ROGERS

4 New Methods and Data for the Study of New Media

The nature of the new media—facilitating communication interactivity with the help of computers (or microprocessors)—generates a host of evaluation issues and motivates a considerable reassessment of communication theories and concepts, as the prior chapter discussed. A reasonable question to ask is whether research on the new media also generates or requires new methods and data. The goals and objects of research, the theories used, the methods applied, and the data analyzed all are interdependent. This chapter considers the question with some suggestions about new methods and new data that might be appropriate for the study of new media.

NEW METHODS FOR THE STUDY OF NEW MEDIA

This section makes several arguments. The first is that traditional research designs may involve elements that limit our possible understanding of the uses and impacts of new media. (Warnings as to the limits of mass media research, particularly in the context of telecommunications policymaking, have been well raised by Meyer and Hexamer, 1982). The second is that the natural contexts of new media may limit how faithfully traditional research designs and methods may be applied. The third argument is that the nature of new media themselves may create limitations, as well as new opportunities, for the kinds of research typically applied to mass media.

It may first be useful to describe the main elements in conventional communication research on mass media effects. Such research represents the dominant approach followed by mass communication scholars over the past 30 years or so. The approach typically involves an experiment or, especially in recent years, a survey on mass media effects conducted by gathering data through questionnaires or interviews. A large number of individual respondents (usually at least several hundred) is often randomly sampled so as to provide data on a large number of variables (perhaps as many as 80 or 100). The reliance is upon quantitative analysis of moderately large data sets. The individual is the unit of analysis and data are gathered cross-sectionally at one point in time. Analysis tends to focus on correlations, partitioning of variance into explained and unexplained portions, or tests of differences.

Figure 4.1 diagrams a somewhat typical research design for studying the impacts of a new communication technology. The main elements in the design are a sample of users of the new technology from whom data are gathered, often by means of personal interviews, both before (at t_1) and after (at t_2) the introduction of a new communication medium. This design is a typical field experiment, based on the kind of experimental design that behavioral scientists have taken from classical agriculture experiments of some years ago (i.e., Fisher's analysis of variance design).

As suggested above, a number of methodological questions, problems, and lessons accompany using this type of research design for investigating new media.

(1) Evaluation activities, informed by communication research, could be brought to bear earlier in the field experiment, to take advantage of their potential contributions. Very seldom is behavioral science research explicitly involved in designing the communication technology or the implementation strategy.

Evaluation research is typically kept separate from the management of new media. Conventional wisdom about evaluation research holds that the evaluators should be independent and separate from the system or program that they are evaluating. Politicians and other policymakers often require such separation, so as to minimize possible biases in the evaluation. The independence of the evaluation research from the design and operation of the system is thought to maintain the credibility of the

FIGURE 4.1 Typical Research Design for Study of New Communication Technology

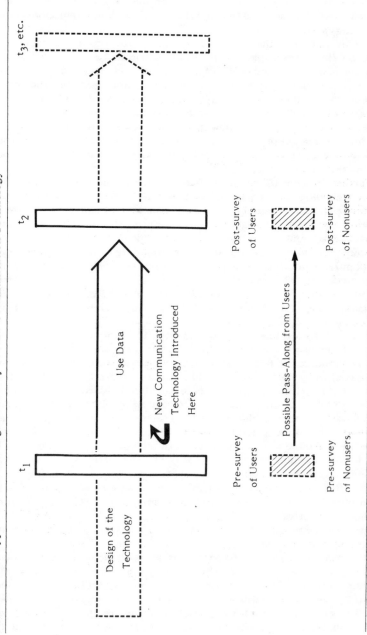

SOURCE: Rogers and Picot (1983).

research results. In many cases such independence and separation may indeed create a healthy tension between the evaluation and system management, and lead to more reliable research findings about the technology's effects.

However, it seems that the system design, evaluation, and management must be closely integrated if an evaluation is to be conducted in an effective manner. For example, if research and evaluation activities are begun after t_1, there may be no baseline data on prior media use, attitudes toward new media, or comparative outcomes (as in Rice and Case, 1983). Then research comparisons at t_2 must depend on users' perceived and remembered impacts of the new media. Research input into the design and implementation process would avoid this limitation; it may even lead to designing the system in ways that facilitate data collection, as the second half of this chapter suggests.

Further, the research findings can be utilized to improve the communication technology through its redesign. Often this redesign occurs during the time period (t_1 to t_2 in Figure 4.1) in which the communication system is being evaluated; the evaluators suggest needed improvements to the technologists, which may then be implemented. When the users are providing formal evaluation feedback, or even reinventing the system (see Chapter 7), then system design, use, and evaluation clearly represent an integrated, ongoing process.

One example is the *Bildschirmtext* Project in the Federal Republic of Germany (Rogers and Picot, 1983). Here the evaluation included an acceptability study of potential users of *Bildschirmtext* and of the actual users in a short test phase of this interactive TV technology. The purpose of this formative evaluation research was to gain understanding of the future acceptance of *Bildschirmtext*, by dealing with such questions as how many (and which) households would purchase the services, at what price, and how the technology should be designed/redesigned for user acceptance. A somewhat similar strategy was chosen for the planning, design, and implementation of the new teletex service in Germany (Picot and Reichwald, 1979). Note that formative evaluation itself grew out of efforts to better design educational and prosocial television (see Chapters 3 and 11).

Such acceptability studies of a new communication technology face many difficulties, stemming from the basic limitations of available social science methods in predicting future behavior. Nevertheless, acceptability studies represent one type of formative evaluation that involves evaluators along with the system designers and managers early in the process of designing and implementing the communication medium.

(2) Typically a new media system is introduced to and used by an ongoing organizational or social context in which the users comprise a specific department or even the whole community. Thus, there is no control group for comparison with the users, so it is impossible to remove the effects of other variables on use of the communication technology or to exclude certain rival hypotheses (see Figure 4.1). It is difficult to introduce new communication systems otherwise, given the network

nature of interactive technologies.[1] Perhaps another unit could be selected as a control group, if it matched fairly well. But even then, the random assignment of respondents to treatment and control groups is usually impossible. There are so many problems involved in having and maintaining true control groups in these situations that they are almost never utilized in evaluations of new communication media. As a consequence, such evaluations consistently overestimate the effects of the medium, because any extraneous effects that may exist are included as a disguised residual in the measured effect. This problem should not be forgotten when analyzing and reporting research results of these studies. Other means of control can be (and are) utilized in evaluating new communication media, such as multivariate statistical control. But such an evaluation design is weaker than an experiment with control groups because all of the variables to be controlled must be measured; in a well-designed experimental design, relevant variables are controlled, whether measured or not. Historical controls, such as comparing a user community at t_0, t_1, and t_2, are another solution.

(3) Users of new communication media often are not representative of the population of future users, so research results cannot be generalized to the wider population. The issue of the generalizability of an experiment's results is illustrated by respondents in an electronic mail study who were the top 110 administrators at Stanford University (Rice and Case, 1983). These administrators were selected, in part, in order to stimulate further adoption by other administrators in the university. Yet are they typical of the next 110 users who accepted Terminals for Managers at Stanford? Hardly. And how representative is Stanford University of other organizations that are expected to adopt electronic mail in the near future? Probably not very.

One specific way in which initial users are not representative is illustrated by the concept of the knowledge gap. In the case of such past communication as television, it seems that it first widened knowledge gaps in society, but eventually closed them, after most everyone had adopted the innovation (Katzman, 1974). The first-widening then-closing sequence occurs if the technology is widely adopted, and the temporary inequalities are less serious when the rate of diffusion is rapid (as with television in the United States). But what about an expensive and complex communication technology like home computers that may never become a consumer item in all households? This case is portrayed in Figure 4.2.

Why does information-gap widening occur?

(a) The new media of home computers, teletext and videotext systems, video recorders, teleconferencing and electronic messaging are expensive. So only the socioeconomic elites can afford them. They adopt them first, and others can only follow slowly, if at all.

(b) Because these new media are computer-based information tools, an individual must in general be a motivated information searcher to use them (at least effectively; though see Chapter 5 for alternative system designs). The information-rich are most likely to be the first adopters, as they are more likely to be computer literate.

FIGURE 4.2 Diffusion Curves for the Adoption of Three Household Communication Technologies

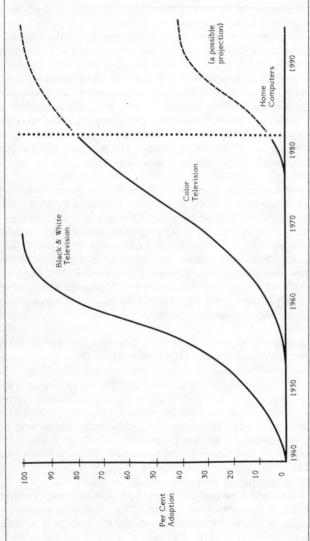

SOURCE: Rogers (1983).

NOTE: At any particular point in time, a new communication technology has the effect of widening the knowledge gaps in society, because the first to adopt are the socioeconomic elites who are already the information-rich. But later, when everyone has adopted the technology, it again has an equalizing effect between the information-rich and the information-poor. But what about a technology like home computers that may not reach 100% adoption?

(c) The new media that support interindividual communication require that potential communicators are equipped with compatible devices (electronic mail, picture phone, teletex, telecopy, computer conferencing, etc.) so that a relevant network can emerge.[2] Thus, a critical mass of users with similar equipment must be involved as respondents in evaluations of the new media.

(d) The information-rich particularly want specialized information, which new media are uniquely able to provide. Thus they increase their information advantage.

The general lesson here is that individuals, families, and organizations that participate in a communication technology experiment are very atypical of the population of potential users. Instead, the users in such an experiment are usually typical of the early adopters of an innovation: information-rich and socioeconomically advantaged (Rogers, 1983). This problem seems a typical and unavoidable aspect of early stages of research on early users of new media.

It is very difficult to avoid this threat to generalizability, even when one tries. For example, in the Green Thumb Project in Kentucky (Case et al., 1981; Paisley, 1983; Rice and Paisley, 1982), the 200 users of this free system were chosen by a local committee from the approximately 400-500 farmers who applied for a Green Thumb Box (in response to a mailed announcement from the local county extension agent to about 2600 farmers in the two counties of study). The committee chose the 200 users so they were approximately representative of three categories of farm size (small, medium, and large sized farmers). This selection procedure guaranteed a range of socioeconomic statuses among the 200 users, but it introduced another bias: The small farmers who volunteered to participate tended to be atypical of all small farmers in the two counties, in that they had a high degree of prior contact with their county extension agent. (Most small farmers do not have much extension contact.) So the Green Thumb selection procedure guaranteed that small farmers were included in out study, but also tended to make these small farmer-users atypical of all small farmers.

A further problem: The Green Thumb system was free to the user in 1981 (thanks to the U.S. Department of Agriculture), but a fee was charged after the end of the evaluation project. Thus, not many small farmers will use Green Thumb in the future. So again our small farmer-users in the 1981 study are a sample whose research results cannot be generalized to future users without considerable qualification.

(4) Quantitative research approaches, particularly manipulated experiments, based on variance research, seldom can provide a satisfactory understanding of the behavioral change process through which a new communication medium has effects. See Monge (1982) for a conceptual discussion of this problem, along with suggested methods, such as structural equation modeling and time series analysis (Monge and Cappella, 1980).

Variance research is a type of data gathering and analysis that consists of determining the covariances among a set of variables but not their time order (Mohr, 1982). A t_1/t_2 pre/post design (Figure 4.1) heads an investigation toward using (a) "difference" statistics (like the t-test between means or analysis of variances) or (b) "correlational" statistics (like zero-order correlation, multiple correlation and regression, or partial correlation techniques) in which the researcher seeks to determine the correlates of dependent variable(s), which often is either acceptance or use of the new medium. This approach typically assumes *linear* associations between variables, and focuses on the impact of a medium. As discussed in the beginning of this section, typical variance research involves a limited number of concepts operationalized by specific questions asked of a random sample of respondents. Thus, some of the limitations of the variance approach include measurement as well as analysis, because completeness in understanding the process is exchanged for representativeness in describing the relations.

Variance research alone usually cannot tell us much about the time order of the variables in a study, other than rather crudely (through the t_1 to t_2 differences in a variable), and seldom can provide a very complete understanding of the over-time process nature of the change behavior effects that are caused by the new communication technology. In this situation, a process research approach may be more appropriate. *Process research* is a type of data gathering and analysis that seeks to determine the time-ordered sequence of a set of events and to explain the process by which the sequence occurs (Mohr, 1982). Data-gathering methods for process research are often more qualitative in nature (like participant observation, case studies, and unstructured interviewing). A special advantage of such qualitative methods is that they allow the investigator (a) to identify unexpected variables and (b) to study the wider context of the user system and of the new communication medium. Case studies may be particularly appropriate in the early stages of a new medium, as process research can be used to obtain understandings of the range of uses, impacts, and applications. For example, the *Bildschirmtext* evaluation involved qualitative data gathering via user diaries and from an in-depth study of 30 low-income users (Rogers and Picot, 1983).

Process research is not necessarily qualitative, however. For instance, the *Bildschirmtext* evaluation included quantitative data gathering from the six-stage panel of 200 users, in which a set of core variables was measured every four months or so. This panel strategy allowed tracing user behavior changes over a number of time periods. (This approach is highly intrusive in that the repeated data gathering undoubtedly conditions the responses that are gathered, although with the large sample of *Bildschirmtext* users that are available, this intrusion may not be too serious.) Rice's (1982) study of over 800 users of a nationwide computer conferencing system involved quantitative log-linear analysis of two years' monthly messaging data.

There are several aspects of "good practice" research that should be included in variance *and* process approaches (Mankin, 1983). These include (a) multiple measures from several independent sources; (b) objective data sources—not just computer-monitored data as discussed below, but corporate records, external agency or association records, and the like; (c) unobtrusive measures, such as absenteeism and turnover as an indicator of job satisfaction; (d) other indicators of measures that typically are collected only via subjective questionnaires—because two external traits may be psychological artifacts of the respondent's attitudes, a researcher might want to use a variable that research has shown to be a good indicator or correlate of another variable of interest, which itself is likely to be confounded with a perceived impact; and (e) measures of organizational climate and work climate, which might also explain contingencies of uses and impacts. Mankin also suggests the development and use of "information primitives," constructs that describe the functions and behaviors of information work. Paisley (1980) has gone a long way toward this goal. By understanding what it is that people do when they do information work, we can better understand how functions migrate across roles and individuals when new organizational media become part of the work life. The use of such standard functional variables would improve compatibility across studies, aid in redesigning office work, and assist in assessing and directing changes.

Indeed, variance and process research are not necessarily mutually exclusive; a research design can include both approaches, with each providing a unique type of data. Hewes (1978), for example, suggests a compromise between the two approaches. His technique

> permits a researcher to describe the impact of a communication process . . . without having panel data. As a result, it has the advantages of both "process" and "variance" approaches without *some* of the disadvantages.

In fact, he suggests several approaches to the problem. The primary technique is discrete-state, discrete-time, Markov analysis. Required data include a vector of probabilities that the sample at time 1 occupies each of several nominal-level categories, and a matrix indicating the probability that the response of the sample (i.e., an "average" subject) will be in a particular category in time 2 given its response in time 1. There are rather severe assumptions for Markov analysis, which Hewes explains well, and for which he shows examples of the effects of transgression. In the examples of effects of stimulated radio interviews, and of political opinion, Markov analysis was remarkably robust.

One aspect of the Markov approach—analysis of a pooled transition matrix—was used by Rice (1982) on the communication linkages from a computer conference to test a model of group role categorization based upon information flows in the system (see Chapter 6). The apparent entropy-laden role structure of the system could not have been revealed without the Markov perspective. In general, though, it is difficult to imagine the theoretical validity of one of the assumptions: that human attitudes or behaviors are dependent only upon attitudes or behaviors from the previous time period, and not related to attitudes or behaviors or prior time periods. Further, Markov analysis requires homogeneous groups for separate analyses, which is a particular problem for the study of new media where clear subgroups have yet to be established by a body of research.

But Hewes's contribution lies in showing how Markov analysis may be applied to independent samples from the same population at different points in time: via simultaneous solution for the unknown parameters by algebra; by ordinary least squares (OLS) estimation, which requires more data but provides better quality estimates; and by more advanced estimation techniques. One of these techniques is pooled cross-sectional time series (Hannan and Young, 1977), which handles some difficulties that OLS regression does not (such as autocorrelation); moreover, it is designed to handle multiwave panel data in time-series fashion. Hardy (1980) successfully applied this procedure to analyzing the relation between the introduction of telephones and economic development. He used UNESCO data on 52 nations in intervals using a variety of lags; his primary use of pooled cross-sectional time series utilized 633 nation-years as the units of analysis.

Insofar as new media may interact with interpersonal communication, the very qualitative nature of such communication may be partially explicated by using the process models of conversation and cognition advocated by Cappella (1980) and colleagues. Their models may easily take advantage of computer-monitored data described later in this chapter.

Consider another approach to combining qualitative and quantitative, variance and process research. Mohrman and Novelli (1983) argue that because

(a)   office technology is still evolving,

(b)   it is becoming more integrated and thus changing and expanding its functionality,

(c)   its consequences and direction are contingent on many factors, and

(d)   simple cause and effect analysis is inferior to a systems perspective in such research,

researchers cannot predict the levels or kinds of change that might occur in an organization implementing such technology. Therefore, they call for "adaptive research." It involves periodic questionnaires as well as in-depth, open-ended interviews with users; the results of prior data gathering (or even of sections of the questionnaire during an interview session) are relayed back to the groups of users. The use of focus groups for impact research, as opposed to product development, has shown great promise in office automation studies as Mohrman and Novelli's (see also Mankin, 1983) and in interactive cable studies (Dozier and Ledingham, 1982; see also Chapter 5). Mankin suggests using guided imagery to help future user groups reveal possible uses, system features, tasks and impacts; these may be further developed in ongoing computer conferences during implementation.

In light of their awareness of the shifting office environments, Mohr-man and Novelli (1983) used factor analyses at different points in time to show shifts in how users of advanced electronic work stations conceptualize the effectiveness of certain office activities. Over one hundred systems analysts, technical specialists, unit managers, and secretaries at a large international organization were asked about their attitudes on these activities before implementation (Pre) and one year after implementation (Post), and, during the post questionnaire, what their attitudes had been a year earlier (Then). Figure 4.3 shows how the activities were conceptualized across the three time frames. The rows are pre factors, columns are post factors, and the boxes are then factors.

We might add at this point that this use of factor analyses at three conceptual intervals provides insight, but may not be methodologically rigorous. Hewes (1983) suggests that LISREL, a full-information maximum-likelihood estimator that can test structural relations across time periods, or GALILEO (Woelfel and Fink, 1980), a metric multidimensional scaling system that can map the development of conceptual spaces overtime, may be appropriate techniques. The use of either would be an appropriate way to establish quantitatively the basis for qualitative analyses of the process of concept reformation involving the implementation and use of new office communication technologies.

The effectiveness of activities in boxes on the diagonal (cells 1A, 2B) was not conceptualized differently at any time period, the activities in column C were generally reconceptualized in the post phase, while activities in columns D and E were reconceptualized in both post and then phases. Activities performed by more than 85% of users (double asterisks) or by more than 33% (single asterisks) appear only in the reconceptualized factors. An example of the utility of this analysis is that, while the mean effectiveness score on activities in columns C-E appeared to remain the same or even decline by the post period, they were scored *much* lower during the then assessment. That is, by time 2, what had been satisfactory before implementation was now seen as unsatisfactory effectiveness; the post measures were based on rescaled dimensions. Further, the ways in which activities were conceptualized were significantly different by time 2. The authors argue that implementation and use of office systems led to changes not only in effectiveness, but perhaps also in the scale upon which effectiveness is evaluated, or even in reconceptualization of what activities are and the dimensions of their effectiveness. They use results such as Figure 4.2 to argue that implementation in organizations leads to unpredictable, shifting situations, requiring adaptive research methods.

This sort of reconceptualization has been found in other studies of office automation. For example, Tapscott (1982: 207) reports that although several measures of "information received" improved between the pretest and posttest periods (nine months) of a pilot office communication system (N of pilot users = 19; N of control group = 26), the perceived "information needed" also increased. "The findings suggest that as access to information improved, so did expectations regarding what is possible and perceived requirements regarding what is necessary."

FIGURE 4.3 Comparison of Pre, Post, and Then Factors of Beliefs about Office Activity Effectiveness

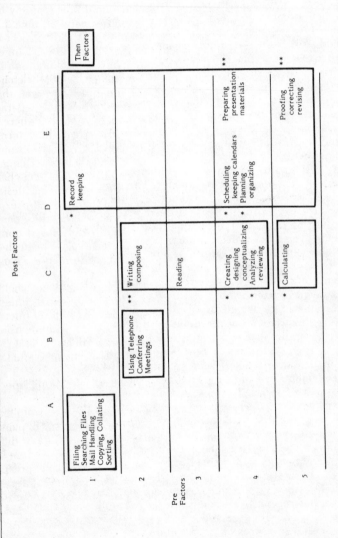

SOURCE: Mohrman and Novelli (1983).
NOTE: ** = Over 85% use office technology for this activity. * = Over 33% use office technology for this activity.

This use of pre, post, and then factors is one solution to a recently identified problem in using attitudinal/self-report data. An exciting and explicit article by Terborg, Howard, and Maxwell (1980) is a good introduction to the problem of alpha, beta, and gamma change. Essentially, they review three kinds of changes that have until now typically been confounded. If the changes in a subject's responses between time 1 and time 2 occur on a scale with constant calibration and with respect to a constant conceptual domain, this is *alpha* change, the kind of change we typically assume and measure. If the changes involve a recalibration of the measurement instrument (the scale), this is *beta* change. And if the changes involve redefining the conceptual domain or some of its criteria, this is *gamma* change. Because these kinds of change, when not separated, represent a misspecification of the change model (as above, where the criteria for information satisfaction changed), it is crucial to determine whether and to what extent each of the types has occurred. For example, beta change represents instrumentation bias, while gamma change is similar to construct invalidity. Terborg et al. emphasize that beta change has in the past been undetectable, even in true experimental designs. Although then/post differences may obtain even if there are no pre/post differences, "there have been no instances where Pre/Post analyses produced significant results while Then/Post analyses produced nonsignificant results" (p. 111). Further, then/post differences have been shown to portray objective ratings of behavioral and performance changes reliably.

After discussing some of the flaws in using multiperiod factor analyses as noted above, the authors critique the few other proposed techniques, and then offer their approach. It involves measurement of level (means), shape (correlations), and dispersion (variance) of the unidimensional measurement instrument at the three different times (pre, post, and then; although time-series assessment is introduced), at both the individual and group level. (One benefit of the individual-level analysis is that it may complement the formative evaluation approach by providing specific feedback to particular respondents.)

For example, to derive evidence for gamma change at the group level, they suggest several approaches. One is to take the correlations of pairs of period profiles (pre/post; pre/then; post/then); then compute raw difference scores between each pair. Under gamma change, the department that implemented office automation, for example, should display a pre/post profile correlation similar to the pre/then correlation (i.e., the difference is small) while displaying a correlation between the post/then correlation that is larger than the other two correlations. Meanwhile, the correlations for the control (nonuser) group should all be approximately equal. Actual significance of differences between the groups could be tested by Mann-Whitney U tests. The other approaches for both individual and group levels are well explained, along with the authors' awareness that these approaches are not perfect but do attempt to assess the kinds of changes that occur—alpha, beta, and gamma—that have been overlooked, but that have the potential for revealing how new media change not only our world but how we look at the world. In sum, the authors suggest ways to employ quantitative methods in order to understand qualitative process.

Organizational media, in their organizational contexts, are not static. In particular, office technology can be designed and redesigned by users in ways that cannot be predicted by implementor, user, or researcher. Chapter 7 considers this ongoing innovation in greater detail.

NEW DATA FROM NEW MEDIA[3]

Many of the new media are possible because of microprocessors or are in fact managed by larger computers, which can facilitate and structure communications. We use these technologies to support routine tasks, from text processing to records management, and to support human communication. Importantly, such systems also provide information about how a medium is used and what it transmits. Refer to Figure 4.1 again. Computer-monitored data can indicate actual usage of the system after the new medium has been implemented. These data may provide a direct measure of user behavior, may complement attitudinal and reported use data, and can be used in ongoing, processual, and quantitative research to supplement some of the qualitative analyses mentioned before. (Sometimes data are gathered by traditional means from a sample of nonusers of the system; these people may be asked about information passed along by users.) *Computer monitoring* of an information or communication system consists of the automatic logging of the type, content, or time of transaction made by a person from a terminal with that system.

Description of Systems and Kinds of Data Possible

Most past monitoring studies involved either (a) information retrieval systems, or (b) computer-based communication systems.

Information retrieval systems. An online information retrieval (IR) system is "one in which a user can, via computer, directly interrogate a machine-readable data base of documents or document representations" (Lancaster and Fayen, 1973: 1). IR systems can be classified either by the type of data base on which they operate or by their search capabilities (Meadow and Cochrane, 1981; Williams, Lannom, and Robins, 1982). Bibliographic data bases include descriptions and accessibility of literature, such as journal articles or books. Nonbibliographic data bases include everything else, such as statistical files, company records, stock exchange activity, and so on. Searching capabilities may allow multiple elements and Boolean logic, or require exact matches on a few characters of input.

More recently a class of IR systems aimed at the consumer market has developed. This class includes videotext and teletext systems that typically require little or no training for use. Such systems are described in Chapters 2 and 5. Many IR systems exist in private organizations and government for the purpose of maintaining internal records and various kinds of management information.

Computer-mediated communication systems. A computer-based communication (CMC) system is a generic term for electronic messaging or computer conferencing as well as for functions of more sophisticated knowledge worker augmentation systems. (See Chapter 6 for a consideration of computer conferencing and Chapter 9 for an overview of electronic mail.) Using a CMC system, people can send text (data, memos, letters, reports) to one another (to one or several individuals or predefined groups of individuals) or may share files (conference comments, working drafts, coauthored papers) while communicating (usually not at the same time) via geographically dispersed terminals (video or hard-copy) in structured ways using a shared host computer and telecommunications lines e.g., national networks and cable (Ellis and Nutt, 1980; Hiltz and Turoff, 1978; Newell and Sproull, 1982; Panko, 1980, 1981b; Uhlig, Farber, and Bair, 1979).

Possible Types of Data

Online monitoring produces large data sets. The precise data elements collected will vary by the type of system, but most data are either transactional (what happened when, where, and by whom) or temporal (what was the pacing of the interaction, how much time is spent in certain activities, and so on).

By collecting a few well-defined "primitive" measures (such as terminal and user IDs, start and end time, commands used, text content, system response, messages sent and received, sender and receivers, matches, and errors), we can generate a variety of useful aggregate and ratio measures of communication behavior.

We can use computer-monitored data to uncover and describe patterns of system usage. Generally, a string of IR commands can be aggregated to comprise a search task, while all commands and results within a single user session may be aggregated to constitute a "session" datum. The data are usually used to look at user behavior within individual sessions and to look for comparisons between users, perhaps across systems or tasks. In CMC systems one research goal may be to describe or model patterns of communication networks, built up from links between senders and receivers, as described below (see Rice, 1982).

We can focus on the analysis of the frequency, type, and context of *errors*. A particular system can identify only certain types of errors (e.g., incorrect entries and commands out of sequence). The system will typically miss logical errors and some content errors that appear correct (e.g., message was sent to wrong person; wrong item was searched for, but matches were made).

We can focus on issues of timing and duration. Some caution must be taken in interpreting user start and end times due to differences between system-clock and real-clock time, or due to system-response time. The elapsed time between transactions may provide useful information about an individual's "think time" associated with specific commands and identify some of the more difficult-to-use features in the system. Also, the choice of time interval affects the meaning of the analysis unit. For example, how quickly does a message recipient have to respond for the message to be considered "answered" or "reciprocated"?

Once the basic data elements have been parsed into user sessions, some aggregate measures can be computed for use in pattern, error, and time analysis. A number of analytical techniques, including Markov and network analysis, may then be appropriate (see Dominick, 1977; Penniman and Dominick, 1980; Rice and Richards, 1984).

Uses of the Data

Researchers and analysts will be concerned with two purposes for such data:

(1) For *evaluations* of the uses and utility of such communication media by individuals, in their social settings, such as organizations or research groups (see Rouse, 1981; Paisley, 1980). Computer-monitored data are clearly only one source of information for system evaluators and researchers, and implications from such data are only one component of a thorough evaluation. Any evaluation of such systems consists of some small intersection of dimensions including (a) the stakeholders, (b) evaluation goals or criteria, and (c) analysis domain. Other issues include historical and methodological approaches (Johansen, Miller, and Vallee, 1975; Penniman and Dominick, 1980); organizational objectives (Hamilton and Chervany, 1981); multiple evaluation perspectives (Carlson, 1974; Dominick, 1977); and constraints in the interaction between systems and users (Chandler, 1982).

(2) For indicators of the *impacts* of such communication media as perceived by the users and within their social settings. Empirical impacts of computer-mediated interpersonal and organizational communications (Rice, 1980a,b; also Chapter 8) or the theoretical foundations of such research (Kling, 1980; also Chapter 3) can be used to help avoid negative impacts and to alter prejudicial attitudes that potential users may have about such systems. Such analyses may also help to understand how such systems are "created" by the organization and users—i.e., how the socioeconomic context of the system affects the nature, design, implementation, and use of the system itself. In this sense, evaluation research and impact research are interconnected: Prior knowledge of potential consequences and typical usage patterns establish baselines for later comparisons and for initial system design and organizational planning.

Advantages of Computer-Monitored Data

From a logistical point of view, using the computer automatically to collect data increases the possibility of analyzing many subjects over time. In addition, having accessible, computer-collected and -maintained large, complex data bases encourages reanalysis by other researchers with differing perspectives. Replications and meta-evaluations are more likely.

Unlike many questionnaires, field experiments or controlled experiments, the collection of computer-monitored data typically involves little or no response bias or demand characteristics from the subjects. It is essentially *unobtrusive*, which may increase the validity of the data (Webb, Campbell, Schwartz, Sechrest, and Grove, 1981). Experiments run on a system are replicable, the timing of commands may be controlled, questions can be randomized, and so on. Consider also the recent controversy as to whether respondents' *reports* of their communication activities diverge widely from their *actual* communication behavior as observed or monitored (see Berger and Roloff, 1980; Bernard, Killworth, and Sailer, 1980, 1982; Nisbett and Wilson, 1977; Shweder, 1980).

A related aspect of computer-monitored data, is that these accurate census data allow us to investigate the *communication networks* of groups of users. Rogers and Kincaid (1981: 346) define communication networks as consisting of relations among "interconnected individuals who are linked by patterned flows of information." These networks link organizations and user groups with each other and with the environment and are, in fact, one picture of an organization's or group's structure (O'Reilly and Roberts, 1977; Rice and Richards, 1984; Richards and Rice, 1981; Tichy, 1981; Weick, 1969).

The servicing computer can capture extensive *longitudinal* network data so that researchers avoid the ungrounded assumption of much cross-sectional research that the system under study is at some equilibrium state. These data may be discrete or continuous; the notion of analyzing continuous time-dependent communication processes is perhaps foreign to most social science researchers precisely because obtaining such data is so difficult. Collection of longitudinal data, particularly if it is continuous or collected at frequent discrete time intervals, allows the researcher to analyze alternative time frames and aggregation schemes. Typically survey data have only a few time intervals, if at all, so different cycles or intervals cannot be compared (Danowski, 1983). Longitudinal network data may be collected and analyzed to an extent simply not possible otherwise (see Danowski, 1982; Rice, 1982).

Finally, the same computer that provides the facilities for human information exchange or retrieval can also administer controlled experiments, collect the data directly, "document the problems, and the decisions made at each stage," and follow up the experiments with joint online authorship of reports (Hiltz and Turoff, 1978).

Disadvantages of Computer-Monitored Data and Collection

The very fact that massive amounts of particulate data can be collected means that someone has to manage all those data. This has serious implications in terms of budgets, time, and expertise. Budgets are affected because preprocessing these data may take quite large sums of computer time, both in the ongoing day-to-day collection and in the conversion of the raw data into analyzable data sets. Evaluators need to integrate plans for using such data into system design to minimize later processing requirements.

Time is involved because, as anyone who has had to handle computer tapes, multiple data files, and custom-developed programming knows, these complex operations generally mushroom into time-consuming activities.

Expertise is involved because some member of the research team must know how to program or execute the necessary routines and transfer sets of data. Penniman and Dominick (1980: 23) strongly recommend that researchers "store monitor data in (data-base management systems) capable of interfacing with external software." Another aspect of expertise is that the researcher needs, perhaps, to be more systematic and theory/hypothesis-driven than usual. Sorting the study down to a manageable set of questions to pursue is a much greater problem in a monitoring study than is a lack of data. For example, Heeter, D'Alessio, Greenberg, and McVoy (1983) in analyzing monitored cable-viewing data, were impressed by having to handle data with 10^7 data points for each day's viewing. They note, "The challenge lies in posing significant questions and reducing the data in meaningful ways."

One related issue salient to the average person is the *ethics* of storage and use of data on that person (Westin and Baker, 1972). People have the right to exchange information in privacy. In some cases it is clear that textual content is *meant* to be public, and analysis is less questionable, such as from publicly-funded pilot research or organizational evaluation of system use. However, we emphasize that subjects must have the right to deny permission for access to portions of the data. A project may limit data collection to the users' commands, with content bypassed, or require the randomization of system identification numbers.

Computer-monitored data obviously do not portray the whole picture of human communication. Studies clearly show the social power and utility of very informal, unmonitorable organizational communication (Wynn, 1979). We also know that much of our human communication occurs on the nonverbal level. And, as the literature on respondent inaccuracy notes, people do apparently base their decisions upon their *attitudes*. But if we are to understand the actual use of such systems, and the impacts of exchanging specific kinds of information, we must study behavior at least as much as attitudes. Danowski (1983) warns, however, of ignoring the fact that a computer-based communication system (therefore its usage patterns and the kinds of data it can collect) are designed and organized by people—perhaps only a group of system designers, or perhaps the user group within an organization. But this limits the meaning of the words "objective" and "behavioral"; the data produced are already constrained in perhaps unknowable ways. Thus, comparisons *across* systems are crucial to verify system-specific data. (See Kerr and Hiltz [1982] for a vigorous multisystem comparison of research findings.)

SUMMARY

The study of new media exists in historical, methodological, and technological contexts. We must understand those contexts in developing research methods and data collection efforts for communication research on new media. Certainly current methods and forms of data are useful and necessary. But we must become aware of new limitations, and new opportunities, in studying new media. One opportunity is to shift to analyses of process rather than strictly of variance. Another is to combine quantitative and qualitative analyses when appropriate. This seems particularly the case in understanding how users reconceptualize their expectations and activities after using new office technologies. Another challenge and opportunity is to design research that can use data collected or monitored by the computer component of new media systems. These data can provide materials for process research, but also require more qualitative data to provide the context for the massive amounts of behavioral data that become available. A severe challenge will come when electronic messaging gives way to voice mail in organizations; data sources may become less accessible. Indeed, one explanation for the dearth of research on telephone use and impacts may be that there is no available record of communication content.

NOTES

1. A particular aspect of many new media is that they provide an improved means for connecting with other individuals (or organizations); thus these technologies essentially are "networking," not "one-way broadcasting" nor "stand alone" technologies. This distinctive aspect affects the acceptance and use of the new interactive technologies. At one extreme, consider the only individual in an organization who has an electronic messaging system; it is worthless as a means of communicating with co-workers. As each additional individual gains access to this technology, its usefulness increases to each of the individuals already on the system as well as to potential adopters.

2. See Note 1.

3. A much longer and more complete version of this section appears in Rice and Borgman (1983). That article references known research that uses computer-monitored data for analysis.

Part II: Individual and Group Communication

Precisely because the new media facilitate, and can structure, human communication interactivity, they necessarily will affect how individuals and groups communicate. However, increased understanding of these potential effects can lead to wiser and more appropriate decisions in design, choice, application, and use of such systems. Thus, as Chapter 3 suggested, "effect" is not necessarily deterministic, and is likely interactive; it may involve the effect of developers and users on the media as well.

Chapter 5 speculates that the current designs of videotex systems, specifically as "electronic newspapers," overlook or misunderstand some indications that a simple translation of newspaper content to a very different medium will meet with very unsatisfactory responses. This is, the chapter argues, because typical designs for information retrieval assume (apparently unconsciously) a very instrumental, goal-oriented approach to information use. Taking a rival perspective—that of newspaper reading as play, habit, or pastime—leads to very different notions of how videotex interfaces might be designed. The available research results from videotex trials and some of the literature on interface comparisons suggest that economic viability of videotex systems may depend on an appreciation of the play inherent in newspaper reading.

There seems to be a similar lack of understanding of the components of small-group decision making that interact with the group's communication medium. Using computer conferencing as an example, two schools of thought on the important factors in group communication are compared. The research results on consensus, time to decision, quality of decision, amount of participation, leadership emergence, and group phases are summarized in an attempt to specify when and how this new medium can aid or obstruct group decision making. Group communication in larger, electronic groups, and across divisional boundaries, is also discussed with an eye to future developments in human interactions.

DAVID M. DOZIER and
RONALD E. RICE

5 Rival Theories of Electronic Newsreading

This chapter explores theories of newsreading in the context of electronic newspapers with respect to system design, adoption, and use. The basic argument put forth is that emerging videotext/teletext news services are presently rooted in a limited theory of newsreading, to the degree that they are based in theory at all. Videotext and teletext technology was briefly described in Chapter 2. Table 2.2 provides a summary listing of known videotext systems—both pilot and commercial, though it does not include the many financial transaction systems. See Tydeman, Lipinski, Adler, Nyhan, and Zwimpfer (1982: Chap. 13) for a review of those services.

Before examining newsreading theory in this context, the "electronic newspaper" requires some description. The electronic newspaper is here defined as any system for distributing textual information on TV screens, where shelf life and manipulability of information permit direct competition with pulp newspapers. To compete directly with pulp newspapers, the shelf life of much of the information must be relatively brief (generally less than 24 hours). While information of a more enduring usefulness might be offered by videotext and teletext systems, such information typically competes with media other than newspapers. Manipulation of information should permit the newsreader *actively* to select subsets of information from the larger textual package in "real time."[1] Thus, continuous scrolling of textual information on a TV screen, which Lowenstein et al. (1982) has categorized as "rotatext," is viewed as fundamentally different from newsreading, where the reader can "scan" and "skip about" at will among the content choices of the newspaper. This interactive character of the electronic newspaper can be achieved through videotext or teletext systems. The ability to display a subset of the available information at will on the screen, through a reader's active choice, is the primary attribute of electronic newspapers.

CONTRASTING PULP NEWSPAPERS AND ELECTRONIC NEWSPAPERS

The emerging electronic newspaper has been the focus of excited scholarly discussion in recent years (see also Neustadt [1982] for a discussion of economic and legal issues). Parker's early scenario of the electronic newspaper provides a useful preview of now-emerging information utilities:

> A fantasy trip into the future may give a feeling for such a communication medium. Sitting at the breakfast table, you might cause the latest headlines to appear on a small display screen simply by touching a key. These headlines may have been written five minutes before. Pointing at a headline might get the story displayed. . . . Suppose you encounter a name of a person you would like to know more about: ask for a bibliographic sketch. Suppose you do not completely understand the economic reasoning behind an action of the International Monetary Fund: there might be available a short tutorial on some aspect of international economics. . . . Suppose you want to search the want ads or supermarket ads. Instead of shuffling pages, you may just ask to have ads displayed in a particular category. . . . Suppose a high school student wishes to search the equivalent of the local public library for information needed to write a term paper. He can quickly search the equivalent of the card catalog and soon be browsing in relevant material [Parker, 1973c].

The emergence of the electronic newspaper draws momentum from inherent problems of pulp newspapers. These problems are perhaps best summarized by Smith (1980: 73–155). The modern American newspaper has a highly computerized news gathering and news editing "front shop."

Vast quantities of textual information of short shelf life are gathered and edited on video display terminals. Most of such textual information (about 90%) is not used (Shaw, 1977). The key bottleneck for pulp newspapers—in production time and costs—is the printing press and systems for distributing to homes of newsreaders. This has become a greater problem with increased migration of subscribers to the suburbs, and the decline in urban newsstands (Carey, 1981a). Some major newspapers have developed complex systems of zoning, microzoning, tailoring, and sectioning in order to distribute subsets of the collected and edited information to ever smaller, homogeneous audience segments. These efforts by cumbersome pulp newspapers herald what Toffler argues is the "de-massification" of the mass media (1981: 155–165). Smith views this effort as an attempt to provide the newsreader with a paper made up of information most directly relevant and useful to the reader. Such individualization of the newspaper provides advertisers with narrowly defined audience segments while reducing distribution of newsprint that isn't read. This process may be called microsegmentation.

The electronic newspaper completely alters the production and distribution constraints of the pulp newspaper. Given the capacity to *address* specific textual information packets to specific newsreading households, the electronic newspaper is, in principle, completely individualized. Once textual information is stored in a machine-readable form, one challenge for videotex systems is to provide access to that information to individual newsreaders in a reasonable time frame. Indeed, one could view the electronic newspaper as providing general reader access to a currently updated newspaper morgue. Such a view mirrors Smith's "electronic Alexandria," where the accumulated information wealth of the newspaper and its wire services are made available to the inquiring reader (Smith, 1980: 300-318). The electronic newspaper, when fully implemented, becomes an electronic library with a constantly expanding wealth of instantly updated information.

However, reading the newspaper is not like using the library. If newspapers were read with the frequency with which people visit libraries, newspapers could not survive economically. Further, to view the electronic newspaper as simply an information storage and retrieval system ignores important characteristics of newsreading.

Carey (1981a) discusses historical consumer behavior with respect to newsreading and telephone usage, both relevant to videotex usage. Price and literacy barriers operated to require a century for newspapers to achieve 50% penetration in the U.S. The act of purchasing is typically a one-time decision to subscribe; home or office delivery requires no action on the part of the newsreader. Furthermore, Carey cites research (mostly by Bogart) showing that the newspaper reading habit develops during adolescence, if at all; after that, the "overwhelming majority of newspaper readers are regular or habitual readers." Reading accompanies daily rituals and is typically performed in the same place at the same time; indeed late deliveries lead to cancellations (Stone and Wetherington, 1979). Readers have individual styles (such as from back to front, or quick scans followed by later follow-up of stories of interest). Berelson (1949) also studied the social uses of newsreading, taking advantage of a citywide newspaper strike. The 60 intensive interviews revealed conscious uses (information on and interpretation of public affairs, a tool for daily living, respite, social prestige, and social contact) and nonconscious uses (pleasure, assurance, ritualistic habit, ameloriation of one's situation, information as power, and even compulsive duty). Only a third could name something they might want to know more about.

The telephone also was too expensive for residential use at first, so local drug stores became a "public telecommunications center," where residents came to use the phone and handle messages. Indeed, two of the early uses for the telephone were as a one-way mass entertainment medium and as an information service. The heavy social aspects of phone use are reflected in the ritual installation of a phone as part of starting a residence. Users pay for potential access and, indeed, are very unsatisfied with usage-sensitive billing methods. Calls are generally short, and to a small number of the same people.

Some aspects of TV viewing may also apply to electronic newsreading. Using computer-monitored data (as described in Chapter 4), Heeter, D'Alessio, Greenberg, and McVoy (1983) analyzed continuous viewing behavior of 197 randomly selected cable subscribers during a June week in 1982. They found (a) channel changing occurs regularly throughout the hour cycle (with understandable peaks at the hour and half-hour; 4.4 channel switches per hour, on the average); (b) there are extended periods (10-15 minutes) of channel sampling not aligned with show or commercial times; and (c) a moderately small set of channels (10 of 36) captured most of this switching. The first two results strongly indicate *browsing* behaviors, while "the uniform consistency across days [of channel profiles] suggests the presence of extremely *habitual* behavior, almost uninfluenced by the day of the week or the program schedule" (p. 18; emphasis added).

Other differences distinguish the pulp newspaper from the electronic newspaper. Pulp newspapers are portable; for now, electronic newspapers are locked inside TV sets connected to cable or phone lines.[2] Perhaps more significant, the pulp newspaper facilitates the "scanning" of news, as the newsreader skips from one part of the newspaper to another, reading a headline here or a lead paragraph there. All this selectivity is under the easy control of the reader. The electronic newspaper, on the other hand, displays information in screen "pages" consisting of about 50–70 words. Once a screen is read, the reader signals the videotex system that another page is desired. Strategies for what happens next need to be rooted in a theoretical understanding of the newsreading process. The next section discusses the theoretical implications of reading the electronic newspaper, followed by a review of current videotex system designs and patterns of adoption and use.

RIVAL THEORIES OF NEWSREADING

Application of two rival theories of newsreading to electronic news-reading suggests alternative design strategies. The alternative designs might then serve as potential experimental interventions in empirical tests of the rival theories.

Uses and Gratifications Research

The uses and gratifications theoretical perspective emerged as a powerful influence in mass communication research in the early 1970s, but its roots date to the 1940s. The uses and gratifications perspective can be argued to have begun with Schramm's (1949) immediate-reward and delayed-reward model of media gratifications. Another seminal work is Katz and Foulkes's (1962) article on media use as escape. Components of the uses and gratifications perspective were spelled out by Katz, Blumler, and Gurevitch (1974). The pivotal assumption of the perspective is the belief that the "audience is conceived of as active, that is, an important part of mass media use is assumed to be goal directed." The authors proceed to make clear the theoretical distinction by contrasting the uses and gratifications perspective with Bogart's (1964) conclusions about media behavior among blue-collar workers that such "experiences represent pastime rather than purposeful activity."

The uses and gratifications perspective, then, starts with the very large assumption that media use, including newsreading, serves some ulterior purpose(s) external to the communication behavior itself. Some of these purposes include pleasure, entertainment, and fantasy, so uses and gratifications theory does imply something of the rival theory of newsreading below. However, some directed or goal-motivated purpose is still assumed. As such, the research perspective suggests that people who read newspapers should be presented with lists of ulterior purposes that newsreading might serve, asking them to indicate which such purposes (gratifications sought) are served by their use of newspapers. Applying this approach to telephone usage was discussed in Chapter 3. A number of factor analytic and other types of studies have been conducted of the various posited purposes served by media use of different media and different content within media (Becker, 1979; Griffin, 1981; Levy, 1979; Rayburn and Palmgreen, 1981; Rubin, 1981a,b). Many uses and gratifications studies tend to be descriptive in nature.

Uses and gratifications research has been sharply criticized on theoretical grounds, such that one discussant at a national scholarly convention urged that nails be driven in the coffin of uses and gratifications research (Wade, 1981). Towers (1982) provides a useful overview of difficulties in uses and gratifications research. These difficulties involve the selection of statements of posited media uses, problems of focal media of study, problems of gratifications *sought* versus gratifications *obtained*, and problems with statistical analysis, and the likely confounding of "audience needs" with "images" of different media on which audiences agree (Lichtenstein and Rosenfeld, 1983).

Other problems have to do with the *normative characteristics* of the data-collection context. Suppose for the moment that newsreading, by and large, serves no ulterior purpose external to the newsreading experience itself *for the individual reader.* This is not to say that newsreading serves no large purposes for society or culture, nor does this imply that newsreading has no effects. This is simply to say that such larger social purposes and effects have little to do with why an individual, for the most part, reads a newspaper. Suppose you then ask such an individual to explain what useful purposes his or her newsreading serves. The social situation demands that the respondent come up with a rational explanation for his or her behavior. This is especially striking in Peled and Katz's (1974) study of uses and gratifications of media behavior in Israel during the 1973 war with Egypt and Syria:

> During the height of the fighting, 40% of the population called
> for television programs that would contribute to their feeling of
> pride in state and army, solidarity with the leadership, and so on.

That respondents should agree with such normative statements in times of stress is not surprising. Whether such responses illuminate much about media usage at the individual level of analysis is open to question.

Returning to the electronic newspaper, uses and gratifications research suggests that the adoption of work-related, purposive storage and retrieval systems to videotex newspapers is theoretically appropriate. Presuming that the system user is actively seeking specific content to gratify an ulterior purpose, then a menu-driven, general-to-specific retrieval system should be put to use by former pulp newspaper readers. Residual problems remain, which are related to hardware designs, initial resistance to the technology, and knowledge of its proper use. Ulterior purposes, however, provide the driving force behind goal-directed, information-seeking behavior using videotex systems.

Play Theory Reconsidered

When Katz et al. contrasted the uses and gratifications perspective of ulterior purpose with Bogart's view of media use as a "pastime," they also set the perspective in sharp contrast with another theory of newsreading. That theory—the *play* or *ludenic* newsreading theory—was developed by Stephenson in the early 1960s and fully detailed in *The Play Theory of Mass Communication* (1967). The failure to apply ludenic newsreading theory to the electronic newspaper—or pulp newspapers, for that matter—has puzzled other scholars. Logan (1982) has theorized that "play as a theory requires too much of a gestalt shift to be 'pleasing' to many scholars and practitioners with other inclinations." Tannenbaum (1980) offers a strong exception to this trend.

While play as a formal theory has been underutilized, the notion of "play" in information systems has received some attention. Marvin (1983) urges that play be considered in telecommunications policy making. She argues that heavy emphasis on utilitarian frameworks such as productivity constrain the social flexibilities inherent in networks. Information as a commodity is pitted against imaginative fantasy in the content and uses of telecommunications. She provides examples such as the officially illicit social messaging on the ARPANET, the emergence of CB radio against strenuous regulatory obstacles to social broadcasting (Marvin and Schultze, 1977), and the transformation of the personal telephone into an "expensive smorgasbord of specialized services for commercial users." Marvin calls upon policymakers and system designers to use the potential of computers to provide "intellectual parks in our computer systems."

The ludenic newsreading theory asserts that the process of newsreading is intrinsically pleasureable, and that intrinsic pleasure is at the root of both a mature, orderly, and highly ritualized form of newsreading as well as a more casual, spontaneous, and unstructured form of newsreading. This theory suggests that people who regard newspapers as information storage and retrieval devices used to accomplish certain tasks are nonpleasure readers who generally tend to be nonreaders as well (Stephenson, 1967: 157). Thus, we do *not* argue that all uses of the *Racing Form* or the *Wall Street Journal* are intrinsically pleasurable for their readers; though we *hypothesize* that strictly task-oriented users may not be *generalized* heavy readers. We do not include electronic journals in our discussion of ludenic reading (see Turoff and Hiltz, 1982a), though something akin to play may be served by such systems.

> The increase in the speed of response, the ability of current responders to view responses to that moment, the private message exchanges resulting from responses, follow-up conference discussion, and most importantly, the ability to view how many relative inquiries and responses any member has made, all make the behavior of individuals and groups in this environment very different than what can be generated in any sort of print medium [Turoff and Hiltz, 1982b].

Play consists of those activities that people perform for their own sake, for pleasure, for recreation, for hobbies, and for self-cultivation. Stephenson argues that work "deals with reality, with earning a living, with production. Play, on the contrary, is largely unproductive except for the self-satisfaction it provides." Play is an "interlude in the day; it is voluntary and not a task or moral duty." Play is "disinterested" and while "attended to with seriousness, it is not really important" (pp. 45-46).

Regarding newsreading, Stephenson argues that the activity "has all the earmarks of play." People volunteer to read newspapers, they become absorbed in the newsreading interlude, "satisfying in itself and ending there" (p. 150). Some people are characterized as *mature* newsreaders, who treat their newsreading interlude as a formal game, following highly individualized paths through different sections of the newspaper. The newsreading interlude is highly ritualized. *Pleasure* newsreaders, on the other hand, engage in free-form play during the newsreading interlude. These readers skip about with no particular ritual, reading fragments of the news here and there. These newsreaders see reading as entertainment, as a way to pass the time.

With pulp newspapers, *nonpleasure* newsreaders also exist, and constitute a large segment of print users. Theoretically, these are nonreaders who do not find newsreading absorbing or enjoyable. They use the newspaper to accomplish tasks, for sales information, for facts that serve purposes outside the newsreading interlude itself. Such pulp newspaper users seem to serve as the videotex designer's model of the electronic newsreader.

Key concepts in the ludenic newsreading theory are *convergent selectivity* and *apperception.* Convergent selectivity involves the individual's selection of something for himself or herself in ways that make the product uniquely individual. Newsreading is a process of convergent selectivity, whereby highly individualized rituals within the newsreading interlude "customize" the experience. Apperception is the characteristic of individuals to perceive only those aspects of a more complex situation that tie in with prior interests. Both concepts are important to the theoretical design of the electronic newspaper.

REVELANT VIDEOTEX RESEARCH:
DESIGN, ADOPTION, USE, AND OBSTACLES

Numerous studies (mostly proprietary) are under way to evaluate the potential of videotex services and electronic newspapers. Tydeman et al. (1982: Chap. 9) suggest prototype videotext and teletext systems design based upon a comprehensive features analysis. We discuss features relevant to this chapter.

Most emerging systems tend to follow similar design strategies. Such systems are generally menu-driven information storage and retrieval systems. The newsreader is initially confronted with a "master menu" or index—a screen/page (or several) that lists topics of information services in the most general terms. The newsreader presses a key corresponding to the item number on the index. The index disappears from the screen, replaced by a second menu listing specific topics that fall under the more general category selected on the master menu. The newsreader selects a topic from this second menu, and so forth. The number of topic menus searched depends on the volume of information stored, its data-base structure, and the general system design. Figure 5.1 shows this process for an imaginary news search. It would take considerable time to read through all the various menus of current offerings, such as the CompuServe videotex service.[3] The sheer mass of this index implies special problems for newsreading or for information retrieval in general.

This "tree structure" or sequential menu approach is generally easy to learn and use, and costs less in terms of system overhead. But this

FIGURE 5.1   An Imaginary News Search on a Videotex System

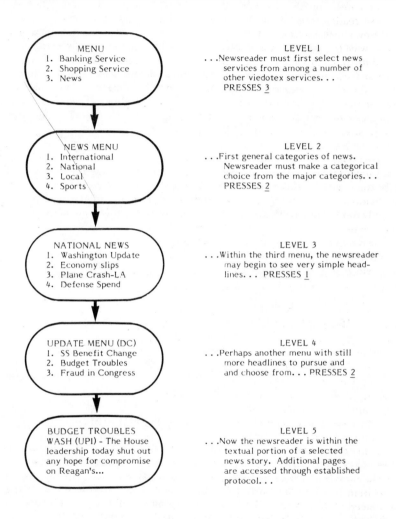

MENU 1. Banking Service 2. Shopping Service 3. News	LEVEL 1 . . .Newsreader must first select news services from among a number of other viedotex services. . . PRESSES 3
NEWS MENU 1. International 2. National 3. Local 4. Sports	LEVEL 2 . . .First general categories of news. Newsreader must make a categorical choice from the major categories. . . PRESSES 2
NATIONAL NEWS 1. Washington Update 2. Economy slips 3. Plane Crash-LA 4. Defense Spend	LEVEL 3 . . .Within the third menu, the newsreader may begin to see very simple head- lines. . . PRESSES 1
UPDATE MENU (DC) 1. SS Benefit Change 2. Budget Troubles 3. Fraud in Congress	LEVEL 4 . . .Perhaps another menu with still more headlines to pursue and and choose from. . . PRESSES 2
BUDGET TROUBLES WASH (UPI) - The House leadership today shut out any hope for compromise on Reagan's...	LEVEL 5 . . .Now the newsreader is within the textual portion of a selected news story. Additional pages are accessed through established protocol. . .

approach places greater emphasis on the first of the objectives that Carey (1981a) and Schabas and Tompa (1983) identified as served by information retrieval designs. These objectives include

(1)   to provide access to particular items(s) — (known by one or more of its characteristics) — to provide a specific answer;

(2)   to group items by common characteristic(s) for browsing: the characteristics of use may be unknown by the indexer and by the user, or may not even be feasibly joined;

(3)   in the extreme, to facilitate consumption of information services as a (pleasurable) habit, rather than to satisfy motivations and needs.

Typically, "browsing is viewed as an integral part of all information and is not clearly distinguished from directed search" (Grusec, 1982: 2). Even when the first two reasons are salient (i.e., information seeking), tree structures make it difficult to scan or browse to find a hidden fact; the user may not know the best source or approach. Videotex search trials show considerable failure in supporting information seeking: its success rate is only about 50%-60% rather than the minimal 80% that Sutherland (1980) deems necessary for the mass audience. Several Dutch experiments reported by Sutherland showed that from 6 to 14 steps were required to find information, and there were one or more errors in the majority of search tasks. Even with only four index steps, the majority of subjects had to "back up" at least once in the search.

There are several reasons for this problem:

(1)   information usually fits into several hierarchies, and thus is susceptible to arbitrary decisions by information providers and users;

(2)   classification may be poor;

(3)   typical screen size provides severe limits to classification limits and increases chances of going wrong;

(4)   users lose track of their spatial information location;

(5)   residential use of information is typically diverse, uncritical, nonrecurrent and based upon alternate sources, unlike business information needs;

(6)   residential users are generally familiar only with the two-step indexing barriers of newspapers and telephones: the page index or the directory (Carey, 1981a; Rothman, 1980; Schabas and Tompa, 1983).

A direct test of effectiveness, efficiency, and satisfaction of menu-driven versus keyword-relational retrieval designs is reported by Geller and Lesk (1981). Users of library information retrieval systems are typically more experienced and more purposeful than residential videotext users; so the authors decided to test the two designs of an actual library data base on real users (N = 779) with real tasks (1952 searches over 59 days, as monitored by the computer.) Users spent more time in keyword searches in an average session (218.1 seconds versus 181.7; p < .001); this extra time is (a) user time, not computer time and (b) is because users get farther and are reinforced. Over time, the keyword approach was more popular, particularly among users with experience in both systems: 79% of the searches were by keyword.

Such searches were more successful, too: If the item was known, 65% of keyword users found it compared to 30% of menu users; if users were browsing, 69% found a book on the subject of interest, compared to 36%

of the menu users; and only 24% of keyword searches resulted in *no* document versus 55% of menu searches.

A parallel controlled experiment by Schabas and Tompa (1983: Supplement) used two groups of eight students to compare hierarchical "tree" searching to multiple-hierarchy "forest" searching. The computer-monitored data showed that there was no significant difference between the success of each group in solving six simple queries (retrieve one document describing a specific course) or in solving six compound queries (find all documents conceptually related.) However, the multiple hierarchy required fewer steps and less time for the simple queries, but more for the compound ones, due to mistakes made by users in the extra step required to display the context. The authors concluded that the forests search is a useful indexing strategy, but that it is important to reduce the number of menu pages required to arrive at a retrieval solution.

Videotex retrieval designs may have long-term cultural consequences, too. In a very creative article Grande (1980) suggests that the online relational/keyword search process has some characteristics of oral culture: Inverted file structure removes words from grammar; meaning is established largely by context; indeed, "grammar and linear subject-predicate-object bonding are antagonistic to healthy search strategies" (p. 128). Given topics are not treated consistently across data bases, indexers, or time, so a user cannot predict all contexts. Search strategies require intuition, typically multiplied over all synonyms. Retrieving unexpected contexts, say by completion of truncated words, is a learning process that is frustrating to novices, but leads to wider associations of concepts. Early training on videotex might lead to "a flexibility in word association and concept analysis that engenders a capacity for dealing with unexpected situations without anxiety" (p. 130), and, we would add, to increased susceptibility to playing with words through electronic newsreading.

Videotex Design Issues: Visual Aspects

Linkage between physiological/psychological studies of visual perception and videotex reading is provided in a thoughtful discourse by Mills (1982). His goal was to extract implications for the use of graphics in videotex from perception research. A few intriguing conclusions follow:

(1)   A general problem is "to understand how a picture can serve as a 'conceptual base' facilitating the comprehension of text and how text can guide the processing of a picture." Visuals tend to generate multiple propositions, and are not good for formulating about past, future, or conditional events, or logical inference chains.

(2)   However, "pictures departing from photographic realism . . . may be more easily and quickly identified than photographs of the real thing," possibly because they are more easily fit to "mental schemas." Thus videotex line graphics may be more effective and efficient (in terms of transmission time) than photo-graphics.

(3)   Complex ideas may be transmitted by simple graphic imagery; this is
        particularly true of dynamic graphics showing transformations that tend
        to aid productive thinking and problem solving. "Sequence" rather than
        "motion" may suffice, and would be possible on videotex.

(4)   Individual differences play a large part in people's ability to use and learn
        from graphics, such as maps.

(5)   Ad hoc use of graphics may only increase transmission time and not
        automatically increase videotex usefulness.

Some related aspects of this body of research were specifically tested in
the WETA Teletext project (Champness and deAlberdi, 1981). They
conducted three rigorous, small-sample experiments to (a) find the main
evaluative dimensions of teletext pages; (b) assess the stability of these
dimensions over people and situations; (c) assess the validity of using slide
simulations of screen graphics by comparing them with actual teletext
graphics; and (d) assess specific page designs on users' reactions and
information recall. The authors found evaluative dimensions to be stable
across situations and subjects. They also found slide simulations of screen
graphics to be comparable to actual teletext graphics.

Champness and deAlberdi's review of the literature on effects of page
layout on readability concluded, in part that (a) segmenting text by
paragraphs and indentations helped, but that bullets did not; (b) underlin-
ing, boldface, and color may help in scanning but not in memory recall or
reading time; (c) color theory is applicable; and (d) readability and
aesthetic appeal are different dimensions.

Champness and deAlberdi report the following three specific findings:

(1)   Based upon 15 semantic differential scales, three dimensions of nearly
        identical strength and composition emerged in each experiment: attrac-
        tiveness (explaining from 50% to 77% of variance), clarity (from 18% to
        31%), and usefulness (from 5% to 12%). Attractiveness included
        colorful, cheerful, dazzling, exciting, bright, interesting, and warm.
        Clarity included organized, straightforward, clear, and easy. Usefulness
        included useful, meaningful, important, and relevant.

(2)   These scales discriminated very significantly among the multiple page
        designs intended to represent a continuum of complexity and graphic
        content.

(3)   Attractiveness increased with increased color and graphics. The maxi-
        mum clarity was obtained with paragraphs and color-coded keywords.
        There were no effects of page design on memory for information (recall).
        Further, Foster and Bruce (1982) found that color-coding columns
        degraded the performance of the 96 subjects attempting to locate a target
        entry, while color-coding of rows had no effect on performance. It seems
        that the attractiveness of color is unrelated, at best, to performance or
        recall.

Merging these findings with ludenic newsreading theory is difficult,
because the methods of inquiry are at great variance. However, it is

interesting that utility (usefulness) is but one dimension along which subjects evaluate teletext screens. The existence of the other dimensions (attractiveness and clarity) is suggested by Stephenson's propositions about communication pleasure in the newsreading interlude.

As a footnote, one major factor in attitude development toward reading is whether the child perceives reading as fun or interesting (Alexander and Filler, 1976; Mason, 1980). Not only do graphics and interactivity stimulate interest, but electronic text itself may be intrinsically more motivating than printed text (Paisley and Chen, 1982). All these notions are consistent with propositions regarding communication pleasure.

Diffusion of Videotex

Some media—for a variety of reasons, including economics, regulatory policy, and technological hurdles—have diffused more rapidly than others. The number of years (rounded) needed to achieve 50% U.S. penetration are given for selected media by Carey (1981a) and Tydeman et al. (1982): newspapers (100+ years), telephone (70 years), color TV (17 years), AM radio (10 years) and black and white TV (10 years). It has taken cable TV 30 years to achieve 20% penetration (see Figure 2.2). The prevailing estimate is that 7% of U.S. households will be using videotex by 1990. (Markoff [1982] and Tydeman et al. [1982] give projections through 2000 for various aspects of videotex.)

Many studies show that at a fair number of pilot users would be willing to pay for actual videotex services—from 43% (Irving, Elton, and Siegeltuch, 1982) to 76% (Eissler, 1981). A survey televised over 16 regional markets showed a willingness to pay for videotex in general by 50% (Marketing News, 1982). The typical monthly dollar amount is around $10-$15 (Rice and Paisley, 1982).

Some primary system attributes deemed important are reduced access time (Elton, Irving, and Siegeltuch, 1982; Ragland and Warner, 1981; Rice and Paisley, 1982), more interactivity than menu selection alone can provide (Drewalowski, 1983; also Gaffner, 1983 ["the presence of menu-oriented news services is in itself not a determining factor"]), good graphics (Drewalowski, 1983; Elton et al., 1982), and the reduction of household time spent in transactions or obtaining news and shopping information (Times Mirror, 1983).

Studies by the Associated Press, the Washington Post research department, and Butler Cox and Partners Limited provide basically the same user profile of the potential videotext subscriber (Broadcasting, 1982; Butler Cox, 1980; Editor and Publisher, 1982a,b,c). Evidence compiled by these firms suggests that the typical (initial) user will be male, white, college educated, between the ages of 25 and 45, of managerial or professional status, and earning in excess of $30,000 per year. These characteristics seem to correspond quite highly with the characteristics of "heavy users" of both magazines and newspapers as determined by Simmons Market Research Reports (1979), except that these users are slightly older (35-54), not specifically professional, and specifically reside in a 1-2 person household for the newspaper reader and in a 3-4 member household for the magazine reader.

In terms of psychographic characteristics, one report termed the potential user as a "vanguard" (Kagan, 1983). While not defined in the report, potential users could be categorized as upwardly mobile, career oriented, and participating in more outdoor and culturally oriented leisure-time activities. Perhaps psychographic characteristics of the potential videotex user will resemble those of the heavy print user. Heavy magazine readership life-style includes: enjoys reading, attends fine-arts activities, self-confident, pro-business attitudes, nonresistant to social change, above-average vacationing and travel, has negative advertising attitudes, and is not typically family oriented (Crask and Reynolds, 1980).

Using adoption categories more familiar to communication research (see Chapters 3 and 7), Dozier and Ledingham (1982) led two two-hour-long focus groups consisting of six couples who were cable subscribers in generating positive and negative attributes of videotex after a half-hour demonstration of a system. Comments were later grouped into the five primary attributes of innovations evaluated by potential adaptors. With respect to *compatibility*, "computerization" was seen as a negative aspect not conforming to current values; there was a perceived trade-off between convenience and privacy. This finding was also reported by Marketing News (1982), although the Times-Mirror survey reported that 87% did not fear lack of privacy. With respect to *relative advantage*, other social functions of activities facilitated by videotex (such as social interaction) were seen as negative by some (such as reducing personal sociability) and positive by others (such as reducing waiting in lines). With respect to *complexity*, videotex was generally seen as complex, involving considerable learning. Tryability and observability would be improved by seeing others use it in their homes. Subjects also discriminated between read-only surveillance services (positively evaluated) and read/write transaction services (more negatively evaluated).

Bolton (1983) tested these adoption categories along with AIO/life-style measures (activity, interest, and opinion), sociodemographic variables, and measures of "innovative" consumers, as part of the Channel 2000 pilot involving 144 people in 71 houses over three months. The service provided free library, encyclopedia, banking, education, and community information and services. Based on upper and lower levels of the amount subjects would pay for the service before, during, and at the end of the pilot, the strongest contributors in the discriminant analysis were the innovation attributes of compatibility and relative advantage. With modest discrimination, and only at two time periods, shopping venturesomeness and positive evaluation of TV for entertainment also contributed. Heavy prior computer users and innovative consumers were less willing to pay—perhaps because they are more critical consumers and thus aware of videotex limitations. Standard sociodemographic indicators did not distinguish among payment levels. Bolton suggests that consumers must understand the relative advantages of videotex, as an aid in one's daily life. Videotex services should fit into and expand current consumer values, needs, and past experiences, including TV as an entertainment medium.

Videotex Usage: Amount and Categories

Usage statistics by themselves are not particularly informative. We typically find a wide range: from 14% of all subjects reporting daily use of televised text as part of a pay cable service (Ruchinskas, 1980), 25% per day for agricultural information (Rice and Paisley, 1982), to over 60% at least once a week for generalized/transactional services (Drewalowski, 1983; Telephony, 1983). Most pilots found decreased usage figures after the initial novelty wore off and technical problems discouraged users (Elton et al., 1982; Rice and Paisley, 1982), although a commercial service reported subsequent continued growth in usage (Times Mirror, 1983). Typically the initially most frequent users show the greatest reduction in usage over time (see also Rice and Case, 1983).

However, correlates of usage may be informative. Ruchinskas (1980) analyzed questionnaires returned by 70% of the 534 Los Angeles residents who were contacted by telephone, from a list of 1097 pay cable subscribers. Those who reported using TV text more often were younger, were more interested in home telecommunications innovations, used radio and TV more, used TV more for excitement, and were generally satisfied with TV. Frequent users were less likely to report that they used TV to learn about themselves; there were no education or income differences. The most frequently updated frames are typically used most frequently, and increased updating influences increased usage in general (Connelly, 1983; Irving et al., 1982). Typically the more pages in a category, the more frequently that category will be used, although requests for the subsequent pages drop off dramatically (Elton et al., 1982; Rice and Paisley, 1982). However, Irving et al. (1982: 6) reported that even though the page contents of their trial system were dramatically changed halfway through the pilot, the level of system use remained the same: "This may be an indication that our sample households had developed *fixed habits of use* which were not affected by the change in system content." The emergence of habitual videotex usage is predicted among mature newsreaders by the ludenic newsreading theory. On the other hand, there was also little variation in the type of frame accessed in the grain county of the Green Thumb pilot, "while livestock county usage showed heavier market frame access during periods of buying, storing and selling of farm products and supplies" (Rice and Paisley, 1982). Utilitarian motives as well as communication pleasure influence usage of videotex services.

From the Green Thumb videotext evaluation (Maloney, 1982; Paisley, 1983; Ragland and Warner, 1981; Rice and Paisley, 1982) the most succinct (discriminant) analyses showed that 40% of the *system-monitored* use was predicted by farmers' being more innovative and valuing weather frames more, while no independent variables significantly entered the equation for *reported* use. Older farmers found more utility in the system. A very similar system and evaluation is reported by Ettema (1983). That pilot involved 188 farmers over an eight-month period. Ettema's analysis of the 74% who returned the mail questionnaire showed that information-seeking benefits were predicted by lower age, lower income, fewer personal contacts, and greater marketing information interest. Positive evaluations of electronic newspapers was predicted by more innovativeness, less newspaper reading, yet greater news interest by respondents. Here, no variables significantly predicted system-monitored use; use was also unrelated to the perceived value of electronic newspapers. Ettema concluded that usage of the farm information and the electronic newspaper systems essentially were not strongly predictable because it is hard to predict who benefits most, yet even the small amounts of variance explained still might indicate potential inequities in access to benefits. (Rice and Paisley argue from a similar finding that benefits are homogenously accessible.) High levels of use may not necessarily be synonymous with high levels of benefit, because some users may value the fact that they can get exactly the information wanted without much tedious use. However, the analysis that described users' evaluations of the *idea* of an electronic newspaper indicates that system usage is not related to specific *actual* information in spite of subjects' reported greater *interest* in news.

Content Categories of Videotex Use

As with frequency of usage, the rankings of content categories vary with respect to use and popularity across systems. Variance may be largely attributed to the fact that services differ in their target audience, in the kinds of information they provide, and in the amount of information they provide. Arlen's (1983) review finds considerable similarity in trial results, with electronic messaging and videogames ranked high, and general interest in news headlines and community reports. Entertainment content (performance, "on view," mind play, "for kids," and electro-art) was accessed second-most frequently in the WETA pilot (Irving et al., 1982); only slightly less than the 41% accesses to index pages. Weather and entertainment were viewed most positively (Elton et al., 1982) and, along with features, were used more than was expected relative to a weighted number of pages. In public places, users tended to scan information items, and seemed to be more instrumental users, particularly with more frequently updated information. Usage figures from the first seven months of Prestel (based upon the top 25 Information Providers, or 60% of all content categories) showed the following percentages of total accesses: amusement 28%, news 27%, leisure 21%, local 10%, and several other categories (Butler Cox, 1980). Ruchinskas (1980) found both browsing and purposeful use in the most popular categories: comparative shopping and weather.

Impacts of Videotex on Usage of Other Media

In all studies except one, no extreme media displacements occurred during the test periods. (See Chapter 12 for a broad discussion of displacement in media environments.) Indeed, 70% of the respondents in the Times-Mirror trial said that they did not want videotex to take the place of other information sources. In the Columbus Viewtel pilot (Harnish, 1981)—a library-oriented service—16% of the 200 homes reported they spent more time reading books during the three-month period and 8% spent more time talking with their children. Ruchinskas (1980) noted 9% of those using TV text channels said they viewed less TV news and read newspapers less frequently. Participants in the Viewtron pilot indicated a 33% reduction in newspaper reading and a 45% reduction in television viewing. Green Thumb farmers ranked their preferred channels for information (Marketing: newspaper, radio, buyers; Weather: AM/FM radio, TV, National Oceanic and Atmospheric Administration (NOAA; "all weather") radio; Farming: magazines, extension services, friends), revealing that videotext never displaced these trusted sources, even if traditional media were more difficult to obtain or less timely. In Ettema's comparable study, greater videotext benefits were associated with less use of other media, but this was perhaps due to prior dissatisfaction with those media, and, in any event, those media were not displaced.

Other Obstacles to Videotex Diffusion

Besides innovation and user characteristics, there are of course other obstacles to the spread of electronic newsreading. While reading is active, viewing video is passive and, thus, may mitigate against some benefits from online information access. Even if a system is designed for browsing, users may be unwilling to do so if they are charged for specific page use. Decoders are expensive. Transactional services using the rapidly-diffusing home microcomputers offer stiff competition. Uncertainties in cable diffusion and incompatible standards will also slow videotex use. Delays in integrated services and networks will not help either (see also Campbell and Thomas, 1981; Easton, 1980; Gollin, 1981; Tyler, 1979).

As indicated, a number of factors unrelated to the internal organization of the electronic newspaper will affect the rate of diffusion, the displacement of other media, and the impact of the electronic newspaper on individual users and society as a whole. All these other factors must be considered and allowed for in analyses of electronic newspapers. At the same time, the internal organization of the electronic newspaper is an important attribute of the innovation. Because internal organization is most directly under the producer's control, considerable attention is properly focused in this area. Here, prior theories of newsreading behavior can provide significant illumination.

THE LUDENIC ELECTRONIC NEWSPAPER

On the surface, organization of the electronic newspaper as a gigantic data base with countless information retrieval options would seem to embrace the convergent selective character of the newsreading interlude. This, however, reflects vulgar extrapolation of the concept to a new situation. The concept of convergent selectivity is properly relegated to the selection of a newspaper title from among a variety of electronic newspaper options. That is, rather than providing individual access to one massive (and forbidding) data base, the "true" ludenic electronic newspaper consists of a number of informational items strung together electronically in a manner that enhances the newsreading play of a particular audience microsegment.

The exact characteristics of an electronic micronewspaper would be determined by the combined behavior of audience segment members and special advertisers, electronic journalists and editors, and data-base providers and indexers. Newsreaders of the artificially "mass" pulp newspaper audience—made mass by the pulp production and distribution demands rather than an objective generic agenda of information "needs" (McCombs and Shaw, 1977)—are set free to select for themselves from a number of electronic micronewspaper titles.

Stephenson provided a number of suggestions to pulp newspapers to enhance play opportunities for readers. These suggestions are equally valid for the electronic newspaper. He suggested that newspapers "induce and encourage . . . regularity, order and perspective" when a developed or mature audience is sought.

> The editor has to make his newspaper interesting; for some readers this can be achieved by primitive play conditions, such as are characterized more by a scattering of the mind than by well-developed absorption. Sophisticated newsreading is contemplative rather than scatterbrained [Stephenson, 1967: 151].

Given the quantum reduction in production and distribution costs inherent in electronic newspapers, convergent selectivity is served through microsegmentation of the newspaper readership. This flows from the technical flexibility to produce an electronic micronewspaper title, using minimal staff who can access various machine-readable data bases.[4] These pieces of information are then assembled—"edited" in the precise sense of the word—in forms that enhance the newsreading interlude for the microsegment.

The key to successful development of electronic micronewspapers is development of forms consistent with the type of play that characterizes the newsreading interlude. Vital to such play (at least for audience microsegments at the "mature" end of the play continuum) is regular and consistent style or form of presentation. *The indexing of information must become part of the subjective play of the newsreading interlude.* True ludenic newsreading cannot be transformed into a task-oriented drudgery of data-base manipulation and intricate information-recovery protocols, as now required by many videotex systems. To do so is to take newsreading out of the realm of play and into the world of work and task accomplishment (see Paisley, 1980). Such systems will attract only nonpleasure readers; mature and pleasure readers will find little communication pleasure.

LUDENIC DESIGN IMPLICATIONS

On a practical level, how does one go about designing a ludenic, electronic micronewspaper? First, one must have a clear idea of the newsreading microsegment for whom the electronic newspaper is to be edited. Smith (1980: 135-157) argues that the newspaper is becoming more like a special interest magazine. He provides an excellent overview of this microprocess in the magazine industry. Stephenson's mature and pleasure newsreaders serve as a starting point. As empirical experience grows, Stephenson's theoretical types will be elaborated into increasingly sophisticated "fixes" of key audience microsegment characteristics. Second, task-oriented, goal-directed menu searches should stop (at least temporarily) with the selection of the micronewspaper title. Recall that the pulp newspaper has developed a number of conventions that ease the reader into the mass of information it contains, conventions that enhance ludenic play throughout the news-selecting process. Sections, indexes, headlines, subheads, boldface, windows—all are techniques used to signal or cue the newsreader as to the relative importance, priority, value, or meaning of the various pieces of information that make up the newspaper. Putting pulp newspaper content on the screen as an electronic newspaper is akin to a radio newscaster's reading the daily newspaper aloud from front to back. A new medium requires a form of presentation unique unto itself. New design forms must vie for support against the formidable "default" design option: simply dumping text from available data bases onto a videotex system.

Despite the absence of an accepted form and grammar for the electronic micronewspaper, some basic design principles flow from ludenic newsreading theory. One such extrapolation is the MORE/NEXT strategy for information presentation. Figure 5.2 provides a model for a ludenic electronic newspaper, using the MORE/NEXT strategy for accessing news. The abbreviated screen pages across the top of Figure 5.2 are similar to the one- and two-sentence indexing descriptions that many newspapers have adopted. For example, the March 12, 1982, issue of the *San Francisco Chronicle* included the following indexing description in the "Top of the News" for a main story and sidebar:

John Belushi's widow has a number of questions about his death. Page 5.

Speedballing—the use of heroine and cocaine simultaneously—is becoming more popular among the well-to-do. Page 5.

FIGURE 5.2 Design for a Ludenic Electronic Newspaper

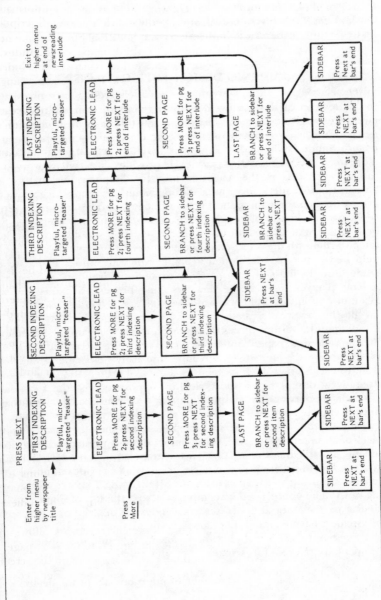

The index descriptions, linked in an electronic chain by the electronic micronewspaper's editors, provide a highly targeted summary of the day's news as well as serving as indexing teasers for additional information about the particular news items. After reading each indexing description, the newsreader is faced with a simple choice: MORE about the same news item or display the NEXT indexing description in the chain. Indexing descriptions should be written in a manner that enhances the ludenic character of the information retrieval process. Rather than using a universal style for such descriptions, each electronic micronewspaper would develop styles consistent with characteristics of its newsreader microsegment that self-selects that newspaper title as its own. The number and length of stories to be included in an electronic micronewspaper would be determined by the characteristics of the self-selecting microsegments. However, style as transmitted by typefaces may be a major problem for electronic newspapers.

If an individual newsreader in the newsreading microsegment apperceives a story to be especially tied to prior interests, then the MORE function key on the keypad is pressed. The reader moves down through the story, learning more detail with each screen page.[5] What happens at the end of the story? Here a new menu appears. Various electronic sidebars —relational indexes— related to the main story could be listed by headline or short description (teaser indexing descriptions perhaps). This provides the reader an opportunity to pursue an apperceived interest in still greater detail, in convergent selective fashion. As indicated in Figure 5.2, various sidebars may be accessed from menus at the end of several main stories. In addition, sidebars can provide their own menus at the end leading to still more sidebars. When reader interest plays itself out, the NEXT function key takes the reader to the next indexing description.

Where does advertising fit into all this? First, microsegmentation and reduced production and delivery costs may permit some electronic micronewspapers to be subscriber supported. On the other hand, experiences of the specialized magazine industry suggest that advertising takes on special attractiveness to the reader when advertisers appeal to the special characteristics, interests, and convergent selective options of a narrow readership. Location of advertising messages in the matrix displayed in Figure 5.2 will depend on the characteristics of the audience microsegment. One ingenious strategy for handling advertising in a communication-pleasure and communication-pain framework allows the reader to skip a screen page of advertising and go on to the next page in the chain. For the reader who calls up the advertising page on the screen, an electronic payment or discount is credited toward the reader's cost of using the videotex service.

These theory-based recommendations should be combined with other findings outlined in previous sections. These other recommendations include

(1) fostering use and diffusion among groups of users, including public places;
(2) stabilizing the location of types of information;
(3) providing index support in portable paper form;
(4) downgrading excessive and sole reliance upon indices;
(5) facilitating browsing habits;
(6) avoiding discrete unit pricing;
(7) blending videotex with prior services;
(8) providing electronic messaging and games perhaps as an integral part of the newsreading service;
(9) shifting marketing philosophies as the service diffuses;
(10) considering individual attitude and physiological differences (such as poor reading skills, bad eyesight, arthritic or large fingers);
(11) increasing designers' awareness of age-specific social responses to system problems;
(12) avoiding prior expectations from other media usage;
(13) fitting content, timeliness, and form of information into a new or complimentary medium rather than a displacing medium;
(14) using graphics appropriately;
(15) differential updating and content access for psychographic user groups and time periods; and
(16) creating nonhierarchical data-base and retrieval processes, including vertical, horizontal, and relational access (Carey, 1981a; Elton and Carey, 1983; Schabas and Tompa, 1983).

TESTING THEORIES OF NEWSREADING

The emerging videotex news services are implicit tests of the uses and gratifications perspective, with the assumption that ulterior motives drive the information retrieval tasks. Ludenic newsreading theory suggests that viewing newsreading as a goal-directed information retrieval task ignores the essential communication pleasure of newsreading as an end in itself. As such, emerging videotex systems— as presently designed—stand ready to service financial and work-related tasks of a small nonpleasure elite who need access to news-type data bases to accomplish certain goals and objectives. This segment may well support such services at a moderate level but is insufficient for widespread, particularly residential, adoption. However, it may be the only segment that can cost-justify videotex usage in the near future.

Mature and pleasure newsreaders, on the other hand, are not well served by such systems. What ludenic newsreaders require is an *edited* product, shaped narrowly enough in form and content to permit convergent selective processes to occur *through* protocols that are pleasurable ends in themselves. The electronic newspaper—like its pulp predecessor—must organize the news of the day in a manner that reassures its reader through its regularity and consistency of style. The electronic newspaper keeps newsreading in the realm of subjective play by taking the work-related and task-related assumptions out of the system design. The ludenic electronic newspaper guides its newsreading microsegment through the playful steps of reviewing the major events of the day, as those events are apperceived by that microsegment.

We may envision overtly playful aspects in electronic newsreading, such as comics taking the form of short videogames, or sounds and visual effects supporting the content as it is browsed.

A modest test of newsreading theory and electronic newspapers was conducted by the Center for Communications at San Diego State University. In that study 107 subjects were identified through random-digit dialing of San Diego households, with selection of subjects stratified by age, gender, and cable subscription status. Using a single-group, pretest-posttest design, subjects were provided a 30-minute demonstration of an electronic newspaper on a computer programmed to simulate an operational electronic news service. In a subset of this study, 50 of the subjects actually operated a fully operational information package. Using specialized function keys, the electronic newsreader could move up and down menu structure, scan stories, and move about at will in that information package. While the study was funded to answer other research questions,[6] a study of newsreading theory was piggybacked.

In a pretest interview, subjects were asked whether they agreed or disagreed with several attitude statements toward newspaper reading. A five-point, Likert-type scale was used. One item stated, "I only read a newspaper when I need to get specific information." The item was adapted from Stephenson (taken verbatim, but used as an attitude statement instead of a discriminating item in a Q-sort) measuring the kind of purposive-only newsreading behavior of the type he termed "nonpleasure reader." The item is also a measure of the goal-directed newsreading that the uses and gratifications perspective suggests motivates all newsreading behavior.

During pretest interviews, subjects also indicated agreement or disagreements with the next statement: "Newspaper reading is a habit for me; I really miss it when I don't read it." This item was again adapted from Stephenson as a measure of the newsreader type he termed "mature newsreaders."

Subjects were also asked to indicate how much they would pay for an electronic news service, in addition to the standard $10 per month basic cable fee. (The initial study was based on the assumption that services would be transmitted via two-way, interactive cable systems. The effort in this item was to separate the cost of electronic text services from other, cable-related charges.) The question was posed in the pretest interview, following a brief, single-page description of such a service, which subjects were directed to read. The average price for the 57 subjects in this portion of the experiment was $8.24. The question was again posed in the posttest interview, after the subjects had experienced an electronic news service for about a half hour. The average price given rose to $12.98.

The relationship between goal-directed, purposive newspaper reading and willingness to adopt an electronic news service is striking, given that two media are involved. Prior to the electronic news service simulation, respondents who read newspapers only for "specific information" were generally willing to pay more for the electronic service. (Pearson $R = .23$; $N = 88$; $p < .05$). Following the simulation experience, the correlation remained largely unchanged ($R = .25$; $N = 92$; $p < .01$).

Interestingly, the mature newsreaders who are habitual newspaper readers and who miss the newspaper when they don't read it were predisposed *not* to adopt an electronic news service. During the pretest interview, willingness to pay for electronic news services tended to be negatively, but only slightly, correlated with a mature newsreading ($R = -.15$; $N = 78$; $p < .10$). After the simulation experience, any relationship between mature newspaper reading and willingness to pay for electronic news services disappeared ($R = -.06$; $N = 81$; $p < .30$).

To put these findings in context, consider the fact that the electronic news simulation was designed to replicate closely videotex services on Cox Cable's Indax interactive cable service. The Indax system is a menu-driven system that reflects the goal-directed, information-seeking characteristics of nearly all prototype videotex systems. Further, the written description of videotex services provided to subjects during the pretest interviews also stressed this orientation to videotex services. Thus, nonpleasure readers do not use newspapers as ends in themselves but as a means of accessing information for other purposes. People who use newspapers this way are also willing to pay for electronic news services. Mature newsreaders who use the newspaper in an elaborate, ritualized play interlude recognize little play in this form of electronic newspaper. When such a service is described to them, mature newsreaders are somewhat resistant to electronic news. This resistance disappears following direct experiences with such an electronic service. However, mature newspaper reading and adoption of electronic news services remain, in the end, orthogonal.

SUMMARY

Several bold suggestions for electronic news services can be drawn from these findings. First, nonpleasure readers who use newspapers only for specific information find videotex news services attractive. Second, an important section of newspaper readership is neither attracted nor repelled by the concept and the simulation of an electronic newspaper. Such newsreaders perhaps remain to be convinced. The ludenic electronic newspaper is more labor intensive and more expensive than the "default" dumping of machine-readable text onto a videotex system. Yet the highly edited ludenic electronic newspaper may be the most prudent investment in the long run. Failure to attract mature and pleasure newspaper readers to the new medium has costly implications for those with financial or other interests in electronic newspapers.

NOTES

The authors gratefully acknowledge the technical assistance and observations of Dean Hallford, Department of Music, and Wayne Towers, Department of Journalism, San Diego State University.

1. Many cable systems provide screen frames of wire copy for a preset length of time. The user experience parallels that of TV and radio news consumption. The user is wholly passive and powerless in manipulating the rate and contents of the news provided.

2. The nonportability of the electronic newspaper is not a permanent technical limitation. Rapid advances in liquid crystal displays and "downloading" of data on a periodic basis to microcassettes or microdisk systems may eliminate the nonportability of the electronic newspaper.

3. CompuServe is a national videotex service based in Columbus, Ohio. CompuServe has entered into agreement with the Tandy Corporation to provide videotex services to purchasers of Radio Shack's TRS-80 personal computers. Radio Shack is a Tandy subsidiary. Complete CompuServe videotext menus appear in *Update* (February 1982), a consumer newsletter of the CompuServe Information Service Division. Related material may be found in *Today Magazine* 1 (July 1981), another publication of the CompuServe Information Service Division, 5000 Arlington Center Blvd., Columbus, Ohio 43220.

4. Rice and Paisley (1982) emphasize, however, that demands on staff to maintain updated information for videotex systems may be far more than an unprepared organization can support, leading to user dissatisfaction and rejection of the system.

5. The style of writing text for screen display is not a developed form. The screen is limited to about 50-70 words. The reader consciously decides at the end of each screen display to branch to the next page in the sequence or go on to new material in another category. Different styles of writing are likely appropriate to different applications and different readerships.

6. The study was funded by HomServ, Inc., a subsidiary of American Can Corporation. The study, "Videotex Topic Preferences Study," sought to identify content interests among potential adopters, as well as to develop principles of screen and system design. Principal investigator was John Witherspoon, director of the Center for Communications. Project director was David Dozier, Department of Journalism.

RONALD E. RICE

6 Mediated Group Communication

As a couple, Romeo and Juliet had a lot to talk about, and their communication has become a part of Western culture. But the process of their communication is interesting, informative, problematic, and in the end tragic because they belonged to different groups. The point is that groups are the fundamental building blocks of organizations, communities, society; they mediate the form, direction, and content of individual and dyadic communication. Influential sociological concepts of "group" include reference groups, kinship groups, group stratification, socioeconomic groups and the like. Here, however, we focus on one locus of group communication—small groups. More specifically, we consider communication as mediated not only by its occurrence within a group but also by new communication technology.

This is an interesting topic precisely for the reason that there are not many group media. Rural party lines are rudimentary telephone conference calls; and audio conferencing is not unfamiliar to many organizations. Video conferencing and computer conferencing (CC) are two other group media; organizational teleconferencing in general is discussed in Chapter 9. There has, however, been considerable research on cross-media comparisons as reviewed by Fowler and Wackerbath (1980); Hiemstra (1982); Johansen (1977); Johansen, Vallee, and Spangler (1979: 141-191); Rice (1980b); Short, Williams, and Christie (1976); Weeks and Chapanis (1976); Williams (1975); and Williams, Paul, and Ogilvie (1957; see also Chapter 3). This literature emphasizes that acceptance, use, and consequences of group media are created from complex interactions of the medium (system design as well as coding attributes and interactivity), task, individual traits and motivations, group size and structure, group rules and rewards, access to alternative media, conduct of the group's meetings, and the organizational environment and goals.

For the purposes of this chapter, the term "task" needs to be clarified. Groups can be classified as task oriented or non-task oriented. A task is a specific goal that the group intends to achieve, whether it be to produce a tangible product or an intangible decision. A *socioemotional* task emphasizes the more social interpersonal skills and outcomes, such as negotiation or getting new members to join. A *technical* task involves more factual or cognitive skills and outcomes, such as exchanging information or arriving at a decision based largely on information gathered and/or evaluated by the group. The problem with this categorization, of course, is that many overtly technical group tasks are heavily laden with political and symbolic purposes. For example, what may appear to be a simple attempt to gather information to make an objective decision may be a politically astute negotiation to acquire symbolic power through conspicuous consumption of information (Feldman and March, 1981).

A group may not necessarily be task oriented, in the strict sense of the above terms. That is, a group may be constituted simply to communicate or be sociable in its own right. Indeed, as discussed in Chapters 3 and 5, information system designs not only seldom consider the more pleasurable or playful aspects of communication but, along with regulatory policy and organizational dictates, may often actively discourage or prevent such uses (Marvin, 1983). While acknowledging these purposes, this chapter primarily considers the effects of mediated group communication on task-oriented groups; we must await experimental results from video-conferenced picnics.

This chapter also primarily considers group communication as mediated by computer-based communication systems, and CC in particular. There are several good reasons for this focus. Audio conferencing is limited to a few people at a time, and video conferencing is quite expensive and not accessible to the casual or informal user. Electronic mail and CC are already in use by thousands of people, and are widely available through public and private networks at generally affordable prices. As Chapter 3 briefly discussed, print media are typically judged to have less "social presence," and they transmit less of the full bandwidth of human communication codes, than do other media. Table 6.1 shows (as does Table 3.2) that, indeed, computer conferencing systems are generally rated more satisfactory for tasks requiring lower amounts of intimacy, conflict, or socioemotional content. Exchanging information and opinions and generating ideas (which *can* be conflictual) seem to be more suitable tasks than bargaining, persuading, or getting to know someone.

There may also be more effort required to achieve facility with such systems. Therefore, many of the research results reported below can be considered to provide the extremes of the possible outcomes; similar research on video conferencing may not reveal strong differences from face-to-face communication.

WHAT IS COMPUTER CONFERENCING?

Excellent descriptions of CC system features, historic development, specific systems, philosophical issues in technical choices, and uses and impacts at the individual, group or social level are provided by Hiltz (1983); Hiltz and Turoff (1978, 1981); Johansen et al. (1979); Kerr and Hiltz (1982); and Rice (1980b). The simplest definition of CC is a computer-facilitated mechanism for recording and using a textual transcript of a group discussion over varying lengths of time, by group members who may be geographically dispersed and who may interact with the transcript either simultaneously or at times of their own choosing. The basic components typically involve a number of terminals dispersed through an organization or a nation, connected through modems and a telephone line to a network's host computer (or directly to the company computer). This computer contains the processing software to connect all users when they log in to the system, and maintains storage of the transcripts.

This is significant: The medium has a memory (Johansen, Miller, and Vallee, 1974). Any user may log in at any time to receive waiting messages, read the latest comments to a common conference, work on a manuscript others have edited, or scan directories and indices for shared interests with other users. Computer conferencing systems may be said to differ from electronic messaging systems primarily because they provide *shared files*. This means that users may jointly contribute to, read, and comment on, a dynamic joint file of text; electronic messaging generally involves sending a discrete file to one or more members, but sharing a file is usually difficult. Because of the shared files, and the processing ability of the computer, a very wide range of communication structures may be offered in a CC system. Basic facilities include messages, conferences, and work spaces—which may be public or private and which may involve specific individuals, a formally defined group, or anyone with access to the system—along with text editing, storage, and printing capabilities. A very public form of CC is developing rapidly. It is called Community Computer-Based Bulletin Boards; there are over 30 in the Washington, D.C., area

TABLE 6.1 Summary of Satisfaction Ratings from Several Sets of Computer Conferencing Users

TASK	Confravision[a]	Conferencing[a]	PLANET[b]	PLANET[b]	MACC-Telemail	Experienced EIES Users[c]	Staff EIES Users[d]	Student EIES Users[d]	Experienced Student EIES Users[d]	Average
Exchanging opinions	1.9	-	1.5	2.1	1.9	2.3	3.5	3.1	2.7	2.4
Exchanging information	2.0	2.6	1.3	2.1	2.0	2.4	3.6	3.2	2.8	2.4
Generating ideas	2.7	-	1.8	2.6	3.8	2.8	3.1	3.4	3.0	2.9
Problem solving	2.7	-	3.0	3.4	4.0	3.9	4.4	4.1	2.8	3.5
Resolving disagreements	-	-	3.2	4.3	3.5	4.1	4.5	3.5	4.1	3.9
Bargaining	3.6	3.9	3.3	4.2	4.4	4.1	4.4	4.2	3.8	4.0
Persuasion	3.6	3.9	3.4	4.6	4.3	4.2	4.1	3.9	4.0	4.0
Getting to know someone	4.0	5.1	3.8	4.5	4.8	3.3	3.9	4.6	4.3	4.3

SOURCES:

a. Pye and Williams (1977).

b. Vallee, Johansen, Randolph, and Hastings (1978).

c. Hiltz (1981).

d. Hiltz, Johnson, and Agle (1978).

NOTE: Ratings based on average of responses to seven-point scale: 7 = completely unsatisfactory. Tasks and groups not generally comparable across studies. Cross-system averages are not weighted for study sample sizes.

alone. Anyone with a modem and a terminal may call in to "post " and read notices or exchange private messages. The rapidly expanding array of online information and communication services available to the public is described by Grossbrenner (1983).

Much more complex facilities include virtual text, online polling, highly structured group communication processes, interactive education courses, computing, experimentation, and the like. An analysis of how uses and users evolve within such a system, along with in-depth charts of system features, is provided by Hiltz and Turoff (1981). The authors report that various system services (such as private or public version of messages, conferences, and work spaces) show significant differences in usage, which indicates that they "have their role and function in the computer augmentation of human communications" (p. 746). Many of these services are not available in electronic mail, and as their importance to users increases with increased experience with such systems, the simpler mail systems will eventually discourage or stunt possible applications (Hiltz and Turoff, 1981).

Computer conferencing, as any medium, has its weaknesses. Some of these include the following:

(1)   the written mode is disliked for certain statements;
(2)   direct interpersonal and nonverbal feedback is missing;
(3)   users may participate in the group infrequently;
(4)   negotiations may be more intransigent or rigid;
(5)   a perceived need to communicate is highly important, as is leadership;
(6)   multiple threads to the conference discussion may develop and create confusion or information overload (Johansen et al., 1979).

The remainder of this chapter will consider more specific aspects of group communication and decision making as mediated by CC.

ALTERNATIVE PERSPECTIVES ON DECISION-MAKING IMPACTS

There are two primary schools of thought on the likely consequences, and thus the appropriate uses, of CC for group decision making (see Barefoot and Strickland, 1982; Kiesler, Siegel, and McGuire, 1982). The first is the classic behavioral/information processing model of decision making, or the "cool" school. This perspective argues that positive and accurate decisions come from groups with low conflict wherein more information than opinion is exchanged, and such exchange is relatively equal and frequent. The idea is that many problems are well solved by a dispassionate discussion of retrievable factual information or informed opinion. Group decisions tend to have higher quality than the average of the decisions of the individual group members, but not necessarily as high as the best member's decision (Davis, 1969). Reducing affective cues will remove "irrelevant" considerations, such as status, charisma, prejudices, and physical or minority personal attributes. For example, a study of actual brainstorming groups showed that group members with high output of ideas perceived fewer status differences in the group (Jablin and Sussman, 1978).

One conclusion from a comprehensive controlled experiment comparing group performance across several media argued that the largest performance differences occurred when the group had, or the channel created, imbalances among members (Weeks and Chapanis, 1976). For example, face-to-face allows the weaker side to enhance its position, and particularly for matters of conflict and opinion rather than of cooperation and fact. The authors also concluded, however, that the presence or absence of voice was the primary differentiation between media, and not visual cues; this possibility is opposed by research showing that "transmitted nonverbal cues tend to increase the positivity of interpersonal evaluation", as tested by controlling for communication channel (Williams, 1975). Groups with high affect may suffer from "groupthink," in which groups avoid conflict and threats to their credibility, even at the cost of making crucial decisions (Janis, 1972).

The "warm" school, on the other hand, emphasizes the human relations inherent in groups and which lead to more integrative solutions. Group norms, affective bonds, trust, and commitment are important both in and of themselves and because they encourage intuitive, experiential solutions. Nonverbal communication aids the transmission of contextual clues, values, and implicit goals. The assumption here is that routinization, explicitness, and efficiency work against the development of appropriate decisions. Negative affect, polarization, flaming, and intransigence may result when communication is not regulated by group affect, or by the warm communications gained in the elevator, at the water cooler, through organizational culture, and in face-to-face encounters. Indeed, if affective and social cues are missing, group discussions can give rise to disinhibition or highly emotional reactions rather than rational decision making.

There are additional distinctions that inform this debate. One is the nature of the task communication. Routine communication may be more susceptible to the advantages of "cool" decision making. Nonroutine communication—handling personal matters, crisis problems, uncertain conditions (the kind of decisions higher-level managers are likely to make)—needs a higher quality of effort, is less amenable to formalized procedures, involves more ambiguous goals, and requires credibility (Kiesler et al., 1982).

One aspect of nonroutineness may be the level of politicization in the group or in the problem; in that case, lack of affect and potential disinhibition may just exacerbate the condition and fragment the group. On the other hand, such increased polarization may *improve* the diversity of solutions and the level of group commitment, particularly in highly novel situations.

Indeed, the psychological distance imposed by mediated communication can allow a greater expression of emotions, especially negative ones (Barefoot and Strickland, 1982). More specifically, extreme levels of intimacy (high or low) tend to be avoided by people, so media that suppress intimate cues may be evaluated as more appropriate for tasks of high intimacy (Williams, 1975). For example, treatment-seeking clients concerned about drug, tobacco, or alcohol use rated a computerized interview (compared to a traditional face-to-face interview or self-reporting) less friendly but shorter, more relaxing, lighter, and more interesting (Skinner and Allen, 1983). Similarly, Griest and Gustafson (1973) found that suicidal patients preferred a computerized interview over an interview with a physician. Thus, the perspective taken on the fundamental nature of group decision making, the nature of the communications, and the acceptability of emotionality all contribute to an assessment of the utility of CC.

We might add that cognitive psychology suggests three other perspectives on the potential interaction between mediated communication, affect, and decision making, according to Sims (1982), who cites the following theoretical considerations.

(a)"Prototype-matching" is a model that assumes that we try to match perceived characteristics of a situation with associations and characteristics held in memory, as a short cut to full processing and recategorization of each new event (Cantor and Mischel, 1977). A reduction in available characteristics (because of reduced medium bandwidth or feedback) might decrease the likelihood of such matches, with attendant frustration and emotional responses.

(b)In some cases we "automatically" evaluate the process stimuli; in other cases we must perform "controlled" processing. Again, with reduced availability of stimuli, users may be forced into slower and less relaxed controlled processing (Bargh, 1982).

(c)Related to these two theories is the notion that we process inputs according to "scripts" or schemas of expected sequential events. Writ large, these scripts mold our most obvious as well as subtle behavior, particularly in public settings. Insufficient cues may lead to the use of inappropriate scripts, or may demand the generation of new ones, both with perhaps frustrating consequences (Abelson, 1981).

Most of the controlled experiments discussed below tend to follow the cool school in their assumptions, but analyses of the results provide information for the warm perspective as well. Of course, the cost of the rigor of controlled experiments is some generalizability. In general, real-world contexts are missing from most of the studies, although one did use organizational staff in their work settings. Other groups, primarily students, did not have any ongoing history in which group norms and affect would have influenced their behavior. This kind of experiment is rather discrete, in that the process of group structuring and development is condensed into a few hours. Further, it may be unlikely that a CC user would "flame" as strongly in an ongoing business context as some subjects did.

These experiments typically utilized either a ranking decision (e.g., rank-order 15 items found in a plane wreck in terms of their importance for survival) as judged by survival experts, or a human relations problem (e.g., decide what to do about an apparently incompetent forest ranger) judged more qualitatively by local experts in personnel management. Perhaps the most detailed model for this kind of cross-media controlled experiment can be found in Weeks and Chapanis (1976). A methodological description of such research, emphasizing the role of the computer in running the experiment, appears in Hiltz, Turoff, Johnson, and Aronovitch (1982).

Subsequent sections will refer to Table 6.2, a summary of several controlled experiments using CC and face-to-face communication as treatments, and various aspects of group decision making as outcomes.

PHASES IN GROUP DECISION MAKING

Groups seem to pass through a regular series of phases on their way to a joint decision (Bales, 1955). Insofar as it seems likely that different kinds of information and resources are crucial at different phases, CC may have differential acceptability and utility in different group phases. This section reports the few CC studies on this topic.

Different authors conceptualize these phases in different ways. Perhaps the best known are those identified by Interaction Process Analysis (Bales, 1950). Bales suggests that there are task and socioemotional components, each comprising three phases, each of which has active and passive forms. The progression, then, has group members who (a) give/ask for orientation, (b) give/ask for evaluation or opinion, (c) give/ask for control, such as suggestions, (d) agree/disagree, (e) manage tension by asking for help, withdrawing or joking, and (f) integrate group comments by showing solidarity or antagonism.

Using this typology, Hiltz, Johnson, and Agle (1978) and Hiltz, Johnson, and Rabke (1980) analyzed the interactions (using audio, video, and textual content) of groups in face-to-face versus CC conditions, and in technical versus human relations tasks, as part of ongoing research (see Hiltz, Johnson, Aronovitch, and Turoff, 1980). The authors found more tension release, agreement, and asking for opinion in the face-to-face condition; the HJA78 experiment also found more disagreement in this condition, along with considerable nonverbal and nonlinguistic communication. The HJR80 experiment found some differences between the kinds of task: The human relations problem elicited more solidarity and greater tension in the face-to-face condition, while the technical task elicited less tension in the face-to-face condition than in the CC group. Note that the face-to-face condition emphasizes the more socioemotional phases (opinion, agreement, tension) and in particular seems to elicit behaviors that can diffuse group tensions (such as agreement, tension release, and asking for opinion). There are few differences in the categories of task management: orientation, exchanging suggestions, and integration (although antagonism is a part of integration). However, the decision phase (agreement and disagreement) is more pronounced in the face-to-face groups. This may support the cool school, because, as Hirokawa (1983)

TABLE 6.2 Results from Selected Controlled Experiments Involving Group Decision Making and Computer Conferencing

Treatments	Time to Decision	Consensus	Amount of Communication	Equality of Participation	Choice Shift	Decision Quality
			OUTCOMES			
KSM82-1[a]	$p < .01$[b]			$p < .01$	$p < .05$	
F[c]	quicker[d]		most	least	less	
C	slower		least	most	more	
CA	slower		medium	medium	more	
KSM82-2	$p < .01$		$p < .01$	$p < .01$	$p < .01$	
F	quicker		more	less	least	
C	slower		less	more	most	
E	slower		less	more	medium	
KSM82-3			$p < .01$			
CE	equal		more	equal	equal	
CS	equal		less	equal	equal	
MURREL83						$p < .05$
CE	equal		equal			higher
CS	equal		equal			lower
JHT81		$p < .01$				
F		higher[e]	more		less	
C[f]		lower	less		more	
HTJ82						
CL		equal[g]	more			equal
CF		equal	less			equal

(Continued)

137

Table 6.2 Continued

Treatments	Time to Decision	Consensus	OUTCOMES Amount of Communication	Equality of Participation	Choice Shift	Decision Quality
HJA78				$p < .05$		
F	quicker	All groups	more	less		
C	slower	Two of six[h]	less	more		
CA	slower	All groups	less	more		
WC76	$p < .01$		$p < .01$			
F	slower[i]		more			
V	slower		more			
A	slower		more			
T	quicker		less			

a.

KSM82 = Kiesler, Siegel, and McGuire (1982).
1 = 18 groups of 3 students each.
2 = sample size not given.
3 = 12 groups of 3 students each.

MURREL83 = Murrel (1983).
18 groups of 4 each. Task had a "correct" ranking. An electronic messaging system was used as a conferencing medium, with entries appearing simultaneously in a "window" on the screen, or appearing sequentially and read after the full message was sent.

HJT81 = Hiltz, Johnson, and Turoff (1981). Fully reported in Hiltz, Johnson, Aronovitch, and Turoff (1980). Portions published in Hiltz (1982).
16 groups of 5 each (wide age range as they were continuing and returning education students). Two tasks: one human relations and one with "correct" ranking.

138

HJT82 = Hiltz, Johnson, and Turoff (1982). Portions published in Hiltz (1982).
24 groups of 5 each, staff members of various organizations.
4 conditions: (no) terminal feedback by (no) formal leader (assigned on basis of group's post-practice evaluations).

HJA78 = Hiltz, Johnson, and Agle (1978).
12 groups, not randomly assigned (pilot experiment). CA included private (one-to-one) messaging.

WC76 = Weeks and Chapanis (1976).
48 pairs of male students. Two conflictive and two cooperative tasks.

b. In some instances significant difference concluded, but level not reported.

c. A = audio only.
C = computer conferencing with messages identified by participant.
CA = computer conferencing with anonymous comments.
CE = computer conferencing with entries appearing simultaneously.
CF = computer conferencing with substantial feedback of group agreement and performance.
CL = computer conferencing with formal group leader.
CS = computer conferencing with entries appearing sequentially.
E = electronic messaging.
T = teletype used like electronic messaging.
V = video conferencing.

d. Rank orders of differences in outcome across treatments when differences are reported as significant. Blank means outcome not tested/reported.

e. In human-relations task, all F reached consensus, only 1 C did; in objective ranking task, half F did, no C did. See text for qualification.

f. Feedback provided on terminal to group in form of each person's ranking.

g. Significant interaction only between feedback/leader—lowest consensus with neither, highest with leader and no feedback.

h. System crash did not facilitate consensus.

i. More communication for conflictive problems versus cooperative ones. Cooperative problems solved by all groups, as intended by researchers. These results for conflictive problems did not speak to group problem accuracy, but to effects of "persuader" on "persuadee."

points out, "successful" groups tend to start their discussions by analyzing the problem (orientation and control) rather than by immediately searching for solutions.

This discussion of group phases needs to be qualified by the fact that Hirokawa, using a different set of phases, found no other phasic differences between each type of group and indeed found no single uniform sequence of phases across groups. Another article came to similar conclusions. Seeger (1983) reanalyzed the original group-phase research (Bales and Strodtbeck, 1951) and found that well-acquainted groups do *not* follow the widely accepted sequential phases. Indeed, the sequential phases occurred *only* in the process of group formation, not in the process of problem solving. Thus, the phasic differences reported by Hiltz and colleagues may apply only to initial group meetings, and may have occurred *precisely* because the groups were not previously ongoing groups with a task history.

Related findings by several researchers at the Institute for the Future have provided the conceptual basis for designing a CC system specifically for mathematical modelers (Lipinski, Spang, and Tydeman, 1980; Tydeman, Lipinski, and Spang, 1980). They identify these tasks or phases in group problem-solving: conceptualizing, searching, structuring, implementing, evaluating, and documentating. Their primary argument is that the structuring, evaluation, and documentation phases require the kinds of task communication better served by CC than by face-to-face (structured, delayed, written responses). Conversely, the suppression of affective and nonverbal cues in the early stages of the group process—just when "phases" may be most crucial—may reduce group members' ability to evaluate others' skills, knowledge, and leadership ability. I will return to this question later in this chapter.

SPEED, CONSENSUS, ACCURACY, AND SHIFT

Research in general finds that it takes longer to transmit the same amount of communication in electronic print form than verbally (Johansen et al., 1979: 148, 152; Krueger and Chapanis, 1980; Hiltz and Turoff, 1978), although this may be an advantage when there is no deadline and users can take more time to reflect before responding. Not only can the verbal channel transmit more words per time unit for a given individual (but not when more than several people are involved), but the mechanics of conferencing necessarily create delays (such as typing speed, transmission speed, and read-out speed; also see Hiltz and Turoff [1978: 412]). The controlled experiments reported in Table 6.2 support this finding: It takes less time to arrive at a decision in a face-to-face group. When the experiments have time limits, this fact also takes the form of less consensus, because the CC groups have had less effective time in which to consider the problem.

The studies also support a common result when comparing decision making by different media: Agreement on the group's decision tends to be lower in CC groups (Kerr and Hiltz, 1982: 155). The difference between media tends to be greater with human-relations tasks, just the sort the warm school feels requires more affective cues. As mentioned above, when groups have longer periods, the level of agreement seems to improve in CC groups; indeed, increasing consensus in CC groups is strongly associated with typing speed and prior experience with terminals (R = .49, .67, respectively; HJT82). The explanation is not that typing per se leads to better decisions, but that operational factors or time constraints can degrade the ease with which group communication occurs; after sufficient training or decision time, the level of agreement is determined by group processes as filtered by the medium.

What is more important is that the face-to-face context both puts more pressure on members to agree, or to agree that they agreed. In the HJT82 study, in half of the face-to-face groups the members reported (in writing after the experiment) different group decisions. Thus, "consensus" may be only apparent. Further, the level of agreement is not necessarily related to the quality or accuracy of the decision. The HJT81 experiment found no significant relationship between the two. Indeed, because there is increased diversity of ideas, and fewer sanctions or effects on deviants in CC groups (HJA78) members can "hold out" for their decision, and they may be right! Indeed, in one study, "the highest-rated solutions . . . were made by the minorities (with respect to the group solution) in the CC condition who refused to agree with the solutions proposed by the majority"(HTJ82).

This does not mean that everyone is intransigent, just that it is easier to be so. In fact Kiesler et al. (1982) and Siegel, Kiesler, and McGuire (1982) found not only that CC group members were emotionally aroused (one measure was that they ate significantly more malt balls while in group discussion than did subjects in face-to-face condition) but also showed greater shifts from their original position.

In summary, then, CC groups may show less consensus, although this may be partially due to technical factors that improve with experience; this lack of consensus may have nothing to do with the group's quality of decision; and the warm aspects of group decision making do operate in the sense that correct members may be able to hold out, while others display riskier behavior than in face-to-face groups or they display disinhibition (Reid, 1977; Remp, 1978). Bales (1955) suggests that in an ongoing series of meetings, initial levels of consensus have strong consequences for later meetings. If it is generally high in the first few meetings, then levels of consensus and ranking of leaders in subsequent meetings oscillate, but eventually stabilize, and antagonism declines. With early low consensus, there is high turnover in later rankings, more inequality in participation, and stable consensus may take a long time to build. An implication of this finding is that initial meetings might best be held face-to-face to mobilize generalized agreement (as well as to provide social introductions to later conference members), but followed up by CC to emphasize problem-solving performance.

LEADERSHIP EMERGENCE AND FUNCTION

Some people regularly emerge as group leaders. This is partly due to identifiable personality traits known as "latency of verbal response"—the delay in a person's response given an opportunity to respond (Willard and Strodtbeck, 1972)—and "response duration"—the extent to which a person tends to talk once the opportunity is available (Koomen and Sagel, 1977). Both of these are highly correlated with one's actual participation in group communication (Hiltz and Turoff, 1978: 107). People differ in these traits; if there were no other factors, people would still have differential participation in group discussion because of such differences. In the early stages of the group process, this differential participation is the greatest influence on the selection and emergence of a group's leader, although a leader must be accepted by the group, which provides reinforcement and a perceptible willingness to follow (Hare, 1976; Strickland, Guild, Barefoot, and Patterson, 1978).

There is evidence that group members can more easily identify who was the group's leader, who provided the best ideas, who was an effective guide to the group's process, and who was most likable, in face-to-face groups than in CC groups (HJA78; Murrel, 1983). Even small distinctions between a leader and followers in a group increase goal and task-oriented behavior (HJT82). Hence, differences in leadership emergence between media have implications for subsequent task performance; so it is significant that the emergence of a leader seems to differ across media and in particular is less likely in CC groups (Kerr and Hiltz, 1982: 155).

The warm school would say these identifiable cues are important for group performance; the cool school would say that in general the choice of leader based upon such cues may not be based on other more relevant attributes. For example, in the HJT82 experiment, the group's choice of leader correlated .45 with the number of comments made by the leader in the pre-experiment practice session, yet there was no correlation between the leader's number of comments and the quality of the leader's decision. Similar findings—that those who talk more are chosen more often as leaders—are found in related literature (Jablin and Sussman, 1978). Further, the quality of the group's decision was highly correlated (.54 to .71) with the quality of the leader's initial ranking, along with the quality of the ranking by the individual with the best actual solution. The implication here is that the fate of a group's performance often depends on its choice of a leader, which tends to be based on sheer amount of early communication, which is largely influenced by two personalty traits having to do with propensity to talk, and not with the characteristics needed to perform the task.

This experiment also helps resolve a question raised by Barefoot and Strickland (1982) with respect to leadership suppression in video conferencing: Do mediated communications suppress leadership *emergence* or, instead, suppress leadership *dominance*? Evidence from this experiment suggests that emergence, rather than dominance, is suppressed, although the capabilities of a CC system allow other group members to diffuse or counter attempts at dominance. One can enter comments at any time, and even choose not to read certain entries; useful comments, no matter who entered them, can be brought to bear on the topic.

It is particularly in the area of human relations tasks, as the warm school argues, that strong leadership seems to be most needed in group decision making (HJT82); Hiltz and Turoff (1978: 107, 123); Johansen et al. (1979: 153); Kerr and Hiltz (1982: 155). Other general tasks for which a leader is needed in CC groups include

(a)   overcoming organization inertia against using such technology (Johansen, DeGrasse, and Wilson, 1978),

(b)   entering new members,

(c)   providing administrative and systems-use comments, and

(d)   providing indexes to comments on a regular basis (Hiltz, 1981).

Indeed, the least "successful" group in a two-year experiment using a nationwide CC system involving several subdisciplines of dispersed researchers was the one with a highly inactive formal leader (Hiltz, 1981, 1983).

FACILITIES FOR FEEDBACK, DOMINANCE SUPPRESSION, AND SIMULTANEITY

Not only does CC have by definition more facilities than electronic mail, but even CC systems should evolve to fulfill the needs of users; indeed, the evidence summarized above shows that users' expectations of and satisfactions with system features change with increased usage (Hiltz and Turoff, 1981). In particular, the authors argue that features especially important to experienced users should include (a) facilitating long-term group communication, (b) allowing active user control of the system, (c) supporting the handling of complex documents, and (d) permitting individual tailoring of the system.

A few experiments have attempted to investigate the consequences of three special features: group feedback, suppression of dominance, and feedback. The HJT82 experiment in Table 6.2 had two treatments: in one, the groups selected a formal leader on the basis of evaluations formed during practice sessions; in the other, a substantial amount of ranking and group agreement information was provided over the terminal as feedback for the group's decision making. There was no significant main effect on consensus or quality of decision, although there was a significant interaction, as discussed in the section on leadership above. The authors suggest that terminal feedback reduces the effect of the most knowledgeable leader (perhaps by forcing a compromise). Also, there were significantly fewer comments in the feedback condition. Perhaps, the report offers, feedback should go to the leader only.

A tangentially related study on the use of a decision support system (such as described in Keen and Scott Morton, 1978) found that the efficacy of feedback by software that facilitated searching for good solutions seemed to depend on the complexity of the problem (Madeo and Schriber, 1980). With only four variables to consider, users receiving feedback performed just as well as users without feedback; but with eleven variables, they reached a significantly better decision (and without more time or effort). Thus, it may be that effects of computer-generated feedback are more salient for *complex* problems, as well as being more useful to a *leader* .

Another facility that may be programmed into the structure of groups using CC is a priority device for allocating entry time based upon past amounts of contribution. This would be more plausible for real-time (synchronous) conferences, and in fact has been developed for video conferences to maximize the benefits from expensive video bandwidth and transmission costs (Stodolsky, 1981). In this manner, communication apprehension may become less of an obstacle to participation by specific (and perhaps expert) group members, over and above the more equal participation that comes from CC use anyway. In the brainstorming study mentioned earlier, group members with higher production of ideas reported less communication apprehension (Jablin and Sussman, 1978). The fear here, of course, is that natural differences in quality of contributions would be suppressed in favor of more equal participation. The programming could easily include weighted priorities, an override mechanism, or just notations of cumulative percentages of comments from each member. A controlled study of the use of an expert-based model for arriving at equitable decisions in awarding social services showed that there was a significant increase in the equity of decisions compared to users without the decision support system. However, when the modeled decisions were programmed to be inequitable, users did not blindly conform to the models, and did not make inequitable decisions (Boyd, Clark, and Hanson, 1980). The idea here is to provide discretionary decision-making aids.

Even with synchronous conferences, differences in the presentation and access of comments are possible. One choice is between presenting the comments sequentially, after each one has been completely entered by the participant, or offering "virtual" commenting, whereby each member's comments appear on all other members' terminals just as they are being entered. The first condition may be termed "sequential" while the second may be termed "entry driven." Table 6.2 shows two such experiments: KSM82-2 and MURREL82. Neither shows many differences, except that in the first one there was more communication in the entry-driven mode, while in the second experiment this mode led to a higher quality of decision. Users preferred the entry-driven mode over the sequential mode (60% to 30%) in the KSM82-2 test.

A related test compares CC, where all comments are public, to electronic messaging, where some comments may be sent to selected individuals and are, thus, private. This facility would be especially consequential in negotiations or decisions susceptible to coalitions or high-affect bonds. In the KJA78 and KSM82-1 trials, these two conditions are similar in their differences with face-to-face, but show a slight difference with respect to amount of communication: There was less in the CC condition in the second trial. This is likely due to the increased generalizability of public comments or to increased motivation in individualized messages.

In general, it seems that refined system features such as these *can* have effects on group processes, but the effects are more limited and are not always present. Groups might want to consider the trade-offs involving feedback, dominance suppression, and simultaneity when they have access to designing the system they will use.

COMMUNICATION LINKAGES

This section considers several components of communication linkages in group decision-making and task performance, although not restricted to controlled experiments. These components include group structure, amount of communication, connectedness, equality of participation, electronic migration, and social structure in an information environment.

Group Structure

The literature on small group networks at first indicated that the more centralized structures facilitated leadership emergence and quicker decisions (particularly for simple tasks) but at the cost of greater errors and less individual satisfaction (Leavitt, 1951; Rogers and Agarwala-Rogers, 1976: 121). These are similar to some of the findings reported in this chapter for face-to-face groups, which, with strong leaders, would be more centralized than CC groups. Later evaluations and replications showed that most effects were due (1) to differences in learning how to use different structures while making decisions, or (2) to nearly unending contingent conditions (Collins and Raven, 1969: 146; Davis, 1969: 103-104; Farace, Monge, and Russell, 1977: Chap. 7; Shane, 1979; Shaw, 1964). However, Doktor and Makridakis (1974) found, through computer simulations, that indeed it took numerous runs for groups to achieve stability in performance, but the groups had inherently different stabilities ranked in the same order as the performance levels of different group structures had been ranked by the early researchers.

Inherent group stability and group performance are not necessarily related, however: Another computer simulation that modeled group behavior over 800 problem-solving runs found that the "all-channel" and "circle" structures resulted in equal performance levels, but that the all-channel structure reached stability in performance level earlier (around 200 runs versus 300)(Shane, 1979). It was concluded, among other findings, that the fewer levels in the group's hierarchical structure, the sooner the stable and optimal performance levels were achieved. Thus, differences in how CC is used to *structure* group communication are likely to affect the group's processes for a good part of its early experiences but

> seem to have the most motivation to expand their professional networks. . . . what matters to the individual is how many other group members available to communicate with have relatively high professional status.

And, rather than low status, late entrance into the information system may restrict access to these resources. How early one enters a communication system may be the major constraint to individual advancement or even survival as an accepted group member. Consider that leaders may be chosen on the basis of early loquacity. "Indeed, individuals and groups who have early access to information may continue to 'occupy' their information-rich positions and thereby function better or have more power than those who have later access to information flows within the system"(Rice, 1982: 927). Groups themselves may have to compete for information resources, both in the form of energy and effort applied to their task, and in the form of specific information needed to coexist with other groups.

Consider also that given that we have limits on how many people or items we can process, and given that time on a CC system may be longer for a given task than in face-to-face mode, and given that use of the system takes away from other work and social activities, there is an upper limit to how much system communication we can actually commit or afford. So members of groups that operate in electronic space are caught between upper limits on their processing limits and lower limits on the amount of information with which they can survive. The consequence of these dual constraints is that new entrants to an "online community" (Hiltz, 1983) must first search the system widely, making contacts with otherwise unknown members to establish rewarding exchanges, but cease unreciprocated exchanges before their processing and resource limits are exceeded. One final variable of import is whether the group is task-oriented or not.

> Members of a nontask group are freer to explore their informational environment, because their activities are not necessarily detractions from the group's sense of cohesiveness or interferences with an ongoing task; a group can prosper by "scouting" the environment as long as they are stable, because the task focuses internal group communication exchanges and cohesion [Rice, 1982: 928].

The conflict comes when a task-oriented group operates in a turbulent environment and must scan that environment for information about how to respond and reduce the complexity of the task (Galbraith, 1977; Weick, 1969).

Three hypotheses were generated from this basic argument and tested by Rice (1982): (a) Information flows within, between, and among groups will significantly define group roles within a CC system supporting their activities; (b) reciprocity will become a significant attribute of systemwide information flows over time in a large CC system; and (c) groups will occupy information-based roles differently depending on whether they are task oriented or not. The data were computer-monitored usage statistics, aggregated by month, from two years' usage by over 800 geographically dispersed researchers comprising 10 groups. (This kind of data is described in Chapter 4). Five groups were task groups, three were non-task groups, one group was the system consultants, and one was an aggregation of users who did not belong to a formal group and, thus, represented a random non-task collectivity. Results follow.

(1) Groups indeed were significantly differentiated on the basis of whether their information flows within, between, and across other groups were higher or lower than average flows. These information-based network roles can be summarized in general as carriers (greater than average on all three dimensions), receivers (greater receivers than the average group), transmitters (greater senders of messages), and isolates (less than average on all three dimensions). Over time, groups tended to either occupy certain roles or drift into isolate status, as shown in Table 6.3.

(2) A model of systemwide structure assuming reciprocity as a primary attribute of information flows quickly became an extremely significant description of the data. Figure 6.1 shows the fit of this model over the 24-month period.

Figure 6.2 is a plot of the systemwide scaling of the group weights from months 12 through 20 (as there were one or two more or fewer groups before and after this period). Whereas the plot of the prior period shows no discernible direction, this three-way INDSCAL solution (with time as the third dimension) shows a progression of the systemwide interaction to a unidimensional state. Because the scaled data are the values of the cross-group reciprocity parameters estimated by the interative log-linear network modeling program used, we may interpret this y-axis as a reciprocity dimension. Figure 6.2 is another portrayal of the increased importance of reciprocity in the CC system over time.

(3) Task groups, even if they entered the system as carriers, quickly became isolates. The systems consultants developed into transmitters, as befitting their purpose; the random group developed from transmitters into carriers, presumably because they had no conscious or functional reason to concentrate communication exchanges solely with other members of their "group." Non-task groups generally developed from isolates into carriers.

From these results we might conclude that (1) information flows are indeed major aspects of group structure in an information environment; (2) individuals and groups must emphasize reciprocal exchanges in large computer-mediated communication systems; (3) if a task group requires information from a changing environment, managers of CC-based groups must support selected members as liaisons who can adapt the group based upon external information; and (4) maintenance of an information-rich role requires constant effort in the form of high levels of transmission and receipt of information.

There is a potentially dark side to all this computer-mediated communication, with respect to group social structure. In Chapter 3 we saw that

**FIGURE 6.2   INDSCAL Solution for Dimensionality of
Systemwide Interaction Based upon Group
Interactions under Model of Reciprocity**

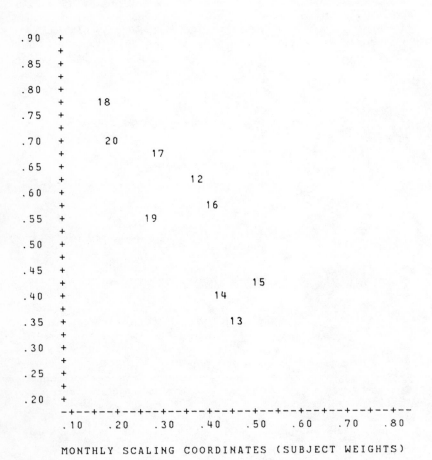

MONTHLY SCALING COORDINATES (SUBJECT WEIGHTS)

NOTE: Both axes portray the range of scaling coordinates (called "subject" weights).
Numbers plotted indicate the relative position of each month's reciprocal system
interaction. S-stress = .17; R^2 = .71.

is also a constituent and symbol of social organization. These cues and roles bias our actions and decisions, to be sure, but in general they serve to help us survive; they obviate the need to reassess risks, costs, and rewards with every interaction. Cognitive and perceptual biases color nearly every personal decision and evaluation we make, and for the same reason (Tversky and Kahneman, 1974). Singer argues that there is a need for barriers against open communications: "The opening of organizational boundaries simultaneously desocializes messages while eroding authority and identity," leading to irrational authority, reduced responsibility, and "crazy" systems.

SUMMARY

Before all the consequences discussed above come about, people have to accept and use computer conferencing systems. Typically, the strongest influences on acceptance include

- the number of people (particularly prestigious or high-status others) on the system known before one begins using it,
- one's anticipated level of use,
- the relative priority of the kinds of tasks to be performed on the system,
- access to the system and to alternative media,
- a perceived need to communicate, and
- an advocate for the group (to be followed by a moderator who maintains the group on the system.

(See Hiltz, 1981; Hiltz, Johnson, and Turoff, 1982; Johansen, et al., 1978; Johansen, Miller, and Vallee, 1975; Palme, 1981; Rice, 1980b).

But even acceptance and use may be problematic, as this chapter has tried to emphasize. A variety of media, as well as face-to-face communication, may be necessary at different phases of the group's progress, to transmit the differentially valuable cues, affect, power, information, facts, decisions, and evaluations needed for good group performance. Roles of individuals and groups may need to be negotiated or understood; particular system designs may facilitate one at the cost of another. A specific instance is the apparent utility of unequal participation that follows from the emergence of a group leader.

On the other hand, group processes may be custom structured to facilitate the desired goals and values of the group. This notion of "groupware" is emphasized by Kerr and Hiltz (1982: 47), based upon work by the Johnson-Lenzes. Groupware is "the intentional group processes and procedures to achieve specific purposes plus the software tools designed to support and facilitate the group's work."

Finally, we have seen that the pervasiveness of computer-mediated communication may even sacrifice social goals and structure to the

functions of teleconferencing to affect adoption success, use, and consequences. This chapter suggests a conceptual approach to understanding the organizational context for uses and impacts of teleconferencing.

BONNIE McDANIEL JOHNSON and
RONALD E. RICE

7 Reinvention in the Innovation Process: *The Case of Word Processing*

Lord Wen-hui watched in amazement as his cook Ting carved the roasted ox with speed, grace, and rhythm. "Imagine skill reaching such heights!" he marveled. Cook Ting replied:

A mediocre cook changes his knife once a month—because he hacks. A good cook changes his knife once a year—because he cuts. I've had this knife of mine for nineteen years. There are spaces between the joints, and the blade of the knife has really no thickness. If you insert what has no thickness into such spaces, then there's plenty of room. . . . However, whenever I come to a complicated place, I size up the difficulties, tell myself to watch out and be careful, keep my eyes on what I'm doing, work very slowly, and move the knife with the greatest subtlety [Watson, translator, 1964: 46-48, rearranged].

filable documents led to written procedures and one-topic memos, specialization in text processing, increased internal correspondence, reduced autonomy, and "corporate memory."

The introduction of the telegraph (first demonstrated in 1844) decreased the effect of distance on business, but did not affect intracity communication traffic much. The telephone did that. Although direct dialing in switched local networks was available by 1899, operator-assisted service was available soon after Bell invented the phone in 1876.

Whalen suggests that railroads and the telegraph, along with increasing vertical and horizontal integration in industry (1880 to 1900), fueled a tremendous growth in transactions, which lead to an insufficient supply of male clerks.

Meanwhile, the aspirations and education levels of women were rising (see Aron, 1981). The introduction of the typewriter was inextricably linked to the insufficient male labor pool and the new female labor pool. The increase in women office workers was concomitantly dramatic. The 1880 census shows that only a tiny percentage of office clericals were women; by 1910, 83% were women (Scott, 1982: 173).

The concept of a typewriter fascinated inventors from as far back as Henry Mill in 1714. Over fifty inventors demonstrated writing machines before Sholes patented his version in 1868; it underwent 50 revisions before being bought by Remington. Typewriting led to a dramatic increase in dictation, hence facilitated the rise of the role of "personal secretary" and the segmentation of handling correspondence. By the turn of the century, shorthand and touch typing were widely used; more than 100,000 typewriters had been sold (Giuliano, 1982). The typewriter was seen at the time as a major revolution equal to the steam locomotive (Bliven, 1954; Curley, 1981).

A spate of inventions in office systems quickly followed. Edison's "business phonograph"—the dictation machine—was introduced in 1913, though it did not replace the stenographer. (That awaited modern office equipment, as stenography jobs declined 50% from 1972 to 1980; Giuliano, 1982: 154.) There were even early "automatic typewriters" based upon the player piano principle, using two rolls for form text and name lists, sold until after World War II (Leffingwill, 1926). Due to the Depression and reduced office work during World War II, there was little development in office products. Many have argued (although, ironically, without much documentation) that the photocopier ranks with the telephone, typewriter, and computer in significance for office work. The mainframe computer of course transformed the way organizations handled transactions and personal computers promise to continue the trend, but those topics are outside the scope of this discussion.

The development of word processing began as the marketing concept of a German IBM products manager (Steinhilter), who saw the magnetic tape/selectric typewriter (MT/ST) as an improvement over the paper-tape Frieden Flexowriter automated typewriter (Curley, 1981). He convinced IBM of the possibilities, and they marketed the term "word processing." They also marketed the idea of reorganizing the office around centralized transcription pools so dictation could take advantage of the costly equipment. Centralization as an organizational concept was advocated by IBM, until recently, and made a permanent mark on the use and design of office technology.

The MTST was introduced in 1964 and used tape cassettes to store short text material. Storage was increased in 1969 with the IBM CMST, or mag card typewriter. WP developments followed rapidly, and included Lexitron's introduction of a video display that allowed correction of errors before printing. Vydec's floppy disks, introduced in 1973, offered random access to text. Programmable WP software appeared in 1977 from Lanier; multiple functions were soon added by the IBM 6670 in 1979. The concept of integrated data and text was manifested in Jacquard's offering in 1979. Prime, Wang, Xerox, and Datapoint introduced networking in 1980. Managerial terminals were available from Xerox the next year. The Wang Alliance system offered multiform data and integrated functions that year as well.

Word processing now takes many forms. Hardware includes electronic typewriters, stand-alone nondisplay or single line-display storage typewriters, stand-alone display processors, clustered systems, hybrids (with multifunction intelligence), time sharing with internal or external mainframes, and now desk-top microcomputers. Uses of word processing also differ widely and seem to result from differing patterns of implementation. The next section describes a project intended to find out more about how organizations adopt and use word processing.

DESCRIPTION OF DATA AND RESEARCH METHODS

The project on innovation in word processing was funded by the National Science Foundation, and had two phases. In phase 1, we conducted telephone interviews with respondents at each of 194 organizations that had adopted WP at least two years before and that had at least four WP terminals. Contact respondents were recruited from lists of members of WP associations, from students in professional night schools, and from directories. Whenever possible, we contacted directly the person with supervisory responsibility of a unit. Respondents were mostly female (70%) holding the title of word processing supervisor or manager (42%) or systems manager or information, administration, or office (24%). The organizations represented a cross section of business: federal (27%), private nonprofit (14%), private profit (50%) and private regulated (7%). These also had a wide range of employee population size: fewer than 100 (14%), 100 to 400 (23%), 401 to 2,000 (32%), 2,000 to 20,000 (20%) and over 20,000 (10%).

Sixty-three percent of the organizations employed fewer than 15 WP operators, and an additional 17% employed fewer than 25. WP centers, with or without satellite work stations, made up 80% of the sample. In the remaining 20%, equipment was distributed among secretaries or professionals. Our sampling approach likely overselects from the more "centralized" units, because it is harder to identify respondents in organizations with distributed WP use.

In a second round of data collection and analysis, we selected 60 sites, for follow-up visits, interviews, and questionnaires with managers, authors, and operators. Case studies were constructed from these interviews, and the questionnaires asked for attitudes, uses, and perspectives specific to each group. Overall, sample sizes of these three data sets are managers—80, operators—302 and authors—243.

We posed three research questions:

(1)   Do organizations vary in their uses of and procedures for word processing?

(2)   How do word processing adaptations evolve?

(3)   What predicts the development of adaptation?

We discuss differences and similarities among organizations with respect to (a) whether or not there is a "standard" form of WP, and (b) four kinds of word processing/information systems. Systems here are considered in light of implementation and innovation theory, and constitute managerial philosophies, supervisory actions, work unit communication, and level of technical integration. The following section considers relevant aspects of implementation research.

FACTORS IN INFORMATION SYSTEM ADOPTION

The literature on innovations in general and on implementing information systems in particular is voluminous (Ackoff, 1967; Bikson, Gutek, and Mankin, 1981; Danzinger, Dutton, Kling, and Kraemer, 1982; King and Kraemer, 1981; Lucas, 1981; Rogers, 1983; Sheposh, Holton, and Knudsen, 1982; Zaltman, Duncan, and Holbek, 1973). Any review of this literature is beyond the scope of this chapter. However, we can note some of the common threads to this research.

The factors most common to implementation success include the rationale(s) for adoption, key actors, the distribution of the innovation within the organization, flexible planning, incremental change, pilots targeted to specific groups, user participation, training and face-to-face facilitation, and incentives for accepting change (Bikson et al., 1981; Keen, 1981; Meyer, 1983a). Hopelain (1982) suggests that successful implementation tends to be stimulated by dissatisfaction with current quality and location (or control) of data, accessibility of adequate organizational resources, and agreement about basic issues (technical, organizational, or interpersonal) on the part of involved parties. Underneath the appearance of administrative efficiency and precise decision making, even the most successful innovation is likely to be an instrument of organizational politics (Bikson et al., 1981; Danzinger et al., 1982; Feldman and March, 1981; Keen, 1981; Kling, 1980).

Dutton (1981), Keen (1981) and Markus (1981) and other authors take the "segmented institutionalist" perspective described in Chapter 3 when analyzing the politics of implementing information systems. Dutton, for example, concludes that "information systems seem to be highly malleable political tools which are utilized to reinforce the interests of the dominant coalition within an organization" (p. 200). He claims that consensus is not a likely outcome or safe assumption when implementing systems because of (a) unavailability of appropriate data for support or rejection of claims or even for the system's requirements; (b) organizational complexity, including too many actors; organizational instability, such as managerial mobility; (c) personalities of the actors; (d) shifting political environments that make the system appropriate or inappropriate at different times for different groups; (e) different stages in the innovation's lifespan which activate different groups; and (f) multiple, changing agendas.

Keen (1981) goes further in reassessing the notion of "rational" rationales for information systems. Information is, after all, only a small component of decision making, and is clearly an intellectual and political resource that affects various groups. Because of pluralism of goals, overt counterimplementation and resistance are not only likely, but even quite rational for the various organizational actors. Resistance is seen as a sign that some group doubts the official cost/benefit ratio of the innovation. (See also Zuboff [1982], who emphasizes that managers should pay attention to the form and source of resistance as guides to implementation, training, and job design.) In general, Keen focuses on politics, negotiation, authority, and coalition-building (as does Meyer, 1983b).

The comprehensive review by Sheposh et al. recognizes the prevalence of resistance, but warns that this may have been overemphasized in the literature. As they summarize (1982: 47), individuals are

> oriented not only toward defense of the status quo, the maintenance of consistency and the reduction of ambiguity, but also toward new learning, self-utilization and development of competence.

We agree, and will discuss how managers can foster these more positive reactions to implementation.[1]

THE PROCESS OF ADOPTING WORD PROCESSING

Implementation, however, is but one aspect of innovation adoption. This section describes a stage or process model of innovation, using word processing data for examples. The adoption process has also been characterized in the form of various stages. These may include a progression from knowledge/awareness, formation of attitudes toward the innovation and decision, to initial implementation and sustained implementation (Zaltman et al., 1973), or from evaluation and implementation to routinization (Hage and Aiken, 1967). We summarize a five-stage model of adoption developed over the years by Rogers (1983) and others (see

Rice and Rogers, 1980), highlighted by data from the WP project and mention of various perspectives that seem useful at each phase.

Agenda-Setting

At this initial stage the organization defines in a general way its problem; this definition includes the development of a common recognition of the problem by interested organization members. Early research assumed, at least tacitly, a rational perspective underlying agenda-setting. Organizations investigated their problems systematically, ordered their goals; and established objective criteria for selecting solutions. We have seen that this perspective is insufficient: "decision-making is multifaceted, emotive, conservative and only partially cognitive" (Keen, 1981: 25); "a WP system is part technology and part ideology" (Williams and Lodahl, 1978: 11).

In our study the initial rationales for considering WP were very utilitarian, yet may in the long run be quite limiting. Table 7.1 shows that the majority of organizations reported "repetitive typing" as the rationale, followed far behind by improving the work unit or employment containment.

A survey by the journal *Word Processing and Information Systems* (1981; based upon 2164 WPIS readers, or a 19% response rate) and another by Curley (1981; based on completed questionnaires from 21 organizations out of 30) found similar rationales: document preparation, documentation, and some data manipulation in the first survey, and faster output, keeping up with increasing paper volume, and better quality output in the second. Curley found that 84% of organizations reported their initial use of WP was for form letters or extensive revisions. These are quite important rationales for justifying the first plunge into an expensive innovation, but the paradox lies in the fact that these uses do not change or improve the organization. Further, although they are based upon notions of increased productivity, secretarial typing costs constitute less than 5% of office costs (Bair, 1979; Tapscott, 1982: 20). Therefore, a narrow focus on repetitive typing misses considerable potential of office automation, even on grounds of narrow productivity measures (see Chapter 8).

Matching

Matching is the stage at which a general problem from the agenda and a possible solution are brought together. The implementation literature emphasizes that top support is important for success; indeed, in most of our sites the initial idea came from top management. In 61.9% of responding organizations the idea for WP initially came from executives or top management, 10.7% from clericals and 10.1% from clients or professionals. The WPIS survey found that 77% of those deciding initially to buy WP were chief officers—fully 25% were the organizations' chief

TABLE 7.1 Rationales for Equipment Installation and Subsequent Change

Rationale	Rationale for Initial Installation	
	First [a]	Second [b]
Repetitive typing	66.3%	15.8%
Improve work unit	13.5	32.7
Reduce or maintain staff	11.0	11.9
A new thing to do	7.4	5.9
Other	1.8	33.7

Rationale	Rationale for Subsequent Change	
	First [c]	Second [d]
Upgrade functions	33.6%	48.5%
Dissatisfaction	26.8	13.9
Add features	22.8	14.9
Added demand	12.8	10.9
Managerial decision	2.0	2.0
Compatibility	—	5.0
Other or none	2.0	5.0

a. N = 163
b. N = 101
c. N = 149
d. N = 101

executive officers. Curley reported less of an influence of top management—only 38%; 46.7% were individual managers. But she notes that subsequent purchases, or companies deciding on WP later than average, were more likely (61.8%) to have top management make the decision.

Computing as well as WP seems to be initiated by a "godfather" who then delegates the idea to lower levels, where support may be less visible or real. On the one hand, this explains the excessive rational perspective behind initial usage justification, but also explains why these justifications rarely consider changing the nature of work: High-level managers are not sufficiently involved in the work process to suggest those kinds of changes. As we will see, such change in work design, rather than in technology, must come from the locus of activity.

In addition to lack of support at the operational level, the person put in charge of the WP unit was typically a secretary or WP operator (72.7%) with no experience outside the organization (61.5%). In many cases it was the executive's secretary, or an operator in the original WP unit who felt someone had to take charge.

During the matching stage, certain characteristics of the innovation influence its adoption. *Relative advantage* is the degree to which a new idea is perceived by the user as superior to the practice it replaces. Clearly reduction of repetitive typing makes it easier to see the obvious relative advantages of WP.

Complexity is the degree to which an innovation is perceived by the user as difficult to understand. The early WP technology was seen as quite similar to typewriters and, thus, was conceptually simple, but was also limited in functions and not easy to operate. Current WP systems are highly functional and, thus, easy to use for certain tasks, but they do allow highly complex procedures. Indeed, the median number of months the operators reported needing to become competent was a short 1.6 (mean = 2.7), but 72.4% reported that they are still learning "some" or "much" about ways to use WP.

Compatibility is the degree to which a new idea is perceived as being consistent with the potential adopter's prior experience, beliefs, and values. Placing WP into stenolike centralized "pools" reduced the initial perceived incompatibility of WP by including it in existing procedures and operations, but the potential of WP is often limited by fitting it to preexisting procedures.

Communicability is the degree to which a new idea is visible to potential adopters. Here the product is quite visible—rapidly produced, correct, formatted, clean copy. Thus, this quickly becomes the standard for demands by authors. However, the process of WP is nearly invisible to clients, so tensions quickly arise between author expectations and WP unit capabilities.

Divisibility is the degree to which a new idea can be given a small-scale trial by a potential adopter, or the extent to which parts of the innovation may be tried. Here there is often a large leap to the first WP equipment, so divisibility is not a strong attribute of WP. Further, attempts to keep initial WP simple also work against developing managerial expertise and effort in designing the unit's structure and procedures.

We see that many of the attributes of WP that facilitate initial adoption during the Matching stage may operate in the long run to either suppress its potential or generate organizational conflicts that must be resolved in later stages.

Redefining

In the redefining stage, attributes of the innovation are defined relative to the organization's needs. Incremental implementation facilitates this redefinition. An incremental approach, particularly through pilot demonstrations (either experiments, which provide more information about the innovation, or exemplary demonstrations, which try to display the innovation and its benefits), will uncover negative meanings and inappropriate design aspects. A system is more likely to succeed if people involved associate with it favorable—and realistic—meanings and expectations of the benefits (Lippit, Miller, and Halamaj, 1980).

In our sample, there seemed to be few extreme cases of either rapid experimentation or lengthy and large-scale initial implementation: The median number of months spent in planning was 6.3, with a mean of 8.1.

No more than half of the organizations spent "much" time in even lease-buy assessments of WP technology; slightly less spent "much" time in cost-benefit or work-flow assessments; less than a third spent "much" time in assessing employee attitudes; and only 12% made site visits (see Table 7.3 below).

Experience with WP leads to better understanding of its potential role within an organization. One measure of this is whether subsequent changes in equipment are motivated by different reasons than the initial rationales. Table 7.1 shows that although general dissatisfaction was responsible for 26.8% of the rationales, and added demand (an extension of the initial rational justifications) represented 12.8% of the changes, upgrading of functions (33.6%) and addition of features (22.8%) represented the majority of reasons. This may be interpreted as slight redefinition of the original concepts of WP, developed through actual use. The WPIS survey also reported what functions users wanted to acquire (thus their question is biased toward functionality). The most mentioned functions included more work stations, communication, additional software, electronic mail, and photocomposition interface. All except the first-mentioned reason imply redefinition of the initial role of WP as a way to reduce repetitive typing. Curley also reported a shift in top uses among her responding organizations: Broad correspondence was ranked first by 55%, word and data processing by 30%, and forms typing by 15%. In general, she concluded that there were no overall differences in initial and subsequent purchase rationales, although five organizations (24%) did argue for "soft" dollar savings, greater managerial productivity, and increased effectiveness as changes in cost-benefit criteria.

Another measure of redefinition is whether the functions that were performed were changed much over the implementation and usage period. Table 7.2 shows that regardless of the WP use, typically only about 10% of the organizations reported "much" change in the way these services were performed.

Thus, while there was a general redefinition of the kinds of reasons for which WP was acquired and reasonable amounts of effort were expended to match and redefine the innovation in a short period of time, the initial ways in which WP was used to perform services typically changed little.

Structuring

In this stage organization members establish the innovation within the organization's structure. Structuring occurs partially through peer pressure, negotiations and social modeling, and partially through formal and informal communication about the innovation (Rogers, 1983; Rogers and Kincaid, 1981).

TABLE 7.2 Word Processing Service Elements, Ranked by Frequency of Organizational Adoption

| | Does Organization Provide Service? | | | |
Uses	Never	Occasionally	Regularly	Was Service Changed Much?
Draft copies	7	26	158	23
Proofread	24	41	125	28
Index files	25	20	145	24
Boilerplates	42	49	99	25
Develop forms	53	51	85	14
Edit and rewrite	55	50	85	22
Fill out forms	61	47	83	20
Keep activity log	65	25	96	13
Maintain inventory	71	25	92	18
Maintain data base	76	27	85	26
Deliver work	69	44	65	4
Process records	82	36	66	15
Write original material	94	42	56	15
Telecommunicate	102	22	60	22
Provide admin. support	110	23	53	6
Provide photocopies	120	20	46	9
Phototypeset	153	9	26	6

NOTE: Figures are number of organizations giving that response, rather than percentage, to avoid difficulties with missing responses. Uses ranked according to total of "occasionally" and "regularly" responses.

A spurt in the acceptance and use of an innovation occurs when the opinion leaders in a system adopt an innovation. On the other hand, top management may encounter peer pressure and norms not to send one's work to another unit or not to use a keyboard. Indeed, among authors in our study there is a barely significant relationship (Kendall's tau = .395, p < .001) between doing any of one's own typing and interest in having WP on one's desk.

With respect to actual organizational structure, although 80% of the organizations had WP centers or centers with satellites, it was not always this way. When asked what was the growth pattern for WP, 28 (41.7%) organizations said "the same", 27 said "to decentralization", and 40 said "to centralization". Curley found about the same shifting, but she commented that the direction tended to be away from whatever structure was devised initially. She concluded that any change in organizational structuring was "reactive" and not necessarily directed by conscious choice or managerial planning.

Interconnecting

More than any other stage, interconnecting requires attending to processes brought into focus by the political and interactionist perspectives (see Chapter Three). Questions about turf, social benefits, control, and access rise; solutions are dictated or negotiated. Markus (1981) argues that adoption resistance can be largely explained by "features of the information system's design which represent a loss in power for affected users." Individuals' rules and departments must be interconnected and integrated within the organization.

The most common interconnection issue in our WP survey centered around the amount of access and contact authors had with operators. At the extreme, some authors lost their personal secretaries upon the development of WP, and thus felt a keen need to maintain contact with their documents and the operators. On the other hand, supervisors quickly became wary of easy access to their operators, and devised ways to protect the operators who were not in a position to negotiate author's demands. This is not to say that operators did not want some contact with authors. Of the word processing operators responding, 167 (62%) said they had "some" or "much" contact with authors, and this correlated (Kendall's tau = .60, p < .001) with how much they would like (they tended to want a little more). Nearly all authors (93%) reported "some" or "much" contact with operators, and slightly more felt that this improved the work. However, 49 of the organizations reported "many" and 88 "few" as opposed to 35 reporting "no" formal procedures for contact with authors. Thirty (65.2%) reported decreases in author contact, with 13 reporting increases.

REINVENTION OF WORD PROCESSING

How and whether WP is adapted *after* it is adopted is an important question. The potential of office communication technology may be facilitated by starting out with WP, but applications and work design must progress past those rationales and designs initially typical in most organizations. Thus, we are interested in reinvention in the innovation process.

Reinvention is the degree to which an innovation is changed by the adopter in the process of adoption and implementation after its original development (Rice and Rogers, 1980: 501). Reinvention as a concept has its roots in educational implementation studies. Berman and McLaughlin (1975), for example, noted the considerable "mutual adaptation" between educational organizations and their innovations. Hall and Loucks (1978) discussed the notion of "innovation configurations" or "the operational patterns of the innovation that result from selection and use of different innovation component variations." Perhaps the first use of the term "reinvention" appeared in Agarwala-Rogers, Rogers, and Wills (1977). As Rice and Rogers (1980: 501) have written,

Reinvention may involve both the innovation as a tool and in its use. Thus, the same technological innovation may be put to a different use than originally intended; alternatively a different innovation may be used to solve the same problem. In addition, the intended or potential consequences of an innovation may be changed through reinvention.

Thus, reinvention may occur at any of the five adoption stages. The nature of reinvention may involve operations and service, technical aspects, or managerial and organizational aspects. Further, reinvention seems to be categorizable into planned (intentional) or vicarious (learning from other's mistakes) and reactive (solving a problem generated by the innovation) or secondary (solving unintended consequences elsewhere in the organization or innovation due to the reinvention).

Measuring Reinvention

A straightforward measure of reinvention is the number of innovation components over and above a "standard" configuration. Here, operation/service components are represented by WP uses or services. Table 7.2 listed WP services, ranked by decreasing frequency of adoption by the 194 organizations. If we define the standard adoption as those components adopted by at least 50% of the organizations, the standard service components include providing draft copies, proofreading, indexing files, and using boilerplates (standard forms and headings).

Technical and managerial/organizational components are included under "role and organizational structure" in Table 7.3.

The standard WP innovation (adopted by 50% or more of organizations) comprises units in centers (or with satellites) staffed by "WP/word specialists/technicians" working for a WP supervisor manager (the plurality category of titles). As we have seen, its main rationale is repetitive typing and is initiated by top management. Only lease-buy assessment is performed. There is much operator-author contact, though the WP unit has its own location and does not share it. Any changes that occur are primarily motivated by the supervisor.

The 50% criterion is rather arbitrary, if useful. Another way to detect the standard form is to inspect the distribution of the number of components adopted by organizations. For this analysis, all service and role/structure variables were dichotomized, then summed for each organization. For the 16 service components, the mean is 9.3, median 9.5. For the 23 role/structure components, the mean is 10.4, median 10.2. These values and Figure 7.1 indicate that the distribution of components is quite normal and we cannot conclude that a specific number of components in each set constitutes a clear standard adoption.

Another approach to identifying a standard configuration is to look for factors underlying the adoption of components. Tables 7.4 and 7.5 portray the orthogonal varimax rotated solutions to the service and role/structure variables.

TABLE 7.3 Word Processing Role and Organizational Structure, Ranked by Frequency of Organizational Adoption

Rank	Role/Structure	Response Frequency			Number of Organizations
	Title				
2	WP unit	Distributed			35
		Center(s) perhaps w/satellites			147
14	Operators	Secretary/Typist/Etc.			94
		WP/Word specialist/Technician			94
15	In charge	Other			104
		Supervisor/Manager			89
	Initial Idea				
9	Rationale	Other			55
		Repetitive typing			108
11	Source	Other			84
		Executive/Top management			104
	Assessments	None	Little	Much	
8	Lease-buy	53	29	82	
12	Cost-benefit	57	26	76	
13	Workflow	66	21	75	
17	Employee attitudes	85	23	39	
	Client Boundaries				
4	Amount of contact	32	31	108	
5	Procedural formality	35	88	49	
		Never	Depends	Always	
20	Chargeback	121	30	17	
	WP Unit Evaluation		No	Yes	
16	Line/Page/Doc Count		120	66	
17	Turnaround time		125	62	
17	Client satisfaction		120	62	
18	Lead to changes		100	61	
21	Errors		151	35	
	Physical Boundaries				
7	Others share WP place		68	120	
10	WP personnel one place		84	105	
	Involved in Changes	None	Some	Often	Usually
1	Supervisor	17	15	25	119
3	Execs/Top admin.	37	68	28	49
6	Clients	49	72	29	28
19	Data processing	103	29	8	21

NOTE: Ranks based upon combined positive responses, or upon most frequent category of response, except for "In charge" variable.

FIGURE 7.1 Distribution of Adoption of 39 Word Processing Components by 194 Organizations

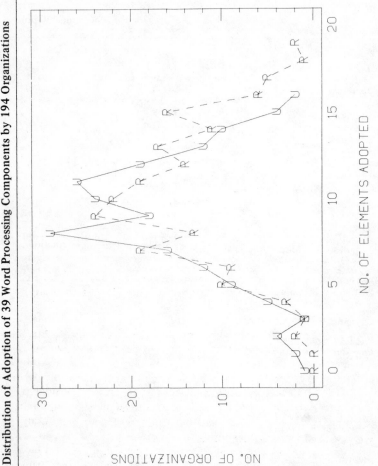

NO. OF ELEMENTS ADOPTED

NO. OF ORGANIZATIONS

TABLE 7.4 Factor Solution of WP Service Components

Uses	Factor 1	Factor 2
Draft copies	Not included due to wide adoption	
Proofread		
Index files		
Boilerplates	.42	
Develop forms	.60	
Edit and rewrite		.50
Fill out forms		
Keep activity log	.40	
Maintain inventory	.46	
Maintain data base	.44	
Deliver work		
Process records		
Write original material		.70
Telecommunicate		
Provide admin. support		
Provide photocopies		
Eigenvalue	2.36	1.03
Variance explained	40.9%	17.9

NOTE: Two significant factors resulted from varimax orthogonal rotation of initial solution, of which six factors were significant (had an eigenvalue greater than 1.00). First principal component of first solution explained 18.6% of the variance; cumulative explained variance of the initial six factors was 57.9%. Only loadings greater than .40 are reported.

Table 7.4 shows almost no structure to the service components. The primary factor (comprising 40.9% of the variance) is a rather passive, warehousing sort of WP use: storage and reduction of repetitive typing of forms material. The second significant factor is a "writing" factor; the WP unit is actively involved in the creation of text. We might consider these two functions as standard WP activities, except that none other than boilerplating is done regularly by at least 50% of the organizations. However, the most common functions are performed by so many organizations that they would likely be distributed across several factors.

Table 7.5 shows some reasonable structure to the role/structure components. The first factor (representing 28.9% of the variance) indicates that early planning and assessment activities were likely performed together. However this planning approach seems negatively associated with later changes due to work unit evaluations. Early planning is external to the WP unit and organized from above; internal changes perhaps do not follow easily in such a structured environment. The second factor represents just such change: A variety of WP unit evaluations occur together, and they tend to lead to changes. The third factor is the general identification of WP in our sample: centers, with WP "operators" or "technical specialists," which established formal procedures for client

TABLE 7.5 Factor Solution of WP Role Structure Components

Role/Structure	FACTORS					
	1	2	3	4	5	6
WP Unit			.81			
Operators			.53			
In charge			.72			
Rationale				.68		
Idea source					.59	
Lease-buy	.81					
Cost-benefit	.57					
Workflow	.68					
Employee attitudes	.63					
Amount of contact						.52
Procedural formality						.40
Chargeback						
Line/Page/Doc./Count		.44				
Turnaround time		.72				
Client satisfaction		.68				
Errors		.56				
Lead to changes		.54			.52	
Others share WP place						
WP personnel one place				.76		
Changes						
Supervisor			.72			
Top Management					.57	
Clients						.63
DP						
Eigenvalues	3.86	2.38	1.84	1.43	1.33	1.06
Variance explained	28.9%	17.9	13.8	10.7	10.0	8.0

NOTE: Six significant factors resulted from varimax orthogonal rotation of initial solution, of which eight factors were significant (had an eigenvalue greater than 1.00). First principal component of first solution explained 18.4% of the variance; cumulative explained variance of the initial eight factors was 71.5%. Only loadings greater than .40 are reported.

contact, but which also took employee attitudes into account when initiating WP. This approach represents a structured attitude toward WP that takes into account its group members. The flip side of this is factor 4: WP members located in the same place but motivated by the initial rationale of reducing repetitive typing. Factor 5 is a standard component: initiation of WP by top management, which continues to be involved in change, and indeed change follows from unit evaluation. The last significant factor is the "client" factor: Clients are involved in changes, and have much contact with operators, but all this contact is regulated by formal procedures. In other words, managerial control directs and facilitates communication and change.

The analyses so far have attempted to detect a standard form of WP and measures of the extent to which it is reinvented. The frequency analyses did not indicate much differentiation in this regard, and the factor structures were not particularly clear or strong, though they did indicate how some components seem to appear together. The lack of strong structure of WP components is mirrored by a cluster analysis of the service components. The SAS version of average link hierarchical cluster analysis did not find any clusters according to its cubic clustering criterion. This result indicates even more forcefully that the components seem to be rather loosely associated.

One implication is that we would not expect to be able to predict the simplest measure of reinvention—the total number of components adopted. Using the same total number of service components (maximum: 16), except coding the value as missing if an organization did not respond to more than two of the service component questions (so as to avoid a bias toward low totals due to pervasive nonresponse by an organization), the total was regressed on variables measuring structure and change. These variables were number of employees, public or private organization, amount of operator contact with clients, executive involvement in change, WP unit a center or distributed, supervisor's involvement in change, influence on change of evaluating WP, and presence of formal procedures for dealing with clients.[2] (The total N after listwise deletion was 107; total $R^2 = .186$; $F = 3.22$; $p < .05$.) Only increased operator contact with authors has a significant coefficient (R^2 increment $= .137$; $F = 14.46$; $P < .001$).

Of course we cannot impute causality from this analysis. More services available might draw the interest of authors; on the other hand, more communication with authors might generate requests and ideas for new applications and functions. In general, though, the total number of innovation components seems to be only a generalized indicator of reinvention, and does not seem to be very predictable, although communication plays a role. One implication of these analyses is that "word processing" is a flexible notion comprising a diverse set of services and roles. Thus, managers can take advantage of this flexibility by reinventing WP to support their organization's goals and to restructure work in positive ways.

From this implication, we now suggest that there may be a more fruitful way to look at reinvention in the adoption of word processing.

FROM TYPEWRITER TO INTEGRATED OFFICE SYSTEMS: FOUR SYSTEMS AS LEVELS OF REINVENTION

If there is one common thread to the office automation literature, at least from those who think deeply about the form and implications of new office media, it is that, as the introductory story suggests, narrow concepts of productivity and technology will stifle the potential for innovative ways to use the media and ways to work. Several typologies have been suggested that trace the progression from manual office work, an assembly-line manufacturing model for work, to mechanization, automation, and integration. These typologies involve concepts such as "contagion" through the organization, "maturity" of the uses of the technology, "transformations" of work, and "fifth-generation" computer-based systems (Emery, 1982; Giuliano, 1982; Landau, 1983; McFarlan and McKenney, 1983: 38; Meyer, 1983a; Strassman, 1980; Tapscott, 1982; Zisman, 1978).

Even the most sophisticated technology may be used simply to increase efficiency, and as we have noted, that is the most common initial rationale. But good management of and innovation in information work can lead to increased effectiveness, successful accomplishment of organizational mission, and perhaps even redefinitions of that mission.

We suggest here that the information system—involving work, technology, and people—may take four forms. Each system exhibits increasing amounts of reinvention. Increased reinvention breaks out of prior constraints on the technology configuration, on how work is done, on what work is done, and how the sociotechnical system is designed. We consider each of the four systems in light of examples from our site visits.

Low-Integration Systems:
Word Processing as Typewriter

This system operates at a level below standard adoption. Basic functions such as boilerplating, global searching, computation, linear graphics, and simple records processing functions are seldom used because their utility is not appreciated. Word processing is seen as a fancy typewriter; even routine work has not been automated.

A critical factor seems to be that low-integration systems lack WP management. From a communication perspective, there is little interaction or sharing of ideas about applications. None of these systems has a supervisor or coordinator of WP services. Further, these tend to be federal sites, largely due to the low job classifications of WP operators in government jobs. One government analyst summarized the findings of a study of federal WP usage: (a) WP increases the unit cost of producing documents; (b) the majority of procurement is for the typing function; (c) there is no training, and people have no conception of how word processing differs from typing; (d) WP is not considered as a general purpose machine; and (e) no one ever evaluates what they do with or for WP.

Many low-integration systems use the ability of the equipment to clock its use for acquisition and evaluation purposes; more advanced systems have the attitude that "anyone can write a program to keep the equipment constantly in use; keyboarding time is no measure of utility." Because of minimal management and little understanding of the capabilities of the technology, all of the sites where the unit's operation was described as "poor" (7%) were low-integration systems.

In brief, at low-integration sites, managers paid little attention to WP capability. Sometimes equipment served no purpose other than as a status symbol. A few people taught themselves to use it; some developed brilliant applications, but without systematic attention to how or to what purpose the equipment should be used, innovative practices seldom spread.

Standard Adopter Systems: Clockwork Systems

Clockworks are mechanical systems known for efficient operation of specific tasks in a stable environment. Standard adopter systems are "successful" but have not moved beyond efficiency, and will likely have little impact on whatever office automation developments occur in their organization. Communication does involve feedback to the operators, but the system does not stimulate using this communication for devising new procedures or sharing insights.

Most of these systems are centers, and all have a supervisor, manager, or coordinator. The goal of these systems is to routinize operations and to save keystrokes. Boilerplating, limited math applications, searching and replacing, and records processing are fairly common services. As one supervisor put it, "My job is to see that this office operates as efficiently as possible. The measures of this would be low turnaround time, reduction of secretarial turnover, and high quality work."

In one of the larger sites we visited, an operator told of how authors used to be allowed in the center. One day an author saw her using the global replace function and asked if she could do a special kind of revision that required rather complex searching. She thought a bit and showed him how she would do it. The author then asked the supervisor for that to be done for some special report he was preparing; he complained that the supervisor had told him it was impossible. After the author left, the supervisor told the operator that she was not to tell authors what the word processor could do. Soon after that, the center adopted a policy preventing authors from entering the center.

The paradoxical result of this emphasis on efficiency in doing the obvious tasks is that clockwork systems typically are reluctant to get new equipment, or to take the time to develop new procedures systematically; both would hamper their efficiency, even if they might do better in the long run. Short-term efficiency prevents long-term reinvention.

Again, we see a problem of attention. Attention is focused on efficient use—getting the most pages of output for the least input of human and machine resources. No one asks if the output serves any useful purpose for the organization. No one asks what they might be doing more productively with the equipment. The appreciation of "what we are doing here" is limited.

Expanding Systems: Supervisory Reinvention

These systems are characterized by supervisors who span their unit's boundaries and motivate reinvention. Applications evolve, equipment is changed frequently for new functions and applications, and the unit's mission is often to provide service to professionals. However, the motivation for change is located in the supervisor, who therefore must rely on political savvy and top management support.

Supervisors in these sites did not emphasize efficiency; instead, they told of changes and improvements. They invest in reinvention, even when it means taking longer. The WP center of a large manufacturing firm got new equipment and is diversifying its services. Using math and automated function keys, the unit has figured out a procedure for automatically updating the catalogue of several thousand products and sending material with typesetting codes directly to the printer. Moreover, the supervisor, after watching departments getting their own equipment and struggling to make minimal use of it, is setting up satellite centers to better meet the needs of departments by being closer to them. She is also starting consulting to people who get their own equipment, seeing this consulting as her future: She's launching "an educational campaign for in-house consulting."

However, supervisors in these systems recognize the tensions that arise from demands for these new services, and work to protect their operators, by managing their unit's boundaries. This involves negotiating formal procedures with clients, as we have seen, and maintaining top-level support for new equipment and the flexibility to suggest new procedures for other departments whose work they process. One particularly difficult boundary to manage is between WP and data communications/processing. Typically, the first substantive human communication between these two starts when one party wants to start communicating between equipment. WP supervisors must then secure cooperation from data services personnel who often show little respect for word processing operations or needs. (See Meyer, [1968] and Zisman, [1978] for a discussion of this particular boundary problem.)

Most reinvention-related communication in these systems is motivated by the supervisors; typically the operators are brought into the change process very little, although the managerial style of the supervisor often motivates sharing of ideas within the unit itself. One reason supervisors are so important is the rapid upward mobility of upper management. The manager who brought in WP may be gone before the technology proves itself. This transience puts a premium on fast early results, but often at the cost of support for explicit goals or specific commitments later. Thus, the supervisor must take charge. In addition, a superior's favorable attitude toward innovation has a significant influence on subordinates' attitudes toward communication technology (Elizur and Guttman, 1976).

Supervisory attention is focused on the customer or author in expanding systems. Performance is monitored by how well the system serves the customer rather than how many pages it produces. By attending to service needed, expanding systems find new uses and procedures for the technology.

High-Integration Systems: Systemwide Reinvention

Reinvention in these systems is a way of life. One subject commented, "We are definitely a service, not a center." Word processing is managed rather than supervised, and increased capability is the primary focus; in particular, augmentation of professional work is a clear goal. With this perspective comes higher risk, more operational uncertainty, and an emphasis on organizationwide communication networks.

The form and function of the work group as well as the equipment are appropriate targets for reinvention. Idea sharing leads to idea development, and then to system development, not in the narrow sense of hardware/software use, but in the broader sense of people working with technology to accomplish a mission. Interaction is the route to innovation as this manager of a work group suggests.

> We also do a lot of proposals. I said to myself, "What would I do if I had a lot of home computers and wanted to do a proposal?" I worked out a concept. I shared the idea with other people. They had an idea of where we could get the computer.

An operator put it this way,

> I always find easier ways of doing my work. With a system this complex, there are lots of ways. We are always telling each other to come over the see a new technique we have figured out. If it is something that has to be standard, we take a vote and the majority rules.

Another said,

> All our fooling around with the equipment has been most useful to us. We have learned a lot about how to do things more quickly, shortcut the machines, do more with fewer entries. To learn charting and graphics you really have to play with the machines quite a bit.

Notice that this kind of activity assumes that there is time to experiment, to learn; that communication and sharing of ideas is encouraged; and that reinvention is tested, implemented, and diffused. Supervisors and operators need to cooperate to help the user participate in system development and operation. But this does not always happen. According to 56% of the operators, tasks in their organization could be done better with WP that are now done other ways. However, only 8% are given much time to find new ways; another 44% do receive some time. Forty-seven percent receive encouragement to experiment; 24% are discouraged from doing so. Only 16% often receive praise for developing new methods from their supervisors, though another 23% do sometimes.

An example underscores the wider implications of such change. In one unit of a loan authorization agency, the process of approving loans was cumbersome and especially used professional time doing essentially clerical tasks. The people in WP found a way of simplifying the process and relieving the loan authorizers of needless copying of information by hand.

At that time, we saw we were typing up loan authorizations and forms by hand when we already had the information stored. Someone suggested to do all of them at the same time. We worked out a procedure, sold it to management. Now the whole information process here is different. The operators who had the idea were upgraded to GS5s because they were making decisions and not just routine typing.

Attention in high-integration systems is on "our work." In high-integration systems there is less emphasis on the technology per se. As one manager put it, "We didn't set out to put in word processing, we set out to get our work done." The attention is on "good work" rather than "good use of tool." The means of doing the work is intensive communication and an appreciation of what the tools (WP) can do.

COMMUNICATION AND REINVENTION

In an attempt to understand the relationship of communication to reinvention in WP in a more quantitative fashion, we analyzed the operator data with a specific focus on the variables discussed so far. We can provide only an overview of that analysis. The primary measure of reinvention was the question "Do you and your co-workers develop new procedures for using word processing?"

Traditional sets of variables did not much predict reinvention. These include technological characteristics (machine reliability, ease of use, and versality), personality traits (play computer games, seek new ways to do things, enjoy being a leader, prefer to communicate directly with authors, have friends elsewhere in the organizations), organizational orientation (talk about organization's or group's product), or participation in certain kinds of decision making (equipment, maintenance, or personnel performance evaluation criteria).

However, the factors that do associate with operator reinvention closely parallel principles of sociotechnical systems analysis (Bostrum and Heinen, 1977a,b; Cummings, 1978; Emery, 1982): training, encouragement of experimentation, communication, and participation in other kinds of decision making (unit productivity, formatting procedures, training). In a well-designed sociotechnical system, there is an emphasis on increasing the "response repetoire" of employees. The emphasis is on increasing the competence of people to do their job, rather than on learning skills per se. For example, the two training questions that relate to reinvention are not questions such as "Did you learn how to operate the machine?" but rather ask whether training increased their ability to make decisions.

A colleague of ours, Cline (1983), subjected 15 communication items, six job satisfaction items, and 13 reinvention items from the operators' data set to principal components factor analysis with varimax rotation. Factors with an eigenvalue greater than 1.00, and items with a loading greater than .60 on one factor and less than .40 on any other factor, were selected.

Three communication factors emerged. The factors were interpreted as "Input into Decisions," "Received Praise," and "Supervisor Friendliness", and accounted for 91% of the common variance. The two reinvention factors that emerged were interpreted as "Discussing New Procedures" and "Shown New Procedures," explaining 72% of the common variance. One "Discontentment" factor emerged from the job satisfaction items.

The correlation between the communication and reinvention sets, when considered as unidimensional (ignoring factor structures), was .51. Other factor-factor correlations appear in Table 6.

Generally, quality of communication and level of reinventiveness in word processing installations were significantly associated. The highest correlation occurred between the frequency with which operators received praise from others and the frequency of discussions of new procedures. The next highest correlation occurred between the degree of friendliness of the supervisor and an attention variable—the frequency with which operators were shown new procedures. Job discontentment is associated with low levels of both communication and reinvention.

SUMMARY

Our conclusions from this analysis of the adoption and reinvention of word processing considerably reinforce the findings of other researchers of new office media. In addition, we emphasize the role of attention and

TABLE 7.6 Correlations Among Communication, Reinvention and Job Satisfaction Factors

	Input into Decisions	Received Praise	Supervisor Friendliness	Discontentment
Discuss New Procedures	.32	.57	.19	n.s.
Shown New Procedures	n.s.	.27	.47	-.40
Discontentment	n.s.	-.25	-.25	

SOURCE: Cline, 1983.
NOTE: Minimum N = 160. Correlations significant at p < .001.

organizational communication in fostering reinvention and, by imputa-
tion, attaining the potential of the office of the future.

Clearly, planning and implementation must fit with—indeed, are
products of—the particular organization culture and context. Part of this
fit includes the negotiation of boundaries and the development of
organizational networks, with support from opinion leaders, and from
personnel in classifying jobs. Often this process includes technology plans
that match business needs, or experimental and exemplary demonstrations.

But to tap the full potential of these technologies and the work groups
requires wider managerial perspectives and more concentrated attention
than we typically encountered in our study. As Curley (1981: 342)
concluded from her analysis,

> There is no evidence to suggest that evolution towards more
> successful implementation occurs in the absence of a specific
> strategy to increase managerial effectiveness. . . . it seems to
> require the active intervention of management who view the
> technology as a catalyst for a variety of job and organizational
> changes which ultimately bring about the more widespread
> productivity gains promised by office automation technology.

Attention may take the form of training, time to experiment, and verbal
praise. Successful managers tend to stress development of the new
abstract and cognitive skills needed for information work instead of a
constrained view of the technology.

Underlying these activities is a managerial philosophy that focuses on
long-term organizational goals rather than narrow visions of efficiency and
productivity. This requires support for co-worker interaction, controlled
interaction with authors, and diffusion of new ways of using WP functions
and doing work. Peters points out that studies of the sources of innovation
emphasize that "the great majority of the ideas for new products come
from users" (1983b: 17). The implication is that those close to the
technology and the work process should have a major role in work
procedures and products. WP units may provide an organizational model
for self-designing work groups: "The essential problem in self-design is to
make a teacher out of a learner" (Weick, 1977). Such groups represent a
return to symmetric dependencies in the organization rather than authori-
tarian and hierarchical ones (Emery, 1982), and generate responsibility,
commitment, and ownership—key factors in innovation (Peters, 1983a,b).

The ultimate implication is that organizational structures and work
forms must be, and will be, changed: Information technology becomes a
cause of and tool for organizational redesign (Keen, 1981; Zuboff, 1982).
As Emery perceives these changes, "the knowledge revolution may be in
the release of human capabilities rather than in microprocessors, optic
fibers and satellites" (1982: 1108).

NOTES

This research was funded by the National Science Foundation, Grant ISI8110779 to Dr. Johnson. Conclusions are not necessarily those of the NSF.

1. There are serious policy issues associated with the introduction of information systems, such as job fragmentation and deskilling, health hazards, exploitation of women workers, and unemployment. These topics are outside the scope of this chapter, but are discussed elsewhere (Downing, 1980; Glenn and Feldberg, 1977; Gregory and Nussbaum, 1982; Harkness, 1978; Johnson and Rice, 1984; Scott, 1982; Smith, 1984; Taylor, 1980; Zimmerman, 1982).

2. The first two independent variables were entered jointly first, to control for possible effects due to the form and sector of the organization. Number of months since implementation seems a likely control variable as well, in the sense that organizations with greater experience with WP might have more software/hardware functions or have had opportunity to develop more services. However, there were too many nonresponses to that question; it reduced the effective analysis sample size to 63. Analysis of residuals found only two cases greater than 2.05 standard deviations from the standardized mean of zero, which is to be expected at the .05 level of significance, and at the .01 level for a two-tailed test.

RONALD E. RICE and
JAMES H. BAIR

8 New Organizational Media and Productivity

Organizations are rightfully concerned with the costs and productivity impacts of new organizational media. Before we can assess the impacts of new organizational information systems on office productivity, however, we need to establish a conceptual framework for identifying and locating such impacts. Information work is different from industrial work. Further, information and communication have attributes that may be productive at one organizational level but quite irrational or ineffective at another. Within a framework of information work behavior, this chapter considers the nature of and opportunities for productivity improvements from office automation in general and electronic messaging in particular.

This chapter begins by briefly noting the concept of productivity and how information work requires a new framework for analyzing productivity. That framework demands an understanding of effectiveness and performance rather than efficiency and product. Further, it requires that communication activities be emphasized. The kinds of productivity benefits stemming from new office media are therefore outlined. A specific medium, electronic messaging, is described in light of such cost and benefit considerations. The general framework also demands an understanding of different levels of organizational performance, in order to specify what kinds of benefits are sought, and how communication activities play a role. The chapter ends with a brief summary of office automation study results with respect to information worker productivity.

UNDERSTANDING AND MEASURING PRODUCTIVITY

Even a summary discussion of the causes of productivity growth and decline—global and national economics, industrial strategies and markets, production engineering, personnel management, job satisfaction, job design, and augmentation of decision making—is well beyond the scope of this chapter (see, for example, Ruch and Ruch, 1982).

We do need to discuss the concept of productivity, however. There are numerous ways of conceptualizing and measuring productivity (see Rees et al., 1979; Siegel, 1980). A common approach is to divide output by input. Each may be "partial" or "total"—measuring one, several, or all known variables. Inputs and outputs are commonly physical in nature, or represented in monetary form or in combined form: the value of the outputs divided by a specific physical input. The cost of capital may be included in the resources used. The value-added component of the output may be measured in a simple way by subtracting the inputs from the value of the output. The value may include subjective pricing by a given market segment. Measures may shift from an emphasis on efficiency to a concern for effectiveness. Such productivity measures may include ratios of work units achieved versus those intended, achievements compared to objectives, or performance compared to resources. One long-run view of productivity assess how well the organization adjusts to changes in the environment while achieving its goals, or even its success in altering its goals in order to survive turbulent environments (see Downs and Hain, 1982; Packer, 1983).

There are problems with many of these classical productivity measures.

(a)   They are not appropriate for custom or small-batch activities.

(b)   They are not easily comparable between products varying in style or consumer tastes and in users' subjective perceptions.

(c)   They tend to focus on outputs rather than outcomes and impacts.

(d)   They do not involve sufficient tools for interpreting data, such as trade-offs between quality and cost or trends and cycles (Packer, 1983).

But for our purposes, the major difficulty is that they cannot be applied to knowledge workers.

INFORMATION WORK AND PRODUCTIVITY

We have entered the information economy, where more than half the GNP is allocated to handling information—an economy that is populated by information workers who represent more than half the labor force. Overall productivity (in 1972 dollars) in the private business economy declined during 1978-1980 and, indeed, has been declining since the mid-1960s (Packer, 1983; Tersine and Price, 1982). Yet productivity is far lower in white collar jobs than in blue collar jobs. The typical figures cited in the literature are that blue collar productivity grew 90% while white collar productivity grew only 4% during the 1960s (though those figures are over a decade old). To begin to improve office productivity, the activities performed and technologies used in organizations must be appropriate for information work. Notions of productivity and ways of measuring productivity need to be appropriate as well. Several authors have begun to outline how to go about this (Bair, 1978, 1980; Business Week, 1982; Culnan and Bair, 1983; Downs and Hain, 1982; Goldfield, 1983; National Bureau of Standards, 1980; Packer, 1983; Patrick, 1980; Strassman, 1976; Tuttle, 1982).

The reasons for this shift in conceptualizing productivity is that information work differs from material-based work (Giuliano, 1982; Paisley, 1980). Information does not itself behave like physical inputs or outputs. Constrained only by the physical markers used to transport its symbolic content, information can be diffused over time and space in ways that material products can never be. On the one hand, its utility may expand the more that it is used by more people; on the other, it may lose all worth when other people obtain it. The quality and timeliness of information may be critical to its use; yet quality may be largely subjective and determined separately by the producer and the user. Overabundance may sap the scarce resource of managerial attention (Simon, 1973). More *efficient* dissemination of information that is incorrect or unneeded will clearly harm the effectiveness of an organization. That is, the *effectiveness* or *outcome* of many information activities is more crucial than its *efficiency*.

As discussed in Chapter 3, use of information by managers may be heavily political and symbolic (Feldman and March, 1981), creating apparent inefficiencies and unjustified costs for the organization as a whole (such as mandating continual information searches or warehousing information for possible justifications) while increasing the status and survivability of a given department. Information use and obstacles may appear quite rational for an organization while appearing quite irrational for a client or customer (Singer, 1980). Organizations may die if they fail to reduce the amount of information that must be processed or fail to increase internal processing capability (Galbraith, 1977). Handling information—filtering, abstracting, storing, retrieving, evaluating it (especially in unstructured situations), deciding how and when to perform information processing tasks, avoiding overload—is a primary process of information workers, yet this means different things, and has different consequences, to different organizational members.

Interpersonal communication of this information is another important component of organizational activity. Communication effectiveness is related to organizational effectiveness. Communication is a fundamental activity in organizations. Studies have clearly shown that researchers' productivity is correlated with more communication within and between work teams and other groups (Allen, 1977; Kerr and Hiltz, 1982; O'Reilly, 1977; Paisley, 1980; Pelz and Andrews, 1976), although increased communication may also lead to information overload or divert work unit members from their tasks.[1]

Many aspects of organizational communication seem to be crucial to improved productivity, and are either essential components to office automation or are likely to be strongly affected by automation—or both. These communication aspects include: purpose of communication, the medium or channel used, timing, organizational communication structure and norms, group and organizational networks, supervisor-subordinate relations, the emphasis on task-related as opposed to more or less socioemotional content, and the like. "Ineffective communication is not the major cause of America's productivity crisis, but effective communication is a major requirement for implementing solutions" (Downs and Hain, 1982: 452). Indeed, of the top eighteen office activities (elicited from on-site interviews) that were perceived by managers as facilitating productivity improvement, eleven were specifically communication related (Culnan and Bair, 1983). The highest-rated need was providing remote information access and retrieval; the ninth was supporting composition; the eighteenth was reducing time for making written records of communication.

Finally, emphasizing a point now quite obvious in the literature on information work and the products of knowledge workers, the *outputs* of such work are often quite intangible. a "good" decision may involve weeks of reading, talking, thinking, near-random contacts, and blind alleys. In output form, it may not even appear in a report or on a memo. Yet it may save a company or motivate a group. On the other hand, countless thick, tangible aspects costing considerable time, energy, and money sit on shelves gathering dust.

PRODUCTIVITY BENEFITS OF OFFICE AUTOMATION

This brief discussion of information and communication in organizational work readily generates a list of potential productivity benefits of office communication technologies or office automation. We can conceptualize these potential benefits in terms of five areas. (Needless to say, outcomes in any of these areas may not necessarily be productive; they represent areas for possible benefits).

The first two areas are crucial components of any cybernetic communication system, such as an organization.

(1) Control: requiring less information to perform a task, better planning, providing a more effective response.

(2) Timing: reduced waiting time for a meeting to commence or for another department to respond to an inquiry; reduced time spent in decision making, initiating action, or responding to the environment; increased flexibility of work schedule. Uhlig, Farber, and Bair (1979: Chap. 3) elaborate on the role of these components of a cybernetic communication system in improving productivity. The other three areas involve the form, transformation, and by-products of communication activities.

(3) Automation: the replacement or elimination of manual processes, such as constant revision of mailing lists, that do not contribute to increased effectiveness (because perhaps the material shouldn't be sent out to the mailing list in the first place).

(4) Media transformations: time, energy, and errors in transferring information from one medium to another may be reduced. For example, a company memo may pass through many media—oral, tape, typewritten, handwritten, revision, typewritten final, photocopies, and mail—before the content is entered into someone's calendar.

(5) Shadow functions: unforeseen, unpredictable, time-consuming activities that are associated with accomplishing any task, but do not contribute to productivity, include telephone tag and unsuccessful attempts to retrieve information from a personal file. For example, Table 8.1 suggests that the real costs of a successful telephone call are considerably greater than the actual telephone charges (Hirschberg, Bossaller, Kerns, Dugan, Sargent, Feltman, Wiseman, and Dutton, 1982, citing an International Resource Development report).

TABLE 8.1 Costs of Telephone Tag

Outcome	Percentage of Calls	Length (minutes)	Labor $	Phone $	Total Cost 100 Calls
No answer	5	1.0	.27	.00	1.35
Answering machine	2	1.5	.40	.65	2.10
Out	20	2.0	.51	.65	23.20
Lunch	18	1.5	.40	.65	18.90
Meeting	20	2.0	.51	.65	23.20
On phone	15	2.5	.62	.91	22.95
Not available	7	1.5	.40	.65	7.35
Put on hold	3	12.5	2.82	2.92	17.22
Reach party	10	10.0	2.27	2.37	46.10

Real cost of each successful call on average: Phone cost = $8.97
                                                  Total cost = $16.24

SOURCE: Hirschberg et al., 1982, adapted from International Resource Development report.

ORGANIZATIONAL USE OF ELECTRONIC MESSAGING:
BENEFITS AND COSTS

This section considers the new organizational medium of electronic mail in light of the kinds of potential productivity benefits discussed above, provides an overview of the benefits of electronic mail in the context of similar and competing services, and summarizes some cost information for productivity assessment.

The use of the term "electronic mail" may be a bit misleading. That is, the term really encompasses far more than the sending and sharing of text files in computer-mediated communication systems. Consider that the first form of electronic mail was the telegraph, demonstrated in 1844, and still transmitting 45 million messages in 1979. However, nearly a quarter trillion telephone messages, 57 trillion first class mail messages, and 25 trillion intracompany letter mail messages were distributed in the same year (EMMS, 1979). Panko (1984) provides a comprehensive summary of the varieties of electronic mail, along with an estimated number of messages sent in the United States in 1979. (Figures from 1978 are available in EMMS [1979] for trend comparisons.)

Facsimile (350 million messages in 1979) is currently the most popular form of electronic mail and typically uses regular telephone lines. Several companies now offer private fax networks with store and forward capabilities. Recent developments in digital transmission will allow exchanges of photographic quality images in seconds, or remote copying, as well as integration of fax with video conferencing and teletext (Posa, 1983). Facsimile thus leads the way into "image processing."

TWX is in wide use in the United States and Canada, but European standards make *Telex* the dominant form outside North America. Telex is a point-to-point, dial-up telegraph service without "intelligence" in the system; i.e., it is primarily a transmission tool, although International Telephone and Telegraph's OMNI VI offers many processing capabilities. Their combined messages were 128 million. *Private teletypewriters* and networks distributed 100 million messages in 1979, and often are part of transaction-oriented data-processing systems, though they are typically limited to terminal-to-terminal transmission.

Teletex is a higher level of service than Telex, as the International Telecommunications Union adopted a standard in 1980 that includes a 2400 bits per second, message-switched store and forward service with broadcast (i.e., multiple recipient) capabilities. Teletex is a significant component of office automation plans in Germany, as it allows communication between office components and interorganizational networks.

The U.S. Postal Service, (USPS) is slowly moving into the area of electronic mail, with *Mailgram* (40 million messages), a joint venture with Western Union, which uses Telex to transmit messages to selected post offices that print and mail messages. *ECOM* (electronic computer-originated mail) takes advantage of batch electronic input from companies, although there are severe format restrictions (still, over 172 thousand ECOM messages were sent in one week in July 1982 [Office of Technology

Assessment, 1982]). The USPS's new Electronic Message Service System (*EMSS*) is much more flexible, and is creating some concern in the private industry.

Communicating word processors sent over 200 million messages in 1979, typically via Telex lines. The more advanced systems, some using centralized message controllers, take care of all aspects of addressing, communicating, and delivery once the file destination is given. *Voice mail* (one million messages) provides editing, indexing, store and forward, and distribution facilities for handling aural/oral content. This recent medium may develop into the messaging service of choice within organizations, particularly for managers who typically prefer talking over writing.

Electronic Messaging: Benefits

Computer-mediated exchange of text—in which computer capabilities are involved in processing the message rather than just transmitting it— constituted 66 million messages on commercial systems in 1979. Hewlett-Packard's private electronic messaging service generated 25 million messages a year worldwide (Panko, 1984). Projections by the Yankee Group call for a rise in the number of service "mailboxes" (formal accounts on commercial services using electronic messaging) from 49,000 in 1981 to 392,000 in 1983 and 882,000 in 1984 (Burstyn, 1983). Comparable figures for private mailboxes (corporate systems) are 80,000, 225,000, and 680,000, indicating a shift to greater use in a service environment after 1983. These figures do not include the rapidly growing use of personal messaging on The Source, CompuServe, or microcomputer networks (estimated number of mailboxes: 77,000 [Sandler, 1983]).

The general notion of computer-mediated communication (CMC) was described in Chapter 6. Electronic messaging allows the creation, editing, sending, receiving, storage, forwarding, and printing of text—all facilitated by the computer. Integration with the computer-file system, command recognition and spelling correction, the ability to request a return receipt, and a reliable computer system, along with a screen-based editor, variable levels of sophistication, general simplicity, good documentation, and related nonmail options, such as calendar or tickler files, have been listed as important or desirable by users (McQuillan and Walden, 1980).

Because of the processing capabilities of the computers, and the interconnections facilitated by telecommunications networks, many commercial messaging systems are marketed (and used) in integrated ways. Computer Corporation of America's COMET integrates with word processing; General Electric's Quik-Comm integrates with data processing; Dialcom's service is viewed as part of an integrated management system; The Source's Sourcemail provides access to diverse information sources. Special features possible include security programming, voice and text integration, spelling checks, automatic report generation, interconnection with other media and networks, managerial calendars, auto dial-out, delayed mailing, prioritizing and filtering of messages, graphics generation, file purging, cancellation of previously sent messages, and even general delivery service (such as MCI's new MCIMAIL).

A particularly innovative application is "Intelligent Electronic Communications," whereby electronic messaging is integrated with relational data bases and executable computer programs. Messages can be sent to a software *function*, which, upon receipt of a message with proper formatting, processes the message as a command with *variables*. Thus, a field report update could automatically generate payroll, inventory, billing, and scheduling processes while entering a progress report maintained as a data base.

It should be apparent by now that electronic messaging has many potential benefits (and some disadvantages) for information work, many of which are listed below.

- permanent, searchable record
- no simultaneous activity necessary
- less meeting scheduling—or meetings
- control over timing and preparation of response
- freedom from geographical constraints—including time zones
- no interruptions
- fast delivery (if recipient logs on)
- automatic headers and message information
- easy reply, further distribution ("carbon copies")
- increased contacts (although possible overload)
- rapid responses (with possible misunderstandings)
- more upward and diagonal organizational communication (possibly by passing approved channels)
- substitution for some other media, under some conditions
- potential for reduction in travel (though possibly generating more travel)
- medium for creation, transmission, and receipt are the same
- fewer nonverbal constraints (though possibility of disinhibition)
- one action (possibly automatic) for multiple distribution (though perhaps before content is ready, and perhaps lacking relevant context for all receivers)
- information search not limited by *known* contacts
- communication can develop around timely or common interests (perhaps reducing chances of "new" topics)

Electronic Messaging: Costs

These potential—or even actual—benefits of electronic messaging must be placed in a multidimensional context before they can be converted into claims of increased productivity. First, for interorganizational messaging, standards must be established and regulatory issues must be negotiated (particularly for international communication). These standards include designs and formats for usage, addressing and delivery, the message itself, and the transmitting networks (Panko, 1981a). Second, the benefits must contribute not only to individual users, but also to the goals of the organization, as discussed below. Third, the costs of such services must be justifiable.

The third point is no less difficult than the preceding two. Many factors are involved: operators and maintenance, transmission and storage, terminals, training, users' time spent in composing and sending, receiving and reading, costs of the software or service or licensing. For example, the National Archives and Record Service (1981) found that one of the five systems they studied generated $1960/month in computer storage costs for electronic mail files. The report concluded that, in addition to a lack of baseline comparative data or even a sufficient conceptualization of the need for and use of office automation in federal agencies, "it appears that current office automation efforts have often led to increased costs with limited tangible benefits"(p.5).

King and Kraemer (1981) postulate that information technologies generate both organizational and social costs far beyond what is commonly estimated and that the decentralizing influences the new telecommunications technologies are likely to have on the world of information use and management will exacerbate what is already nearly uncontrolled growth in costs from these technologies. For example, according to the authors, the costs of computing are typically 20% higher than they are usually estimated to be.

Several attempts have been made to specify electronic messaging costs. Montgomery and Benbasat (1983), assuming $150/month for subscription to COMET, $60/month for service, and $90/month for terminal rental, concluded that for a $50,000/year managerial salary (plus 30% overhead), only 12.5 minutes/day needed to be saved in order to cost-justify the service. Crawford (1982) analyzed a variety of cost components for organizational communication, including labor, shadow costs, materials, communications facilities, system use, peripherals, and access. Total cost for a phone call was $4.31; for an electronic message entered and sent by the originator, $4.70; for an electronic message entered and sent by support staff for the originator, $6.70; and for an interoffice memo, $7.60.

Panko's (1981b) cost analysis is the most thorough to date. He suggests that there are cost opportunities in *handling* messages—at $30/hour, the cost of managerial time spent writing is nearly $60 (see Table 8.3 below)—and *transmitting* messages—the sending and receiving costs of a business letter are about $15. Based on actual costs in 1977 of two systems, with adjustments for up-to-date hardware, continuing reductions in communications costs, and operator and transmission costs, Panko suggests that the cost per message (assuming three per day) for two extant systems would drop from $1.34-$6.72 in 1977 to $.07-$.27 in 1985. Adding in terminal costs, the costs per message in 1985 (assuming five per day) would range from $.17 to $.27. Panko offers $.25 to $.50 in a later paper (1983). These figures do not include software, training or local communication costs.

Table 8.2 summarizes costs of the major commercial electronic messaging services (Hirschberg et al., 1982).[2] Not included in these cost figures are hardware, labor, or operator support; these are all assumed to be sunk costs and in place before the service is implemented. Investigation of the table shows that some services are more cost-effective for certain kinds of messaging activity. For example, Quik-Comm is more cost-effective for single copies and short messages; Dialcom and Sourcemail have declining unit storage costs; and Infoplex puts all cost burdens on the message.

Comparing electronic messaging to the more traditional services, it can be shown that Telex is not as cost-efficient for multiple messages; Fax has lower message unit costs at higher transmission rates, but this requires the more expensive "Group Two" and "Group Three" machines; telephone costs are distance-sensitive and of course provide no written record; the USPS is weight-sensitive and has long delivery time; further, most traditional "mail" services cannot provide processing capabilities—only transmission.

The implication of these analyses is that productivity benefits—in terms of quality, effectiveness, and value-added output—provide the rationales for using messaging systems, as strict cost comparisons show relatively similar orders of magnitude among media at this time.

LOCATING PRODUCTIVITY IMPACTS: A MODEL OF ORGANIZATIONAL COMMUNICATION PERFORMANCE

So far we have emphasized that the welter of productivity conceptualization and measures are, as yet, not sufficient for understanding the potential productivity impacts of office automation. We have noted some aspects of two components of organizational information work: information and communication. Using the example of electronic mail, we have briefly mentioned some of the potential benefits of office automation for information work, and located five areas for communication benefits. The cost benefits for electronic messaging are not, as yet, overwhelming, unless criteria more relevant to knowledge work are also considered.

We have, thus, introduced some of the concepts and variables needed to understand and measure information productivity. Finally, we need a model to provide the context of organizational information work: what goes on in information work. Paisley (1980) provides a comprehensive review and analysis of the more cognitive aspects of information work; we here provide a model of behavioral communication performance. This model will aid in using the concepts above to locate behaviors—organizational performance—that may be appropriate contexts for analyses of information work and changes in its productivity. Finally, a review of office automation productivity benefits will be structured according to this model.

TABLE 8.2 Cost Analysis Matrix (EM Systems)

Costs					SYSTEMS				
	CCA's COMET	GFISCO's Quik-Comm	Dialcom	Telenet's Telemail	Compuserve's Infoplex	Ontyme	BBN's Infomail	Source	Notice
Initial account charge		$500		$100	$500 (includes training)		DEC or VAX UMS: $30,000	$100.00	(SRU=44¢ fee standard user, or 30¢ on discounted volume rate)
Software/ License fee	DEC: 40,000 (includes installation, documentation & 1 user-training class) IBM: 60,000 (includes installation, documentation, class)					$80-100,000	IBM VM/CHS: $50-70,000		
Documentation	(included above)		$30.00		(included in initial acct.)				
User training	(included above)		$100-200						
Maintenance	DEC soft. fees:450/month IBM soft. fees: 750/month							$1.00/acct.	

(Continued)

Table 8.2 Continued

Costs		CCA's COMET	GFISCO's Quik-Comm	Dialcom	Telenet's Telemail	Compuserve's Infoplex	Ontyme	BBN's Infomail	Source	Notice
						SYSTEMS				
Monthly fee for standard usage		$100/organ. +60/indiv. user (includes 9 hrs connect time & 500 stored messages)			None	None	$200			
Minimum monthly fee		None		$100	None	$2,000 (or 2,500 w/filing system after 4 month period)	$500		$9/Acct./Month	$250/subscriber organization
Common carrier (phone) lines included?		Not included	Not included	No	Not included	Not included (but 50% discount on all rates if use GTE WATS line)				
Connect time		$7/ hour	0 (costs based on activities or functions performed) $.10/hr (prime time) $.05/hr. (non-prime time)	$6-$8.00/hr. (prime time) $4.00/hr. (non-prime time)	$14/hr. (business hrs.) $7/ hr. (non-peak hrs.) $4/hr (night hrs.)		$3.40/hr. high density areas $6.00/hr. low density areas		$20.75 (prime) $300 baud $25.75 (prime) 1200 baud $7.75 (weekends, evenings, holidays) 300 baud $10.75 (weekends, evenings, holidays)	$16.50/hr. (average (prime time) $.05/hr. (non prime time)

	(1)	(2)	(3)	(4)	(5)	(6)	(7)
Log on fee	None	$.50 to log on	1200 baud $5.75 (non prime) 300 baud $8.75 (non prime) 1200 baud				
Log off fee							
Composing fee		$.09/line	2 SRU's	None			
Cost for multiple copies		Basic .40 + .02 per line	1 SRU ½ SRU per line (CL) .25 (7/10 Sru)		.40/600 chars.		
Forward/send				No charge for first	.20/(+ .15 per 600 chars.) .40/600 chars. .40/600 chars.	.04/1000 chars.	
Editing fee		No charge					
Use file for further processing		No charge					
Transfer charge to storage				.05/message	.05/message	.10-.15/message (.03/1000 chars.)	
Storage charge	.02 per message per month (after standard 500 messages)	2.00 per month per user acct.	0-2500 units = .40 over 10,000 units = .10 (unit = 2048 chars.) (so, cheaper with more use)	.01/day per 2000 chars. (No charge 1st 3 days)	.02 per 600 chars. (after 3 days)	.03 per 1000 chars. (14 days free)	1-10 blks-.50/mo. per blk 11-99 blks.-.20/mo per blk. 100-999 blks.-.15/mo. per blk. 1000-9999 blks.- .10/mo. per blk. 10,000-99,999 blks.- .05/mo. per blk.

Table 8.2 Continued

| | | | | | SYSTEMS | | | | |
Costs	CCA's COMET	GFISCO's Quik-Comm	Dialcom	Telenet's Telemail	Compuserve's Infoplex	Ontyme	BBN's Infomail	Source	Notice
Store/ Confidential					.25+ .25/600 chars.				
Store/ Priority					.25+ .25/600 chars.				
Printing			.05 per page						
Discount available w/volume	Yes. Over 25 mailboxes. pay 1 fee based on # of boxes. Then, monthly costs $20 per box per month		Yes. 0-15,000 fees no discount 15-20,000 fees 5% dis. Over 20,000 fees 10% dis.	Yes	Yes. $10,000/ mo.=10% 25,000/ mo=15% dis. 40,000/mo & over=20% discount	Yes		No	
Pilot program offered			Yes, but no discount		Yes				
File					.40 per text file (or .20 per 600 chars.)				
Display					.15 per text file (or 600 chars.)				
Delete/Cancel messages		5.00/ message			$3.00 per text file				

Check status of messages	.03/line		
Scan messages	.03/line	.10/text file	2.3 SRUs ($^1/_{10}$ SRU per line)
Retrieve messages		No charge	.03/1000 chars.
Broadcast delivery		.05/ addressee	
Define a group	5.00/group		2 SRUs
Add/delete user (Admin. functions)	10.00/first time 2.50/ after	40.00/con- nect hr.	

SOURCE: Hirschberg et al. (1982).

The model of organizational communication performance is one level of a four-level model of information work performance.

(1)   Equipment performance—includes error rate, percent of manufacturer's specifications, reliability, response time, overload threshold, features, cost per unit, and the like.

(2)   Throughput performance—includes the interaction of operators and equipment, such as how individual worker differences are facilitated or constrained by the equipment (and vice versa), work flow, learning rates, effects of variances in input and output, cost per unit processed, resources required for maintaining man-machine interaction maintenance communication.

(3)   Organizational performance—discussed below.

(4)   Institutional performance—includes organizational-environment interactions such as economic conditions, labor costs, competitions, resource inputs and dependencies, total productivity, seasonal variations, vendor resources.

Any measurement of information work productivity and the impacts of office automation would naturally consider all four levels of performance. Further, an in-depth analysis would have to consider the interactions among the levels. For example, if regulatory changes allow more vendors to offer equipment with incompatible standards, an organization's ability to network information work internally may be reduced, or the organization may be less competitive with respect to multinational organizations that own their own private networks. The remainder of this chapter concentrates on level 3—organizational communication performance.

A Hierarchy of Organizational Communication Performance

We suggest that organizational performance occurs, and may be measured, at six levels: mission, purpose, function, process, activity, and action. This hierarchy provides a tentative framework for making sense of the difficult concept of knowledge worker productivity, by identifying possible interactions among variables and across performance levels. Figure 8.1 summarizes these levels.

(1) The *mission* of the organization is what organizational members perceive as "the business" of the organization. This is not straightforward. For stockholders, the mission may be to increase dividends; for a clerical worker, it may be unknown. In terms of criteria for beneficial impacts of office automation, corporate stockholders may emphasize short-term return on investment, perhaps through labor reduction or better dissemination of research results, while the marketing department may emphasize how new technology mirrors the innovative culture of the organization. If corporate policy maintains a narrow and industrial definition of productivity, the "mission" of the organization may appear to be in conflict with the introduction of office automation.

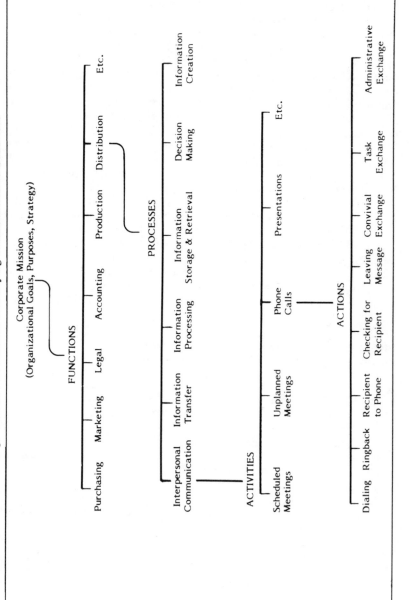

FIGURE 8.1 Model of Organization Performance Identifying Communication Behaviors

Corporate Mission
(Organizational Goals, Purposes, Strategy)

FUNCTIONS

Purchasing   Marketing   Legal   Accounting   Production   Distribution   Etc.

PROCESSES

Information   Information   Information   Decision   Information
Transfer   Processing   Storage & Retrieval   Making   Creation

ACTIVITIES

Interpersonal Communication

Scheduled   Unplanned   Phone   Presentations   Etc.
Meetings   Meetings   Calls

ACTIONS

Dialing   Ringback   Recipient   Checking for   Leaving   Convivial   Task   Administrative
          to Phone   Recipient   Message   Exchange   Exchange   Exchange

(2) Organizational *purpose* represents decisions to focus corporate resources, and includes what are commonly known as organizational goals—strategic targets for accomplishment of mission. Figure 8.1 shows purpose subsumed under mission, as they are often difficult to separate operationally. An example of an organizational purpose is to reduce operating expenses and overhead; an inventory control system providing instant updating and ordering (such as at Sears) can have impacts deemed beneficial for this goal. The goal of reducing customer turnover through improved quality of service may be obtained by the same information system, but the impacts would be measured in very different and longer-term ways.

(3) *Functions* include the traditional division of labor within an organization (such as accounting, purchasing, and planning). Within an organizational function, the information that is processed and communicated may be relatively homogeneous and sequential. Quick, isolated, and cryptic electronic messages may improve the productivity of this function. However, organizational structure may be redesigned around products instead of functions. For example, a matrix organization may pull together persons with complementary skills into a temporary organizational structure. Particularly in consulting or research organizations, coordination of information and communication is crucial in this organizational form. Separate computer conferences for ongoing projects would allow group members to stay updated, but would require attention only from participants, who could retrieve information for performance assessment by project code or time period. Without a formally instituted documentation process, as might exist in a function, a product group might maintain online, ongoing documentation as a by-product of the work.

(4) *Processes* define the form of organizational behavior, while the higher levels describe the content of organizational behavior. Processes are the means for achieving the missions, purposes, and functions of an organization. Differences across organizations affect the nature of processes and, thus, the media used. For example, some companies (perhaps due to their environment, corporate philosophies, or nature of their business) are more oriented toward meetings, and others to telephones. Different organizations foster different norms for information sharing, leading to variations in media use (Dewhirst, 1971).

Information work processes include information creation, processing, storage, retrieval, and transfer; decision making and problem solving; interpersonal communication, and the like. Processes tend to be dynamic, ongoing behaviors, yet may be quite structured, depending on the organization. Some processes may be repetitious, while others have a "life cycle." For example, a report, from its inception to final use, has a life cycle involving many people, revisions, and media. Office automation may facilitate the process, perhaps by removing some of the repetitive steps. Other processes occur in the form of human communication networks. The recurring patterns of relations provide a structure through which information dynamically flows.

(5) *Activities* are the observable behaviors that comprise each process. For example, the process of interpersonal communication may include activities such as unplanned meetings, using various media for communication interactions, presentations, negotiating, interviewing, supervising, and relaying orders. These activities are specific, measurable behaviors. For example, the time and money spent in attending regional meetings may be directly compared with the same for teleconferences. Other important components of attending meeting—such as satisfaction, quality of decision, increased contacts, and the like—can also be measured, although perhaps more subjectively.

This example also highlights an important aspect of this model: Different activities may accomplish the same process (just as different processes may support the same function, and different functions may support the same purpose and mission). Thus, office automation impacts may show up in reduced media transformations, more control, fewer interruptions, when a set of activities is transferred to or integrated in, one information system. Such potential benefits, of course, are subject to constraints such as advantages of some activities over others (there are personal benefits to travel), attributes of different activities (such as easy accessibility of and familiarity with the telephone compared to a terminal down the hall), and differences in activities across organizational roles and levels.

(5A) Intraorganizational communication activities. Such differences in activities across organizational roles and levels are, we believe, a crucial element in assessing the appropriateness, and likelihood of productivity improvements, of CMC systems. There are several reasons for this belief.

The first reason is due to the nature of managerial processes and activities. These tend to be less structured, more informal, more diverse, and higher in uncertainty for upper management than for staff managers and specialists. Intuition and politics, as well as a reliance on nonverbal affect cues, are important in managerial communication along with negotiating, getting to know contacts, creating a corporate image, and discussing confidential information (Downs and Hain, 1982; Kotter, 1982; Newman, 1981; Rice and Case, 1983). "Middle management . . . calls for the ability to shape and utilize the person-to-person channel of communication, to influence, persuade, facilitate" (Volard and Davies, 1982). One study of organizational communication training needs showed that the primary communication difficulty reported by supervisors involved the crucial task of listening. Computer-mediated communication systems are less likely to be appropriate for these kinds of tasks than are more traditional channels (see Chapter 3).

The second reason is that managers differ among themselves according to activity styles: some are emissaries, writers, discussers, troubleshooters, committee persons (Stewart, 1976). So, while CMC systems may aid some, they are not likely to aid all managers even in the bulk of their activities. Therefore, office automation may have greater productivity benefits for the more clerical and transactional processes (or for interorganizational information exchange) and less so for more managerial processes. This different potentiality for application must be weighed against the fact that a single manager costs the organization more than a single clerical worker, so a greater payoff in terms of an organizational purpose of decreased labor costs is likely to come from increased augmentation of managerial information work (Bair, 1979).

The third reason follows from descriptions of how managers actually do allocate their time, particularly with respect to communication activities. Table 8.3 summarizes many of the studies of managerial time allocation.

The gross conclusion from these studies is that, indeed, managers spend most of their time communicating (about 75%-80%) and most of that time in oral communication (about 60% face-to-face within dyadic discussions or in meetings, or via the telephone). Another conclusion— not surprising—is that secretarial and clerical workers spend considerably less time communicating, and the bulk of that in reading and writing. Scientific and technical workers fall somewhere in between.

(5B) Interorganizational communication activities. An analysis of communication activities should also include cross-organizational media use, because CMC systems may play a role in improving productivity involving interorganizational relations. Picot, Klingenberg, and Kranzle (1982) studied four German suborganizations in two large companies involving 30 locations with 640 principals and 150 secretaries. The authors found that as the direction of communication went from intra- to inter- to extraorganizational, the percentage of communications spent in phone usage varied (22%, 53%, 46%), face-to-face usage decreased (73%, 28%, 11%), mail increased (5%, 15%, 32%), and Telex also increased (0%, 3%, 10%). Another European study (Dormois, Fioux, and Gensollen, 1978) aggregated data over 60 organizations to find 47% of interorganization communication by mail, 46% by telephone, 7% face-to-face, and 1% by Telex. Of particular interest, respondents claimed that over one-third of the calls required a written follow-up, while over two-thirds of the letters and Telex were sent to authenticate a telephone call. That is, uses of some media have attributes that lead to additional use of other media. Steinfield's (1983) analysis of 220 CMC users and 176 nonusers, found 55% of their average monthly communications with members of other companies was by telephone, 12% by memo, and 15% by face-to-face.

Thiessen's (1978) study of 26 Kansas organizations summarizes the usage of 11 different media (including closed circuit TV and WATS lines) by five types of organizations, and describes the kinds of difficulties experienced with each medium. For example, written media may require additional drafts because of lack of initial clarity, or may duplicate other information; difficulties with oral media include the unavailability of the individual called, and the marring of instructions by bad telephone connections or verbal ambiguities. Other research shows that private organizations tend to use more face-to-face and technical literature than do public organizations (Volard and Davies, 1982), and that different academic departments may rank their usage of media very differently (COST, 1980).

TABLE 8.3 Percentage Allocation of Managers' and Professionals' Working Day to Communication Activities

| | COMMUNICATION CHANNEL | | | | |
| | Oral | | | Written | |
Source and Sample Notes	FTP[a]	Phone	Reading		Writing[b]
Advanced Systems (1981) N = 30	42	36		—22—	
Booz et al., cited in Panko and Sprague (1982); Poppel (1982) N=300; 90,000 time samples	26	20	8		13
Burns (1954) N=76 managers	—52—			—24—	
Brewer and Tomlinson (1964) N=6 Managers	meetings=37 discussion=14	6	13		17
Carter (1980)[c]	meetings=27 discussion=29	11	8		15
Case Institute (1958) N=1500 Chemists	—40—			mail=9 —29—	
Conrath (1973b) N=115 Managers 4086 events	66	13		—21—	

(Continued)

Table 8.3 Continued

Source and Sample Notes	COMMUNICATION CHANNEL			
	Oral		Written	
	FTF[a]	Phone	Reading	Writing[b]
Coulter and Hayo (1978)	51.6	18	—6.8—	
Croston and Goulding (1967) N=6 Managers	56	7	—18—	
Dubin and Spray (1964) N=8 Managers	55	6	—5—	
Ganz and Peacock (1981) managers and professionals	—23—		—47—	
Goetzinger and Valentine (1962) N=40 faculty and staff	40	37	11	12
Hinrichs (1964) N=58 supervisors	49	8	10	14
N=20 technical	27	6	11	16
Horne and Lupton(1965) N=66 managers	54	9	10	14
Klemmer and Snyder (1972) N=3132 observed events	35	7	12	14[d]
N=2626 reported events scientists and engineers	20	8	20	22[d]
Lowenstein (1978); Engel et al.		R	R&W[c]	W	T

(1980)						
N=396 managers[g]	27	16	11	18	11	—
N=1066 managers[g]	27	10	11	18	12	—
N=1074 managers	14	12	7	21	16	4
N=297 managers[h]	14	4	10	19	11	10
N=363 secretaries[i]	5	9	4	40	3	29
Mintzberg (1973)						
N=5 managers	64	6			—20—	
Olson (1982)						
N=6 d.p. managers	48	9			—?—	
Palmer and Beishon (1970)						
N=1 manager	54	6			—15—	
Ruchinskas (1982)						
N=795 exempt employees	27	15		17		
Steinfield (1981)						
N=357 supervisors						
receiving	78	3			—6—	
transmitting	59	4			—14—	
Steinfield (1983)						
N=220 CMC users	19[j]	7		15		manual=6 computer = 20[k]
N=176 nonusers	19	14		13		CMC=10 manual = 16 computer=9
Stewart (1967)						
N=160 managers	44	6			—36—	

(Continued)

Table 8.3 Continued

Source and Sample Notes	COMMUNICATION CHANNEL			
	Oral		Written	
	FTP[a]	Phone	Reading	Writing[b]
Talbott et al. (1982) N=20 managers				
observation	meetings=34 other[c]=25	7	4	8
questionnaire	meetings=28 other[c]=13	5	9	16
Volard and Davies (1982)	61	6	—21—	
Wofford et al. (1977) averaged 10 studies	—72—		—?—	
Xerox[m] Panko and Sprague (1982) N=17,000	18	5	—47—	

NOTE: Data were collected by a variety of means (observations, self-report questionnaires, event-driven diaries, time-sampling diaries, etc.) for different durations (one time, up to two months) and therefore are not conceptually similar across studies. However, most studies using multiple data collection methods report good correspondences between observational data and self-report data on *overall* time spent communicating (Goetzinger and Valentine, 1962; Hinrichs, 1964; Klemmer and Snyder, 1972; Roberts and O'Reilly, 1974). However, several studies found that allocations to specific *channels* showed discrepancies. Typically these involved overestimates of time spent writing or phoning and underestimation of time spent in face-to-face contact (Dahl and Lewis, 1975; Hinrichs, 1964, 1976; Kay and Meyer, 1962; Klemmer and Snyder, 1972). The most comprehensive analysis of such comparisons, based upon an average of 603 observations of each of 36 office workers, as well as task identifications, task sorting, and time estimation, concluded that subjects can reliably identify which tasks they perform, only moderately well rank each task according to the time spent in each task, and are not reliably able to estimate specific amounts of time allocated to each task (Hartley, Brecht, Pagerey, Weeks, Chapanis, and Hoecker, 1977).

a. Primarily meetings; also informal discussions, conferring with working partners, etc.
b. Includes general document preparation.
c. Carter's figures are weighted averages of figures from Brewer and Tomlinson, 1964; Burns, 1954; Carlson, 1951; Copeman, Luijk and de P. Hanika, 1963; Dubin and Spray, 1964; Horne and Lupton, 1965; Lawler, Porter, and Tennenbaum, 1968; Sproull, 1977; Stewart, 1967; and Stogdill and Shartle, 1955.
d. Data analysis and programming included.
e. That is, searching, filing, dictating, proofing, copying, record-keeping, and mail handling.
f. Use of terminal, or typing.
g. Organization was meeting-oriented.
h. Used interactive computing.
i. From same organization as N=1066 managers; other three secretarial samples included in sources.
j. Management=28%.
k. Management=12%.
l. Supervising, training, consulting, coordinating, information-gathering.
m. Same organization as reported in Steinfield (1983); note similarly low FTF figures.

The implication of these interorganizational media usage studies is that there is considerable potential for the use of CMC systems *between* organizations. This potential is due to two reasons. First, more of cross-organizational communication is transmitted by text or telephone, rather than face-to-face. The kinds of content and communication exchanged by text or sound are more easily transmitted by CMC systems than are face-to-face communication contents. Second, interorganizational communications seem to require (or generate) the use of complementary media for successful exchanges. CMC systems may provide the marginal capabilities needed to satisfy such needs.

(6) *Actions* constitute the sequential stages in performing activities. For example, making phone calls involves finding the number, dialing, encountering busy signals or wrong numbers, having the target person called to the phone (or giving a short message and verifying its content), exchanging social or task communication, recording, and following-up the conversation. Many actions are shadow functions, which have cost. As shown in Table 8.1 these shadow costs may be estimated and averaged over a managerial day, just as the costs of preparing letters can be, in order to compare with as opposed to sending costs for alternate media, such as electronic messaging.

It is at this stage that strict labor-saving benefits (in the sense of reducing time spent in performing activities) of office automation can easily be understood. Because of the ease with which system usage may be monitored (see Chapter 4) and because of the explicit nature of such productivity comparisons, much office automation planning concentrates on this level. For example, as described in the preceding chapter, the primary rationale for most organizations in adopting word processing is to reduce repetitive typing. This is laudable and, depending on the organization's productivity criteria, may justify word processing. However, this emphasis limits the scope of office automation application and may in fact solidify ineffective activities and processes; they may even inhibit the performance of organizational purposes and missions.

Such justifications may prevent the organization from using software that automates or reduces actions involved in the creation, revision, and organization of text (such as the UNIX system's Writer's Workbench; See Cherry, Fox, Frase, Gingrich, Keenan, and Macdonald, 1983). As the beginning of the chapter noted, it is necessary to avoid focusing solely on improvement in efficiency. However, if avoiding inefficient communication activities than frees organization members to apply their time and skills to more effective activities, then such improvements are crucial.

SUMMARY OF OFFICE AUTOMATION BENEFITS WITH RESPECT TO COMMUNICATION BEHAVIORS

This section summarizes the primary results from available field studies on office automation impacts, specifically those results concerning productivity and communication behaviors. Table 8.4 lists the studies and their key impacts; only the primary or key cost benefits explicitly cited by each study are noted, although there often were other explicit benefits and may have been other implicit, qualitative, or long-term benefits. Computer conferencing studies are not included, as they are considered in Chapter 6.

The following major positive findings are highlighted as a summary of those benefits that were common across many of the studies:

(1) Electronic mail capabilities increased asynchronous communication activity within functional groups and in superior-subordinate relations.

(2) Remote communications enabled executives to work outside the office during nontraditional work hours.

(3) Word processing reduced document preparation turnaround time.

(4) Office automation systems produced a daily time savings by reducing the number of clerical tasks per activity and reducing the number of clerical tasks per activity and reducing wasteful shadow functions.

(5) Users perceived a qualitative improvement of their work frequently in the form of greater control, improved communications, and greater access to information.

Some of the studies have sufficiently detailed information that their impacts can be categorized according to classes of communication activities and benefits.

(1) Reduced shadow functions—telephone calls (Bair, 1974; Bullen, Bennett, and Carlson, 1982; Edwards, 1978; Gardner, 1981; Rice and Case, 1983; Steinfield, 1983; Tapscott, 1982; Uhlig, Farber, and Bair, 1979).

(2) Reduced media transformations—handwritten to computer (Melton, 1981; National Archives and Records, 1981).

(3) Reduced tasks per job—retyping (Cramer and Fast, 1982; Crawford, 1982; Dahl, 1981; Dunlop et al., 1980; Edwards, 1978; EIU Informatics, 1982).

(4) Eliminating manual tasks—handling mail (Edwards, 1978; EIU Informatics, 1982; Tapscott, 1982).

(5) Increased speed of information creation and turnaround—composing documents (Bamford, 1978, 1979; Dahl 1981; Dunlop et al., 1980; Edwards, 1978; EIU Informatics, 1982; Gardner, 1981; Talbott, Savage, and Borko, 1982).

(6) Increased information control—reduced information float (EIU Informatics, 1982; Gardner, 1981; Mertes, 1981; Melton, 1981; Steinfield, 1983).

(7) Decreased time to process information—responding to requests (National Archives and Records, 1981).

(8) Decreased time to manage information—managing personal information (Gardner, 1981; Talbott et al., 1982).

(9) Increase in outputs—quantity of documents (majority of studies).

(10) Decreased cost per unit output—typesetting (Dahl, 1981; Dunlop et al., 1980; EIU Informatics, 1982).

TABLE 8.4 Key Productivity Impacts of Office Automation

Study Reference	Key Impact
Bair (1974)	Changes in communication patterns: decreased face-to-face contact and increased vertical communication
Bair (1980)	Reduction of telephone shadow costs
Bamford (1978,1979)	Decreased document turnaround time and increased document output
Bullen et al. (1982)	Improved work flow with time saved
Canning (1978)	Increased volume of communications
Conrath and Bair (1974)	Reduction in telephone and face-to-face; increased upward communication flows
Cramer and Fast (1982)	Considerable secretarial time saved
Crawford (1982)	Decline in menial, clerical tasks
Curley and Pyburn (1982)	Greater organizational productivity when seen as more than a way to increase secretarial output
Dahl (1981)	Annual cost savings and 8% increase in knowledge worker time
Dunlop et al. (1980)	Striking productivity gains from 50-100+ percent in document preparation
Edwards (1978)	Change in working mode based on ability to work at home
EIU Informatics (1982)	
Rank Xerox	Large reductions in telephone use, 1 hour/day labor saved for attorneys
German Computer Services	Joint information sharing and editing
British Dept. of Education and Science	50-100% productivity gains in word processing after 6 months
England—various organizations	Many sites did *not* reach cost-justifying wp productivity levels
British travel agents	Booking rose significantly
Scotland	WP output rose 150%
Engel et al. (1979)	5-25% knowledge worker and 15-35% secretarial time saved
Gardner (1981)	Decreased turnaround time in document preparation and scheduling
Gutek (1982)	More creative, challenging, complex, organized work

TABLE 8.4 Continued

Study Reference	Key Impact
Helmreich and Wimmer (1982)	High user acceptance
Leduc (1979)	Changes in communication patterns: ability to work at home and increased vertical communication
Lippitt et al. (1980) Miller and Nichols (1981)	Reduction in memos and phone calls
Melton (1981)	Improved communication and decreased information float
Mertes (1981)	Cost and time savings via central library
National Archives and Records (1981)	Concept, scope, and potential of office automation ill-defined in government
case-processing	Reduced backlogs, more timely and accurate reports
electronic messaging	Too few terminals—no benefits identified
optical character scanning	More cost-beneficial than word processing
Panko and Panko (1981)	Many perceived benefits—more for managers and professionals using system directly than for secretaries; highest benefit for long-distance communications
Rice and Case (1983)	Reduction in paper and telephone traffic; increased work quantity and quality; but depends on "media style"
Steinfield (1983)	More timely and accurate information, increased coordination
Steward (1983)	13% daily time saving; 35% increased document output
Talbot et al. (1982)	Less time in communication activities
Tapscott (1982)	Changes in communication patterns: decreased telephone usage and meetings
Tucker (1982)	Implementation failure primarily due to shortened initial analyses phase
Uhlig et al. (1979)	Reduction of telephone shadow costs

SUMMARY

In discussing the various levels of organizational performance, we emphasized that a specific concept of productivity benefits at one level of organizational performance may detract from performance at another level. This is crucial, for increases in office worker effectiveness and efficiency are possible, but not guaranteed, either within a level or as a cumulative effect across levels. Office automation represents *opportunities* for management and workers to improve task productivity, worker satisfaction, and organizational viability. Most managers spend most of their time in communication, but most of that time involves oral communication. So the opportunities for improved organizational productivity by managers lie in specific and appropriate augmentation of oral communications (preparation, some substitution for phone, documentation), improving or replacing the remaining mediated communication (memos, meeting notices, reviewing documents, some conferencing), and in facilitating support staff in aiding managerial communication. Developments in integrated multimedia systems may have greater significance for improved managerial communication, because they will facilitate the kinds of communication to which most managers allocate most of their time. Interorganizational communication, which must overcome obstacles such as distance, technological incompatibilities, and noisy or inappropriate media, may be a productive area in which to apply computer-mediated systems.

Organizational managers of these systems should remember that media are only one component of the organization. They are part of the *total information system* used by people of varying roles for tasks within and across organizations.

A suggestion made a decade ago might be relevant here. Mason and Mitroff (1973) wrote,

> What is information for one type (of person) will definitely not be information for another. Thus, as designers of MIS, our job is not to get (or force) all types to conform to one, but to give each type the kind of information he is psychologically attuned to and will use most effectively.

If we change "information" to "an appropriate medium" and change "MIS" to "computer-mediated communication systems," this good advice is brought up to date. Management can implement and use office automation in ways that will achieve missions and purposes through more appropriate functions, more responsive processes, and more effective activities and actions. We must be careful to avoid measuring the wrong thing well, but we also must be responsive to opportunities to improve performance through the use of new organizational communication media.

NOTES

The authors would like to thank the staff of Bell Northern Research for their help in preparing the review of office automation impacts.

1. Researchers are not representative of typical organizational information workers. However, communication is central to both kinds of workers. The relationships between communication and effectiveness found in studies of the former provide useful foundations for analyzing media use of the latter.

2. Other major systems not listed include Electronic Mail Information System by Medical Information Technology, Inc.; Mailbox by I. P. Sharp Associates, Ltd.; APL Plus Message Processing System by STSC, Inc.; Mailcall by Telecomputing Corporation of America (offered through The Source); Mailbox by United Computing Services; and MCIMAIL by MCI. (MCIMAIL already has over 80,000 subscribers, according to Communications Week [1984].) The Survey of Electronic Mail Systems, Edition II, 1982, by Hannigan and Associates lists over 70 commercial electronic messaging systems and services. Most major information utilities — including specialized services such as library networks — will soon offer electronic mail.

LYNNE L. SVENNING and
JOHN E. RUCHINSKAS

9 Organizational Teleconferencing

Rarely does an individual or an organization have an opportunity to create something of broad utility that will enrich the daily lives of everybody. Alexander Graham Bell with his invention of the telephone in 1876, and the various people who subsequently developed it for general use, perceived such an opportunity and exploited it for the great benefit of society. Today there stands before us an opportunity of equal magnitude—Picturephone service [Molnar, 1969: 186].

Teleconferencing. That is another trend that will not happen. Talking with people via television cannot begin to substitute for the high touch of a meeting, no matter how rational it is in saving fuel and overhead. If it is of little importance, use teleconference. Be appropriate. But we have to face it: There is no end to

meetings. TELECONFERENCING IS SO RATIONAL, IT WILL
NEVER SUCCEED [Naisbitt 1982: 46].

Somewhere between the promising projections for the Picturephone
and the pessimistic perspective of Naisbitt (1982) lies the truth about
organizational teleconferencing. This chapter casts a realistic eye on the
status of the teleconferencing modes as emerging communication media
in organizations and raises some important questions about the acceptance, use, and impacts of these new meeting modes.

Teleconferencing is interactive, electronic communication among three
or more people in two or more separate locations. All four teleconferencing modes (computer, audio, audiographic, and video) are communication
tools that facilitate meetings among people in different locations. The
geographic dispersion of many modern organizations and the need for
groups of people in these varied locations to work together in a timely
fashion makes teleconferencing an increasingly appealing alternative to
face-to-face meetings and two-party phone calls.

Promise Versus Reality

As far back as the 1930s, teleconferencing was heralded as a cost-
beneficial way to conduct business across geographically dispersed locations. Early experiments with teleconferencing were conducted mainly in
educational and governmental agencies (Olgren and Parker, 1983). Very
few business organizations jumped on the bandwagon. Those that did try
teleconferencing in the 60s and 70s (e.g., First National City Bank, Union
Carbide, and Allied Chemical) often discontinued use after a brief trial
period. Discontinuance was attributed to a number of factors, including
technological problems or insufficiencies, poor human-technology interfaces, insufficient training, cost, inadequate management support, and
unidimensional impact assessments. Teleconferencing appeared to be a
failed innovation in the organizational context. As we write, teleconferencing has yet to penetrate the business community in any depth. Olgren and
Parker (1983) estimate that less than 1% of all organizations in the private
business sector use teleconferencing on a regular basis.

There appears to be a new flurry of activity on the teleconferencing
front. The Wall Street Journal (1983) reported that 84% of the Fortune
500 companies planned teleconferencing installations in the near future.
Research firms making market projections for the teleconferencing industry are bullish. Growth in teleconferencing use is variously estimated to
climb from 1% of all potential office applications in 1980 to 90% by 1995
(Strategic Inc., 1981); or from 575 installed teleconferencing rooms in
1981 to 4340 installed teleconferencing rooms in 1986 (Quantum Science,
1981); or from $50 million in expenditures, 1980, to $900 million in
expenditures, 1990 (Gnostic Concepts, 1982); or at a rate of 61% a year
(Predicasts, 1982, as cited in Olgren and Parker, 1983: 51).

While it seems logical to assume, as do these market analysts, that use
of teleconferencing modes will grow (a) in response to increasing travel

costs and decreasing communication costs, (b) as a by-product of office automation, and (c) by virtue of impressive advances in teleconferencing technologies, we have yet to see evidence of the "promised" take-off in the adoption and implementation of these new communication modes.

In the next section we explore some of the reasons teleconferencing remains an innovation, rather than a well-accepted practice for organizational communications. Taking an innovation perspective we discuss the multiple faces of organizational teleconferencing, the process of organizational adoption and individual acceptance, and the factors influencing the choice of teleconferencing over more established communication alternatives. Then we look at how the various teleconferencing modes are being used in organizations, by whom, and for what purposes. Finally, we cast a quick glance at what is known about the effects and impacts of organizational teleconferencing and propose an agenda for future research.

NEW TOOLS IN AN ESTABLISHED CONTEXT

Why does teleconferencing remain a relatively "new" organizational phenomenon after a 50-year existence? The answers are myriad, ranging from the "time hasn't been right" to "the technology wasn't quite up to snuff" to "a lack of concern with human-technology interface." This discussion looks at three different sources of complexity and uncertainty to explain further why teleconferencing has not yet reached the critical take-off point (Rogers, 1983: 11) in diffusion among organizations with cross-locational work and communication requirements.

Teleconferencing is not a single innovation. It comes in four modes (computer, audio, audiographic, and video) and a bewildering array of possible configurations within each of the modes. Thus, organizations not only have to decide in favor of teleconferencing, they must also determine which mode will best serve their communication requirements and needs. Depending on the choices the organization makes with respect to mode and facility configurations, teleconferencing will vary on important attributes such as utility, accessibility, convenience, ease of learning, and ease of use. Individuals, in turn, will make their own assessments of teleconferencing attributes relative to the other options available. These individual perceptions will also vary with mode and facility configurations.

Organizational teleconferencing requires both organizational adoption and individual/group acceptance. Although teleconferencing can result from an individual's decision and action (e.g., using a speakerphone or bridging service for an occasional meeting), teleconferencing systems usually require organizational decisions, commitments, and action. Even then the acceptance and use of teleconferencing cannot be assumed. Individuals and groups must be willing to meet and work via the new media. There is a double adoption jeopardy when it comes to organizational teleconferencing.

Teleconferencing is/will be just one of several communication options. Once adopted and/or accepted, teleconferencing takes its place in a well-established social system, complete with well-defined role and status structures, communication practices, and time-honored ways of doing business (relating, meeting, and coordinating). It must fit the established organizational and work context, yet yield observable advantages over the accepted and habitual communication alternatives.

As we delve further into each of these arenas, keep in mind the complexity and uncertainties in the other two. Successfully designing and implementing organizational teleconferencing requires a planned change perspective that considers the users, the context, and the innovation (Svenning and Ruchinskas, 1982). (Since this chapter format precludes a detailed discussion of planned innovation, see Chapter 7, which considers some of the issues associated with introducing and supporting the use of new communication alternatives.)

The Multiple Faces of Organizational Teleconferencing

Teleconferencing is a meeting process that varies with the mode, system and facilities configurations, and transmission networks. There are four basic modes: computer, audio, audiographic, and video. These modes can be provided through either fixed or ad-hoc facilities located either in-house or off-premises, and linked together via available or specially arranged permanent or ad-hoc transmission networks. The commonality underlying the myriad varieties of teleconferencing options is the interactive, telecommunication connection of multiple people in multiple locations. The differences among the modes are highlighted briefly in the following descriptions.

Computer. Computer conferencing is unique among the teleconferencing modes. It depends on the written word and facilitates both simultaneous and asynchronous meetings of users. Chapter 5 describes its capabilities, uses, and impacts in detail.

Current usage seems confined to a subset of professionals who use computing for such other purposes as statistical analysis, technical design, variable forecasting, and text processing. Future usage is likely to grow as computer networks and facilities within organizations expand and incoming management, technical, and professional personnel arrive with improved degrees of computer competence. Clearly, the overwhelming success of electronic mail in select organizations (Steinfeld, 1983) portends an increase in the use of computer conferencing.

Audio. The voice-only teleconferencing mode is the simplest, least expensive, and most widely used form of organizational teleconferencing. Audio teleconferencing can be as simple as using speakerphones in two locations to permit an exchange among three or more people, or using the call-transfer feature of modern switching equipment to add a third person to the basic two-party telephone call. More sophisticated versions of audio teleconferencing involving more people or more locations may be set up through an operator who gets everyone on-line ("dial-up conferencing"), or by the participants' calling a central conferencing number provided by a bridging service at a prespecified time ("meet-me bridge"). Olgren and Parker (1983) report that most regular business users employ dial-up conferencing (44%) or meet-me bridging (37%). Less than 5% of those using audio conferencing employ a dedicated or leased network.

Some organizations making regular use of audio teleconferencing have acoustically treated rooms and special microphone equipment to enhance sound quality and encourage meeting effectiveness. Others use portable equipment moved into offices or conference rooms as the need arises.

Generally, audio conferencing proves to be an efficient and effective communications medium. Short of investing in an audiographic system, users can overcome this mode's visual limitations by sending copies of visual aids (slides, overheads, written materials) in advance of the meeting and displaying them at each location when called for. Many of those most experienced in using this medium (Baird and Monson, 1982; Threlkeld and Pease, 1982) stress the importance of training to achieve maximum effectiveness.

Since audio teleconferencing seems to bear a close resemblance to plain old telephone communications, users must be encouraged to recognize the uniqueness of this communications medium. For example, with many people online, it is easy to "lose" people during the course of the meeting. Use of names to introduce comments or direct questions is a commonly recognized technique for overcoming the lack of visual presence and encouraging participation of the more quiet members. Effective use of this medium does require some adjustment from typical telephone or meeting behaviors. Carey's study of interaction patterns and information flows in audio conferences reinforces the notion that this is "is a distinct mode of communication with its own properties and associated codes of behavior" (1981b: 314).

Audiographic. As the name implies, audiographic systems add a graphic or visual component to audio conferencing. Typically, additional telephone lines or other "narrow band" channels are used to transmit the visual images. Thus, meeting in this mode maintains the advantage of being almost universally accessible at relatively low cost, while providing an interactive visual channel for the presentation of complex information.

Audiographic devices include facsimile machines; telewriting devices, such as electronic pens, scratchpads, and blackboards; computer displays; random access microfiche or slide projectors; slow-scan/freeze-frame video; and video annotation systems. Some systems on the market combine several of these options into a single audiographic work station. (More detailed descriptions of these technologies can be found in Bretz [1983], Olgren and Parker [1983], and Telespan Newsletter [1981: vol. 1, nos. 7 and 8]). Slow-scan and freeze-frame video are classified under audiographic teleconferencing primarily because "snapshot" images, which are refreshed every 10 to 60 seconds, are transmitted using narrowband channels. These two characteristics make this type of teleconferencing more akin to the other audiographic devices listed than to either compressed or full-motion video, which provide moving images and require wider bandwidth for transmission.

Although these audiographic devices share the trait of narrowband transmission, they vary rather dramatically in the degree of interactivity permitted and the amount and kind of visual material that can be sent. For example, *facsimile* machines, which provide high-speed (as fast as 10-second) document transfer between distant locations, are used to transmit existing documents and in some cases to amend such documents during the conference. However, the requisite machine feeding and transmission delay make interaction over such materials somewhat stilted. On the other hand, the *telewriting devices* are particularly useful for creating or modifying materials (drawings/numbers) during a meeting, but cannot transmit images of existing materials.

Interaction over the *electronic blackboard* is particularly cumbersome, since the blackboard image is transmitted not to a blackboard in the other location, but a TV monitor. Thus, if people in the distant location want to amend the image sent, someone at that end must recreate the original image along with the amendment. *Slow-scan* or *freeze-frame* video differ from all other audiographic systems since they can be used to show participant images. However, the display of still-person images as an accompaniment to a moving discussion can be very distracting. Research and experience indicate its true value lies in the display of other visual adjuncts to the meeting, such as charts, blackboard/chalkboard writings, or three-dimensional objects.

One of the most interesting trends in this arena is the merger of various graphic options. For example, scratchpad annotation systems are being linked with freeze-frame video allowing almost real-time annotations of existing documents, diagrams, objects, and maps from each location. The greater interactivity permitted by these emerging options may make audiographic teleconferencing an even more popular option, since audiographic systems remain significantly less costly and easier to implement than fully interactive video teleconferencing systems. Olgren and Parker (1983: 159) report "AT&T estimates that audiographics can be used for over 70 percent of all teleconferences." Similarly, needs-assessment research we have conducted in both business organizations and government agencies indicates many potential users feel audiographic systems are acceptable, even preferable, for the majority of their tasks requiring cross-locational communications.

Video. Teleconferencing via video provides moving images for multilocation meetings. It is the most expensive and currently least-utilized teleconferencing mode. There are two basic versions of video teleconferencing. (1)Point-multipoint video conferencing is essentially a closed circuit TV broadcast. An originating site sends out a video and audio signal to any number of remote locations, which in turn have the ability to feedback in audio only.[1] (2) Fully interactive two-way video allows participants in two locations to both see and hear one another. This is more akin to the other teleconferencing modes we have been discussing, in that it facilitates "relatively" small group communication. It is currently limited to two-location connections for all practical purposes.

Two-way interactive video conferencing comes in basically two formats: *continuous presence*, which provides a view of all participants in the conference room (within camera range), and *voice-switched*, which focuses primarily on the person speaking. Our formative evaluation research with Atlantic Richfield, as well as that of Bell Labs (Brown, Limb, and Prasada, 1978; Hoecher, 1978) and others (Wilkens and Plenge, 1981) shows that potential users prefer the continuous presence option. Users seem to feel they are missing important visual cues from other meeting participants when the camera focuses only on the person speaking. Continuous presence seems more like a regular meeting, where all participants are in view at all times.

Given the costly nature of installing dedicated video conferencing systems, many organizations experimenting with this communications mode make use of publicly available conferencing rooms, such as those provided by AT&T's Picturephone Meeting Service (PMS) in approximately 42 major cities. PMS facilities use the voice-switched option. Other experimenters opt for in-house portable equipment and ad hoc networks. This "inexpensive" version of video teleconferencing brings with it trade-offs in technical quality, obtrusive equipment, and problems in the availability of the necessary transmission links and bandwidth.

Only a few organizations have braved the expense and uncertainties associated with video teleconferencing technology to install dedicated conferencing facilities and establish dedicated transmission links. Organizations linking relatively close locations can take advantage of lower-cost microwave links, while those organizations linking either many locations or extremely distant sites must make use of significantly more costly satellite links, leased trunk lines (T1 carrier), and/or compressed video signals.

The cost of video conferencing facilities often results in companies' installing only one room in each location, which means video conferencing may very well be less accessible and convenient than audio conferencing. Video conferencing systems often have a full complement of graphic options, which may require more learning for effective operation. While this makes video conferencing more flexible and applicable to a wider range of uses, it may mean a greater learning investment for those wishing to make effective use of the graphics.

It is hoped that this brief overview provides some feel for the differences among the various teleconferencing options. Table 9.1 highlights these differences with specific reference to their comparative cost, means of transmission, display, advantages, and disadvantages.

As this discussion illustrates, organizations face a bewildering array of possibilities once they decide to consider teleconferencing. Even though a user needs to, and requirements analysis can, "reduce" the number of viable alternatives the organization has to examine, the available options,

TABLE 9.1 A Comparison of Teleconferencing Modes

Types	Cost*	Transmission	Display	Advantage	Constraints
Computer	Highly variant (network expensive, each new user .5-2K)	Phone and/or cable	Text/Graphic	Can meet without being present. Can be used from home.	Requires keyboard skills. May require conference management. Most "impersonal" mode.
Audio	.5-3K	1-2 phone lines	None—sound only	Most prevalant. Equipment readily available. Extension of "familiar" technology. Can be used from home.	Works best when participants know each other. Limited perceived benefits. Training requirements not obvious. Graphic, visual support must be sent ahead.
Audiographic —Facs —Blackboard —Scratchpad —Slow scan/ Freeze frame —Annotated slow scan/Freeze frame	2-8K 9.6K yr/lease 4-10K 10-45K 35-65K	2+ phone lines " " Microwave, data line, or phone line	Documents Drawings Drawings Still image of documents, objects Still image with annotation	Visual support for meeting. Can meet many functional requirements. "Perceive" as enhancement. Substitutes for least desirable business travel.	Needs graphics compatibility. Graphics interaction may be slow, stilted. Not particularly good for people-centered meetings.

	Cost*	Technology	Content	Advantages	Considerations
VIDEO —Point-Multipoint one-way video two-way audio	Typically 50-200K	Satellite	Real time image of people, objects	Good for reaching wide audience. Cost-efficient. Point-multi-point. Keeps top officials in view.	Most often requires production. Extensive planning/preparation. Best for formal presentations.
—Full Motion Two-way	200-700K	Satellite, T1 carrier, microwave, cable	Real time image of people, documents, objects.	Most like face-to-face. Most flexible. Most glamorous.	Point-to-point. Long lead time. Limited availability. May require "selling" to realize benefits.

*Per location for basic equipment.

configurations, and operational possibilities can still be challenging. The lack of one clear teleconferencing answer, plus the rate of technological change among the teleconferencing technologies, may be one reason teleconferencing remains a tool of innovators and early adopters, rather than the majority of geographically dispersed organizations.

Adoption and Acceptance Decisions

Organizational teleconferencing implies that electronic meeting is accepted by organization members as a means of accomplishing organizational ends. Securing both the organizational and individual commitments necessary for teleconferencing to take its place among the already accepted avenues of organizational communication, such as writing and reading, traveling and meeting, and telephoning, is at best complex. The following discussion approaches teleconferencing as an organizational innovation, requiring both an organizational commitment to provide the means and support for teleconferencing and individual willingness to use teleconferencing when it becomes available and is appropriate.[2]

The organizational decision to adopt teleconferencing. An innovation must gain organizational attention, be determined beneficial, tailored to match the organizational context and needs, and supported through a fair-trial period before it becomes a routinized aspect of organizational operations. We have already alluded to the complexity in the technological arena, which may forestall organizational action. The following discussion highlights some other forces that influence the organizational adoption process.

The adoption process begins with awareness. How the organization becomes aware of teleconferencing can be instrumental in determining whether and when teleconferencing reaches the organization's innovation agenda. Rogers (1983) suggests that organizations are continually agenda setting, that is, identifying performance gaps and scanning the environment for new ideas that may prove beneficial to the organization. Our experience indicates that teleconferencing most often appears on the organizational scene as a solution in search of a problem, which is not atypical for organizational innovations (March, 1981). Usually teleconferencing is championed by someone focused on a specific teleconferencing technology with little reference to the communication context it must fit (Svenning and Ruchinskas, 1982). Obviously, when the teleconferencing champion is someone very high in the organizational hierarchy, the way to the organizational agenda is easy. This was the case at Atlantic Richfield. On the other hand, when teleconferencing is advocated by a vendor and/or enthusiastic underling, they must arduously work their way up the corporate decision ladder, trying to cost-justify teleconferencing every step of the way.[3]

The slow emergence of organizational teleconferencing may in part stem from the difficulty of establishing its benefit; "innovation is instrumental—it is supposed to achieve a better state" (Downs and Mohr, 1979: 392). Unfortunately, demonstrating that a given innovation yields an improved state at an absorbable cost is often more difficult than it sounds. When one is dealing with a general communication process, rather than a specific product or production process, the problem is even more difficult (for examples, see Chapter 8). Typically, those responsible for cost-justifying teleconferencing focus on cost issues, relating the costs of teleconferencing technology to the costs saved through reduced travel or the costs avoided through trips not taken (Charles, 1981). However, after reviewing the research on teleconferencing and travel substitution, Gold (1979) concludes that the evidence does not warrant total reliance on travel substitution models for teleconferencing cost-justifications.

Switching from a cost focus, which relies on travel avoidance/reduction, to a benefit focus—which means tallying multiple and often subjective indicators of organizational advantage—presents more problems. It is extremely difficult to identify, value, and measure the outcomes of using a given communications medium, much less compare the costs-benefits of using one medium over the other. Interestingly, many experts suggest that cost-justifying teleconferencing may be most difficult at the lower levels of the corporate decision ladder (Telespan Newsletter, 1982: vol. 2, no. 12 special supplement). The person with budget authority for implementing a teleconferencing system, usually a middle manager, is far more interested in the nitty-gritty cost evaluation than is the top-level executive, who is more likely to see the value-added benefits of a new communications option. Unfortunately, the lack of solid "bottom-line" cost-benefit evidence for the middle manager means teleconferencing is often relegated to the back burner rather than presented to upper-level management.

An organizational decision to seriously consider teleconferencing usually sets in motion a needs assessment/feasibility determination, which begins matching the organization's needs/requirements with the available and affordable technology. In the case of teleconferencing, this process usually spans the watershed point between initiation and implementation identified by Rogers (1983). The feasibility of teleconferencing is often dependent on how well the organization can tailor teleconferencing to its needs/requirements. The goodness-of-fit between the jobs to be done and the capabilities of the chosen teleconferencing mode will be instrumental in determining its utility and, thereby, its successful implementation. Downs and Mohr (1979) suggest that utility, one of the much-ignored variables in innovation research, is extremely important in organizational adoptions of new technologies. Other factors related to the installation of the technology, such as accessibility, convenience, and ease of use, will be extremely important in determining the success of a new communications option (see "the Established Context—Choosing to Teleconference" section below).

The organizational adoption battle is not won with the choice of an appropriate teleconferencing mode. Teleconferencing will be innovation for most of the organization's members. They too must accept the notion of teleconferencing and be willing to give it a fair trial (Downs and Mohr, 1979; Svenning, 1982). A fair trial means a potential user gains "enough experience with the innovation to assess its costs and benefits accurately" (Downs and Mohr, 1979: 387), before deciding to accept or reject it as a viable option for themselves. The organization must sponsor this new communications option through the fair-trial period and beyond—creating awareness, persuading, motivating, and supporting use of this "foreign" medium. It must foster individual acceptance and utilization.

Individual/group acceptance. The organization's adoption of teleconferencing in no way guarantees member acceptance and utilization. Both academic and trade journals are rife with examples of failed teleconferencing systems. Teleconferencing succeeds only when individual members of the organization accept and effectively utilize it in appropriate situations. A process view of the individual's response to an organizationally adopted innovation such as teleconferencing might be helpful (Figure 9.1).

Upon becoming aware of teleconferencing, the individual makes an initial assessment and forms preconceptions that are manifested in a readiness or willingness to try teleconferencing. This points the way to a fair-trial period, during which the individual gains experience with the new communications option and develops a real basis for making a general acceptance/rejection decision. Acceptance is the decision that precedes routinized use. The individual acknowledges that teleconferencing is a viable option. It is the demarcation between experimental and normalized use of an innovation. The factors influencing readiness and the decision to give teleconferencing a try may differ significantly from those influencing acceptance and/or routinized use. In fact, individuals may accept teleconferencing but have relatively little need of its use in the course of their work.

A recent study conducted in a large, geographically dispersed organization committed to implementing a video teleconferencing system sheds some light on factors influencing both the acceptance and probable use of teleconferencing (Svenning, 1982). In line with the trend toward the multivariate view of factors influencing communication and innovation behavior in organizations (Baldridge and Burnham, 1975; Katz and Kahn, 1978; Monge, Edwards, and Kirste, 1978; Roberts, Hulin, and Rousseau, 1978; and Van de Ven and Ferry, 1980), this study assessed the influence of individual, contextual, and innovation factors on attitudes toward, intentions to use, and projected frequency of teleconferencing usage. Table 9.2 summarizes the factors analyzed in this study.

The data collected from 795 managerial-level employees shows a similarity—yet a uniqueness—in the factors explaining an individual's attitudes toward teleconferencing, intentions to try/use this new medium, and projected frequency of use (Table 9.3). Positive attitudes toward video telconferencing seem firmly linked to perceptions of utility, ease of use, ease of learning, and cost. The decision initially to try teleconferencing is further explained by expectations of improved productivity, the importance of relative advantage over other media, and convenience. Actual use

FIGURE 9.1 Model of Individual Acceptance Process

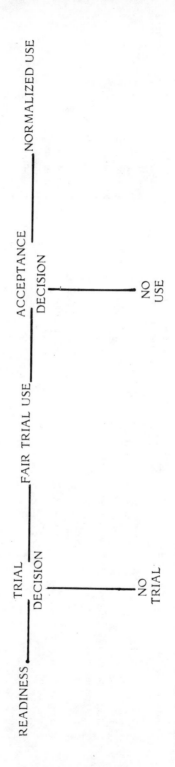

TABLE 9.2 Variables Assessed in Organizational Baseline for a Video Teleconferencing System

DEPENDENT VARIABLES

INDEPENDENT VARIABLES

Pre-dispositions Toward Video Conferencing:	Individual	Contextual	Innovation
1. Attitudes	Background/Status Age Education Organizational tenure Job tenure Hierarchical level	Current Communication Requirements/Practices Trips Phone Calls Meetings (cross-loc.)	Perceived Attributes Formality Expense Usefulness Sociability Reliability Accessibility Comfort
2. Intentions Eagerness to try Intention to use	Beliefs/attitudes about: Communication Travel Change/Innovation	Perceived Needs Organizational Norms Communication Innovation	Ease Effectiveness Convenience Personalness Flexibility
3. Projected Frequency of use		Work Characteristics Standardization Pressure Innovativeness Task diversity	Simplicity Sensitivity to detail Ease of learning

Work Activities
Negotiating
Persuading/Selling
Problem solving/Decision
making
Giving presentations
Generating/Brainstorming
Coordinating/Monitoring
Appraising/Reviewing

Expected Impacts
Productivity
Meeting effectiveness
Visibility

Decision Factors
Importance of:
Relative advantage
Convenience
Comparability with face-to-face

of teleconferencing options over time, as indicated by projected frequency of use, is far more likely to depend on the communication or information requirements of one's work and the ability of teleconferencing to serve the requirements.

Interestingly, while the relative advantage decision factor is important in explaining attitudes and intentions, convenience or operational ease of use is the decision criterion important in explaining projected teleconferencing usage. Evidently, as one moves from a general evaluation of teleconferencing to more specific considerations of how frequently one might use it, operational concerns such as convenience become significantly more important. Such a trend appears consistent with other research examining use of "routinized" communication channels (Ruchinskas, 1982).

Teleconferencing is a group communications tool. This discussion of individual acceptance obviates the importance of group acceptance in successfully implementing organizational teleconferencing. There has been no research to date examining issues related to group willingness to use this new medium. However, the probable importance of referent-group favorability in explaining individual predispositions toward teleconferencing was demonstrated by Svenning (1982). Explained variance in attitudes, intentions, and projections all increased markedly when the individual's perceptions of how favorable their superiors, peers, and subordinates were toward teleconferencing were included in the regression equations. This finding is consistent with Elizur and Guttman's (1976) work on individual responses to computers and Goldman's (1979) analysis of factors affecting the acceptance of telecommunication innovations in vocational rehabilitation agencies.

The Established Context—Choosing to Teleconference

Once teleconferencing takes its place among viable options for organizational communication, individuals and/or groups must decide when teleconferencing is the most appropriate means of communicating. In some instances the choice will be coerced by meager budgets, organizational policy, or time pressures that preclude the travel/face-to-face meeting alternative. In other instances the choice will be volitional and rest on the individual's or group's assessment of teleconferencing relative to other available communication options. The question then becomes, what factors influence this choice?

Researchers have approached this question of media choice in organizations from several different but related perspectives that seem to converge on two basic foci. The first focal point is the work context, where the question is basically, "What aspects of individuals' work activities or work environment influence communication behavior?" The second focal point concentrates on the dimensions, attributes, or characteristics of different media and how these affect choice.

TABLE 9.3 Predictors of Attitudes Toward, Intentions to Use, and Projected Frequency of Use for Video Teleconferencing

	UNIQUE VARIANCE*		
Independent Variables	Attitudes	Intentions	Projected Use
Individual Factors	.018	.026	.015
Background/Status			
Educational level		.009	
Attitudes—Travel			
Negative evaluation scale	.018		.015
Attitudes—Change/Innovation			
Wait till others succeed		(-).017	
Contextual Factors	.037	.078	.109
Communication Requirements			
Total communication behavior			.056
Node communication behavior		.014	
Cross-locational meetings			.036
Perceived Needs			
Want more f-f contact		.033	
Organizational Norms			
Organizational innovativeness	.022		
Work Characteristics			
Standardization scale	.015		
Task diversity		.018	
Work Activities			
Appraising/Reviewing			.017
Presenting		.013	
Innovation Factors	.421	.440	.227
Perceived Attributes			
Utility	.252	.296	.107
Ease of use			.044
Inexpensive	.025	.029	
Ease of learning	.032		
Expected Impacts			
Increased productivity	.080	.079	.060
Decision Factors (Importance)			
Relative advantage	.032	.036	
Convenience			.016
Total Explained Variance R^2	.477	.544	.352
df	8/628	10/626	8/628
F	71.50	74.57	42.72
Sig	p < .001	p < .001	p < .001

*The table presents the product of the betas multiplied by simple Pearson product-moment correlations.
Sample size = 637.

The nature of work and communications. Teleconferencing is a tool that facilitates the meeting of individuals who work in different locations. Its utility and desirability can, in part, be determined by looking at the reasons for current cross-locational communications. Cross-locational communications is conceptually related to the constructs of "task interdependency" and "coordination modes" in organizational research literature. Task interdependence is the degree of collaboration required to produce or deliver the work product or service (Thompson, 1967: Mohr, 1971). Coordination modes are the means of integrating or linking together different parts of the organization. Van de Ven, Delbecq, and Koenig (1976) found that as task interdependency increased, all types of coordination modes were used more, with unscheduled and scheduled meetings increasing most dramatically. Traditionally, meetings have been viewed as the most inefficient and costly coordination mode (March and Simon, 1958). Cross-locational, in-person meetings are particularly costly and inefficient means of coordination. Teleconferencing offers opportunities to meet coordination needs while decreasing costs (Shulman and Steinman, 1978).

A large number of trips and cross-locational phone calls in an organization's and/or individual's communications profile indicates cross-locational task interdependencies. Current trips and telephoning demonstrate both organizational and individual "needs" for teleconferencing and indicate which individuals and groups in the organization can be expected to make most use of this communications option. Svenning (1982) showed that current cross-locational communication behavior (number of trips and phone calls) and the number of cross-locational meetings attended were important variables in discriminating individuals who projected no use of video teleconferencing from those who projected light or regular use of the new medium.

Beyond the mere presence of cross-locational communication, there may also be a level of dissatisfaction, or latent inefficiency, in current practices. Needs are discrepancies between what is and what is desired. March and Simon (1958) describe needs as gaps between the expected and the actual. Typically, they are manifested in perceived problems or expressed dissatisfactions. For an innovative alternative to be adopted in place of the present strategy, it is necessary for the present strategy to be considered in some sense unsatisfactory; otherwise, individuals and organizations opt for the status quo (Dickson and Slevin, 1975).

Perceived need has been generally associated with innovation and change (Brief, Delbecq, Filley, and Huber, 1976; Evans and Black, 1967; Gruenfeld and Foltman, 1967; Radnor, Rubenstein, and Tansik, 1970; Utterback, 1974) and specifically associated with predispositions toward telecommunication innovations (Goldman, 1979). Telecommunication planners have also noted the importance of perceived needs in gaining acceptance (Elton and Carey, 1978) and supporting use (Casey-Stahmer and Havron, 1973). Perceived communication difficulties due to the organization's geographic dispersion were helpful in discriminating among individuals with resistant, neutral, and receptive attitudes toward video-conferencing, while the desire for more contact with those in other locations helped discriminate those who intended to try teleconferencing from those who did not (Svenning, 1983).

Obviously, job responsibilities and requirements influence communication behavior and needs in organizations (Monge et al., 1978). Ruchinskas (1982) demonstrated that both the amount of communications and the use of various communication modes varies significantly with job type. In general, research shows that scientists and engineers tend to communicate less than those engaged in nontechnical fields (Case Institute, 1958; Hinrichs, 1964; Klemmer and Snyder, 1972). Scientists and engineers also show greater use of written channels (Rosenbloom and Wolek, 1970; Bodensteiner, 1970; Ruchinskas, 1982), while administrative and non-scientific managers are heavily oriented to verbal channels (Horne and Lupton, 1965; Stewart, 1967; Palmer and Beishon, 1970; see also Chapter 9). Functional specialty has also been shown to influence the amount of travel (Westrum, 1972).

Svenning and Ruchinskas (1981) demonstrated the influence of job type in predicting the use of video teleconferencing. Conducting separate regression analyses for specific job types increased their ability to predict the amount of expected teleconferencing use. Interestingly, the predictor variables also changed with job type. For example, usage for employee relations personnel was predicted not only by teleconferencing's perceived utility, ease of use, and sensitivity to detail, but by the desire for more contact with people in other locations and the degree to which their jobs involved cross-locational work contacts and finding novel solutions to problems. For engineering personnel, the current number of trips and phone calls, a dissatisfaction with the current amount of travel, and perceived open organizational communication norms combined with perceptions of teleconferencing's utility and cost to predict usage.

One's organizational status also shows clear impacts on communication behavior. The Porter and Roberts (1976) review of communication literature finds organizational status to be the most important individual determinant of communication behavior. In general, managerial employees spend more time communicating and conduct more of their business through face-to-face exchange that do nonmanagerial employees (Hinrichs, 1964; Engel, Groppuso, Lowenstein, and Traub, 1980; Ruchinskas, 1982; Walker and Guest, 1952). Hierarchical level is positively related to telephone use (Conrath, 1978), and is also positively and strongly associated with the amount of business travel in which one engages (Westrum, 1972).

Organizational tenure, which is another indicator of organizational status, has also been associated with communications behavior. Senior people, in general, communicate more across all modes (Pye, 1974). Rosenbloom and Wolek (1970) and Steinfield (1981) demonstrate a positive relationship between tenure and face-to-face communications.

Dutton, Fulk, and Steinfield (1981) found actual video-conferencing use to be related to hierarchical level, with a disproportionate number of users (one-third) upper-level managers. Higher organizational level helped discriminate between those who were eager to try video-conferencing and those who were not (Svenning, 1983). Svenning and Ruchinskas (1981) also improved the prediction of teleconferencing use by analyzing the data from lower, middle, and upper management in separate regressions. The different predictor variables for each equation seem to reflect the different task and work environment factors of each management level. For lower management personnel, who presently travel least, the desire for more contact with people in other locations combined with perceived utility and evidence of strong speakerphone use to predict teleconferencing usage. Middle manager teleconferencing use was predicted by feeling one currently traveled too much, as well as a desire for more contact with other locations, perceived organizational norms favoring open communications, and teleconferencing's perceived utility and inexpense. Teleconferencing use for upper-level managers was predicted not only by teleconferencing's perceived utility, but perceived ease of use and current cross-locational communications behavior.

Work activities have also been used to discriminate among jobs and differences in communication behavior (Dormois, Fioux, and Gensollen, 1978; Goddard, 1973; Irving, 1981). Examining the current communications behavior of the employees in an organization considering teleconferencing, Ruchinskas (1982) showed that work activities accounted for major portion of explained variance in time spent communicating via face-to-face, phone, and written channels. Persuading/selling and appraising/reviewing were associated with face-to-face communications; negotiating, giving presentations, and brainstorming predicted telephone use; and written communications associated with negotiating and giving presentations. Svenning (1982), in turn, found that intentions to use teleconferencing were related to the amount of presenting associated with one's work, and projected frequency of teleconferencing use was influenced by the amount of appraising/reviewing one did (see Table 9.3).

A more theoretical approach to the relationship between work activities and use of organizational media is manifested in the "social presence" research tradition (Short, Williams, and Christie, 1976; also described in detail in Chapter 2). The social presence paradigm suggests a one-to-one relationship between the degree of interaction intensity associated with a particular activity and the ability of a particular medium to accommodate it. While this paradigm has shown some success in explaining results from laboratoratory settings, it has proven less fruitful in explaining the more complex web of business communication.[4]

Work is also characterized by a number of other factors that appear to influence communication behavior and, as a result, the need for or utility of teleconferencing. For example, the amount of pressure (time constraints, crises, unexpected events) experienced in one's work affects communication behavior (Hall and Lawler, 1970; Mintzberg, 1973; Ruchinskas, 1982; Wright, 1974). Generally, as pressure increases there is a tendency to turn to oral channels, particularly the phone. Teleconferencing is often pictured as a tool that may alleviate pressures, permitting faster responses to crises and eliminating the need for travel in order to respond to important or timely matters (Green and Hansell, 1981). Contrary to expectations, Svenning (1983) found a lesser degree of pressure to be helpful in discriminating those who were eager to try teleconferencing from those who were not.

Task diversity, or the amount of variability in one's work, is another characteristic often associated with variances in communication behavior. Wilson (1966) and Lawrence and Lorsch (1967) suggest that task diversity leads to creative dialogue, and thus, more communications. Task diversity has been linked to the amount of communication in a variety or organizational settings (Hage, Aiken, and Marrett, 1971; Hrebiniak, 1974; Tushman, 1979) and specifically to greater use of oral communication channels (Hrebiniak, 1974). Task diversity also helps predict intentions to use teleconferencing (Table 9.3).

Task uncertainty, routineness, and standardization all relate to use of written versus oral communication channels. Routineness and standardization were related to greater use of written channels (Hage et al., 1971; Form, 1972; Randolph and Finch, 1977), and lower levels of face-to-face exchange. Conversely, Van de Ven et al., (1976) found as task uncertainty increased, so did the use of horizontal communication channels and group meetings. The amount of standardization in one's work is a minor predictor variable of one's attitudes toward teleconferencing (Table 9.3). Neither task uncertainty or routineness influenced predispositions toward teleconferencing. Perhaps these variables become important only in explaining actual use of organizational communications media.

Teleconferencing use may also be influenced by less obvious "communication norms," or expectations about what is the "correct" behavior in a given situation. Different organizations, and indeed different subunits, have specific norms and operating environments, resulting in unique patterns of communication and behavior (Tushman, 1979). "Open" communication norms, evidenced by information sharing among organizational units, have been associated with greater use of oral communication channels (Dewhirst, 1971; O'Reilly, 1977; Wofford, Gerloff, and Cummins, 1977). Since teleconferencing is another oral communications mode, it is not surprising that perceived openness of the organization's communication norms helps distinguish between those who intend to use teleconferencing and those who do not (Svenning, 1983).

The established work and communications context can be either a stimulus or barrier to the acceptance and use of teleconferencing. The variety of work and organizational factors shaping the context for communications are numerous, as this discussion indicates. Many of these variables will be instrumental in distinguishing among the communication requirements and needs of different organizational members. The appropriateness of any given teleconferencing mode or facilities configuration may vary widely within the organization, as a result of these varying communication patterns. It is important to understand the current nature and interplay of these factors to ensure that the teleconferencing options selected and or designed by the organizations serve the established context and provide organizational members with a choice that can improve the status quo.

Media attributes or characteristics. An alternate research perspective on media use in organizations begins with the assumption that individuals have a need to communicate, and asks what characteristics of the channel interact with the need to favor use of one medium over the other. This research has shown a number of interesting dimensions or characteristics of media that appear to shape strongly media use. Two distinct approaches have emerged in this area, the first focuses on characteristics such as utility, accessibility, convenience, and ease of use, and the second centers on the social presence of media.

Convenience, accessibility, and ease of use emerge as key factors in communications and information-seeking research. Allen's initial work (1966) showed the surprising outcome that there was no relationship between the perceived effectiveness or utility of eight available information channels and the extent that they were used by engineers. Rather, the perceived accessibility of a channel (Allen, 1966; Gerstberger and Allen, 1968), or its perceived ease of use (Rosenberg, 1966; Werner, 1965) proved to be the primary factors influencing use by engineers. O'Reilly (1982) found accessibility to be the primary predictor of information source use for 163 welfare professionals. Studies on other subject populations, ranging from research chemists to consumers to farmers, also confirm the importance of accessibility or ease of use in information channel selection (Case Institute, 1958; Lee, 1968; McEwen and Hempel, 1977).

Utility has been proposed as an important construct for assessing communication channel use in organizations (Melcher and Beller, 1967). However, as in innovation research, it rarely emerges in empirical studies. Atkin (1973) does use utility in theoretical and empirical explanations of information-seeking behavior. He found a modest relationship between information seeking and the perceived utility of the information. Technical quality of information was a secondary influence in media choice in Gerstberger and Allen (1968), while Fett (1975) and McEwen (1978) showed utility to be the primary characteristic affecting consumers' choice of information sources.

Actual use of communication modes has also been associated with accessibility and operational ease of use. Champness (1973) found accessibility to be a key determinant of managers' use of speakerphones. Steinfield (1983) showed similar effects of accessibility on use of electronic mail, while Ruchinskas (1982) found operational ease of use to be a minor influence on time spent using the telephone.

The dominance of accessibility, convenience, and ease of use in prior research may indicate that the economic model of man (which assumes that we seek to maximize our gain) may be less suited than a satisficing model of information seeking (March, 1978; March and Simon, 1958; Simon, 1957). It appears we are more sensitive to the cost side of the equation than to potential benefits when we choose our information sources or communication channels. Accessibility and ease of use may be barrier conditions; if the effort required to overcome them is too great, the alternative is not considered, whatever the potential improvement in benefits. It may be only after the accessibility criterion is met that utility and other factors are weighed to choose among the remaining alternatives (see Gerstberger and Allen, 1968: 277).

Varying teleconferencing modes will have differing degrees of accessibility and ease of use, ranging from the readily accessible dial-up audio conferencing to the less accessible one room per location video-conferencing systems. Nonexperimental studies of media attributes involving business personnel are presently limited. Ruchinskas's (1982) examination of media utility suggests that employees use three basic dimensions in assessing communications media: ease of use, utility, and sociability. Employees expected that using video conferencing would be significantly lower than the phone or face-to-face in utility and ease of use, though only slightly less sociable than face-to-face. It was also rated equal to, or significantly higher than, written communication. In all cases video conferencing rated above the midpoint on the seven-point scale, calling into question whether its "low" ease of use score was below employees' threshold level. It should also be pointed out that face-to-face ratings were not solely directed toward *travel-based* face-to-face communications.

Ruchinskas's sociability dimension suggests the other major school of thought in the media attributes arena—the social presence concept— which attempts to explain media use based on the "personalness" of the channel to the communication (See Chapter 3). Short et al. (1976) asked respondents to rate different media (face-to-face, video conferencing, audio conferencing, telephone, and written communication) on a series of semantic differential scales, with their results leading them to hypothesize a single dimension named "social presence" as the key differentiating factor in individuals' evaluations.[5] Later research concentrated on the relationship between the social presence of the task and the social presence of the media.

Several early teleconferencing studies, guided by the social presence notion, showed expected patterns of task-medium relations in the activities of actual teleconferencing users (Champness, 1973; Noll, 1977). A recent study of Picturephone Meeting Service (PMS) users, not bound by the social presence rationale, found video-conferencing meetings were dominated by surveillance (e.g., exchanging information/opinions, giving presentations, brainstorming/ generating ideas) and/or consensus-building (e.g., monitoring performance, appraising/reviewing, coordinating) activities. Little time was spent negotiating, persuading, socializing (Dutton, Fulk, and Steinfield, 1982). The authors suggest that the dominance of surveillance or consensus activities in video-conferenced meetings may be a function of how often these activities occur in the conduct of business rather than social presence of the activity or the medium.

In the case of teleconferencing, social presence may be an important differentiator among media, though clearly it is not the only aspect of the medium promoting its use. For example, the visual component of audiographic and video systems may be the key determinant of its ability to accommodate certain exchanges of technical information. Both our needs-assessment work and prior examinations of communication patterns show that scientists and engineers' low use of the telephone result, in part, from its inadequacy for discussing technical drawings or figures (Ruchinskas, 1982). Further, participants often seem willing to trade-off on the social presence dimension for higher speed, or other functional capabilities, offered by new electronic media. This trade-off seems particularly likely when the activity is part of an ongoing process that will involve further exchange by face-to-face and other media.

It is also important to recognize that media are rated relative to one another. The ratings of different channels change when respondents are exposed to wider range of media (Short et al., 1976: 66). This interplay among channels was demonstrated in a business setting by Steinfield (1981), who found managers' use of telephone and written channels for gathering performance information was largely a function of the accessibility of face-to-face communication. Thus, in attempting to assess the effects of channel characteristics on teleconferencing use, it may be the relative accessibility, ease of use, utility, and so on of the various media that will govern use.

The fact that media are rated in comparison to one another also suggests that *context* must be taken into account in assessing a medium's characteristics. Teleconferencing systems, perhaps more so than any of the other "new" communications technologies, can be shaped to reflect any number of organizational cultures and applications. They allow greater scope for reinvention, as discussed in Chapter 7. How the organization chooses to implement teleconferencing within its operations will dramatically influence the ways people perceive and use it. For example, many organizations have audio-conferencing systems, yet this same mode is rated far differently depending on the organization one looks at. In certain companies, audio conferencing is an accessible, simple, operational-level tool. Conversely, other organizations have built special acoustically treated conference rooms among the executive suites to serve the needs of upper management (e.g., Equitable Life and Bank of America). Bank of America's choice to place its audio conferencing facility in a plushly apportioned room on the executive floor virtually precluded its use by lower-level personnel. Employees likely viewed this system as expensive and inaccessible. Thus, the "characteristics" of a given communication mode are only partially technologically determined, and can be dramatically altered by how the system is introduced, and what other options are available to users.

In sum, the need for any given teleconferencing system is likely to be unevenly distributed within the organization, based on current work requirements. The attributes of any system are shaped by how it is positioned within the organization and what other options are available to the user, not merely by its technological characteristics. The result is a great deal of uncertainty at the organization-adoption level, and many opportunities for misapplication at the individual level. Successful teleconferencing systems require matching the right teleconferencing configuration in the right setting with the right users, a task whose vagueries and permutations currently seems to deter many potential adopters.

WHAT WE KNOW ABOUT TELECONFERENCING USE AND IMPACTS

After having examined some of the factors influencing the acceptance and use of organizational teleconferencing, a brief look at how organizations are using audio, audiographic, and video teleconferencing is in order. (Chapter 5 looks at the use of computer conferencing.) We will also consider what little is known about the impacts of organizational teleconferencing in this section.

Current Teleconferencing Use

Two recent studies of teleconferencing use provide much of the data reported in this section. In late 1981 the Center for Interactive Programs at the University Wisconsin-Extension conducted a study of 147 organizations using interactive teleconferencing. The questionnaire survey included 62 companies in business and industry; 55 colleges, universities, and medical groups; 19 government agencies; and 11 other organizations that eluded categorization (CIP, 1981). As part of a study designed to project the future demand for teleconferencing, the East Lansing Research Associates (ELRA) interviewed the telecommunication managers in 341 organizations currently using teleconferencing and in 291 potential user organizations. The user population included 164 business organizations, 108 educational organizations, 20 government agencies, 14 associations and 35 unclassifiable groups (LaRose, 1983). A more descriptive review of current usage can be found in Olgren and Parker (1983).

Audio. Audio teleconferencing is clearly the most popular and most frequently utilized from of teleconferencing in American organizations. LaRose (1983) and CIP (1981) report, respectively, that 56% and 44% of the business organizations are regular users of audio-only teleconferencing. Although audio conferencing is used for a variety of purposes ranging from national sales meetings to crisis management to multisite training and education sessions, most often it facilitates day-to-day business functions such as staff meetings, project coordination, information exchange, and problem solving. This everyday, operational-type usage is evidenced in an average of well over 1000 audio-conference meetings per year, per utilizing organization reported by LaRose (1983).

Audiographic. Recent activity in organizational teleconferencing seems centered on audiographic systems, which are currently the second most popular teleconferencing media. Interestingly, it is the business users who seem to account for most of this action. For example, 47% of the business organizations in the CIP (1981) study used audiographic teleconferencing, while only 27% of the total survey population employed this mode. Gnostic Concepts (1982) projects audiographic teleconferencing will claim 35% of the teleconferencing market by 1990, a figure that may even understate future demand should full-motion video remain significantly more costly than audiographic systems.

Audiographic systems are used primarily for operational-level meetings, such as cross-locational staff meetings, project and coordination meetings, technical conferences, problem solving, and information updates (Olgren and Parker, 1983). The recent advances in audiographic technology, which allow "real-time" annotations to be added to a still image (i.e., a chart, graph, figure, or passage of text), have significantly added to this mode's utility. As we indicated earlier, our needs-assessment research in a variety of organizations suggests audiographic teleconferencing may meet most of an organization's current communication requirements, since many operational level meetings focus on alphanumeric or graphic documents, rather than the personalities involved.

Video. Given the expense and rapidly changing technologies associated with this mode, regular use of full-motion video teleconferencing is relatively limited compared to audio or audiographic teleconferencing. Only 10% of the 62 business teleconferencing users surveyed in the CIP study employed full-motion video. An identical percentage of the 164 business users interviewed by LaRose used full-motion video. As noted previously, it has been used for a full range of business activities, with surveillance functions predominant among users of public video teleconferencing facilities (Dutton, et al., 1982; Noll, 1977). The Satellite Business Systems (SBS) study of 165 video teleconferencing users from 10 organizations with in-house facilities indicated video teleconferencing was used for both routine (44%) and special purposes (56%); primarily for discussion sessions (76%) rather than presentations (24%); and subject matters ranging across engineering/technology (30%), project management (24%), administration (14%), business/finance (13%) and data processing (10%). Full-motion video seems to serve all the functions facilitated by other teleconferencing media, as well as a number of "person-centered" activities. Initial experience at Atlantic Richfield has included use for introducing employees to new management, getting to know co-workers in distant locations, and other activities that the social presence notion would suggest are not compatible with teleconferencing. Organizational use of video teleconferencing is still in the experimental phase, with people trying a variety of cross-locational sessions to determine what works and doesn't work via video. Essentially, the jury is still out.

Ad hoc or special-event video teleconferencing (one-way video, two-way audio) serves unique purposes requiring the broadcast of a common message to many locations. The LaRose (1983) study indicates that 19% of all teleconferencing users employed this mode, including 17% of the business users. This mode claims more than a third of the users among the educational, associations, and other nonbusiness, nongovernment organizations contacted in the LaRose study. As the name indicates, this teleconferencing mode is most often used on an occasional basis, for such purposes as large-scale sales presentations (ie., introducing new products to the sales force), seminars, training, and other educational applications.

Analyses of teleconferencing use show few clear patterns by job type or organizational position. The lack of specific findings about users themselves is due in part to the way teleconferencing use had been studied. Most often telecommunications managers or people in charge of systems are interviewed or surveyed about usage. While these individuals can provide a good overview of usage, they most often do not have specific job type or hierarchical position data about the users. In our survey of a large, geographically dispersed organization, we examined current use of the speakerphone and conference calling for meeting purposes. In general, speakerphones were far more accessible to middle and upper management personnel. Thus, it was not surprising to find that upper-level managers were significantly heavier users of this medium (35 speakerphone meetings per year) than were lower-level management employees (5 speakerphone meetings per year). Interestingly, conferencing calling, (where more than two locations are linked together in a telephone meeting) was utilized more by middle managers than either lower or upper management personnel.

Our job type analysis showed the heaviest users of speakerphone meetings to be corporate officials and legal personnel, who held approximately 40 speakerphone meetings a year, compared with an average use of about 8 per year. Job types making below-average use of speakerphone meetings included technical and scientific personnel. Above average use of conferencing calling was made by legal people, sales, and marketing personnel, purchasing employees, and supply operations personnel.

Research in other organizations shows a range of audio-conferencing users. There are examples of audio-conference use for virtually every type of organization member with access to a telephone or speakerphone. In some instances these are upper-level executives conferring on crisis situations, in others operational-level personnel doing such things as monitoring airplane maintenance (Republic Airlines) or coordinating refinery output and fuel transportation (Atlantic Richfield). In certain companies, usage patterns are dictated by the design of specific conferencing facilities (e.g., Equitable Life, International Harvester, Bank of America), where special acoustically treated rooms were located in or near the executive suites for upper management to facilitate tasks such as financial or board meetings (Hough, 1976; Olgren and Parker, 1983). This variety of uses and use situations for audio conferencing points to the critical importance of organizational culture and organizational context to system use and impacts.

Although audiographic systems also serve varied users, they seem to be employed more heavily by scientific and engineering personnel. The graphics adjunct to the telephone suits technical discussion well. Engineering and technical employees also tend to be somewhat less concerned with the interpersonal aspects of the exchange that drives many users to consider full-motion video.

Given the small number of operating full-motion video-conferencing systems, it is difficult to generalize about user patterns. The two recent studies of video teleconferencing users (Dutton et al., 1982); Hansell, Green, and Erbring, 1982) indicate that video teleconferencing is utilized by all levels of management, with middle- to upper-level people generally more prevalent in meetings. The SBS study of in-house video teleconferencing reported that respondents from research and development, engineering, and data processing dominated their sample (Hansell et al., 1982), while the public room video teleconferencing respondents were primarily marketing/sales, general management, program or project managers and legal personnel, with a smattering of users from personnel, finance, research, design/development, planning, accounting, and production. It is clear that these systems serve a full range of users.

We know teleconferencing is being used by a variety of organizations, for a variety of purposes by a wide range of users within organizations. There is some indication that users are making appropriate use of the technology, with scientific and technical people leaning away from audio systems and toward audiographic systems, and people-oriented managers leaning more toward video. Perhaps the most interesting observation we can make about current usage is that organizational users seem to be willing to explore a variety of uses, under a variety of meeting conditions, with little attention to the constraints suggested by earlier laboratory studies. Users appear particularly adept at making teleconferencing serve their needs. A more comprehensive assessment of teleconferencing use awaits the inclusion of teleconferencing in studies of communications behavior in organizations.

Impacts

Does organizational teleconferencing make a difference? We wrote earlier of the difficulties surrounding the measurement of organizational benefits accruing as the result of teleconferencing use and the tendency to concentrate on travel reduction and avoidance estimates to establish organizational benefit. There are numerous examples of organizations demonstrating travel costs saved as a result of teleconferencing. Olgren and Parker (1983) catalogue a number of hypothetical and real examples of travel savings. Almost two-thirds of the telecommunication managers in the LaRose (1983) study cite reduced costs as an advantage of teleconferencing. Of the video teleconferencing users in the SBS survey, 75% produced a "resounding chorus" of agreement on perceived decreases in travel expense and "overwhelmingly approved such saving" (Hansell et al., 1982: 74).

Data on other effects of organizational teleconferencing gathered in organizational settings are sparse. LaRose (1983) reports 61% of the telecommunication managers perceived improvements in the flow of information/decisions and use of time. Since the SBS study gathered data from actual users and was more focused on impacts, there is some evidence of a wider variety of perceived differences as a result of video teleconferencing. One of the most interesting aspects of this study was the attempt to determine whether users viewed these differences as personally beneficial, neutral, or detrimental. Of course, the 75% who perceived improvements in their personal productivity as a result of teleconferencing saw this effect as beneficial. Even the impacts on meetings characteristics (decreases in length, lead time, privacy, and increases in frequency, size, and access to resource people) and meeting effectiveness (increases in decision quality, task orientation, cooperation, preparation, and decreases in decision time) were generally perceived as personally beneficial. "Greater task orientation was viewed as overwhelming beneficial, and was seen as the key to greater decision quality. Increased cooperation was also widely valued, and was perceived as the key to greater meeting effectiveness' (Hansell et al., 1982:74). Fifty percent of the users also noted increases in the amount of communication among various parts in the organization. Other corporate performance indicators affected positively by teleconferencing were organizational responsiveness, competitive advantage, management visibility, worker morale, and shorter time for completion.

Although the assessment of personal benefit derived from observed changes is a step forward in impact evaluation, we also need to devise additional measures of organizational benefit. The problem of empirically determining the organizational benefit of an observed impact, such as shorter meetings, decreased decision time, and increased communications remains one of the knottiest for researchers examining the effects of new media in organizations.

AN AGENDA FOR FUTURE RESEARCH

The opportunities for research on organizational teleconferencing are many, and varied, and, most of all, challenging. One of the biggest drawbacks to the available teleconferencing research is that so much of it has been conducted in laboratory settings with little resemblance to real-world organizations. Another limiting characteristic is the cross-sectional nature of most work. Keeping in mind the need for organizationally based, longitudinal studies we suggest the following areas of needed research (not necessarily in order of importance):

Organizational adoption and implementation. Since organizations may be the initial adopting unit for teleconferencing and ultimately bear the responsibility for successfully integrating teleconferencing into the communication behavior of their employees, it would be useful to have better information about (1) the forces influencing decisions to adopt teleconferencing; (2) organizational characteristics that may influence the consideration of teleconferencing; (3) the key decision makers for organizational teleconferencing and how they perceive organizational benefits and costs; (4) the length of the fair-trial period necessary to determine whether teleconferencing will by accepted and utilized by organizational members; and (5) organizational variables associated with successful implementation.

Organizational benefit. Theoretical and practical value can be derived from research focused on the organizational benefit of teleconferencing. One might use a theoretical framework such as that proposed by Downs and Mohr (1979), which classifies organizational benefits as (1) programmatic—those associated with increases in the efficiency and effectivness of work-related performance; (2) prestige—related to value gained from recognitions and approval from being earlier rather than later adopters; and (3) structural—internal advantage realized through greater worker satisfaction and better internal relationships. This approach recognized that benefits are not intrinsic attributes of innovations, such as teleconferencing, but rather variable attributes of the choice situation, which will be different for each organization.

The problem then becomes one of not only measuring these benefits, but identifying the determinants of these benefits and their relative weights in the decision to adopt teleconferencing. Research on the organizational benefits of teleconferencing must be balanced with similar investigations of costs and risks associated with this innovation.

The role of the "group" in the acceptance and use of teleconferencing. Given that teleconferencing is essentially a group communications mode, it is surprising that so little attention has been paid to the group factors influencing acceptance and use. How is the decision made to use teleconferencing? Is it a group decision or the decision of the group "leader"? What happens when some members of the group are uncomfortable with teleconferencing? Surely group norms, expectations, and leadership will all influence use of this medium, yet most of the research dealing with acceptance focuses only on individual factors.

Effects of teleconferencing on the organization of work. Given the linkages permitted by teleconferencing, the whole process of organizing and conducting work in geographically dispersed organizations may change. Assessing differences in (1) the organization of work teams; (2) access to and use of organizational resources, both human and information; (3) the process of coordination; and (4) the nature and structure of cross-locational decision-making activities resulting from teleconferencing use may yield important insights about the interaction between communications and work and, in particular, use of organizational media and work.

Changes in group work and communication dynamics. Most of the research dealing with group dynamics and use of various communication modes has been conducted in laboratory settings. There is much to be gained from examining the extent to which teleconferencing effects interaction patterns within the group, leadership, credibility of members, and so on in real organizational settings. Just as we find the laboratory findings on appropriate activities for teleconferencing challenged by "real world" usage, we may also find the dynamics of ongoing work groups to differ significantly from laboratory groups.

Effects of teleconferencing on expectations associated with communication norms. Teleconferencing may alter the very nature of organizational norms associated with appropriate communications behavior. For example, expectations may change with respect to time required to transact business and acceptable mode choices for given tasks. The need to be there in person may change dramatically as people adjust to "being there" via video. Research assessing changes on communications norms as the result of adopting and implementing new communication technologies will produce useful insights on the factors shaping communication norms in organizations.

CONCLUSION

After 50 years of existence and several decades of active experimentation, teleconferencing remains a seemingly underutilized mode of organizational communication. Current interest in teleconferencing seems justified, given existing applications, which demonstrate some of the many potential benefits attributed to this medium. Yet uncertainty continues to be the dominant operating force, with organizations unsure about how to apply which type of teleconferencing technology, and what benefits they can expect.

This uncertainty can be reduced by focusing on the nature and pattern of present organizational communications. No matter what proponents claim, teleconferencing is merely another possible communications tool for business employees. It has unique attributes, which may facilitate its individual and group acceptance, but these attributes will come into play only with proper adoption, placement, and implementation within an ongoing organizational setting. Only when organizations approach the adoption and implementation of teleconferencing with a sure knowledge of their own communication interests will teleconferencing be successfully incorporated into everyday business operations.

NOTES

1. Occasionally, several different locations may serve as originating sites over the course of a conference. However, the interaction remains one-way video and two-way audio, despite changes in the originating location.

2. There are instances in which teleconferencing is used by organization members without a significant organizational adoption, such as a small group of employees conducting audio conferences with existing phone equipment. However,

most teleconferencing applications require organizational decisions on equipment purchase, space utilization and the like.

3. In those instances in which teleconferencing reaches the corporate agenda through a felt need by some work group in the organization, the entire adoption and implementation process can be short-circuited. Several of the most successful examples of organization teleconferencing happened just this way (Boeing, Ford, Honeywell, to mention a few).

4. Media use in organizations is determined by several factors, with the social presence of the medium only one of them. Communication acts in organizations are part of an ongoing process, where any single transaction may support, promote, or result from other communication activities. Laboratory experiments, which isolate participants from any context of ongoing communication processes, do not accurately reflect the myriad influences on channel choice (see Irving, 1981; Pye and Young, 1982; Ruchinskas, 1982).

5. Social presence is at best a vague concept, never clearly defined by its proponents. See Chapter 3 for criticisms of social presence.

Part IV: Communicating Within Institutions and Environments

Individuals may choose to adopt and use new media, within economic and social constraints. Organizations may feel pressured to adopt word processing or office automation and, depending on the implementation approach taken, to begin integrating the media within its activities shortly thereafter. Institutional change is by necessity, or perhaps by definition, slower.

In this section "institution" is not a specific place or entity; it is, rather, a locus of social norms, goals, and activities that are deemed significant by that society. For example, library services, education, and media industries are all institutions that operate within their own constraints—political and economic constraints, and those set by their particular environments. Thus, communication activities such as integrating new media within extant institutional structures are subject to a variety of constraints and pressures. Each of the chapters in Part IV discusses some of the institutional trends related to new media.

Chapter 10 argues that not only must libraries take advantage of new information technologies for their survival, but libraries have a tremendous opportunity to play an institutional role in providing information access to all segments of society. The history of libraries shows continual expansion and technological development. Many of the information systems appropriate to library services are described within the context of content, audience, and use, and technological trends relating to input, storage, transmission, and output. However, both the constraints and opportunities are significantly influenced by economic and political forces over which libraries have only limited control. Research into some of these forces, such as determining the value of information and regulations about information flow, is explored.

The institution of education is the context for Chapter 11, which looks at the future of educational computing in the context of past television research. There are historical, economic, theoretical, and empirical similarities as well as differences between these two media, and the benefits for educational use of computers depends on a proper understanding of these similarities and differences. For example, television diffused rapidly, but in individual homes; educational microcomputing is diffusing through educational institutions and, thus, has very different implications for diffusion speed, social equality access, and application. Rather than focusing on the antisocial effects, as was the case with early television studies, contemporary researchers emphasize the positive potential of computers for augmenting children's active cognitive processes. Thus, interactivity and involvement become the focus for this new area of research, but also require cross-disciplinary research efforts.

Chapter 12 closes the book by providing theoretical and analytical tools for understanding the effects of different media upon each other. Only with such a conceptual and methodological framework, based upon empirical analyses of prior mass media, can we begin to understand the institutional consequences of new media. Notions such as niche, niche overlap, niche breadth, displacement, and survival are introduced to explicate the argument that media compete for resources (such as advertising dollars and content), and that the entry of new media necessarily create shifts in distribution and utilization of these resources. It may well be difficult to predict what the effect of new media such as music video will have on radio, or videotex on newspapers, but we are beginning to develop tools for understanding what happens in the past and present.

W. DAVID PENNIMAN and
MARY ELLEN JACOB

10 Libraries as Communicators of Information

In the United States there are over 85,000 publicly available libraries in communities, public schools, and colleges or universities (Information Hotline, 1978). These institutions represent a major storehouse of human knowledge. Their value, however, rests not in their facility to store information (which was a primary role in medieval times) but to disseminate it in large quantities to a knowledge-seeking public (see, for example, Branscomb, 1979). New library media today can provide the mechanism for this large-scale dissemination, and this chapter will discuss research on how humans interact with the new technology in libraries. But the technology also offers a great deal more. Modern technology offers libraries the promise of becoming the communications links between institutions, communities, and even countries as new computerized library systems are linked together. That also is the topic of this chapter.

HISTORY OF LIBRARIES AND LIBRARY-RELATED TECHNOLOGY

To set the stage for the rest of this chapter, a brief chronology of the development of libraries and library technology appears in Table 10.1. The items chosen for this table are meant to represent benchmarks, not a comprehensive list of events. What these benchmarks illustrate, however, is a steady, inexorable progression of technologies and social change leading us to today's situation where libraries are poised at the brink of a revolution. They are faced with new opportunities and challenges. If they do not evolve and adapt, their very survival may be threatened. Static entities have little chance for survival.

Asimov (1977: 33-34) describes the progression illustrated by Table 10.1 as follows:

> [I]n 650 B.C. Ashurbanipal of Assyria collected bricks in his palace—stacks and stacks of bricks marked with fine cuneiform imprinting that held the gathered knowledge of 2500 years of culture in the Tigres-Euphrates Valley. Four centuries later, Ptolemy of Egypt . . . began the process of accumulating the papyrus rolls that were to make up the largest library the world had seen up to that time.

> Down to well into modern times that was the pattern of the storehouses of knowledge—they were the private property of kings and of great noblemen, and were available for use to a very few.

> But now the smallest town can have a collection of books that rivals all but the greatest libraries of past ages, and, considering the advance of knowledge, contains in its least reference work wonders undreamed of by the great minds of the past.

> So we must conclude that the most democratic place of learning in the world is the public library. It is there that we can find information on any subject, reading what we will, and how we will. And I look forward to the time when computerization will place in every home a terminal connected to some central library which will place, in facsimile, or on the television screen, the resources of human generations at the very fingertips of even the least of humanity.

For libraries, the invention of writing, paper, and printing with movable type are landmark events. Writing, whether on clay, tablets, papyrus, or skin led to the establishment of libraries to house, organize, and transmit the cumulative heritage of mankind. The Gutenberg press led to mass communications on a scale unknown and probably inconceivable before then. It placed in the hands of scholars and commoners information previously restricted to the few.

The impact of books such as the English translation of Spanish sailing knowledge in promoting exploration and settlement is of obvious signifi-

TABLE 10.1 A Brief Chronology of Library-Related Historical Events

Period	Event
–30,000 to –15,000	Cave paintings, earliest sculpting of animals
–15,000 to –10,000	Formal spoken language
–10,000 to –5,000	Rock paintings and engravings
–5,000 to –2,500	Pictographic writing in use (clay tablets)
–2,500 to birth of Christ	Recorded evidence of libraries
	Public libraries in Athens
	Foundation of great library of Alexandria
	Public libraries in Rome
	Oldest known computer made of bronze used for navigation
Birth of Christ to 1000	Development of paper-based records as a result of paper manufacturing in China
	Large library founded at Caesarea
	Library in Alexandria destroyed
	First printed book
1000 to 1500	First printing from movable type
	Encyclopedia produced by B. Anglicus showing state of knowledge of his day
	First European paper mill
	Gutenberg press
	Vatican library started
1500 to 1800	Spanish sailing knowledge first published in English
	Johnson's Dictionary of English Usage
	Wooden printing press replaced by metal one
1800 to 1900	Telegraph printer developed
	Hollerith developed electric tabulator for Census Bureau
	Wireless telegraphy
1900 to 1940	First television demonstrated
	Turing machine
	TV development
1940 to 1950	General purpose digital computers
	Commercial TV
	Xerography
	Photo typesetting

(Continued)

TABLE 10.1 Continued

Period	Event
1950 to 1960	Commercial computers
	Educational TV
	Video tape recording
1960 to 1970	Computer utilities
	Resource sharing computer networks (including OCLC)
	Data-base management systems
	Computer typesetting
	Laser printing
	Public TV
	Satellite telecommunications
	Spreading use of microforms for information storage and dissemination
1970 to 1980	Integration of software functions into hardware
	Interactive television systems
	Large screen TV
	Videodisc
	Information utilities and search systems (including The Source, DIALOG, BRS, Prestel)
	Widespread use of value added networks
1980s	Personal computers
	Artificial-intelligence-based software
	Laser communications

cance. The Dictionary of English Usage by Dr. Johnson facilitated the standardization of language and spelling.

Recently the development of telecommunications, computers, and networks is changing the way libraries organize, operate, and serve users. No longer must a library acquire for its own collection all the possible materials its users may demand. Now it can tap the resources of other libraries through resource sharing networks such as Online Computer Library Center (OCLC) and Research Libraries Information Network (RLIN). It can acquire full text of some journal articles from Bibliographic Retrieval Service (BRS) or Mead's NEXIS.

The rapidly increasing development of communications technology should not be surprising. Nor should the possible warning that it holds:

> If today we use our shiny new tools in ways that glorify their limitations—if we seek to get our news from machines rather than from people—then our tools may enslave and befuddle us more than they serve us. It would be all too easy to spread darkness with the speed of light [Lovins and Lovins, 1981].

Given this historical perspective, where are libraries and information services today, and how should they be developing? We start with an overview of current systems, user developments, and studies followed by the impact of technology, economics, and politics. Finally, we look at where the present situation and trends are leading us and what this implies for the future of libraries.

CURRENT SYSTEMS

There are many ways of viewing and categorizing current library-oriented information systems. Two ways used in this section will deal with the information *content* and with intended *audience*. Content will separate bibliographic systems from nonbibliographic systems and audience will separate business and special purpose use from general or mass use.

Content

Bibliographic systems are primarily oriented to information about information, i.e., citations to reports, journals, books, or other print form information. Such systems had their genesis during the sixties, when computer storage was still limited and grew from systems designed to produce abstracting and indexing publications such as Chemical Abstracts or Index Medicus, or from union catalogs of machine readable data such as OCLC or RLIN.

Newer systems with significantly increased storage and processing capability are focusing on storing and accessing full-text information. Examples of full-text systems include Mead's LEXIS and NEXIS, the American Medical Association's MINET, and the American Chemical Society's mounting of selected journals on BRS. Mead's LEXIS contains the full text of laws and statutes and NEXIS includes a variety of newspapers. MINET, in conjunction with General Telephone, provides access to medical journals, handbook data, and *Excepta Medica* (Electronic Publishing Review, 1982a).

Most of the bibliographic systems were developed during the sixties, although they did not come into widespread use until the seventies. There are two major groups of bibliographic systems: *information search* services, providing content access—DIALOG, BRS, and System Development Corporation (SDC)—and *technical support* services—OCLC and RLIN. DIALOG mounts over 200 data bases, primarily based on abstracting and indexing publications including Chemical Abstracts, Educational Resources Information Clearinghouse (ERIC), the Monthly Catalog of Government Documents, and Magazine Index. The data bases and their content are accessible through title key-word, index, and subject terms. Users may obtain printed copies of searches or individual records. DIALOG does not contain location information for items, although its ordering service (Dialorder) does provide access to potential suppliers.

OCLC, in contrast, does not provide subject access. Its main function is resource sharing and catalog support. It contains location information for all the items in its file as well as a system to facilitate transfer of items between institutions. In addition to online access, it provides catalogue cards, accession lists, printed labels, and machine-readable tape copies of records for individual institutional use.

The last several years have seen a significant increase in systems and data bases developed for *nonbibliographic* uses. Such uses include numeric and statistical analysis, economic or demographic forecasting, market research, and scientific experimentation. Such data include the U.S. Bureau of the Census data, econometric and statistical data, physical constants, and a variety of other types of data. DIALOG and BRS offer access to some of these files, and use of these is growing faster than use of bibliographic files (Electronic Publishing Review, 1982b).

Several new entrants have recently started offering services, including Dow Jones, Dun and Bradstreet, Reuters, and I. P. Sharp. Many of these new entrants are financial or business firms primarily interested in economic, financial, or business measures. As executive use of microcomputers and time-shared services grows, these firms will expand their offerings.

Public data-base publishers are enjoying strong and continuous demand, averaging 30% customer growth during a nine-month period in 1982 (Russell, 1983). Six of the 17 companies reported by Russell serve more than 20,000 users each; over 700 publishers provided 1,450 different data bases by means of over 220 online services. This represents a growth of 53% in data bases and 61% in online services in the past two years. Cuadra Associates (1983b) reported a rise to 1878 online data bases by November 1983, involving 272 vendors and 927 data-base producers.

Audience

As might be expected, content and audience categorization overlap. Some of the use of nonbibliographic files are by mass or general user, although most fall in the professional or business user class.

MASS AUDIENCE

A number of systems, originally aimed at the mass marketplace, have since changed their orientation. The Source and Prestel both started out as mass market information services. Both have since found that the majority of their users come from the business or professional community and have been repositioning their offerings toward this group.

There are several difficult questions to be asked by anyone contemplating mass market services (Forbes, 1983). Various studies have explored this issue, but while intentions to use have been assessed, there are no real use data available, because commercial offerings are not yet operating or have only just started. Questions that must be answered by the marketplace include the following:

(1)   What kinds of information will the general user pay for?

(2)   Are there uses beyond education and entertainment?

(3)   What is the perceived value of such information services, and how much will the user pay?

(4)   Are most subgroups such as professional/business users already satisfied by work-related services?

DIALOG and BRS are both offering services aimed at the mass market. They have repackaged existing services and offered special pricing for use after 5:00 p.m. Both have been advertising in professional and scientific journals, but so far no data have been published to verify the success of these offerings nor the volume of use by general users.

Another entry into this mass market is the Knight-Ridder Videotex offering introduced in the fall of 1983 in Coral Gables. (See Chapters 2 and 5). This offering is aimed at upscale users and is intended to be personalized. If it succeeds it will signal likely success for similar offerings.

BUSINESS AUDIENCE

The only successful offerings to date have been to the business and professional audience. Both The Source and Prestel, originally targeted to mass use, have since reoriented themselves to this group of users. The Dow Jones and other financial quoting services are aimed at those investing in stocks or other financial instruments. Users include professional financial analysts as well as private investors.

Another group which has shown an interest in and a willingness to pay for information are agribusinesses and farmers. Information on the weather, agriculture and commodities markets, futures, and prices are offered. Project Green Thumb was sponsored by the Department of Agriculture (Rice and Paisley, 1982), and similar services are being offered commercially by Agridata (Electronic Publishing Review, 1982c).

OCLC and RLIN are targeted toward library staff. They focus on known item searches; that is, the user has some information about the specific book, report, article, film, or other item desired. A major function is the support of cataloging activities. Each library maintains a record of its collection in the form of a catalog. Creating the records for the catalog is costly and time consuming. Using such systems, a library staff member can locate, if available, an existing record and use it. If no record is available, a work form may be completed. Once the record is created it can be manipulated to produce catalog cards, magnetic tape records, book labels, accession lists, or other products.

OCLC has over ten million bibliographic items in its data base representing over 152 million locations. New records are added at the rate of over one million per year. This vast resource allows libraries to use records created by others 94% of the time, which means that on the average, out of one hundred new books, a library need create only six new records. This increases library staff productivity and provides more rapid access to new materials. The location data provide library staff and scholars access to materials regardless of physical location. Esoteric or rare items held by only one or two institutions can be located easily. Libraries can spend funds more wisely knowing what materials nearby libraries have.

Public access terminals are available but account for only a small percentage of total activity. Similarly, most of the searching done on BRS and DIALOG is either research- or work-related.

LIBRARY USE AND USERS

While it can be argued that librarians were the first information professionals long before there was an "information age," the real question is whether or not libraries will survive in this age and, if so, in what form. A visit to most public libraries shows little improvement in the "user interface." While there may be a microfilm or microfiche reader in lieu of a card catalog, most would argue there has been little change and no improvement. Despite the apparent lack of change, libraries are poised on the brink of radical restructuring of the user interface and the ways the library is perceived by users. The forces leading to this restructuring include (a) increased automation behind the scenes within libraries, which now makes possible online public access catalogs and (b) increased computer literacy among the portion of the population using library services most heavily. In the following paragraphs some of the recent research that will influence library use and users is discussed.

The Council on Library Resources can be credited with providing the leadership and resources for a series of cooperative studies of online catalogs in the early 1980s. These studies attempted a comprehensive look at such catalogs and their use within academic and public library settings. The results were far-ranging and have yet to be fully felt in terms of impact on library systems and, ultimately, on library users, but the studies have already served to raise the level of consciousness of librarians through numerous reports, conferences, and briefings.

Earlier studies, such as the comprehensive evaluation by Markey (1980) of previous work in the area of subject access, pointed up the major problems of the access systems now within libraries (i.e., card catalogs). These systems are difficult to use effectively, provide little in the way of user aids, and do not lend themselves to rapid iterative searching with varied strategies. With the council's concerted efforts, progress is likely in the development of tools for searching provided by libraries. Of greater concern is the context in which these tools will be used.

The Library of Congress Network Advisory Committee, concerned about how people would locate information in the year 2000, sponsored a study to look at possible library scenarios (Crooks, 1982). While Crooks saw reason for serious concern about the survival of libraries, she also felt the vital roles for libraries would continue. Other researchers have questioned the future of one of the mainstays of the academic library—the scholarly journal. Hickey (1981) describes the journal in the year 2000 as an electronic document tailored to the needs of the user (see also Turoff and Hiltz, 1982a). Libraries will be pressed to provide more such user-tailored products without significantly increasing their investment (Lindquist, 1977). As a result, libraries will have to move from free to fee-based services in many areas. This change will require significant research in areas currently foreign to most libraries, such as pricing strategy, marketing, and value analysis. It is likely that library-oriented studies such as the one by Ramsing and Wish (1982) concerned with value measurement methods will increase, and that libraries will turn to market-oriented techniques to meet user needs.

While the card catalog may disappear in the years to come, the problems of providing effective user interfaces will not. The new access devices (i.e., computer terminals) are not without shortcomings. Seldom did the user find a card drawer already in use. With terminals instead of card files, the user may have to wait for access to a terminal, or the library must invest in enough terminals to reduce the likelihood of a lengthy wait for users during peak load hours. The study of this problem is reported by Kaske and Sanders (1983) and some techniques for meeting user needs are presented; but there is no general rule of thumb, and each library must carefully study its own operating conditions.

The commands and query languages used in the new access devices within libraries are not universally easy to use. Studies involving monitoring of online use (e.g., Borgman, 1983; Dominick, Penniman, and Rush, 1980) have indicated surprisingly high error rates. Users often have problems gaining access to the system, and when they do they often give up too early in a search, even though the system does contain information relevant to their query. The literature on "user friendly" interfaces abounds, yet most of our current information-retrieval technology still demands that the user adapt to the machine. According to Baker and Eason (1981: 131),

> In short we may characterize the interaction witnessed as a computer dominated process in which the intermediary and to some extent the customers adapt their behavior to suit the computer.

Attempts to develop uniform user interfaces have met with limited success, and compromise solutions involving intermediate devices for achieving uniformity are now being proposed (see, for example, Treu, 1982). Comparisons of command, menu selection, and natural language approaches have failed to provide conclusive results (Hauptman and Green, 1983; Small, 1983).

Experiments with relatively simple menu-selection approaches for mass access to information sources (e.g., OCLC, 1981; Bolton 1980) indicated that this approach was easy to learn but soon proved frustrating to the user (see Chapter 5). Library catalog access approaches built on the same principles may provide easy access initially, but could lead to user frustration on a mass scale, resulting in ultimate rejection by consumers. Should this occur, the void would likely be filled by more responsive information providers in the commercial sector.

Among the most recent developments that may offer both opportunity for and threat to libraries is the emergence of knowledge-based or expert systems (Duda and Shortliffe, 1983; Nav, 1983). While current technology limits application of such systems to high-value areas such as medicine, engineering, and defense, there is no reason why some of the more labor-intensive areas involving user-library interaction (e.g., reference questions) cannot also be addressed with these emerging systems. The opportunity is one of reducing cost of operation while improving the service that libraries can provide. The threat is that someone else may do it earlier and better than libraries, leaving libraries with the costly, but not cost-effective remainder.

TECHNOLOGY

A number of technologies affect information systems, including telecommunications, computers and peripherals, and optical and video technology. These include such diverse devices as communicating copiers, satellite transmission, local area networks, cable TV, electronic mail, the Kurzweil Reading machine, optical character readers, printers, videodisc, computer microfilm technology, computers, and associated peripheral equipment. This list is by no means exhaustive. Such diverse disciplines as electronics, printing, librarianship, communication sciences, data processing, publishing, optics, and records management are concerned with the many problems of information storage, retrieval, and delivery.

Information systems are storing vastly larger quantities of information than ever before. System operators must also be able to access it quickly and efficiently and transmit it without error to users. Processing full-text information and delivering quality graphics are possible but are pushing the limits of commercially available technology and the price level users will support.

Much of current technology is either still in the developmental stage or too costly to be used in the library or home environment, but this picture is changing rapidly. What is not changing so quickly is user behavior and patterns of information access and use. Many users still have biases against machines and machine-assisted processes. This "high tech, high touch" phenomenon was noted by Naisbitt (1982).

It is difficult to provide an ideal categorization for discussing technology for information services and delivery. There is overlap no matter what approach is chosen. Some devices and technology provide a continuous process, not a discrete one. Nonetheless, we have considered four major areas: input, storage, transmission, and output. These are purely arbitrary but fit familiar actions and activities.

Input

Input devices depend on where in the process the data are captured. Many new journals are being created in machine-readable form through existing computer technology (Doebler, 1980; Frank, 1982; Hickey, 1981). Of major interest to libraries is how older information not currently in machine-readable form can be converted or at least transmitted electronically. Considerable activity is under way in the area of videodisc, electronic imaging (including digitizing cameras), and optical storage. These areas are discussed further under the section on storage.

Two areas of particular interest to libraries are the development of the Kurzweil Reading machine and optical character readers. The Kurzweil machine converts printed text into spoken word for use by blind or visually impaired people. It will accept a variety of printed materials, including bound books. It operates on optical character reading (OCR) and pattern matching techniques. Continued development of the Kurzweil machine as well as language translation uses indicates more improvements will be forthcoming (Cushman, 1980; Weinberg, 1980).

Optical character reading continues to improve. More fonts as well as hand printing and, in certain instances, cursive scripts can be handled. Unfortunately, a low-cost machine providing even all printed fonts is not yet available. Digitizing of images and their transmission may reduce the need to actually convert print material to machine-intelligible or interpretable information. The ability to scan it and transmit it without further manipulation may be sufficient for many document delivery applications.

Another area of interest for input is the development of communicating copiers, an extension of present photocopying processes (Arnett, 1981; Computerworld, 1982; Fukae, 1980; Hanson, 1980). With such facilities, instead of making and mailing a photocopy, a library making a copy can simultaneously create a copy on a machine located in another library. Xerox has announced a table-top model for under $5000 (Wall Street Journal, October 19, 1983). This device will function as a copier, computer printer, and telefacsimile machine. Such a device eliminates the need for a separate, single-purpose machine. A communicating copier can be used for both copying and telefacsimile.

Telefacsimile has been around some time, and several experiments have been undertaken in the library community (Boss and McQueen, 1983; Lerner, Mick, and Callahan, 1980; Marcum and Boss, 1981; Saffady, 1978; Waters, 1979). These studies indicate that lack of use of telefacsimile is primarily due to the attitude and choice of library staff, as a reaction to cost, quality problems, and inconvenience. These factors are changing rapidly. While costs are still higher than most librarians would like, they are affordable for certain uses. Many businesses are beginning to use telefacsimile, and as locations of machines increase so does their accessibility to libraries. Bound volume problems will eventually disappear, reducing the damage to materials and making the process more efficient, but it is not yet clear where and when telefacsimile will merge with communicating copiers.

Storage

Much has been written about the potential of videodisc for use in libraries and for information storage (see Chapter 2). The Library of Congress, The National Library of Medicine, and numerous other organizations are active in applications of this technology. The Library of Congress has been experimenting with videodisc for preserving library materials. They also use it for storing images of catalog cards for reproduction of individual cards on demand.

Technologies such as videodisc, optical and digital image storage, and magnadot, to name a few, offer interesting facilities for document preservation, storage, and distribution. The image quality, the cost, and ease of use are improving.

In addition to video storage, we will see continued development of other storage technologies. We will see greater capacity in all storage, including 50 million bytes on floppy disks. Hard disk, which is used on most larger computer systems, will also increase capacity and reduce costs. More exotic memory storage technologies will also appear. Holographic image memory has some interesting potential for nontraditional materials storage, particularly for art objects, engineering models, and other three-dimensional objects.

Transmission

Transmission media are also developing and improving, as outlined in Chapter 2. Satellite communication, fiber optics, and digital techniques are providing more, lower-cost options that are less distance dependent. Continued developments and reduced costs in this area are essential for effective information-delivery systems. Pressure for continued development will come from all aspects of society.

A number of factors will affect future developments and availability of transmission technology. Not least among these are the social and political factors associated with the recent settlement of the antitrust suits against IBM and AT&T and with AT&T's divestiture. The latter is of particular importance to the development of telecommunications. The cost implications of divestiture are indicating substantial rises in library telecommunications costs for the next several years. This may halt or slow the use of local systems requiring dedicated telecommunication; it also could affect access to systems like OCLC and, to a lesser degree, those relying on value-added networks.

Output

Output may be of two main types: soft or hard. *Soft* ouput would normally appear on some type of display unit, such as a conventional cathode ray terminal (CRT) or television screen. Such displays are adequate for much material, but not for high-quality graphics. Quality graphic displays are expensive, but prices are dropping.

Limited amounts of printed information can be displayed effectively on a television screen. These limitations are a function of present U. S. and European signal standards controlling display resolution. A full encyclopedia page would have to be displayed in small segments requiring a number of screens. The Japanese have developed a higher-resolution television screen, which would increase screen capacity and capability for graphics displays, but it is not yet available in the United States. In addition, there have been numerous studies documenting the fatigue effects of long hours of CRT use (see Note 1 in Chapter 7).

Technology will improve, and certainly access and available alternatives will have much to do with user acceptance of soft copy output. It is well suited to conveying ready access to information of a limited volume. Electronic mail and conferencing systems indicate users can overcome inherent deficiencies, although there are a number of users of such systems relying on printer units instead of CRTs.

The slow acceptance and use of microform technology, which requires use of reading devices, indicates some of the problems to be faced and overcome before soft copy can be viewed as a substitute or an effective replacement for hard copy, printed output. Some aspects of these problems are discussed by Line (1981). Many users simply do not like using CRTs or mechanical devices.

The second major type of output is *hard* copy. Printed output is a relatively bright spot in the technological area. Better quality, cheaper, more reliable printers are being developed and marketed. Newer technology such as ink jet and laser printing offer more improvements for the future. Communicating copiers offer potential in not only paper output, but also microform (Computerworld, 1982). This could be useful in allowing high-speed transmission between distant libraries while using conventional services, such as mail or United Parcel Service between libraries and users. This would be an interim solution reducing overall costs of delivery until low-cost units for library and home use were available.

ECONOMIC AND POLITICAL ENVIRONMENTS

The economic and political environments are changing and will change even more. The two are inextricably intertwined. In a full-fledged service economy there are fewer products to tax, and services become the primary revenue source. Some governments and states have already begun to tax services. (For instance, California taxes software.) Foreign governments are considering taxing information flows.

Libraries and users face major challenges in how to maintain equity of access to information when information becomes an economic good. What rights have citizens to electronic information services? Are these available only to those with the funds to pay, or does government provide subsidized access for some users? Several reviews of this issue have appeared recently, including Braunstein (1979), Buckwell (1983), Drake and Olsen (1979), Griffiths (1982), and King (1979, 1982).

Economics

This review of information economics is divided into four sections. First, the problems of determining and defining value are considered. Second, the costing of information and property rights are discussed. Third, the problem of substitutes is considered. Last, limitations of analysis techniques and data are outlined.

VALUE

There is probably no area of concern that has more ambiguity associated with it than the economics of information. The application of such economic analysis to information services is discussed by Griffiths (1982). She highlights the problems of the subjective aspect of value, the time dependencies of information, and the user context. She does not mention the frequent discrepancy between purchasers' reported intent and their actual behavior when offered a choice requiring payment. It is sometimes difficult to trace the source of information, its direct influence on both our attitudes and our later contributions, and, consequently, its value. Information is context-dependent, but it has other characteristics that create further confusion. The value of information may be diminished by sharing, or it may be unchanged. This depends on the information and the context in which it exists. Further, sharing may add value to information.

COST OF INFORMATION CREATION AND GENERATION

Most information services involve not the creation of information but its repackaging. In some instances this enables a fairly straightforward estimation of costs, in others it does not. Again, aspects of this are discussed in the Griffiths paper and in other studies done by the King research staff in determining costs for the Department of Energy (King, 1979, 1982). Cost allocation here, as in other areas of economic concern, are somewhat fuzzy, and decisions are often based on experience and subjective judgment.

There are, in the engineering and business literature, well-documented studies on opportunity costs of information. Given a specific project that will provide a given return with certain levels of risk and ambiguity associated with it, the cost of acquiring information to reduce that ambiguity can be determined or estimated. However, such a determination or estimate is only as valuable as the underlying assumptions on which it is based. Typically these studies assume that certain interest rates will prevail, which depends on the stability of the economy and the current rate of inflation. The King (1982) study did demonstrate savings to the user, but these savings depended on what cost was assigned to user time and on the validity of the benefits derived.

There is considerable discussion about the nature of information itself and whether in economic terms it can be considered a commodity, a public good, or other type of economic good. Several writers have explored the concepts of what makes information valuable to the user. An interesting concept put forward by Gordon Thompson of Bell Northern Labs is that information has value to the extent that we give our attention to it. He suggests that we need new ways of charging for information and that we should look at some of the parallels that exist in radio and music broadcasting, such as the various licensing and royalty fees when a radio station plays a piece of music or when a local orchestra plays a piece of copyrighted music.

At present, library users do not pay an explicit fee besides taxes when they use library materials. If materials are in electronic form, will users have to pay to access information, to copy all or selected portions of the data, to reformat or manipulate it? Some of the services allow copying and manipulation of information, others do not. Keplinger (1980) surveys the relationships between copyright issues and information technology.

Librarians are defensive on the topic of copyright issues. They are caught between users' wanting information and the property rights of authors and publishers. Most of the problems relate to photocopying of journal articles. The questions associated with electronic forms of information are troubling because of the ambiguity associated with these forms. Data bases can and are being copyrighted. Access to electronic data often requires signing contracts that have more restrictions than does copyright law. The ability to copy, extract, and manipulate electric data easily creates more opportunities for abuse. Cuadra Associates' recent study (1983a) indicates that the problem, while not yet major, is real.

In looking at the value of information, copyright is intended to protect the expression of ideas but not the ideas themselves. Patents can protect certain ideas, but do not apply to much of the data in information systems, although they do apply to a physical representation or process. That is, another individual or organization can say the same thing using different words. This applies most clearly in the case of works of fiction, where the same plots may be used over and over again by different authors, without plagiarism. However, if the words used or the expressions are too close, then copyright infringement may occur.

Others have indicated that information value in the future will be provided by those removing redundancy from information and providing required information without all of the overload that may otherwise occur. Information-analysis centers or others will, in response to a user's query for information, be able to provide not just sources where that information may be found, but the actual information itself. This service verges on becoming a fact retrieval system or expert knowledge system.

SUBSTITUTES

Alternatives to or substitutes for particular media or information also confuse the issue. Differing user populations are willing to pay differing amounts based on their differing perceived values of the information package. This is particularly apparent in the case of government information, which may be available direct from the government or via repackaging services (such as census data). In a number of instances the repackaging services charge substantial amounts for their collection, indexing, and presentation of the information in a form more readily accessible to users than is provided by the government information service. Because of the availability of substitutes or alternatives for information provision, users often are highly sensitive to price.

LIMITATIONS

Because so much is context- and user-dependent, the rules available through decision and information theory, while providing a guide, do not fully satisfy suppliers' and users' needs in determining price or value. They can, however, be used to determine an upper limit on price; because of the subjective aspects of information, users, and information uses, however, they can only remain guidelines.

Online systems offer both new opportunities and new threats to information providers. It is possible to control access to information in ways not previously possible with print media. This will come to the fore with electronic publishing as publishers are able to control who has access to their files and what type of access they have (Page, 1983). Monitoring of usage will be much more effective than in the past.

On the other hand, information in electronic form can be readily copied and reproduced. Better monitoring techniques may be developed as well as software protection codes and materials. Further, the security of information systems seems rather permeable; there have been increasing cases of individuals and groups illegally tapping into online time-sharing systems and gaining access to various data bases and programs.

Innovation in the area of access, monitoring, and protection will affect cost of operation and pricing of services. Dialogue will continue on fee versus free services. Because of continuing costs pressures on libraries, differentiation will occur between base-level services and value-added services. Base-level services will be provided either free or at a subsidized rate. Value-added services, such as reducing the delay in delivery of information or adding further to its analysis or packaging, will incur additional charges.

Politics

Political concerns are diverse and include not only U.S. policy, but international policy as well. U.S. moves to deregulate telecommunications are being followed in the United Kingdom, but not elsewhere. Much of the international concern relates to the influence of information on cultural heritage, political stability, and economic survival (see, for example, Schiller, 1982).

Many of the political issues relate to economics. These include subsidies, fees for services, taxation, and who provides services. Libraries are mainly tax-supported institutions. Sources of funding and changes in the tax legislation are of critical concern to libraries. They are under increased pressures to charge for services, particularly for new or innovative services such as information-search services and electronic document delivery. Libraries have concerns related to their ability to access and acquire the information sources needed by their users. This debate has been sharply focused on the Depository Library Program from the Government Printing Office. Maintaining the provision of free copies for libraries is costly. These costs must be balanced against citizens' rights to information about or generated by government agencies.

Changes in U.S. and state regulatory policies will affect the speed and pattern of library development. This is particularly so in relation to telecommunication and services requiring the use of telecommunication. Local telephone access charges will slow the development of computerized services in multibranch library systems until economic alternatives are available.

Politics also shape and are shaped by society. The library, to be effective, must respond to its political realities as well as societal needs. Its services and functions are not determined in isolation, but in response to the articulated needs of its particular user community. It may be more responsive to some elements of that community than to others, particularly to those elements having control over economic resources.

THE COMING DECADE

The form and uses of communication media will continue to change. We have an aging population. This will increase the need for continuing education, lifelong learning and retraining, entertainment, and medical services, which will generate opportunities and challenges for libraries as well as a variety of other professionals. We will continue to have stubborn pockets of unemployment and an imbalance between people available and the job skills needed. We will need fewer people for factories and traditional offices, but more for providing personal and information services.

We will inevitably move to more information systems and linkages among systems. Public data networks and protocol and interface standards will make it easier for users to access a variety of systems via a single access device. More information will be accessible. Major challenges exist in the organization and timely delivery of information. There will be greater emphasis on the analysis and synthesis of information. This, in turn, will require the employment of more highly skilled staff with more subject knowledge in libraries and information centers.

It is unlikely that we will completely abandon printed information, but, where time is critical, softer electronic forms will take over. Information format will be more flexible and task related. Some information will appear in a variety of media and formats. Some will appear only in a single form, such as electronic.

So, where are we at present? Do we have the technology to improve information services within libraries? Yes. Can libraries afford this technology? Only in a few cases. Is there sufficient material in a suitable form to use these technologies? No.

In the near term we can see improvement. Technology is offering more capability with improved quality at a reduced cost. Current information is being created and stored in machine-readable or digitized form. Research by institutions like the Library of Congress, the National Library of Medicine, OCLC, Xerox, AT&T, IBM, and Battelle, as well as computer, information science and library schools, and others will provide more cost-effective technology applicable to library and information system use.

Major problems, it seems, are related more to people and their needs than to technology per se. We must consider how we preserve and make existing collections accessible. How can we either overcome user preferences or, better, how can we adapt the technology to more effectively meet user needs and preferences? Libraries have a choice of many roles, as do publishers, printers, and information services. All can try to retain traditional roles, or they can work together seeking new patterns of relationships and activities. None will have a monopoly on all information needed by users.

Our most difficult problems will be in the political and economic areas. National and international information policies will affect our ability to access, use, and share information. This, in turn, will affect our technologies and our economies. There is a need to recognize the mutual dependencies and to overcome purely parochial interests. There is also a need for better understanding of why the present differences exist.

Economic issues lie at the heart of many of the problems. As we move to a service and information economy, new opportunities are created, but the most advanced users and countries are more likely to benefit from these than are the less affluent. We will have to develop new measures of wealth and of exchange and do so where not all partners are content with the roles assigned them.

If we are to achieve what Asimov (1977) predicted when he foresaw

in every home a terminal connected to some central library which will place, in facsimile, or on a television screen, the resources of human generations at the very fingertips of even the least of humanity,

then libraries must adapt, change, and become leaders in bringing these changes to society. They have the opportunity to provide information rights as well as privileges.

MILTON CHEN

11 Computers in the Lives of Our Children: *Looking Back on a Generation of Television Research*

THE HISTORICAL AND ECONOMIC CONTEXT

More than twenty years ago the landmark study of *Television in the Lives of Our Children* (Schramm, Lyle, and Parker, 1961) heralded a new era of research in the United States on a new technology known as television. Today, we stand in a similar moment in research history, roughly five years after the introduction of a new group of computer-based technologies including microcomputers, videotext, teletext, interactive cable, and microcomputer/videodisc systems. Since it appears that microcomputers will take the lead as a subject of research with children, this chapter will focus on that technology.

Children have demonstrated a remarkable affinity for both television and microcomputers. While they have not been considered a primary audience for much of the television they watch, children have been strong and loyal devotees of the medium. Recent Nielsen data indicate that children between the ages of 2 and 11 spend an average of 26 hours per week watching television (Nielsen, 1982b). This figure, as many have noted, exceeds the amount of time they spend in classrooms and surpasses every other activity of children, save sleep.

Already microcomputers are enjoying a similar popularity with children. Young people have been enthusiastic users of micros since their appearance in the late 1970s. As with television, while the marketing of computers is directed toward adults who hold the purchasing power, children are frequent and knowledgeable computer users. (TV ads for computers have taken to acknowledging this phenomenon, with children instructing the likes of Alan Alda and Dick Cavett.)

We know as little today about the effects of computers as we did about TV's effects in the mid-1950s. However, based on the pace at which children are beginning to use computers and the anecdotal accounts of their appeal and educational effects, children's learning from microcomputers has become an important topic for research. The first empirical studies of microcomputers and children are now under way at many universities and research centers.

This chapter considers this new era of research in light of the past decades of research on children and television. While the two media certainly differ as technologies, a comparative examination can illuminate answers to some useful questions. For instance, how do television and computers differ in their historical and economic contexts? How do such differences affect their ability to serve children? What are some developing differences in research perspectives and emphases given to television and microcomputers? And, given a common research focus on children, what can we apply from our knowledge of children as television viewers to their behaviors as computer users?

Diffusion Patterns for Television and Microcomputers

This point in the history of microcomputer usage by children is comparable to the period of television's diffusion into American society in the mid-1950s. Figure 11.1 shows the percentage of U.S. households with a TV set, for every five-year period from 1940 to 1980.

As the figure indicates, near-saturation levels for television's penetration were reached in the early 1960s, with TV sets in more than 90% of American homes. A. C. Nielsen also reports that as of 1982, 86% of American households had a color TV set, 52% were multiple-set households, and 44% had cable TV. The largest rate of diffusion occurred between 1950 and 1955, when TV ownership surpassed the criterion of ⅓ market penetration often deemed necessary for a popular and profitable innovation.

FIGURE 11.1 Television Sets in U.S. Households, 1940-1980

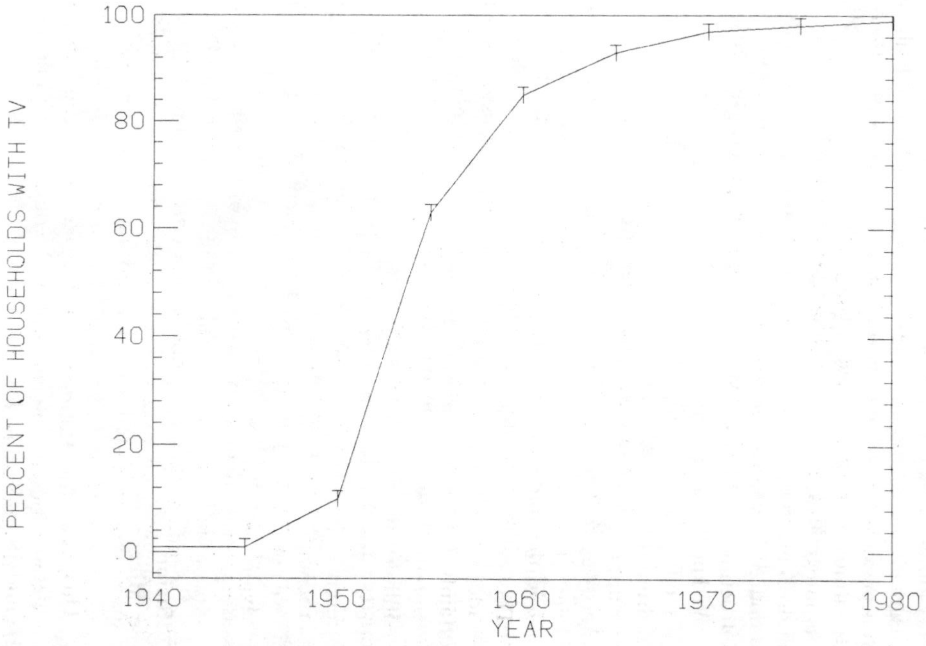

SOURCE: Liebert, Sprafkin, and Davidson (1982).

271

In 1984 microcomputers will be in the midst of their first decade of availability. While figures on the penetration of microcomputers into American homes change every six months, conservative estimates at the end of 1983 estimate that micros were available in 8% of American homes.

A recent survey by Becker (1983) of a probability sample of 2209 public, private, and parochial schools offers a more detailed look into the diffusion of microcomputers in schools. Figures 11.2 and 11.3 summarize data separately for the adoption of microcomputers in elementary versus high schools during the past three years.

As the figures indicate, 42% of elementary schools had one or more microcomputers being used for instructional purposes as of January 1983; less than 10% had five or more micros. At the high school level, 77% of secondary schools had at least one microcomputer, while 40% had five or more.

Comparison of Economic Characteristics of TV and Microcomputers

While the figures above suggest that micros may follow television's path in rapidly diffusing into American homes and schools, they belie some very different processes by which this diffusion is taking place. Adopting an economic framework, important differences in the supply and demand functions of the television and microcomputer "markets" are affecting these diffusion and use patterns. While a full discussion of the industry structures and economics of these markets is beyond the scope of this chapter, the general distinctions are apparent and useful to state here.

The history of domination of the television industry by the three commercial networks has been well documented (Barnouw, 1970; Brown, 1971); Network profits derive from the sale of audiences to advertising sponsors, rather than from the direct sale of individual programs to their consuming audiences. Since children do not control a major portion of family spending, they have not been a crucial audience for the supply of programming from networks and their sponsors. Commercial network programming intended for children has been relegated to Saturday morning cartoons and occasional afternoon specials. The child advocacy group Action for Children's Television has been among the most outspoken critics of the amount and educational value of commercial network programming for children.

The federal regulatory mandate over broadcast television has enabled formal governmental inquiry into the effects of television on children. In 1969 congressional concern over the possible deleterious effects of children's viewing of a high degree of television violence led to the formation of the Surgeon General's Committee on Television and Social Behavior. Under the auspices of that committee, the most extensive program of social research on a communication medium was undertaken from 1970 to 1972 (Surgeon General's Scientific Advisory Committee, 1972).

FIGURE 11.2 Microcomputers in Elementary Schools, 1980-1983

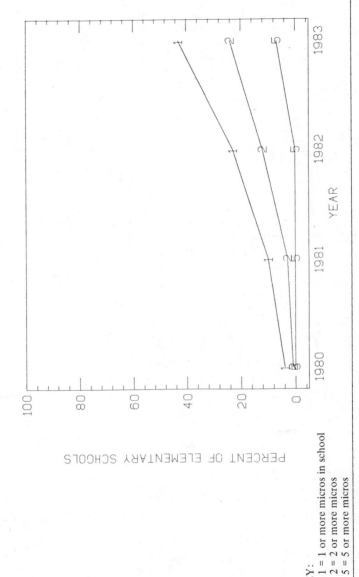

KEY:
1 = 1 or more micros in school
2 = 2 or more micros
5 = 5 or more micros

SOURCE: Becker (1983).

FIGURE 11.3   Microcomputers in Secondary Schools, 1980-1983

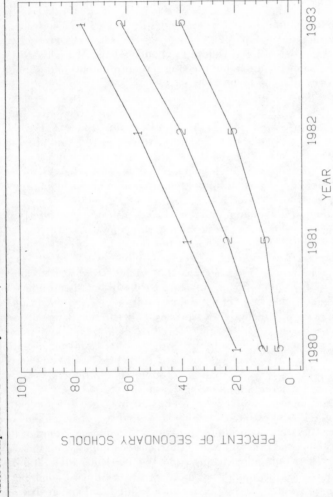

KEY:

1 = 1 or more micros in school
2 = 2 or more micros
5 = 5 or more micros

SOURCE: Becker (1983).

Without the profit-making constraints of commercial broadcasters, public television has provided a daily presence of educational programming for children. Programs such as *Sesame Street, The Electric Company, 3-2-1 Contact,* and *Mister Rogers' Neighborhood* are among the better-known Public Broadcasting Service (PBS) programs for children. In recent years cable television has offered children's channels (e.g., Warner's Nickleodeon, The Disney Channel), but the long-term profitability and viability of these services remains to be seen.

From the demand side of the television economy, there is essentially no direct cost (beyond the purchase of a TV set) to the consumer for the reception of broadcast television. The consumer pays indirectly to advertisers and networks through the increased price of goods due to advertising costs. Cable television reception does require direct costs to consumers, typically a one-time connect fee, monthly charges for basic services, and additional costs for special programming, including movies, sports, or children's channels.

Microcomputers present a different market picture. As with television, there is a distinction between the manufacture of hardware versus the provision of software (programming), but the industry relationships are more complex. The industry is dominated by several of the largest computer manufacturers (e.g., Apple, IBM, Atari, Radio Shack, Commodore). These firms not only manufacture hardware but also produce and commission software, both of which are paid for directly by consumers. Since industry standards have yet to emerge, certain microcomputers can run only certain software designed for their own operating systems.

The question of which software programs are available on which machines becomes a critical question for the adoption of computers in homes, offices, and schools. Analogous to television production, software design is itself a large and growing business.

The educational software market is in its infant stages. It is too early to predict how the market will mature, but some first steps have already been taken in the design of educational programs for children. Some of these programs go beyond drill-and-practice formats descended from a previous generation of mainframe machines and the curricular style known as "programmed instruction." The more creative formats combine the entertainment features of computer games with educational goals (sometimes labeled "discovery" software).

These early exemplars of educational software correspond to successful children's television programs such as *Sesame Street* produced in the late 1960s and early 1970s, nearly two decades after the introduction of television. In contrast, educational software for children has become an active sector of the microcomputer market only a few years after the technology itself became available. This early progress in educational software is an encouraging sign that microcomputers may go beyond the limitations of commercial television in expanding educational opportunities available to children.

Factors Affecting Demand and Utilization of Micros

As with most technological innovations, the supply and production of microcomputers and types of software will be driven by demand. While the demand for television has been largely a demand for entertainment, usage of microcomputers is based upon more instrumental purposes. Mainframe computers, forbears to today's micros, have an impressive legacy of business, scientific, and military applications. This historical image of computers as an information and educational technology is being carried over in the current educational demand for microcomputers. Among legislators, parents, teachers, and educators, there is growing opinion that "computer literacy" represents an important set of skills in children's preparation for future schooling and work.

A look back at the experience of instructional television (ITV) in schools lends some perspective to the current enthusiasm for microcomputers. In 1977 Dirr and Pedone (1979) conducted a comprehensive survey of ITV utilization and school personnel attitudes towards ITV. Among a national probability sample of 1700 elementary, junior, and senior high schools, 72% of teachers had ITV available for use in their classrooms ("availability" defined as the presence of both signal and equipment).

Fifty-nine percent of teachers used ITV during the 1976–1977 school year, with 46% being regular users of at least one ITV series. Usage was highest at the elementary level. Teachers responded with positive attitudes toward ITV, based on its appeal and motivational interest with students, its educational value, and easy access to reliable equipment. Teachers cited inconvenience of broadcast schedules and lack of appropriate programming as the most common barriers to use.

Even by the standard of this favorable reception for ITV, the current enthusiasm of schools for acquiring microcomputers is astonishing. Compared to television, micros are an expensive technology. Three TV sets and videotape recorders can service the minimal needs of an elementary school, for roughly the same price (under $10,000) as three microcomputers, disk drives, and printers. But this latter set of equipment would scarcely be sufficient for an entire school's computer needs.

Despite the higher per-pupil cost, support for microcomputers is being generated at federal, state, and local levels. For instance, a number of computer manufacturers—including Apple, IBM, Tandy, and Hewlett-Packard—have donated equipment and training to elementary and high schools, supported by special legislated programs of tax credits.

At the local level as well, school funds are being earmarked for computer purchases. It is not uncommon for computers to be donated by PTA, community groups, or individual parents. In some cases the rush to purchase computers has led to a situation in which schools have acquired computer equipment but face shortages of software and staff expertise (Wall Street Journal, 1983). Computers are becoming a favored technology at home as well. Parents who might otherwise control and restrain the family's television viewing are encouraging their children's computer use at home and in school.

The fate of microcomputers in classrooms is still very much the province of individual teachers. Based on initial studies such as Becker (1983), it is likely that a similar set of factors to those cited by Dirr and Pedone (1979) will affect teachers' decisions to use or not to use microcomputers. While the inconvenience of broadcast schedules presumably does not apply to stand-alone microcomputers, other factors of availability of equipment and desirable software will still be critical. One interesting difference between the two technologies is that, while ITV found its highest utilization at the elementary level, thus far the early stages of microcomputer adoption favor high schools.

In terms of teacher training and preparation, microcomputers require more investment from teachers, relative to television. A teacher giving instruction in computer-programming, word-processing, or other popular uses of micros must devote substantial energy to mastering the hardware and software of that application. Only minimal amounts of technical expertise and preparation time are required to use ITV.

There are some signs that teachers are rising to accept the substantial challenges posed by inviting microcomputers into their classrooms. Increasing numbers of teachers are pursuing computer training and restructuring curricula to accommodate computer applications. Several research reports have pointed to the new roles and responsibilities presented to teachers through microcomputers (Becker, 1982; Sheingold, 1981). For many of them, the use of microcomputers is injecting a new sense of occupational prestige and professionalism into a tradition-bound profession. For teachers as well as their students, computers are infusing new life into old classroom routines.

These economic, social, and attitudinal factors are affecting not only the ways in which television and computers have entered children's lives. They affect the conduct of research on these media as well. In the next section we consider some emerging differences in emphasis in television and microcomputer research.

A COMPARISON OF RESEARCH ON TV AND MICROCOMPUTERS

Through the 1960s and 1970s, research on the effects of television with children was an active area of social research and, judging from the sheer numbers of studies, the most active area of media research. To date, television has been the most closely studied communication medium; children have been its most highly researched audience. The research has attracted scholars from various disciplines, including psychology, sociology, communication, and education. Its progress was substantially aided by federal concern with the effects of television violence and one million dollars in research funds provided through the Surgeon General's Committee on Television and Social Behavior.[1] Several recent books provide reviews of this substantial body of research (Comstock, Chaffee, Katzman, McCombs, and Roberts, 1978; Liebert, Sprafkin, and Davidson, 1982; National Institute of Mental Health [NIMH], 1983).

A Typology of Television Research

A typology of the topics on which television research with children has been conducted provides an interesting basis of comparison for micro-computer research. The recent summary of television research by the National Institute of Mental Health (1983) cites a 1980 bibliography compiled by Murray (1981) of 2800 research articles, books, and other materials published in English between 1946 and 1980. Before 1970, 300 titles were published; between 1970 and 1980, 2500 were published, with more than two-thirds published since 1975. NIMH estimates that since 1980 another 200 publications have been completed, indicating a continuing level of research interest and activity.

The NIMH report classified the 2800 studies into these categories, which suggest the outcome or "effects" variables studied:

(1) Cognitive and Emotional Functioning
     Cognitive processing
     Forms and codes of television
     Arousal
     Emotional development and functioning
(2) Violence and Aggression
     Violence in television content
     Effects of televised violence
(3) Imagination, Creativity, and Prosocial Behavior
(4) Socialization and Conceptions of Social Reality
     Sex-role socialization
     Age-role socialization
     Race-role socialization
     Occupational role socialization
     Consumer role socialization
     Conceptions of violence and mistrust
(5) The Family and Interpersonal Relations
     Television's families
     Television's effects on the family and social relations
(6) Television in American Society
     Production of prime time television
     Public's attitude toward television
     Television's effects on American social institutions
(7) Education and Learning About Television
     Educational achievement
     Television and reading
     Education aspiration
     Learning about television

(8)   Health-Promoting Possibilities
       Health portrayals
       Television's influences on health
       Health campaigns
       Television for therapeutic purposes

Not all of the eight categories have attracted equal research interest. The two that have been the subject of the most extensive research have been the effects of television violence on children's aggressive behavior, and the relationships between viewing of the social world portrayed on television and children's socialization. The latter category includes not only content analyses of the social world portrayed on television, but also studies of the effects of television advertising on children's socialization as consumers.

Early Directions of Microcomputer Research

We cannot yet build a similar typology for the effects of microcomputers, based on completed studies.[2] However, at least a dozen studies of microcomputer usage and learning now exist, having been conducted during the past five years.

Consider the research topics addressed by this new group of studies:

• the diffusion and utilization of microcomputers in schools (Becker, 1983; Sheingold, 1981);

• the effect of computer games on children's motivation and learning (Levin and Kareev, 1980; Malone, 1980);

• the impact of learning a computer programming language on planning and problem-solving skills (Papert, 1980; Pea, 1983);

• the effect of using a word-processor on composing and writing skills (Kane, 1983; Levin, Boruta, and Vasconcellos, 1983);

• the effect of peer teaching and collaboration in programming classes on cognitive and social skills (Hawkins, 1983);

• high school students' attitudes toward computers and the role of computers in society (Anderson, Klassen, Krohn, and Smith-Cunnien, 1982; Chen et al., in preparation).

Based on this small sample of studies, a noticeable divergence is appearing between the initial research directions for microcomputers and the existing body of television research. Research on microcomputers and their various applications is proceeding without much reference to studies of children's reactions to television. Neither the types of effects explored nor literature referenced in these studies builds on research on the older medium.

Most obviously, research on microcomputers has not begun with television research's emphasis on the antisocial effects of the medium.

While complaints have been heard from parents, teachers, educators, and even the surgeon general about possible effects of violence in computer games (see Chapter 3), effects on children's aggressive behavior have not dominated the research thinking of these early studies.

The topics that *are* being addressed in the first microcomputer studies suggest some different research emphases. New "effects" variables are being conceptualized. The nature of the microcomputer stimulus appears wholly different from television. As the studies of computer programming and word processing suggest, there are specific applications of microcomputers for which no analogue exists in television programming.

For instance, much current debate and research examines the cognitive consequences of learning to program. Against the grander claims of LOGO's effect on problem solving and higher-order cognitive functioning (Papert, 1980) are some findings that children encountered conceptual difficulties in the design, coding, and debugging of programs (Pea, 1983). It seems likely that future studies will continue to enlighten this debate as well as expand to other innovative uses of computers in art, music, science, and other curriculum areas.

In addition, the Hawkins (1983) study points to the substantial research interest in group processes surrounding microcomputer use. Since the economics of computers have not yet allowed schools (and families) to purchase a computer for each child, learning with computers typically occurs through small groups collaborating around a single machine. One outcome has been that traditional classroom structures are being altered to allow students to converse and work together. Claims for the benefits of such collaborative activity are both cognitive and social. Relying on the theories of Vygotsky and Piaget, the verbal and other interaction with peers may be providing children with opportunities to formulate and organize their knowledge. Social effects on communication skills and self-image are also hypothesized.

Hawkins's study confirmed that peer collaboration occurred more frequently for classroom computer tasks than for noncomputer work, but found fewer instances of actual peer teaching. Her study points to the need for closer examination of the nature of peer-group interactions, the types of information exchanged, and students' beliefs about the appropriateness of collaboration versus working alone.

While group viewing of television is common, these processes have not been well studied by television researchers. We know surprisingly little about the group interaction that occurs when a family or a group of children sits down to watch television. The logistics of conducting observations of viewer behavior in private homes have presented substantial obstacles to such research. Fortunately, due to the diffusion of microcomputers in schools, these group phenomena have become accessible to convenient research inquiry.

Common Issues in TV and Microcomputer Research

There are, however, some hidden commonalities. Much of the early microcomputer research focuses on their potential educational and prosocial effects. Research on educational aspects of discovery software is the computer analogue to studies of educational television that combined instruction in entertaining formats. For instance, a reading of Malone's (1980) findings on motivational features of computer games comes close to identifying some attributes of appeal discussed in research conducted for *Sesame Street* (Lesser, 1974; Palmer, 1974, 1981).

Early surveys of computer use, learning, and attitudes (Anderson et al., 1982; Chen et al., in preparation) are in some respects the computer descendants of the first surveys of television use by children (Himmelweit, Oppenheim, and Vince, 1958; Schramm et al., 1961). Studies of the diffusion and utilization of microcomputers (Becker, 1983; Sheingold, 1981) are similar in spirit as well as substance to earlier work on school utilization of ITV.

It is revealing that research on television versus microcomputers has taken such differing views on the thinking and behaviors of children. At the risk of generalizing to make a larger point, television research on TV violence and advertising looks at the child under a "media effects" paradigm. The child faces a TV screen in which the programming presents a heavy diet of violent and commercial messages. The challenge for research has largely been to uncover the extent to which children are also able to resist the learning of antisocial or undesirable content. As Reeves and Wartella (1982) point out, much of the research has been directed toward the mediating influences between television messages and child viewers and the conditional nature of media effects.

With computers the child is portrayed as a thinking child. Researchers appear to begin with assumptions of the child as a perceiver and processor of visual and textual information. Their perspectives have benefited from recent advances in research on cognitive science and child development. Their work reaches into the fields of computer science and artificial intelligence. They are as likely to cite Herbert Simon or Marvin Minsky as television researchers are to reference Albert Bandura or Wilbur Schramm.

The emphasis on children's cognitive processes is one area in which television and computer research appears to be coming together. While the computer research begins from this perspective, only recently has television research begun to address questions of the processes by which children learn from what they see. (Collins [1983] estimates that this research area has attracted only 75 published articles or books since 1970.)

In the past few years television researchers, by focusing upon these cognitive variables, have begun to unveil a new view of the child as an active information processor (Anderson and Lorch, 1983; Collins, 1983; Salomon, 1983). These "active theories of television viewing" offer new evidence to counter views of the passive television viewer presented in past research and lay opinion. The attention to television viewing as a complex cognitive task begins to resemble the perspective taken by microcomputer researchers. As Collins (1983:9 points out,

> The implications of these views [of the more active viewer] for the study of responses to television have recently caused many researchers to shift their attention from a focus on program content and outcomes of viewing to an analysis of the cognitive tasks involved in viewing particular programs and the ways in which viewers of different ages, with different cognitive abilities, might accomplish these tasks.

Different emphases in research perspectives can be found not only in the types of effects variables addressed, but in attention to characteristics of children's background and experience that act as predictor or mediating variables for such effects. For instance, the variable of age has been the subject of much television research. Much of this concern with age is directed toward achieving an understanding of the development nature of children's understanding of television plots, characters, and messages (Roberts and Bachen, 1981; Wartella, 1980). This research has had practical policy implications for regulation of advertising and types of television violence viewed by children of various ages.

Whether research on computers will adopt a similar developmental perspective remains to be seen. As yet, little research concerned with tracking the developmental trends in children's understanding of software has emerged. However, this research area seems a likely one for future studies.

In contrast, the child variable of immediate concern for microcomputer research appears to be sex. Television research also was centrally concerned with boy-girl differences, but the concern with gender differences in microcomputer usage appears to be more pervasive and linked to questions of social equity. It is commonly observed that girls enroll in computer courses, camps, and other computer-related opportunities in fewer numbers than boys (Hess and Miura, 1983; Kiesler, Sproull, and Eccles, 1983; Williams and Williams, 1984; Chen et al., in preparation). Speculation as to reasons for such differential usage and interest ranges from perceptual and cognitive differences to social and cultural factors. These latter factors point to a computer culture dominated by males and lacking in strong female role models. Other common observations find that many of the current crop of microcomputer games present themes of aggression and competition that are more compelling for boys than girls. Some researchers point to the differential encouragement given by parents to their daughters and sons to undertake computer activities.

Interestingly, one of the earliest studies of computer interests and attitudes provides some countervailing evidence on gender differences in computer competence and attitudes. In their large-scale survey of Minnesota students, Anderson et al. (1982) found minimal differences in computer literacy and programming skill between eighth- and eleventh-grade girls and boys. The authors speculated that this lack of sex differences could be traced to Minnesota's statewide commitment to providing widespread computer opportunities for students. Based on the data for eighth graders, they also hypothesize that computer learning may not be justifiably categorized with math and science learning. While a dropoff in girls' math achievement and interest typically occurs in the junior high school years, the Minnesota eighth-grade girls continued to perform on an equal basis with boys on the computer items.

Computers are not yet the ubiquitous technology that television has become. Given the higher costs of microcomputers relative to TV sets,[3] the effect of a child's socioeconomic status on differential access to and learning from microcomputers has become another issue for study.

The concern is tied not only to theoretical interest in how children of varying backgrounds can learn from computers, but to policy issues of the equitable distribution of the technologies. In one popular view, competence in using a computer is viewed as a critical skill for a child's future progress and success. Competence with computers is viewed as an "enfranchising" qualification for the information society. Differences in the patterns of adoption and use of computers poses a form of unequal educational opportunity for children from less advantaged backgrounds. Studies by Rogers, Daley, and Wu (1982) and Becker (1983) support beliefs that microcomputers are being purchased in greater numbers by higher-SES families and schools.

Television researchers in the past have also focused on SES, racial, and cultural variables in analyzing television's effects (Greenberg, 1983). But the concern did not reach the question of unequal opportunities. In fact, evidence indicates that children from minority and lower SES educational backgrounds have at least equal access to TV and view as much if not more television than other children (Comstock et al., 1978).

IMPLICATIONS FOR FUTURE RESEARCH AND PRACTICE

On the Nature of "Interactivity"

The arrival of computer-based media may enable us to revise some previous notions about older media. In particular, videotext, teletext, interactive cable, and videodisc all are altering the ways in which we have regarded what was formerly only a TV screen. As a case in point, consider this often-cited distinction: Television is passive while computers are interactive. The distinction is also captured by our terminology for those making use of these media. Those sitting in front of TVs are referred to as "viewers," while those sitting at computers are "users."

As discussed above, recent research supports as a view of television viewing as more than mere passive absorption of images, but an active cognitive process. Studies of educational programming such as *Sesame Street, The Electric Company,* or *Zoom* have also provided evidence of children's active participation in physical movement, singing, gesturing, oral recitation, and other forms of imitation (Gibbon, Palmer, and Fowles, 1975; Lesser, 1974).

We begin to see that passivity and interactivity are qualities of individuals making use of media, not the media themselves (see, for example, the discussion in Chapter 3). We also begin to see the need for a more precise explication of these concepts. For instance, we need to distinguish between behavioral and cognitive activity. A range of overt behaviors can be conceptualized for viewers/users of both media, ranging from spoken utterances to physical gestures, both overt motoric behaviors and micromomentary eye movements directed at the screen. Similarly, a range of cognitive activities that may or may not be accompanied by overt behavior can be specified.

Future research on television, microcomputers, and other media can benefit by moving away from a view of these media as distinct packages of technology to a focus on the specific features of these media that are linked to specific child outcomes. Salomon (1979:5-6) has provided the most coherent articulation of this view:

> Indeed, from institutional, political, or sociological points of view, media are appropriately conceived of as invariant entities. Newspapers are "an institution" and so is television. . . . However, such a global definition of the medium-stimulus is insufficiently differentiated for cognitive-psychological and education purposes. . . . Something *within* the mediated stimulus, possibly shared to some extent with other media, makes the presented information more comprehensible or better memorized by learners of particular characteristics.

Features analyses of media move us along the path to an improved understanding of the complex and interrelated nature of television and computer-based media (Bretz, 1971; Paisley and Chen, 1982). Salomon (1979: 14) further suggests that analyses of media and their effects address four classes of media attributes:

> all media convey *contents*; the contents are structured and coded by sometimes shared and sometimes more medium-specific *symbol systems*; they all use *technologies* for the gathering, encoding, sorting, and conveying of their contents; and they are associated with different *situations* in which they are typically used.

As the new technologies merge and the video screen becomes a window into an increasing range of entertainment and information alternatives, older distinctions between media will need revision. Research that looks beyond the technology of each new medium to its underlying content and symbols will enable theoretical progress that does not stop at the borders of each machine.

The Need for Cross-Disciplinary Research

This developing marriage of technologies may also lead to a merging of research traditions. However, a surprising division is occurring between research communities that studied television and the incipient group of researchers beginning to study the effects of computers with children. The technologies are moving closer together, but few researchers are bridging the gap from the wealth of research on television to the new questions posed by the new media.

As with television, microcomputers pose cognitive, affective, and behavioral questions that are not limited by the ways in which universities classify the behavioral sciences. Television research has certainly been strengthened by contributions from sociologists as well as psychologists, educational as well as communication researchers. It is important that this cross-fertilization between fields continue into research on the new computer technologies and that opportunities for exchange of knowledge across professional specialties be encouraged. As Paisley (1984) and the Preface of this book point out, research on these computer-based technologies offers a significant opportunity for the field of communication research to break out of its "ethnocentrism" and expand its impact to other social and behavioral sciences.

The move toward greater cross-disciplinary research may be aided by the need not only for new theoretical perspectives, but methodological ones as well. The new media offer opportunities for innovative research designs, less constrained by previous limitations of technology (Williams and Rice, 1983; see also Chapter 4). One study that may point the way for future research on microcomputers utilized the computer as both stimulus material and data collection device (Levin et al., 1983.) The analysis of children's keystrokes during writing, together with field observations of children's behaviors, provided a new view of children's thought processes and problem-solving strategies. This is but one example of the uses of computer-monitored data (Rice and Borgman, 1983).

A final observation on the application of research to practice: While the decades of television research have contributed substantially to our theoretical knowledge of television and its effects, relatively little of it has seen its way to an impact upon programming ideas or practices. With the exception of evaluation research conducted for specific educational children's series, such as *Sesame Street*, *3-2-1 CONTACT*, and *Freestyle*, television production proceeds largely without application of the extensive academic research on children's reactions to TV. The reasons for this atheoretical approach reside in a combination of both producers' resistance to research and the inability to specify practical recommendations from theoretically motivated studies.

The case with computers may differ. There is some cause for optimism that research on the educational effects of microcomputers may yet be applied in practice. Because the focus of much software for children involves educational aims, research holds promise for illuminating some guidelines, suggestions, and alternatives for software. Opportunities exist for collaborative testing of theory in practical settings at many universities and research centers. These include Berkeley's Lawrence Hall of Science, the Study of Stanford and the Schools, and the Minnesota Educational Computing Consortium (MECC). Such research on classroom use of microcomputers may point to more effective ways of organizing and presenting computer instruction.

In addition, the flexibility with which computer programs can be modified permits revisions based upon child reactions. Several educational software groups are including a formative research function in their design processes, testing their ideas at various stages of production with target-audience children. These include educational software groups at Bank Street College of Education and CTW's Children's Computer Workshop.

The unique quality of microcomputers is their potential to abolish previous media distinctions by incorporating features of the book, the newspaper, the still picture, and animation. Combing microcomputer control with videodisc or videotape further offers full audio and visual features of film and television. By studying these features acting in concert rather than isolation, research can address broader issues of optimal combinations of text, pictures, and sound that enhance learning. These systems provide us with new microcosms for studying some fundamental questions of education and leaning. In that sense, the new media promise excitement not only for the lives of our children, but our lives as researchers as well.

NOTES

1. While a comparable level of funding may not become available for microcomputer research, several government agencies and foundations have been early supporters of this research. These include the National Institute of Education, the National Science Foundation, the Spencer Foundation, and the Carnegie Corporation.

2. The term "effects" has had a long and durable history in media research generally and in research on television and children specifically (Reeves and Wartella, 1982; Roberts and Bachen, 1981). Its usage can imply a spectrum of relationships ranging from direct and unilateral effects to more indirect and conditional effects. Recent research on television and microcomputers is directed toward the latter, more complex, types of relationships. For lack of a better term, "effects" is used here, acknowledging its ambiguity.

3. While microcomputers are available for less than $200, their memory and processing capabilities do not enable them to run much of the useful software for popular and more powerful applications. At this writing, a fully configured microcomputer system with disk drive and printer system ranges between $1500 and $5000.

JOHN DIMMICK and
ERIC W. ROTHENBUHLER

12 Competitive Displacement in the Communication Industries: *New Media in Old Environments*

On the first day of August 1981, Warner Communications premiered its stereo rock music channel, Music Television. MTV is a unique blend of video and stereophonic sound, satellite distribution to cable systems, and an album-oriented rock format adapted from radio complete with contests, music, news, and VJs (video jockeys). Significantly, the inaugural video was titled "Video Killed the Radio Star" by a group called Buggles. The lyrics of the first video played on MTV, though couched in the past tense, represent Buggles's (and presumably MTV's) vision of the future impact of video music: They say to "put the blame on VTR" for killing the radio star.

It seems appropriate that the opening lyrics of the new music channel sounded themes recurrent in discussions of today's and tomorrow's communication industries—themes of competition, survival, and obsolescence. MTV's use of "Video Killed the Radio Star" to launch the new channel rather self-consciously symbolizes the challenge posed by the new forms of communication to the established media industries.

The development of the new industries of communication raises a number of questions concerning their impact on the existing media forms. Will radio and its superstars be replaced by video music channels and musical actors? Or, to pose similar questions bearing on different industries, will videotex displace some of the current uses of the printed page? How adversely will network television be affected by cable?

Frankly, we do not know the answers to these questions. We do not pretend to be able to supply accurate long-range forecasts on the fate of the new media. Our more modest aim is to report progress in the conceptualization and measurement of the impact of new media on the existing order. This is a traditional inquiry in communication research; we might inquire about the impact of videotex on the printed page in the same spirit that Lazarsfeld (1940) and his colleagues studied the effect of radio on the printed page. Discussion of "new" media in the context of "old" media is useful for two interdependent reasons. First, as discussed in Chapter 1, newness is a relative quality; it only exists in at least implicitly comparative statements. Second, newness as a social phenomenon—the societal conditions under which it arises and its societal impacts—shows a certain structural stability. Newness is a property that can be investigated regardless of the phenomenon that exhibits it or the time period in which it is exhibited.

In other words, we are confident that, precisely because interactions among media occurred in the past and there is, therefore, more available information about them, we can learn more about the possible impacts of new media in old environments by studying, for example, the invasion of the print and radio media community by the new medium of television than by studying the currently new media, about which we have had no opportunity to gain perspective or gather appropriate data.

When attempting to explain change in media systems it is traditional to look to the *audience*—the underlying logic is that it is they who need, choose, and affect the evolving systems. This market logic is a powerful mode of explanation, and it has contributed much to our understanding. We are, however, advocating a reconsideration of the evolution of media systems in *ecological* terms—the study of evolving populations, dependent on differentially available resources, interacting, in changing environments. In ecological terms, the audience is one of a number of resources available to a *population* of businesses, typically called an industry. A poorly served audience, in the conventional terms, becomes, in the ecological terms, an underexploited resource.

This is a study of ecological succession in the communication media community of the United States. We examine a number of media, the various sources of the income that supports them, and the patterns of dependence on these sources and competition over them. Our unit of analysis is, for each medium, the aggregate of the individual businesses engaged—e.g., television stations, cable facilities, movie theatres—which we call the industry and consider equivalent to an ecological population.

The following section briefly examines the history of the development of ecological theory and how the concepts have come to be applied in studies of communication systems. This is followed by a sketch of the theoretical terrain, concentrating most attention simply on the definition of terms. Readers interested in more detailed discussions should consult the sources cited there and our other works. In the central sections of the chapter we examine the competition for advertising income between the radio and television industries from 1935 to 1980, and the nascent competition between broadcasters and cablecasters. This is followed by a discussion of the environmental conditions faced by new members of the communication industry community. We close with a brief discussion of the implications of our findings in the areas of theory and research, commerce, and policy.

ECOLOGY AND HUMAN ECOLOGY

Ecology, as applied to the human social order, arose as a distinct field of study in the 1920s (Hawley, 1968; also, see, e.g., McKenzie, 1933, 1968; Park, 1936). For social scientists interested in the relationship between human aggregates and their environment, ecological concepts provided a new set of lenses through which to view macro-level social organization. Bioecologists of the day had delved deeply enough into plant and animal associations to develop an awareness of the complexity and intricacy of their subject matter. This awareness was expressed in a rich descriptive vocabulary such as "community," "dominance," "succession," "symbiosis," and "commensualism." Early social scientists interested in phenomena at the molar levels of analysis viewed human life through the macroscope of such concepts and observed the same organized complexity in the urban centers spawned by the industrial revolution that the bioecologist had discovered in the pastoral settings of wood and field. A central image in the writings of early human ecologists (e.g., Park, 1936) is the Darwinian notion of the "web of life"; evidently it struck them as an apt metaphor for the interconnectedness and interdependence of human social organization.

The term "human ecology" was at times overgeneralized and sometimes used as if it encompassed most of the social sciences. Quinn's (1940) overview of the field, however, limited its major headings to terms such as dominance, spatial distributions, succession, and migration and mobility. As some of these topics suggest, human ecology was evolving into a field of study closely akin to demography (see Hawley, 1981). The persistence in human ecology of these concepts over the last four decades is demonstrated by the fact that some of the major headings in Quinn's catalog of studies in human ecology also appear in Hawley's review of the field. Indeed, as Dimmick and Rothenbuhler (1983a) point out, the use of the dominance concept by contemporary human ecologists is much closer to the meaning of the term when it was originally borrowed from bioecology in the 1920s than it is to current bioecological usage.

Bioecology and human ecology have long since gone their separate ways. The close connection that once prevailed is indicated by the frequency with which early human ecologists (e.g. Park, 1936) cited the work of bioecologists. In contrast, the work of contemporary human ecologists (e.g., Lincoln, 1977) is devoid of such references.

Clearly, the original motive for adopting ecological thought and applying it to the human social world was that the level of generality of ecological concepts transcended the boundary between the human and the nonhuman. Ecologists, in attempting to build theory that applies to plant populations as well as to animals, have constructed conceptual frameworks sufficiently general to apply in the realm of human organization as well. On the grounds of the theoretical unity of the areas of study, Hawley (1944: 399) castigated his colleagues for their failure to maintain close ties with the parent discipline:

> Although it seems almost too elementary to mention, the only conceivable justification for a human ecology must derive from the utility of ecological theory as such.

The self-isolation of human ecology from bioecology did not deter the bioecologists Ehrlich and Holm (1962: 652) from suggesting

> there is much to be gained from taking a broad view in the study of populations, in which emphasis is on the many similarities in the phenomena studied by the taxonomist, the ecologist, the geneticist, the behaviorist, the economist, and perhaps the mathematician as well.

What they seem to suggest is that if the unification of science or even of ecology as a whole is an elusive goal, it may be possible to unify in the middle range around the study of such theoretical entities as populations. What we will call the "new wave" of human ecology is made up of a loosely integrated group of researchers in various social sciences who treat the concepts and models of population ecology as central to their work.

In the 1970s, social scientists working in the area of macro-organizational behavior have returned to ecological thought as a source of theoretical models. Appropriately, the work of Amos Hawley (1950) provided the link between the older form and the new wave of human ecology. His influence is apparent in the work of Hannan and Freeman (1977), Aldrich (1979), and McKelvey (1982), three of the major theoretical statements of the new wave. Hawley's emphasis on populations and organizations is manifested in the study of what Hannan and Freeman term "the population ecology of organizations."

As the introduction to this chapter implies, our interest in ecological theories and models was stimulated by the lack of conceptual and empirical tools for assessing the impact of fledgling industries such as cable television or nascent industries such as videotex on the existing industries of communication. We have applied an ecological theory—the theory of the niche—to the historical and contemporary competition between media industries. Our experience to date is that the theory of the niche is a general, reasonable, and powerful explanation of competition between populations and that its domain extends well beyond its bioecological origins.

DEFINITION OF TERMS

Populations are aggregates of unique individuals, each member of which shares some attributes allowing high relative probabilities for special kinds of interaction within but not between populations (Mayr, 1982: 46; Pianka, 1983: 100; Ricklefs, 1979: 507). In biology this special type of interaction is breeding; in the sociology of organizations it may be the trading of members (see McKelvey, 1982: 143-218). In the social science realm there is as yet difficulty with the rigorous definition of theoretical populations; McKelvey's work has been devoted to rectifying this situation. In the meantime, McKelvey and Aldrich (1983) recommend common-sensical categories, and Hannan and Freeman (1977: 934) recommend attention to a "unit character . . . [and] common fate with respect to environmental variations." For any given study, the goal should be to define local populations that exhibit optimal homogeneity on the characters of interest. In our work, this leads to such categories as the newspaper population, the radio population, the television population, and the cable population.

The *environment* is all that which is external to the members of the population. Elements of the environment, of course, may or may not be relevant to the population under consideration. Home videogame consoles are now an aspect of the environment of the television industry, as are the Federal Communications Commission, inflation, and the advertising industry.

Resources are the elements of the environment that are required for the maintenance of the population (Ricklefs, 1979: 878). For media industries in our society, a minimal set of resources would include capital, content, and audience.

The fundamental concept of modern ecological theory is the niche. While the term has a fair history and much common language usage, its current formal usage follows Hutchinson's (1957) set-theoretic definition and the elaborations of Levins (1968), Whittaker and Levin (1975), and others. Ricklefs (1979: 875) defines the *niche* as "all the components of the environment with which the organism or population interacts." Pianka (1983: 253) defines it in evolutionary terms as "the sum total of the adaptations of an organismic unit." McKelvey and Aldrich (1983) follow Pianka and adapt this to organizational science as

> the activity space of an organization or population or community
> of organizational forms that reflects the sum total of both its
> adaptation *to* environmental forces that are not subject to its

influence and adaptation *of* environmental forces that are subject
to its influences [original emphasis].

What is clear is that the niche is a *space* of *interactions.* Thus empty niches do
not exist, nor can they be found in environments to be subsequently
occupied.

Conceptually *niche breadth* is precisely what it implies, a measure of the
area of a niche. In a two-dimensional niche, it is the distance through it. In
a three-dimensional niche it is its volume. In an n-dimensional niche it is a
little tougher to picture, and we suspect it is no accident that most studies
operate on three dimensions, even as a willing degeneration of the true
complexity of the situation (in animal studies it tends to be food, space,
and time; see Pianka, 1983; Ricklefs, 1979). There are also operational
difficulties with niche breadth that are addressed below. For the community of media industries, let us hypothetically say that a three-dimensional
niche would consist of types of capital, types of content, and types of
audience. In many of the analyses that follow, we examine advertising
dollars as some of the types of capital because they are (a) reliably
measured, (b) comparable across a number of media, and (c) available.

Figure 12.1 provides a simple illustration of niche breadth. As the
figure shows, population A uses two resource categories X and Y with the
relative frequencies, .6 and .4, respectively, while population B is totally
dependent on resource Y. Neither population uses resource Z. A glance at
the figure conveys the intuitive notion that A's niche, since it is more
spread out along the horizontal axis, is broader than B's niche. This
intuition can be tested by applying a formula for niche breadth (Levins,
1968) to the two populations' resource utilization patterns.

$$\frac{1}{\sum_{h=1}^{r} P_h^2} \tag{1}$$

Where P_h is the proportion of resources utilized in each category h of the
resource dimension. The measure B ranges from a low of 1 to an upper
limit equal to the number of resource categories used by the population. B
approaches its maximum when resource utilization is distributed rectangu-
larly across resource categories. Applying formula 1 to the data in Figure
12.1 for population A yields:

$$B = \frac{1}{(.6)^2 + (.4)^2} = 1.92$$

while for population B, niche breadth is

$$B = \frac{1}{(1.00)^2} = 1.00$$

FIGURE 12.1   Niche Breadth and Overlap Illustrated

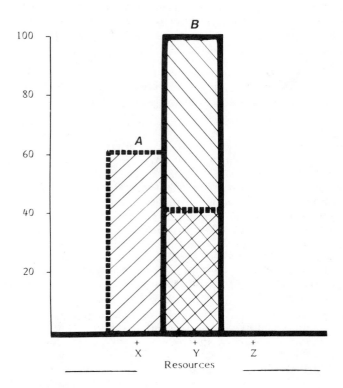

NOTE: Volume of bars arbitrary. Height represents proportional utilization.

Hence, the calculations confirm the graphic impression gained from the figure that A has a broader niche than B.[1]

   Niche overlap has the same seeming conceptual clarity and operational difficulty of niche breadth. Essentially we can think of it as the extent to which the adaptedness of two media industries to their environment is shared; "overlap" is the area of niche space shared by adjacent niches. Populations with highly similar ecologies or resource utilization will overlap strongly, while those that are dissimilar in resource utilization display less ecological similarity and, as a result, lower overlap.

Figure 12.1 also portrays a simple example of overlap between populations A and B. Here, population B overlaps or occupies significant areas of population A's niche. In Figure 12.1 the cross-hatched portion of the figure represents the area of resource overlap between A and B.

While the figure conveys an intuitive idea of the overlap concept, a more precise idea of the degree of overlap can be conveyed by utilizing one of the measures of niche overlap from Levins (1968). The overlap between two populations i and j is given by the geometric distance: n

$$\text{Overlap} = d_{ij} = \sum_{h=1}^{n} (P_{ih} - P_{jh})^2 \qquad [2]$$

Calculated in this way, where $d_{i,j}$ is the distance between populations i and j calculated by summing the squared differences between their proportional utilizations of each of n resources h. High overlap is denoted by values near 0. Applying formula 2 to the data in Figure 12.1 yields $(.6 - 0.0)^2 + (.4 - 1.0)^2 = .72$, a moderate overlap between populations A and B (see Note 1).

If the resources are not superabundant, overlap may be construed as a measure of the degree of competition between two populations. Two media industries that depended on highly similar audiences would exhibit high overlap on at least that dimension; two industries with similar advertising income structures would overlap on that dimension. (But see Pianka [1983: 263-265] on the need for, yet difficulty of, evaluating on all dimensions simultaneously.) *Competition*, in ecological parlance, is the extent of which the use of a resource by one population prevents its usage by another, and thereby decreases the viability of the second population.

A *community* is all of the populations co-occurring in an area (Ricklefs 1979: 668 ff.). It is a useful but sometimes messy term perhaps best seen as the delimiter of a particular study. We make extensive use of the term media industry community, we hope with no confusion.

Generalism and *specialism* are two ideal types of resource utilization patterns. Generalism is activity, or the capacity for activity, in varied environmental conditions, in reference to elements of varied attributes within an environment, or in environments of varied attributes. The payoff of generalism is the ability to withstand any environmental changes within the range of one's generalism. Specialism is activity that is restricted to one or a few elements or areas within an environment. The payoff of specialism is adaptation, which leads to highly efficient resource exploitation. The cost of each strategy is the mirror image of the opposite strategy's benefit; and there are environmental conditions under which each is the optimally adapted pattern. In the media industries, television is a relative generalist, able to draw income, contents, and audiences from a diversity of areas, while the pretelevision movie industry was a relative specialist; surviving solely on the income derivable from direct consumer sales.

ANALYSIS

In the late 1920s summary quantitative data on communication industries began to be compiled, and these data make it possible to begin to assess the impact of the newer media on the older forms. As McCombs's (1972; McCombs and Eyal, 1980) work on the principle of *relative constancy* shows, the media compete for a limited number of dollars. The constancy principle states that the amount of money spent on the media is a relatively constant proportion of the gross national product. As McCombs (1972: 61) has written,

> Only a small and fixed proportion of the economy is available to finance mass communication. Over the years the pie has grown, but at the same rate as the economy which produced the pie was growing. New media in the marketplace did not produce a bigger pie; instead the old pie was resliced to feed the newcomer.

Such a reslicing of the pie is illustrated in Table 12.1, which shows the share of total national advertising for five media from the late 1920s through the late 1930s. By the late twenties, radio had emerged as a national network medium, and the data in Table 12.1 enable a rough assessment of its competitive impact on other media carrying national advertising.

The only medium showing growth over the time series is radio. Its share of national advertising grows from less than 2% to almost 19% over the twelve-year period. Both the outdoor advertising industry and farm

TABLE 12.1 Share of National Advertising By Five Media, 1928-1939 (in percentages)

Year	Newspapers	Magazines	Radio	Outdoor	Farm	Total
1928	68.2	19.3	1.8	7.6	3.1	100%
1929	66.9	20.2	3.3	6.7	2.9	100%
1930	65.7	19.7	5.6	6.2	2.8	100%
1931	65.9	18.1	8.5	5.3	2.2	100%
1932	66.3	16.3	10.8	4.8	1.8	100%
1933	67.7	16.5	9.8	4.5	1.5	100%
1934	64.1	18.6	11.6	3.9	1.8	100%
1935	63.4	18.0	12.6	4.1	1.9	100%
1936	62.0	18.2	12.8	4.8	2.2	100%
1937	60.0	19.0	14.5	4.5	2.0	100%
1938	59.3	16.6	16.6	5.6	1.9	100%
1939	57.7	16.4	18.6	5.4	1.9	100%

SOURCE: The raw data on which the percentages are based are from Lazarsfeld (1940: 273, Table 50).

publications show slight decreases, but the newspaper industry exhibits the largest decrease in share of national advertising. While newspapers are still the largest consumer of national advertising, the industry's share drops from 68% to 57%.

The impact of radio on newspapers shown in Table 12.1 is an example of *competitive displacement*; the newspaper has yielded a portion of its niche space to a competitor. A more precise example of displacement can be given using the theory of the niche to analyze television's impact on radio.

In our analyses to date (Dimmick and Rothenbuhler 1982; 1983a,b) the resources upon which these populations depend are defined as various categories of advertisng revenues—local, national spot, national or network, and classified advertising. Estimates of each industry's revenues in these categories have been collected and disseminated by McCann-Erikson, Inc. from 1935 to the present, and these figures constitute our data base. (These are the standard data reported in *Statistical Abstracts of the United States, Editor & Publisher,* and elsewhere.) In the case of the radio and television industries, which we will use to illustrate displacement, these populations utilize local, spot, and network advertising. The principle of relative constancy effectively sets a limit on the advertising dollars or resources available and allows us to use niche overlap as a measure of competition.

The appearance of a new population in an ecological community is, appropriately enough, termed *invasion.* Although the invasion by television affected other industries to some extent, its impact on radio was dramatic and pronounced (see Dimmick and Rothenbuhler, 1982). Measures of niche overlap and niche breadth for the two industries are graphed in Figures 12.2 and 12.3, respectively. The measures were computed by the formulas given earlier in the chapter.

As Figure 12.2 shows, television and radio are initially quite high in ecological similarity. The overlap index for 1949 is .036. Obviously the industries are in strong competition. If overlap were maintained in this region the result would be lowered population size or, at the extreme, extinction for the outcompeted population. However, as Figure 12.2 shows, the overlap decreases quickly as indexed by values of .049 in 1950 to .210 in 1954 and to .38 by 1960. In the last two decades the overlap values have remained reasonably stable, hovering around the .4 mark. The sharp decline in overlap and, hence, in competition between the two industries averted potential disaster for the radio industry. In Figure 12.3 the breadth measures for radio shows how the decline in overlap was accomplished.

In 1949, radio's niche breadth is at its peak of 2.8, having risen to this point from 2.2 in 1936 (Dimmick and Rothenbuhler, 1982). When television invaded the community and overlapped strongly with radio, the response of the latter industry was to shift its resource utilization pattern. This shift is reflected in the breadth indices in Figure 12.3. As the figure shows, radio's breadth drops precipitously from its high point of 2.8 to 1.7 in 1980. Conversely, the television industry has broadened its niche to

FIGURE 12.2 Niche Overlap of Radio and Television, 1949-1980

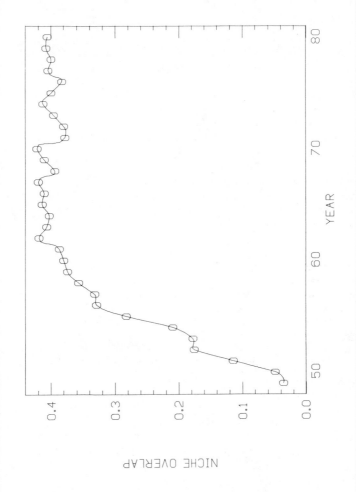

NOTE: The overlap measure ranges from 0.0 to 1.0.

FIGURE 12.3 Niche Breadth of Radio and Television, 1949-1980

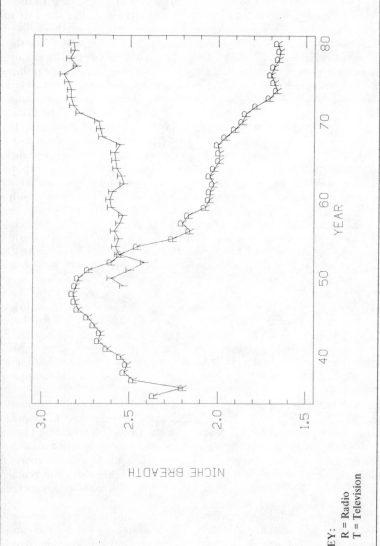

KEY:

R = Radio
T = Television

about the same level achieved by radio when television invaded the community.

The changes in both overlap and breadth result from changes in proportional utilization of the three categories of advertising. In the years 1949 through 1980 the population of radio stations decreased its initial utilization of the network or national category from a little over one third of its total resource utilization to less than 5%. To compensate for the loss of network advertising, the industry increased use of the local category over time to its current level of about 70% of its total resource utilization.

The changes in radio's niche as a result of competition with television constitute competitive displacement; radio surrendered a portion of its niche to television. Competitive displacement or lowered niche breadth is the typical result of strong competition (Colwell and Futuyma, 1971).

Although radio was displaced by television, it survived as an industry, and the key to its survival was its generalism. Radio's rather broad niche—its utilization of three resource categories—enabled it to respond to displacement from one niche component by utilizing another more intensively. In contrast, the specialist movie industry, which used only one resource category—consumer spending—had nowhere to move in the resource space when television invaded, and it paid the price of specialism.

The pattern from invasion to community dominance is clearly evidenced by the competition between radio and television between 1949 and 1980. The phenomenon of critical niche difference is neatly demonstrated by examining the indices for the cable and broadcast industries.

The data here are drawn from the following sources. The data on advertising revenues for television and radio are the McCann-Erickson estimates reported in *Advertising Age* (March 22, 1982), except for the 1983 figures, which were obtained from Coen (1984). The figures on cable advertising revenues were supplied by the personnel of the cable TV Advertising Bureau Office in New York and are available only for 1980 through 1982. These and intermediate computed measures appear in Table 12.2.

The niche breadth measures for the radio, TV, and cable industries are displayed in Table 12.3. As the table shows, television is the population with the broadest niche, followed, in order, by radio and cable. The cable industry's rather narrow niche reflects its current specialization in the national or network category. Currently the industry draws more than 80% of its advertising revenues from this category, with the remainder from spot. For the three years 1980-1982 the industry reported no revenues in the local category.

The measures of ecological similarity of the three industries—niche overlap—are shown in Table 12.4. The overlap between TV and cable are the strongest, followed by the TV/radio and radio/cable overlaps. However, even the highest overlaps indicate no more than moderate competition between the TV/radio and the TV/cable industries. The rather weak competition between radio and cable is due to the specialization of these two industries on different resource categories. As noted earlier, cable is currently drawing most of its resources from national

TABLE 12.2 Raw Data Measuring Resource Utilization and Computed Niche Measures, Among Three Media, 1980-1982

| | RESOURCE UTILIZATION BY TYPE | | | | | | | | |
| | CABLE | | | TV | | | RADIO | | |
Year	Net	Nat	Loc	Net	Nat	Loc	Net	Nat	Loc
1980	50.4*	8.0	0	5310	3629	2967	183	779	2740
1981	112.3	16.7	0	5575	3730	3345	220	896	3096
1982	210.0	31.8	0	6210	4360	3759	255	923	3492

| | TOTAL RESOURCE UTILIZATION | | |
Year	Cable Total	TV Total	Radio Total
1980	58.4*	11726	3702
1981	129.0	12650	4212
1982	241.8	14329	4670

| | PROPORTIONAL RESOURCE UTILIZATION WITHIN MEDIA | | | | | | | | |
| | CABLE | | | TV | | | RADIO | | |
Year	Net	Nat	Loc	Net	Nat	Loc	Net	Nat	Loc
1980	.863	.137	0	.437	.309	.253	.049	.210	.740
1981	.871	.129	0	.441	.295	.264	.052	.213	.735
1982	.868	.132	0	.433	.304	.262	.055	.198	.748

KEY:
  Net = network advertising
  Nat = national spot advertising
  Loc = local advertising
  * = figures in millions of dollars

advertising, while more than 70% of radio revenues are drawn from the local component of its niche.

Although the overlap measures indicate that the strongest ecological similarity is between the TV and cable industries, the competition between the two populations is currently only moderately strong. The overlap of .225 between TV and cable is still far from the high overlap values between radio and TV (.036) in 1949, the point at which TV began competitively to displace radio from portions of its niche space. As cable grows in total revenues and broadens its niche into the local category, the

TABLE 12.3 Niche Breadth of the Television, Radio, and Cable Industries for 1980-1982

Year	TV	Radio	Cable
1980	2.85	1.68	1.31
1981	2.85	1.70	1.29
1982	2.87	1.66	1.30

NOTE: Maximum niche breadth here is 3.00.

TABLE 12.4 Niche Overlap Between Cable, TV and Radio, 1980-1982

Year	Cable/TV	Cable/Radio	TV/Radio
1980	.275	1.216	.398
1981	.282	1.218	.380
1982	.287	1.225	.390

competition will no doubt heighten. If present trends continue, cable will compete most strongly with the TV industry.

Our work to date leads us to believe that we can state the conditions under which future competitive displacement will eventuate. First, the two industries will exhibit high ecological similarity or niche overlap. Second, the competitively superior population is likely to displace its competitor from portions of its niche or exclude it entirely. The overlap measures indicate that none of the industries for which we have data is approaching the point at which one would expect displacement to occur (Dimmick and Rothenbuhler, 1983a,b).

FUTURE DISPLACEMENT: PREDICTING THE FLOOD

It should be emphasized that the "predictions" of displacement that can be made using the ecological concepts are short-term predictions. If these measures had been applied to the television and radio industries in the late forties and early fifties it would have been possible to predict the displacement, but by only a few years at best, depending on when one judges the displacement to have begun. Further, the measures cannot indicate in advance the depth of the displacement nor if the displacement will escalate into exclusion. Clearly the sort of prediction that can be made is so weak that it is perhaps more correctly termed a sort of anticipation.

In a well-known essay, Scriven (1959: 477) contrasted those fields of inquiry in which precise prediction is possible with what he called "irregular subjects," in which explanation of the past and present is often feasible while prediction is possible in only a weaker form. Among the irregular subjects Scriven includes biology as well as social sciences such as psychology and anthropology. As Hardin (1960) points out, ecological theory, such as the theory of the niche, falls under Scriven's description of evolutionary theory. To Scriven, evolutionary theory is the paradigm of the explanatory but only weakly predictive sciences.

While evolutionary theory provides explanation, it supplies only limited potential to predict. Suppose, says Scriven, that a desert environment is suddenly and completely flooded. In such a case, members of populations who possess the ability to swim have a higher probability of survival than members of populations who lack this capacity. While we can use the ability to swim as a factor in explaining survival of certain populations after the flood, we would have been hard put to predict such an outcome before the flood. Scriven (1959: 478) has written,

> Naturally we could have said in advance that *if* a flood occurred, they would be *likely* to survive; let us call this a hypothetical probability prediction.

Although they are not actual predictions, hypothetical probability predictions are useful for anticipating what *could* happen. Corporate planners in the communication industries, for example, are no doubt formulating such predictions and writing contingency plans that envision a number of possible futures. However, in order to make actual predictions—rather than hypothetical probability predictions—one must be able to specify how the environment will change. In other words, we must be able to predict the flood.

This is the crux of the problem in predicting the outcome of competition among communication industries in the future. While there is little doubt that the environment *will* change we do not know exactly *how* it will change and to what extent. For example, ABC's Mike Dann (quoted in DeSante, 1982: 14) gave this pithy summary of the uncertainties facing the national cable channels:

> No one knows what people will look at. And after that, we don't know what people will buy or what advertisers will buy and for how much.

While we cannot predict the state of the environment or the future, we can specify the sectors of the environment that are critical in determining the outcome of future competition.

One key environmental sector upon which the outcome of future competition depends is the national economy. As the constancy principle (McCombs, 1972) states, a constant proportion of the gross national product is spent by consumers and advertisers on the media. As a consequence, new-media industries succeed at the expense of the older forms. Constancy implies that if the economy grows, more money will be available to the media industries as a whole, and populations that are perhaps marginal in competitive ability may retain their viability. On the other hand, if economic growth is relatively flat, the competition for resources may result in lowered population levels within the competitively disadvantaged industry as individual organizations fail. At the extreme, the outcompeted population could follow vaudeville into extinction.

Another sector of the environment that may enhance or constrain the competitive ability of industries is the legal and regulatory system. The decision of the courts, the regulatory agencies, or the copyright tribunal—while grounded in the constitution or on legal precedent, antitrust legislation, or the public interest—are often not benign nor neutral in their practical effect on communication industries. Banning cigarette ads from the airwaves may have been justified in the public interest, but it was certainly of benefit to the print media, whose revenues from cigarette advertising jumped sharply upward. More recently, Pool's (1983) analysis of the legal battle between the newspaper and telephone industries over the control of electronic publishing makes it clear that the contest has as much to do with practical competitive advantage as it does with the more lofty ideal of the freedom to publish. Industries that can arrange a favorable environment for their operations secure for themselves a valuable competitive advantage.

A third sector of the environment that is not only relevant but obviously critical to the outcome of future competition is the behavior of consumers and advertisers. Here, consumer behavior is primary since, even in advertising-supported industries, advertisers—whether they employ audience size, demographics, or life-style characteristics—choose their vehicles based on audience attributes. The key questions, then, in determining the outcome of competition between industries revolve around the number and characteristics of consumers who choose to allocate their time and money to the various media alternatives.

These are turbulent times in the communication industry community. The most obvious contributors to this turbulence are the new companies, the mergers and buy-outs, the AT&T divestiture, the IBM settlement, and so on (see Fombrun and Astley, 1982). This is primarily intraindustry turbulence. This activity does have, however, interindustry effects that are of interest in the ecological frame. To the extent that this organization-level turbulence alters the nature of the resource base for an industry (the aggregate of organizations in question), then the nature of survivorship in that industry has been altered.

Consider a few examples. When Warner Cable became Warner Amex Cable, the operation gained two things: corporate capital and corporate management. Here American Express was making its resources, mined in one ecological community, available to an entity competing in another ecological community. By this, it may have altered the nature of the community and the competition. What Fombrun and Astley, and others who engage in the microecology of examining organizational formations, fail to account for is that when IBM moved into the personal computer business, it was broadening its market, but it remained within the bounds of the industry community niche. Here IBM brought vast resources and much experience to bear and is probably having huge impacts on the viability of individual companies within the community. But we suspect that IBM has not fundamentally altered the resource base of the community. If AT&T were to use capital accumulated in telephony to enter the computer business, however, we may find the resource base altered.

The principle to extract from these examples is this: Though the ecological conception acknowledges that interorganizational intraindustry changes may have important impacts on the economics of individual firms, it is skeptical that these changes have impact on societal-level resource distributions. When strong members of one community make viable entrances to another community, however, the ecological conception predicts changes in the societal distribution of resources.

Whether competition is conceptualized and measured in terms of consumer needs or advertising dollars it is doubtful that the outcome is amenable to long-range prediction. Predicting the long-run effects of competition among present and future industries would require simultaneous predictions of the behavior of the legal and regulatory institutions, the state of the national economy, and the decision-making patterns of consumers and advertisers. In short, we do not believe it is possible to predict the flood. Rather than attempting to predict the outcome of future competition, the approach we have taken and will continue to pursue is to develop means of conceptualizing and measuring competition among communication industries.

NOTES

We thank our editor, Ron Rice, for his energy and patience; he has persevered through missed deadlines and not always kind conceptual arguments. Ron has also been our most prolific respondent to the previous papers in this series. We also thank the many others who have criticized, encouraged, or commented on our previous papers. We consider this, and all of our papers on ecology, reports of works in progress.

1. The measures we use are by no means without controversy. The bioecological literature sometimes seems more rich with measures, models, and simulations than with data analyses. The biologists are currently entrenched in a divisive debate, not only over usable measures, but the epistemological status of ecology as practiced following Hutchinson's work (Lewin, 1983; see also Colwell and Futuyma, 1971; Feinsinger, Spears, and Poole, 1981; May, 1975; Schoener, 1974; also some of the articles in Whittaker and Levin, 1975). In the social science literature, Hannan and Freeman and their students do not use the same measures we do (see, e.g., Freeman and Hannan, 1983), and the most challenging and, thereby, best comments we have had on our previous work have been in relation to the choice and use of niche measures. Until the controversy settles, we use these measures because they are simple and widely disseminated. Parsimony is important not only in theory but also in analytic technique. Any reader can understand our work by simple investigation of the formulas; any reader can replicate our work with scratch pad and pencil.

References

Abelson, R. "Psychological Status of the Script Concept." American Psychologist, 1981, 715-729.

Ackoff, R. "Management Misinformation Systems." Management Science, 1967, 2, 4, 147-156.

Adams, E.; Laker, D. and Hulin, C. "An Investigation of the Influence of Job Level and Functional Specialty on Job Attitudes and Perceptions." Journal of Applied Psychology, 1977, 62, 335-343.

Advanced Systems Laboratory. "Office Communication: A Study of Networks and Impediments." Lowell, MA: Wang Laboratories, 1981.

Agarwala-Rogers, R.; Rogers, E.M. and Wills, R. Diffusion of Impact Innovations from 1973-76: Interpersonal Communication Networks Among University Professors. Stanford, CA: Applied Communication Research, 1977.

Albertson, L. "Telecommunication as a Travel Substitute: Some Psychological, Organizational and Social Aspects." Journal of Communication, 1977, 27, 2, 32-43.

Albertson, L. "Trying to Eat an Elephant." Communications Research, 1980, 7, 387-400.

Alexander, J. and Filler, R. Attitudes and Reading. Newark, DE: International Reading Association, 1976.

Aldrich, H. Organizations and Environments. Englewood Cliffs, NJ: Prentice-Hall, 1979.

Allen, T. Managing the Flow of Scientific and Technological Information. Unpublished Ph.D. dissertation, Cambridge, MA: Massachusetts Institute of Technology, 1966.

Allen, T. Managing the Flow of Technology. Cambridge, MA: MIT Press, 1977.

Allen, T. and Gerstberger, S. "Criteria for Selection of an Information Source." Cambridge, MA: Sloan School of Management, MIT, 1967. See also "Communication in the R & D Lab." Technological Review, 1967, 70, 31-37.

Anderson, D. and Lorch, E. "Looking at Television: Action or Reaction?" in Bryant, J. and Anderson, D. (eds.) Children's Understanding of Television. New York: Academic Press, 1983, 1-33.

Anderson, R.; Klassen, D.; Krohn, K. and Smith-Cunnien, P. Assessing Computer Literacy. Computer Awareness and Literacy: An Empirical Assessment. Minneapolis, MN: Minnesota Educational Computing Consortium, 1982.

Arlen, G. "The End of the Beginning: What Will We Do With What We Learned on the Trial Trail?" in Videotex '83 Proceedings. New York: London Online, 1983, 337-343.

Arnett, T. "Intelligent Copiers-Printers Can Save You Time and Labor." The Office, 1981, November, 155-158.

Aron, C. "To Barter Their Souls for Gold: Female Clerks in Federal Government Office, 1862-1890." Journal of American History, 1981, 67, 4, 835-853. (Cited in Whalen, 1983)

Asimov, I. The Beginning and the End. New York: Simon and Shuster, 1977.

ASIS. Perspectives on Library Networks and Resource Sharing. (Special Issue) Journal of American Society for Information Science, 1980, 31, 6, 404-445.

Atkin, C. "Instrumental Utilities and Information Seeking," in P. Clarke (ed.) New Models for Communication Research. Beverly Hills, CA: Sage, 1973, 205-243.

Baker, C. and Eason, K. "An Observational Study of Man-Computer Interactions Using an Online Bibliographic Information Retrieval System." Online Review, 1981, 5, 2, 121-132.

Bair, J. "Evaluation and Analysis of an Augmented Knowledge Workshop." Final Report for Phase I, Rome Air Development Center, RADC-TR-74-79, 1974, April (NTIS AD 778 835/9).

Bair, J. "Productivity Assessment of Office Information Systems Technology, "in Trends and Applications: 1978 Distributed Processing. Washington, DC: IEEE and National Bureau of Standards, 1978, 12-22.

Bair, J. "Communication in the Office of the Future: Where the Real Payoff May Be." Business Communications Review, 1979, 9, 1, 1-11.

Bair, J. "An Analysis of Organizational Productivity and the Use of Electronic Office Systems," in Proceedings of the American Society for Information Science, 1980, 43, 4-9.

Baird, M. and Monson, M. "How To Tackle Training for Teleconferencing Users." Educational and Instructional Television, 1982, 14, 45-50.

Baldridge, J. and Burnham, R. "Organizational Innovation: Individual, Organizational, and Environmental Impacts." Administrative Science Quarterly, 1975, 20, 165-176.

Baldwin, T.; Greenberg, B.; Block, M. and Stoyanoff, N. "Rockford, Ill.: Cognitive and Affective Outcomes." Journal of Communication, 1978, 28, 2, 180-194.

Bales, R. Interaction Process Analysis: A Method for the Study of Small Groups. Reading, MA: Addison-Wesley, 1950.

Bales, R. "How People Interact in Conferences." Scientific American, 1955, 192, 3, 31-35.

Bales, R. and Strodtbeck, F. "Phases in Group-Problem-Solving." Journal of Abnormal and Social Psychology, 1951, 46, 485-495.

Bamford, H.E., Jr. "Assessing the Impact of Computer Augmentation and the Productivity of a Program Staff." Washington, DC: National Science Foundation, 1978.

Bamford, H.E., Jr. "Assessing the Effect of Computer Augmentation on Staff Productivity." Journal of the American Society for Information Science, 1979, May, 136-142.

Bamford, H.E., Jr. and Savin, W. "Electronic Information Exchange: The National Science Foundation's Developing Role." Bulletin of ASIS, 1978, 4, 12-13.

Barefoot, J. and Strickland, L. "Conflict and Dominance in Television-Mediated Interactions." Human Relations, 1982, 35, 7, 559-566.

Bargh, J. "Attention and Automaticity in the Processing of Self-Relevant Information." Journal of Personality and Social Psychology, 1982, 425-436.

Barnouw, E. The Image Empire: A History of Broadcasting in the United States from 1953. New York: Oxford University Press, 1970.

Becker, H. "Microcomputers in the Classroom: Dreams and Realities." Baltimore, MD: Center for Social Organization of Schools, Johns Hopkins University, 1982.

Becker, H. "How Schools Use Microcomputers: First Report from a National Survey." Baltimore, MD: Center for Social Organization of Schools, Johns Hopkins University, 1983. Paper presented to the American Educational Research Association, Montreal, 1983, April.

Becker, L. "Measurement of Gratifications." Communication Research, 1979, 6, 1, 54-73.

Bell, D. The Coming of Post-Industrial Society. New York: Basic Books, 1976.

Berelson, B. "What Missing the Newspaper Means," in Lazarsfeld, P. and Stanton, F. (eds.) Communications Research, 1948-49. New York: Duell, Sloan and Pearce, 1949, 111-129.

Berger, C. and Roloff, M. "Social Cognition, Self-awareness and Inter-personal Communication," in Dervin, B. and Voigt, M. (eds.) Progress in Communication Sciences, Vol. 2. Norwood, NJ: Ablex, 1980, 2-49.

Berman, P. and McLaughlin, N. Federal Programs Supporting Educational Change. Vol. IV.: The Findings in Review. Santa Monica, CA: Rand, 1975.

Bernard, H.; Killworth, P. and Sailer, L. "Informant Accuracy in Social Network Data IV." Social Networks, 1980, 2, 191-218.

Bernard, H.; Killworth, P. and Sailer, L. "Informant Accuracy in Social Network Data V." Social Science Research, 1982, 11, 30-66.

Bikson, T.; Gutek, B. and Mankin, D. Implementation of Information Technology in Office Settings: Review of Relevant Literature. Santa Monica, CA: Rand, 1981.

Blake, W. The Portable Blake (Kazin, A., ed.). New York: Viking Press, 1946.

Blau, P. The Dynamics of Bureaucracy. Chicago: University of Chicago Press, 1963.

Blau, P. Inequality and Heterogeneity: A Primitive Theory of Social Structure. New York: Free Press, 1977.

Bliven, B., Jr. The Wonderful Writing Machine. New York: Random House, 1954.

Blumler, J. and Katz, E. (eds.) The Uses of Mass Communication. Beverly Hills, CA: Sage, 1974.

Blundell, G. "Personal Computers in the Eighties," Byte, 1982, 8, 1.

Bodensteiner, W. Information Channel Utilization under Varying Research and Development Project Conditions: An Aspect of Inter-organizational Communication Channel Usage. Unpublished Ph.D. dissertation, Austin, TX: University of Texas, 1970.

Bogart, L. "The Mass Media and the Blue Collar Worker," in Shostak, A. and Gomberg, W. (eds.) Blue Collar World: Studies of the American Worker. Englewood Cliffs, NJ: Prentice-Hall, 1964, 416-428.

Bolton, T. "Discriminating Characteristics of the Videotex Innovator." Submitted to Journal of Communication, 1983.

Bolton, W. "The Home Book Club: Experimental Phase Completed." Cable Libraries, 1980, 8, 5, 2-3.

Borgman, C. "Theoretical Approaches to the Study of Human Interaction with Computers." Stanford, CA: Stanford University Institute for Communication Research, 1982.

Borgman, C. "End User Behavior on the Ohio State Libraries' Online Catalog: A Computer Monitoring Study." OCLC/OPR/RR-83/7. Dublin, OH: OCLC, 1983.

Boss, R. and McQueen, J. "Document Delivery in the United States: A Preliminary Report to the Council on Library Resources." ISCI, 1983, October 10.

Bostrum, R. and Heinen, J. "MIS Problems and Failures: A Socio-technical Perspective. Part I: The Causes." MIS Quarterly, 1977a, September, 17-32.

Bostrum, R. and Heinen, J. "MIS Problems and Failures: A Socio-technical Perspective. Part II: The Application of Socio-Technical Theory." MIS Quarterly, 1977b, December, 11-28.

Bowes, J. "Japan's Approach to an Information Society: A Critical Perspective," in Wilhoit, G. and de Bock, H. (eds.) Mass Communication Yearbook, Vol. 2. Beverly Hills, CA: Sage, 1981, 699-710.

Bowers, R. "Communications for a Mobile Society," in Schement, J.; Gutierrez, F. and Sirbu, M., Jr. (eds.) Telecommunications Policy Handbook. New York: Praeger, 1982, 275-306.

Boyd, L.; Clark, M. and Hanson, S. "A Worker-Centered Information System." Evaluation Review, 1980, 4, 5, 637-640.

Brahan, J. and Godfrey, D. "A Marriage of Convenience: Videotex and Computer Assisted Learning." Computers and Education, 1982, 6, 33-38.

Branscomb, L. "Information: The Ultimate Frontier." Science, 1979, 203, 143-147.

Braunstein, Y. "Costs and Benefits of Library Information: The User Point of View." The Economics of Academic Libraries: Library Trends, 1979, Summer, 79-87.

Brenner, D. and Logan, R. "Some Considerations in the Diffusion of Medical Technologies: Medical Information Systems," in Nimmo, D. (ed.) Communication Yearbook 4. New Brunswick, NJ: Transaction Books, 1980, 609-623.

Bretz, R. A Taxonomy of Communication Media. Report R-697-NLM/PR (Rand Corporation). Englewood Cliffs, NJ: Educational Technology Publications, 1971.

Bretz, R. Media for Interactive Communication. Beverly Hills, CA: Sage, 1983.

Brewer, E. and Tomlinson, J. "The Manager's Working Day." Journal of Industrial Economics, 1964, 12, 191-197.

Brief, A.; Delbecq, A.; Filley, A., and Huber, G. "Elite Structure and Attitudes: An Empirical Analysis of Adoption Behavior." Administration and Society, 1976, 8, 227-248.

Broadcasting. "Teletext and Videotext: Jockeying for Position in the Information Age." Broadcasting, 1982, June 28, 37-49.

Brooks, B. "Survey by Dr. Brooks Sheds Light on Effects of Videos on California Youth." Replay, 1983, April, 95-96.

Brown, E.; Limb, J. and Prasada, B. "A Continuous Presence Video Conferencing System." Murray Hill, NJ: Bell Laboratories, 1978.

Brown, L. Television: The Business Behind the Box. New York: Harcourt Brace Jovanovich, 1971.

Buckwell, L., Jr. "The Economics of Information Processing." Journal of Micrographics, 1983, 16, 1, 13-16.

Bullen C.V.; Bennett, L. and Carlson, D. "A Case Study of Office Workstation Use." IBM Systems Journal, 1982, 21, 3, 351-369.

Burns, T. "The Directions of Activity and Communication in a Departmental Executive Group: A Quantitative Study in a British Engineering Factory with a Self-Recording Technique." Human Relations, 1954, 7, 73-97.

Burstyn, H. "Electronic Mail: Evolving from Intracompany to Intercompany," in Smith, A. (ed.) AFIPS Conference Proceedings: 1983 National Computer Conference. Arlington, VA: AFIPS Press, 1983, 52, 379-383.

Bush, V. "As We May Think." Atlantic Monthly, 1945, 176, 101-108.

Business Week. "The New Broader Gauges of Productivity." Business Week, 1982, 19, 44B-44J.

Butler Cox and Partners. Videotex: The Key Issues. Videotex Report Series No. 1. London: Butler Cox, 1980. (Updated from 1980 on)

Byte. "Personal Computers in the Eighties." Byte, 1983, 8, 1, 171-182.

Cablevision, 1983a, September 19, p. 86.

Cablevision, 1983b, April 4, p. 143.

Campbell, J. and Thomas, H. "The Videotext Marketplace: A Theory of Evolution." Telecommunications Policy, 1981, 5, 2, 111-120.

Canning, R. "The Automated Office. Part II." EDP Analyzer, 1978, 16, 10.

Cantor, N. and Mischel, W. "Traits as Prototypes: Effects on Recognition Memory." Journal of Personality and Social Psychology, 1977, 38-48.

Canadian Ministry of Supply and Services. Telidon Trials and Services. Canada, 1983.

Cappella, J. "Talk and Silence Sequences in Informal Conversations II." Human Communication Research, 1980, 6, 2, 130-145.

Card, S.; Moran, T. and Newell, A. The Psychology of Human-Computer Interaction. New York: Erlbaum, 1982.

Carey, J. "Consumer Information Habits." Presented to Online Conference, New York, 1981. New York: Greystone Communications, 1981a. See also Carey, J. "Videotex: The Past as Prologue." Journal of Communication, 1982, 32, 2, 80-87.

Carey, J. "Interaction Patterns in Audio Teleconferencing." Telecommunications Policy, 1981b, 6, 304-314.

Carlson, E. "Evaluating the Impact of Information Systems." Management Informatics, 1974, 3, 56-67.

Carlson, S. Executive Behavior: A Study of the Work Load and the Working Methods of Managing Directors. Stockholm: Stromberg, 1951.

Carlson, T. "Pac-Mania Can't Hurt You, Professor Says." Los Angeles Herald Examiner, 1982, April 2.

Carpenter, E. Oh, What a Blow that Phantom Gave Me. New York: Holt, Rinehart & Winston, 1973.

Carter, G. The Implications of Empirical, Managerial Attention Data for Computer-Mediated Communication Systems. Ph.D. Dissertation, Pittsburgh, PA: Carnegie-Mellon University, Department of Engineering and Public Policy, 1980.

Case, D. "Videodiscs: An Emerging Information Technology." Stanford University Institute for Communication Research, 1981.

Case, D.; Chen, M.; Daley, H.; Kim, J.; Mishra, N.; Paisley, W.; Rice, R.E. and Rogers, E.M. Stanford Evaluation of the Green Thumb Box Experimental Videotext Project. Stanford, CA: Institute for Communication Research, 1981.

Case, D. and Daley, H. "Personal Computers: The New Academic Medium." Paper presented at the meeting of the International Communication Association, Dallas, Texas, 1983.

Case Institute of Technology Operations Research Department. An Operations Research Study of Scientific Activities of Chemists. Cleveland, OH: Case Institute, 1958.

Casey-Stahmer, A. and Havron, M. Planning Research in Teleconferencing Systems (HRR-RR-73/10-88-X). McLean, VA: Human Sciences Research, September, 1973.

CIP [Center for Interactive Programming]. "CIP Survey of Teleconferencing Users." Madison, WI: University of Wisconsin Extension, 1981.

Champness, B. The Assessment of User's Reactions to Confravision: Analysis and Conclusions (Rep. E/73250/CH). London: University College, Communications Studies Group, 1973.

Champness, B. and deAlberdi, M. "Measuring Subjective Reactions to Teletext Page Design." NSF Grant DAR-7924489-AO2. New York: Alternate Media Center, New York University, 1981.

Chandler, J. "A Multiple Criteria Approach for Evaluating Information Systems." Management Information Science Quarterly, 1982, 6, 1, 61-74.

Charles, J. "Approaches to Teleconferencing Justification." Telecommunications Policy, 1981, 5, 296-302.

Chen, M. et al. "Computer Attitudes and Experiences of Students in Five California High Schools." Stanford, CA: Stanford University School of Education. Study of Stanford and the Schools Report, in preparation.

Cherry, L.; Fox, M.; Frase, L.; Gingrich, P.; Keenan, S. and Macdonald, N. "Computer Aids for Text Analysis." Bell Laboratories Record, 1983, 61, 5, 10-16.

Cherry, S. "The New TV Information Systems." American Libraries, 1980, February, pp. 94 ff.

Chu, G. and Schramm, W. Learning from Television. Stanford, CA: Institute for Communication Research, 1967. (Revised form: Schramm, W. Big Media, Little Media. Beverly Hills, CA: Sage, 1977.)

Clarke, P.; Kline, T.; Schumacher, H. and Evans, S. "Rockford, Ill.: In-Service Training for Teachers." Journal of Communication, 1978, 28, 2, 195-201.

Cline, T. "Work Group Communication in Word Processing." Baltimore, MD: College of Notre Dame. Presented to Speech Communication Association, Washington, DC, November 1983.

Coen, R. Telephone interview with Eric Rothenbuhler, 1984, January. (Coen is employed by McCann-Erickson.)

Collins, B. and Raven, B. "Group Structure: Attraction, Coalitions, Communication, and Power," in Lindzey, G. and Aronson, E. (eds.) Handbook of Social Psychology Vol. 4. Reading, MA: Addison-Wesley, 1969.

Collins, W. "Cognitive Processing in Television Viewing," in Pearl, D.; Bouthilet, L. and Lazar, J. Television and Behavior: Ten Years of Scientific Progress and Implications for the 80s. Washington, DC: National Institute of Mental Health, 1983, 9-23.

Colwell, R. and Futuyma, D. "On the Measurement of Niche Breadth and Overlap." Ecology, 1971, 52, 4, 567-576.

Communications Week. 1984, January 30, p. c1.

Computerworld. "Datagraphix COM Unit Offers Remote Imaging." Computerworld, 1982, January 25, 65-66.

Comstock, G.; Chaffee, S.; Katzman, N.; McCombs, M. and Roberts, D. Television and Human Behavior. New York: Columbia University Press, 1978.

Connelly, T. "TAFT Broadcasting Company Findings from Cincinnati Teletext Experiment," in Videotext '83 Proceedings. New York: London Online, 1983, 139-146.

Conrath, D. "Communication Patterns, Organizational Structure, and Man: Some Relations." Human Factors, 1973a, 15, 459-470.

Conrath, D. "Communications Environment and Its Relationship to Organizational Structure." Management Science, 1973b, 20, 4, 586-603.

Conrath, D. "Organizational Communication Behavior: Description and Prediction," in Elton, M.; Lucas, W. and Conrath, D. (eds.) Evaluating New Telecommunication Services. New York: Plenum, 1978, 425-442.

Conrath, D. W. and Bair, J. "The Computer as an Interpersonal Communication Device: A Study of Augmentation Technology and its Apparent Impact on Organizational communication." Proceedings of the Second Internatinal Conference on computer Communications, Stockholm, August 1974, 121-127.

Consumer Reports. "How Our Readers Are Using Computers." Consumer Reports, 1983, 48, 9, 471.

Cook, T. and Campbell, D. "The Design and Conduct of Quasi-Experiments for Field Settings." In Dunnette, M. (ed.) Handbook of Organizational and Industrial Psychology. Skokie, IL: Rand-McNally, 1976.

Cook, T. and Campbell, D. Quasi-Experimentation: Design and Analysis Issues for Field Settings. Chicago, IL: Rand-McNally, 1979.

Copeman, G.; Luijk, H. and de P. Hanika, F. How the Executive Spends His Time. London: Business Publications Limited, 1963.

COST. A Network-Based Text System For Stanford University. Stanford, CA: Stanford University Center for Information Technology, Committee on Office Systems and Technology, 1980.

Coulton, B. and Hayo, G. "Executive Time Management II. How to Budget Your Time." S.A.M. Advanced Management Journal, 1978, Winter, 41-48.

Cramer, J. and Fast, K. "System Justification Specific to the Pacific Power's Rate Department." Portland, OR: IBM, 1982, February.

Crask, M. and Reynolds, F. "Print and Electronic Cultures?" Journal of Advertising Research, 1980, August, 47-51.

Crawford, A., Jr. "Corporate Electronic Mail—A Communication-Intensive Application of Information Technology." MIS Quarterly, 1982, 6, 3, 1-13.

Crooks, S. Libraries in the Year 2000: Document Delivery—Background Papers. Network Planning Paper 7. Washington, DC: Library of Congress, 1982, June.

Croston, J. and Goulding, H. "The Effectiveness of Communications at Meetings: A Case Study." Operational Research Quarterly, 1967, 17, 1, 45-47.

Cuadra Associates, Inc. Downloading Online Databases: Policy and Pricing Strategies Study Report. Santa Monica, CA: Cuadra Associates, 1983a, October.

Cuadra Associates, Inc. Directory of Online Databases. Santa Monica, CA: Cuadra Associates, 1983b.

Culnan, M. and Bair, J. "Human Communication Needs and Organizational Productivity: The Potential Impact of Office Automation." Journal of the American Society for Information Science, 1983, 34, 3, 218-224.

Cummings, M. "Medical Information Services: For Public Good or Private Profit?" The Information Society: An International Journal, 1982, 1, 3, 249-260.

Cummings, T. "Self-Regulating Work Groups: A Socio-Technical Synthesis." Academy of Management Review, 1978, 3, 3, 625-634.

CSP International. World Census of Videotex and Teletext. New York: CSP, 1982, April.

Cushman, R-C. "The Kurzweil Reading Machine." Wilson Library Bulletin, 1980, 54, 5, 311-315.

Curley, K. Word Processing: First Step to the Office of the Future? An Examination of an Evolving Technology and Its Use in Organizations. Unpublished Ph.D. Dissertation, Cambridge, MA: Harvard University Graduate School of Business Administration, 1981.

Curley, K. and Pyburn, P. "Intellectual Technologies: The Key to Improving White Collar Productivity." Sloan Management Review, 1982, Fall, 31-39.

Dahl, S.C. "Implementing a Word Processing/Administrative Support System." Auerbach Publishers, Inc. Electronic Office: Management and Technology. 005.0001.020, 1981, 1-12.

Dahl, T. and Lewis, D. "Random Sampling Devices Used in Time Management Study." Evaluation, 1975, 2, 2, 20.

Danowski, J. "Computer-Mediated Communication: A Network Analysis Using a CBBS Conference," in Burgoon, M. (ed.) Communication Yearbook, 6. Beverly Hills, CA: Sage, 1982, 905-924.

Danowski, J. "Automated Network Analysis: A Survey of Different Approaches to the Analysis of Human Communication Relationships." Presented to International Communication Association, Dallas, 1983.

Danzinger, J.; Dutton, W.; Kling, R. and Kraemer, K. Computers and Politics: High Technology in American Local Government. New York: Columbia University Press, 1982.

Davis, J. Group Performance. Reading, MA: Addison-Wesley, 1969.

DeFleur, M. and Ball-Rokeach, S. Theories of Mass Communication, 3rd edition. New York: McKay, 1975.

Delgado, E. The Enormous File. Norwhich, Great Britain: Fletcher and Son, 1979. (Cited in Whalen, 1983)

Dertouzos, M. and Moses, J. (eds.) The Computer Age: A Twenty-Year View. MIT Bicentennial Studies, Vol. 6. Cambridge, MA: MIT Press, 1980.

Dervin, B. "Mass Communicating: Changing Conceptions of the Audience," in Rice, R. and Paisley, W. (eds.) Public Communication Campaigns. Beverly Hills, CA: Sage, 1981, 71-88.

DeSante, E. "Who Will Survive?" Multichannel News, 1982, 3, 28, II, pp. 6-11, 15, 59-61.

Dewhirst, H. "Influence of Perceived Information-Sharing on Communication Channel Utilization." Academy of Management Journal, 1971, 14, 305-315.

Dickenson, R.M. "System Alternatives for Office Automation: Distributed Office Systems." AFIPS Office Automation Conference Digest. Arlington, VA: AFIPS Press, 1982, 593-597.

Dickson, J. and Slevin, D. "The Use of Semantic Differential Scales in Studying the Innovation Boundary." Academy of Management Journal, 1975, 18, 381-387.

Diebold, J. Beyond Automation. New York: McGraw-Hill, 1964.

Dimmick, J. and Rothenbuhler, E. "The Theory of the Niche: Quantifying Competition Among Mass Media Industries." Paper presented at the Association for Education in Journalism, Athens, Ohio, 1982. (Revised version in Journal of Communication, 1984)

Dimmick, J. and Rothenbuhler, E. "The Niche and Dominance in Media Industries: Competition, Displacement and Coexistence." Paper presented at the Culture and Communication Conference, Philadelphia, 1983a.

Dimmick, J. and Rothenbuhler, E. "The Theory of the Niche: Measuring Competition Between the Cable and Broadcast Industries." Paper presented at the International Communication Association Convention, Dallas, 1983b.

Dirr, P. and Pedone, R. "Uses of Television for Instruction, 1976-1977: Final Report of the School TV Utilization Study." Washington, DC: Corporation for Public Broadcasting, 1979.

Dizzard, W. The Coming Information Age: An Overview of Technology, Economics and Politics. New York: Annenberg/Longman, 1982.

Dizzard, W. "Reinventing the Telephone." Intermedia, 1983, 11, 3, 9-11.

Doktor, R. and Makridakis, S. "Computer Simulation of the Communication Network Experiments: An Application of Stability Theory." General Systems, 1974, 19, 195-199.

Doebler, P. "The Computer in Book Distribution." Publisher's Weekly, 1980, 218, 11, 25-41.

Dominick, W. "User Interaction Monitoring as a Multi-Level Process," in Proceedings of American Society for Information Science, 1977, 14, 63.

Dominick, W.; Penniman, D. and Rush, J. An Overview of a Proposed Monitoring Facility for the Large-Scale Network-Based OCLC Online System. OCLC/OPR/RR-80/1; ERIC ED 186042. Dublin, OH: OCLC, 1980.

Dordick, H.; Bradley, H., and Nanus, B. The Emerging Network Marketplace. Norwood, NJ: Ablex, 1981.

Dordick, H. and Rice, R. "Transmission Systems," in Meadow, C. and Tedesco, A. (eds.) Telecommunications for Management. New York: McGraw-Hill, 1984.

Dormois, M.; Fioux, F. and Gensollen, M. Evaluation of the Potential Market for Various Future Communication Modes Via an Analysis of Communication Flow Characteristics," in Elton, M.; Lucas, W. and Conrath, D. (eds.) Evaluating New Telecommunication Services. New York: Plenum Press, 1978, 367-384.

Dorros, I. "Evolving Capabilities of the Public Switched Telecommunications Network," in Schement, J.; Gutierrez, F. and Sirbu, M., Jr. (eds.) Telecommunications Policy Handbook. New York: Praeger, 1982, 11-26.

Downs, C. and Hain, T. "Productivity and Communication," in Burgoon, M. (ed.) Communication Yearbook 5. New Brunswick, NJ: Transaction Books, 1982, 435-454.

Downs, G. and Mohr, L. "Conceptual Issues in the Study of Innovation." Administrative Science Quarterly, 1976, 21, 700-714.

Downs, G. and Mohr, L. "Toward a Theory of Innovation." Administration and Society, 1979, 10, 379-408.

Downing, H. "Word Processors and the Oppression of Women," in Forester, E. (ed.) The Microelectronics Revolution. Cambridge, MA: MIT Press, 1980, 275-287.

Dozier, D. and Ledingham, J. "Perceived Attributes of Interactive Cable Services Among Potential Adopters." Paper presented to the Human Communication Technology Special Interest Group, International Communication Association Annual Convention, Boston, 1982, May.

Drake, M. and Olsen, H. "The Economics of Library Innovation." The Economics of Academic Libraries: Library Trends, 1979, Summer, 89-105.

Drewalowski, H. "German Videotext Experiment Finds Wide Consumer Approval." Direct Marketing, 1983, January, 36, 40-41.

Driscoll, J. "Office Automation: The Organizational Redesign of Office Work." Cambridge, MA: MIT Center for Information Systems, Research, Report 45, 1979.

Drucker, P. The Age of Discontinuity. New York: Harper & Row, 1969.

Dubin, R. and Spray, S. "Executive Behavior and Interaction." Industrial Relations, 1964, 3, 99-108.

Duda, R. and Shortliffe, E. "Expert Systems Research." Science, 1983, 220, 261-268.

Dunlop, J. (ed.) Automation and Technological Change. Englewood Cliffs, NJ: Prentice-Hall, 1962.

Dunlop, R.A. et al. "Results from the Leesburg Probe, Initial User Reactions and Estimates of Productivity Gains." Xerox Business Systems, 1980, January.

Dupuy, J.P. "Myths of the Informational Society," in Woodward, K. (ed.) The Myths of Information. Madison, WI: Coda Press, 1980, 3-17.

Dutton, W. "The Rejection of an Innovation: The Political Environment of a Computer-Based Model." Systems, Objectives and Solutions, 1981, 1, 179-201.

Dutton, W.; Fulk, J. and Steinfield, C. "Utilization of Video Conferencing." Telecommunications Policy, 1982, 6, 3, 164-178.

Easton, A. "Viewdata—A Product in Search of a Market?" Telecommunications Policy, 1980, 3, 4, 221-225.

Edelstein, A.; Bowes, J. and Harsel, S. Information Societies: Comparing the Japanese and American Experiences. Seattle, WA: University of Washington Press, 1978.

Editor and Publisher. "Viewtron Users Rate News as Top Choice." 1982a, July 10, 15.

Editor and Publisher. "Electronic Newspaper Found Unprofitable." 1982b, August 28.

Editor and Publisher. "AP Finds Meager Demand for Electronic News." 1982c, October 2, 10.

Edwards, G.C. "Organizational Impacts of Office Automation." Telecommunications Policy, 1978, June, 128-136.

Ehrlich, R. and Holm, R. "Patterns and Populations." Science, 1962, 137, 131-139.

Eissler, C. "Market Testing Videotext: Oak's Miami Teletext System." Oak Communications, Inc., 1981.

EIU Informatics. Office Automation in Europe: Survey of European Office Automation Pilot Trials. (22 Pilots summarized.) Sweden: Teldok (Telecommunications Administration), 1982.

Electronic Business. "Computers: Changes Fail to Dampen Market Outlook." Electronic Business, 1982, May 15.

Electronic Publishing Review. "After the Lawyers Come the Doctors." Electronic Publishing Review, 1982a, 2, 4, 249-250.

Electronic Publishing Review. "Business Information Market Growth Will Be Lead by Online Database Services." Electronic Publishing Review, 1982b, 2, 4, 250-251.

Electronic Publishing Review. "Dreams of Electronic Sheep." Electronic Publishing Review, 1982c, 2, 4, 256.

Elizur, D. and Guttman, L. "The Structure of Attitudes toward Work and Technological Change within an Organization." Administrative Science Quarterly, 1976, 21, 611-622.

Ellis, C. and Nutt, G. "Office Information Systems and Computer Science." Computing Surveys, 1980, 12, 1, 27-60.

Elton, M. and Carey, J. Interactive Telecommunication Systems: A Working Paper on Implementation Problems. New York: Alternative Media Center, School of Arts, New York University, 1978.

Elton, M. and Carey, J. Implementing Interactive Telecomms Services. New York: New York University Alternate Media Center, 1980.

Elton, M. and Carey, J. "Computerizing Information: Consumer Reactions to Teletext." Journal of Communication, 1983, 33, 162-173.

Elton, M.; Irving, R. and Siegeltuch, M. "The First Six Months of a Pilot Teletext Service: Interim Results on Utilization and Attitudes." New York: New York University Alternate Media Center, 1982.

Emery, F. "New Perspective on the World of Work: Sociotechnical Foundations for a New Social Order?" Human Relations, 1982, 35, 12, 1095-1122.

EMMS. "Making Electronic Mail Pay off in the 1980s." Electronic Mail and Messaging Systems, 1979, 3, 20, 1-9.

Engel, G.G.; Groppuso, J.; Lowenstein, R. and Traub, W. "An Office Communication System." IBM System Journal, 1979, 18, 3, 402-431.

Engel, G.; Groppuso, J.; Lowenstein, R. and Traub, W. "An Office Communications System," in Cotton, I. (ed.) 1980 Office Automation Conference Digest. Washington, DC: American Federation of Information Processing Societies, 1980, 301-313.

Englebart, D. Augmenting Human Intellect: A Conceptual Framework. Summary Report. Menlo Park, CA: Stanford Research Institute, 1962.

Ettema, J. "Information Equity and Information Technology: Some Preliminary Findings from a Videotex Field Trial." Minneapolis, MN: University of Minnesota School of Journalism and Mass Communication. Presented to Association for Education in Journalism, Corvallis, OR, 1983.

Ettema, J. and Kline, F. "Deficits, Differences and Ceilings: Contingent Conditions for Understanding the Knowledge Gap." Communication Research, 1977, April, 179-202.

Ettema, J. and Whitney, D. (eds.) Individuals in Mass Media Organizations: Creativity and Constraint. Beverly Hills, CA: Sage, 1982.

Evans, W. and Black, G. "Innovation in Business Organizations. Some Factors Associated with Success or Failure of Staff Proposals." Journal of Business, 1967, 40, 519-531.

Farace, R.; Monge, P. and Russell, H. Communicating and Organizing. Menlo Park, CA: Addison-Wesley, 1977.

Feeley, J. "Telidon Trials and Operations—Results, Experiences, and Future Trends," in Videotex '83 Proceedings. New York: London Online, 1983, 73-84.

Feinsinger, P.; Spears, E. and Poole, R. "A Simple Measure of Niche Breadth." Ecology, 1981, 68, 27-32.

Feldman, M. and March, J. "Information in Organizations as Signal and Symbol." Administrative Science Quarterly, 1981, 26,

Fett, J. "Situational Factors and Peasants' Search for Market Information." Journalism Quarterly, 1975, 53, 429-435.

Fombrun, C. and Astley, W.G. "The Telecommunications Community: An Institutional Overview." Journal of Communication, 1982, 32, 56-68.

Forbes. 1982, October 11, 123.

Forbes. "Technology for Technology's Sake." Forbes, 1983, May 9, 196-204.

Forester, T. (ed.) The Microelectronics Revolution. Cambridge, MA: MIT Press, 1981.

Form, W. "Technology and Social Behavior of Workers in Four Countries: A Sociotechnical Perspective." American Sociological Review, 1972, 37, 727-738.

Foster, J. and Bruce, M. "Looking for Entries in Videotex Tables: A Comparison of Four Color Formats." Journal of Applied Psychology, 1982, 67, 5, 611-615.

Fowler, G. and Wackerbarth, M. "Audio Teleconferencing versus Face-to-Face Conferencing: A Synthesis of the Literature." Western Journal of Speech Communication, 1980, 44, 236-252.

Frank, J. "New Electronic Developments Abound at 'Laser' Conference." Publishers Weekly, 1982, January 1, 35, 37.

Freeman, J. and Hannan, M. "Niche Widths and the Dynamics of Organizational Populations." American Journal of Sociology, 1983, 88, 1116-1145.

Freeman, L. "Q-Analysis and the Structure of Friendship Networks." International Journal of Man-Machine Studies, 1980, 12, 3, 367-378.

Fukae, K. "What Computer Technology is Doing for Copying Machines." The Office, 1980, March, 104.

Gaffner, H. "What is This Thing Called Videotex," in Videotex '83 Proceedings. New York: London Online, 1983, 1-16.

Galbraith, J. Organization Design. Reading, MA: Addison-Wesley, 1977.

Ganz, J. and Peacock, J. "Office Automation and Business Communications." Fortune, 1981, October 5, 7ff.

Gardner, P.C., Jr. "A System for the Automated Office Environment." Auerbach Publishers, Inc. Electronic Office: Management and Technology. 005.0001.018, 1981, 1-18.

Gause, G. The Struggle for Existence. Baltimore, MD: Wilkins and Wilkins, 1934.

Geller, V. and Lesk, M. "How Users Search: A Comparison of Menu and Attribute Retrieval Systems on a Library Catalog." Murray Hill, NJ: Bell Labs, 1981.

Gerstberger, P. and Allen, T. "Criteria Used by Research and Development Engineers in the Selection of an Information Source. Journal of Applied Psychology, 1968, 52, 272-277.

Gibbon, S.; Palmer, E. and Fowles, B. "Sesame Street, The Electronic Company, and Reading," in Carroll, J. and Chall, J. (eds.) Toward a Literate Society. New York: McGraw-Hill, 1975.

Giuliano, V. "The Mechanization of Office Work." Scientific American, 1982, 247, 3, 148-165.

Glenn, E. and Feldberg, R. "Degraded and Deskilled: The Proletarianization of Clerical Work." American Journal of Sociology, 1977, 25, 52-64.

Gnostic Concepts. "Digital Communications." Menlo Park, CA: Gnostic Concepts, 1982.

Goddard, J. "Office Linkages and Location," in D. Diamond and J. McLoughlin (eds.) Progress in Planning. Oxford: Pergamon Press, 1973, 111-231.

Goetzinger, C. and Valentine, M. "Communication Channels, Media, Directional Flow, and Attitudes in an Academic Community." Journal of Communication, 1962, 12, 23-26.

Gold, E. "Attitudes to Intercity Travel Substitution." Telecommunications Policy, 1979, 3, 88-104.

Gold, E. "Trends in Teleconferencing Today Indicate Increasing Corporate Use." Communications News, 1982, 48-49.

Goldfield, R. "Achieving Greater White-Collar Productivity in the New Office." Byte, 1983, 8, 5, 154 ff.

Goldhaber, J.; Yates, M.; Porter, D. and Lesniak, R. "Organizational Communication: 1978." Human Communication Research, 1978, 5, 1, 76-96.

Goldhamer, H. "The Social Effects of Communication Technology," in Schramm, W. and Roberts, D. (eds.) The Process and Effects of Mass Communication. Urbana, IL: University of Illinois Press, 1974, 897-951. (First edition, 1971)

Goldman, R.J. Factors Influencing Acceptance of Telecommunications: A Study of Vocational Rehabilitation Practitioners. Unpublished Ph.D. dissertation, University of Southern California, Annenberg School of Communications, 1979.

Goleman, D. "The Electronic Rorschach." Psychology Today, 1983, February, 36-43.

Gollin, A. "Consumers and Advertisers in the Electronic Marketplace." Telecommunications Policy, 1981, 5, 3, 171-180.

Gordon, G. and Fisher, G. (eds.) The Diffusion of Medical Technology. Cambridge, MA: Ballinger, 1975.

Gotlieb, C. and Borodin, A. Social Issues in Computing. New York: Academic Press, 1973.

Gottschalk, E. "Firms are Cool To Meetings By Television." Wall Street Journal, July 26, 1983, pp. 25, 39.

Grande, S. "Aspects of Pre-Literate Culture Shared by Online Searching and Videotex." The Canadian Journal of Information Science, 1980, 5, May, 125-131.

Green, D. and Hansell, K. "Teleconferencing: A New Communications Tool." Business Communications Review, 1981, 11, 10-16.

Greenberg, B. "Television and Role Socialization: An Overview," in Pearl, D.; Bouthilet, L. and Lazar, J. Television and Behavior: Ten Years of Scientific Progress and Implications for the 80s. Washington, DC: National Institute of Mental Health, 1983, 179-190.

Greenberger, M. (ed.) Computers and The World of the Future. Cambridge, MA: MIT Press, 1962.

Gregory, J. and Nussbaum, K. "Race Against Time: Automation of the Office. An Analysis of the Trends in Office Automation and the Impact on the Office Workplace." Office: Technology and People, 1982, 1, 197-236.

Griest, J. and Gustafson, D. "A Computer Interview for Suicide—Risk Prediction." American Journal of Psychiatry, 1973, December, 1327-1332.

Griffin, R. "Refining Uses and Gratifications with a Human Information Processing Model." Paper presented to the Theory and Methodology Division, Association for Education in Journalism Annual Convention, East Lansing, MI, August 1981.

Griffiths, J-M. "The Value of Information and Related Systems, Products, and Services," in Williams, M. (ed.) Annual Review of Information Science and Technology, Vol. 17. White Plains, NY: Knowledge Industry Publications, 1982, 269-284.

Grossbrenner, A. The Complete Handbook of Personal Computer Communications, New York: St. Martin's Press, 1983.

Gruenfeld, L. and Foltman, F. "Relationship Among Supervisors' Integration, Satisfaction, and Acceptance of a Technological Change." Journal of Applied Psychology, 1967, 51, 74-77.

Grusec, T. "Theory and Methodology for Research into Browsing with Special Reference to Videotex Data Bases." Report to Department of Communications Scientific Authority, March 1982.

Gutek, B. "Effects of Office of the Future Technology on Users: Results of a Longitudinal Field Study," in Mensch, G. and Niehaus, R. (eds.) Work, Organizations and Technological Change. New York: Plenum, 1982.

Guterl, F. and Truxal, C. "The Wonderful World of EPCOT." IEEE Spectrum, 1982, September, 46-52.

Hage, J. and Aiken, A. "Program Change and Organizational Properties: A Comparative Analysis." American Journal of Sociology, 1967, 72, 502-519.

Hage, J.; Aiken, M. and Marrett, C. "Organization Structure and Communications." American Sociological Review, 1971, 36, 860-871.

Hall, D. and Lawler, E. "Job Characteristics and Pressures and the Organizational Integration of Professionals." Administrative Science Quarterly, 1970, 15, 271-281.

Hall, G. and Louchs, S. "Innovation Configurations: Analyzing the Adaptations of Innovations." Austin, TX: Research and Development Center for Teacher Education, 1978.

Hamilton, S. and Chervany, N. "Evaluating Information Systems Effectiveness—Part 1: Comparing Evaluation Approaches." MIS Quarterly, 1981, 5, 3, 55-70.

Hannan, M. and Freeman, J. "The Population Ecology of Organizations." American Journal of Sociology, 1977, 82, 929-964.

Hannan, M. and Young, A. "Estimation in Panel Models: Results of Pooling Cross-Sections and Time Series," in Heise, D. (ed.) Sociological Methodology 1977. San Francisco: Jossey-Bass, 1977, 52-83.

Hanneman, G. and McEwen, W. (eds.) Communication and Behavior. Reading, MA: Addison-Wesley, 1975.

Hansell, K.; Green, D. and Erbring, L. "A Report on a Survey of Teleconferencing Users." Educational and Instructional TV, 1982, 14, 70-76.

Hanson, R. "Copiers: Intelligent and Otherwise." Administrative Management, 1980, December, pp. 32, 33. 73.

Hardin, G. "The Competitive Exclusion Principle." Science, 1960, 131, 1292-1297.

Hardy, A. "The Role of the Telephone in Economic Development." Telecommunications Policy, 1980, 4, 4, 278-286.

Hare, P. Handbook of Small Group Research, 2nd edition. New York: Free Press, 1976.

Harkness, R. "Office Information Systems: An Overview and Agenda for Public Policy Research." Telecommunications Policy, 1978, June, 91-104.

Harnish, T. "Channel 2000: Description and Findings of a Viewdata Test Conducted by OCLC in Columbus, Ohio, October-December 1980." Dublin, OH: Online Computer Library Center, 1981.

Harris, S.; Brightman, H. and Hicks, C. Research on the Organizational Impacts of Local Network Technology. NSF:1ST-8201455. Atlanta, GA: Georgia State University. Decision Sciences Lab, 1983.

Hartley, C.; Brecht, M.; Pagerey, P.; Weeks, G.; Chapanis, A. and Hoecker, D. "Subjective Time Estimates of Work Tasks by Office Workers." Journal of Occupational Psychology, 1977, 50, 23-36.

Hauptman, A. and Green, B. "A Comparison of Command, Menu-Selection and Natural-Language Computer Programs." Behavior and Information Technology, 1983, 12, 2, 163-178.

Hawkins, J. "Learning LOGO Together: The Social Context," in Chameleon in the Classroom: Developing Roles for Computers. Symposium presented to the American Educational Research Association, Montreal, 1983.

Hawley, A. "Ecology and Human Ecology." Social Forces, 1944, 22, 398-405.

Hawley, A. Human Ecology. New York: Ronald Press Company, 1950.

Hawley, A. "Human Ecology," in D. Sills (ed.) International Encyclopedia of the Social Sciences. New York: Macmillan, 1968.

Hawley, A. "Human Ecology: Persistence and Change." American Behavioral Scientist, 1981, 24, 3, 423-444.

Heath, T. "Alternative Videodisc Systems." Videodisc/Videotex, 1981, 1, 4, 228-238.

Heeter, C.; D'Alessio, D.; Greenberg, B. and McVoy, D. "Cable Viewing." Ann Arbor, MI: Michigan State University College of Communication Arts. Presented to International Communication Association, Dallas, 1983.

Helmreich, R.K. "Field Study with a Computer-Based Office System." Telecommunications Policy, 1982, June, 136-142.

Helmreich, R. and Wimmer, K. "Field Study with a Computer Based Office System." Telecommunications Policy, 1982, June, 136-142.

Herman, J.; Dunham, R. and Hulin, C. "Organizational Structure, Demographic Characteristics, and Employee Responses." Organizational Behavior and Human Performance, 1975, 13, 206-232.

Hess, R. and Miura, I. "Gender and Socioeconomic Differences in Enrollment in Computer Camps and Classes." Stanford, CA: Stanford University School of Education, 1983.

Hewes, D. "Process Models for Sequential Cross-Sectional Survey Data." Communication Research, 1978, 5, 455-482.

Hewes, D. Comments on ICA Presentation by Rice, R. and Rogers, E. Dallas, TX, May 1983.

Hickey, T. "The Journal in the Year 2000." Wilson Library Bulletin, 1981, December, 256-260.

Hiemstra, G. "Teleconferencing, Concern for Face, and Organizational Culture," in Burgoon, M. (ed.) Communication Yearbook 6. Beverly Hills, CA: Sage, 1982, 874- 904.

Hiltz, S.R. "The Impact of a Computerized Conferencing System on Scientific Research Communities." Newark, NJ: New Jersey Institute of Technology Computerized Conferencing and Communications Center, 1981.

Hiltz, S.R. "Experiments and Experiences with Computerized Conferencing," in Landau, R.; Bair, J. and Siegman, J. (eds.) Emerging Office Systems. Norwood, NJ: Albex, 1982, 182-204.

Hiltz, S.R. Online Communities: A Case Study of the Office of the Future. Norwood, NJ: Ablex, 1983.

Hiltz, S.R.; Johnson, K. and Agle, G. "Replicating Bales Problem-Solving Experiments on a Computerized Conferencing System." Report 8. Newark, NJ: New Jersey Institute of Technology Computerized Conferencing and Communications Center, 1978.

Hiltz, S.R., Johnson, K.; Aronovitch, C. and Turoff, M. Face-to-Face Computerized Conferences: A Controlled Experiment. Vol. 1: Findings. Vol. 2: Methodological Appendix. Research Report No. 12. Newark, NJ: New Jersey Institute of Technology, Computerized Conferencing and Communications Center, 1980.

Hiltz, S.R.; Johnson, K. and Rabke, A. "The Process of Communication in Face-To-Face vs. Computerized Conferences: A Controlled Experiment Using Bales Interaction Process Analysis." Newark, NJ: New Jersey Institute of Technology Computerized Conferencing and Communications Center, 1980. (Portion of Hiltz, Johnson, Aronovitch and Turoff, 1980.) Proceedings of the Association for Computational Linguistics, 1980.

Hiltz, S.R.; Johnson, K. and Turoff, M. "The Quality of Group Decision Making in Face-to-Face vs. Computerized Conferences." Newark, NJ: New Jersey Institute of Technology Computerized Conferencing and Communications Center, 1981. Paper presented to the American Sociological Association, Toronto, August, 1981.

Hiltz, S.R.; Johnson, K. and Turoff, M. "The Effects of Formal Human Leadership and Computer-Generated Decision Aids on Problem Solving via Computer: A Controlled Experiment." Newark, NJ: New Jersey Institute of Technology Computerized Conferencing and Communications Center, 1982.

Hiltz, S. R. and Kerr, E. (eds.) Studies of Computer-Mediated Communications Systems: A Synthesis of the Findings. Final Report to the Information Science and Technology Division, National Science Foundation (IST-8018077). East Orange, NJ: Upsala College, 1981.

Hiltz, S. R. and Turoff, M. The Network Nation: Human Communication Via Computer. Reading, MA: Addison-Wesley Advanced Book Program, 1978.

Hiltz, S.R. and Turoff, M. "The Evolution of User Behavior in a Computerized Conferencing System." Communications of the ACM, 1981, 24, 11, 739-751.

Hiltz, S.R.; Turoff, M.; Johnson, K. and Aronovitch, C. "Using a Computerized Conferencing System as a Laboratory Tool." SIGSOC Bulletin, 1982, 13, 4, 5-9.

Himmelweit, H.; Oppenheim, A. and Vince, P. Television and the Child. London: Oxford University Press, 1958.

Hinrichs, J. "Communications Activity of Industrial Research Personnel." Personnel Psychology, 1964, 17, 193-204.

Hinrichs, J. "Where Has All the Time Gone?" Personnel, 1976, 53, 4, 44.

Hirokawa, R. "Group Communication and Problem-Solving Effectiveness: An Investigation of Group Phases." Human Communication Research, 1983, 9, 4, 291-305.

Hirsch, P. "Occupational, Organizational and Institutional Models in Mass Media Research," in Hirsch, P.; Miller, P. and Kline, F. (eds.) Strategies for Communication Research. Beverly Hills, CA: Sage, 1977, 13-42.

Hirschberg, L.; Bossaller, B.; Kerns, P.; Dugan D.; Sargent, L.; Feltman, C.; Wiseman, S. and Dutton, W. The Notice Market: A Comparative Analysis of Electronic Message Systems. Los Angeles: University of Southern California, Annenberg School, 1982.

Hoecher, D. "A Behavioral Comparison of Communication Using Voice Switched and 'Continuous Presence' Videoconferencing Arrangements." Murray Hill, NJ: Bell Laboratories, 1978.

Homans, G. Social Behavior: Its Elementary Forms. New York: Harcourt Brace Jovanovich, 1961.

Home Video and Cable Yearbook. White Plains, NY: Knowledge Industry Publications, 1982.

Hopelain, D. "Assessing the Climate for Change." Systems, Objectives, Solutions, 1982, 2, 55-65.

Horne, J. and Lupton, T. "The Work Activities of "Middle" Managers—an Exploratory Study." Journal of Management Studies, 1965, 7, 14-33.

Hough, R. Teleconferencing Systems: A State of the Art Review. Menlo Park, CA: Stanford Research Institute, 1976.

Hrebiniak, L."Technology, Supervision, and Work Group Structure." Administrative Science Quarterly, 1974, 19, 395-410.

Hutchinson, G. "Concluding Remarks." Cold Spring Harbor Symposium on Quantitative Biology, 1957, 22, 415-427.

Information Hotline, 1978, 11, 1, 1.

Innis H. Empire and Communication. London: Clarendon Press, 1950.

International Data Corporation. "Business Communication: Alternatives for the Eighties." Fortune, 1980, February 25, 25-46.

International Data Corporation. 1983 Information Processing Industry Briefing Session. Framingham, MA: International Data Corporation, 1983.

Irving, R. "Computer-Assisted Communication in a Directorate of the Canadian Federal Government," in Elton, M., Lucas, W. and Conrath, D. (eds.) Evaluating New Telecommunications Services. New York: Plenum, 1978, 455-469.

Irving, R. Mode Choice in Dyadic Communication. Unpublished Ph.D. dissertation, University of Waterloo, Canada, 1981.

Irving, R.; Elton, M. and Siegeltuch, M. "The Last Five Months of a Pilot Teletext Service: Interim Results on Utilization and Attitudes." New York: New York University Alternate Media Center, 1982.

Ito, Y. "The 'Johoka Shakai' Approach to the Study of Communication in Japan," in Wilhoit, G. and de Bock, H. (eds.) Mass Communication Review Yearbook, Vol. 2. Beverly Hills, CA: Sage, 1981, 671-698.

Jablin, F. and Sussman, L. "An Exploration of Communication and Productivity in Real Brainstorming Groups." Human Communication Research, 1978, 4, 329-337.

Jacobsen, E. and Seashore, S. "Communication Practices in Complex Organizations." Journal of Social Issues, 1951, 7, 3, 28-40.

Jaffe, A. and Froomkin, J. Technology and Jobs: Automation in Perspective. New York: Praeger, 1968.

Jaffe, J. and Feldstein, S. Rhythms of Dialogue. New York: Academic Press, 1970.

Janis, I. Victims of Groupthink. Boston: Houghton-Mifflin, 1972.

Johansen, R. "Social Evaluations of Teleconferencing." Telecommunications Policy, 1977, 1, 5, 395-419.

Johansen, R.; DeGrasse, R., Jr. and Wilson, T. Group Communication Through Computers, Vol. 5. Effects on Working Patterns. Menlo Park, CA: Institute for the Future, 1978.

Johansen, R.; Hansell, K. and Green, D. "Growth in Teleconferencing—Looking Beyond the Rhetoric of Readiness." Telecommunications Policy, 1981, 5, 289-303.

Johansen, R.; Miller, R. and Vallee, J. "Group Communication Through Electronic Media: Fundamental Choices and Social Effects." Educational Technology, 1974, August, 7-20. Also in Linstone, H. and Turoff, M. (eds.) The Delphi Method: Techniques and Applications. Reading, MA: Addison-Wesley, 1975, 577-534.

Johansen, R.; Vallee, J. and Spangler, K. Electronic Meetings: Technical Alternatives and Social Choices. Reading MA: Addison-Wesley, 1979.

Johnson, B. and Rice, R. "Policy Implications of New Office Systems," in Mosco, V. (ed.) Telecommunications Policy Handbook. Norwood, NJ: Ablex, 1984.

Johnson, B. and Rice, R. "Redesigning Word Processing for Productivity," in Vondran, R. (ed.) Proceedings of the American Society for Information Science. Washington, DC: ASIS, 1983, 187-190.

Johnson, J. and Ettema, J. Lessons from Freestyle: Creating Presocial Television for Children. Beverly Hills, CA: Sage, 1982.

Journal of Communication. Special issue on cable television, 1978, 28, 2.

Kagan, P. "Videotex America Signs Chronicle Publishing." Kagan Newsletter Electronic Publisher, 1983, February 28, p. 5.

Kane, J. "Computers for Composing," in Chameleon in the Classroom: Developing Roles for Computers. Symposium presented to the American Educational Research Association, Montreal, 1983.

Kaske, N. and Sanders, N. A Comprehensive Study of Online Public Access Catalogs: An Overview and Application of Findings. Final Report to the Council on Library Resources, Vol. III. OCLC/OPR/RR-83/4. Dublin, OH: OCLC, 1983.

Katz, D., and Kahn, R. The Social-Psychology of Organization, 2nd edition. New York: Wiley, 1978.

Katz, E.; Blumler, J. and Gurevitch, M. "Utilization of Mass Communication by the Individual," in Blumler, J. and Katz E. (eds.) The Uses of Mass Communication. Beverly Hills, CA: Sage, 1974, 19-34.

Katz, E. and Foulkes, D. "On the Use of Mass Media as 'Escape': Clarification of a Concept." Public Opinion Quarterly 1962, 26, 377-388.

Katz, E.; Gurevitch, M. and Haas, H. "On the Uses of the Mass Media for Important Things." American Sociological Review, 1973, 38, 164-181.

Katzman, N. "The Impact of Communication Technology: Promises and Prospects." Journal of Communication, 1974, 24, 47-58.

Kay, E. and Meyer, H. "The Development of a Job Activity Questionnaire for Production Foremen." Personnel Psychology, 1962, 15, 411-418.

Kearsley, G. "Videodiscs in Education and Training: The Idea Becomes Reality." Videodisc/Videotex, 1981, 1, 4, 208-220.

Keen, P. "Information Systems and Organizational Change." Communications of the ACM, 1981, 24, 1, 24-33.

Keen, P. and Scott Morton, S. Decision Support Systems. Reading, MA: Addison-Wesley, 1978.

Keplinger, M. "Copyright and Information Technology," in Williams, M. (ed.) Annual Review of Information Science and Technology, Vol. 15. White Plains, NY: Knowledge Industry Publications, 1980, 3-34.

Kerr, E. and Hiltz, R. "Cognitive Impacts of Computer-Mediated Communication Systems Upon Individuals," in Lunin, L., Henderson, M. and Wooster, H. (eds.) 1981 Proceedings of the American Society of Information Science: The Information Community, Alliance for Progress. White Plains, NY: Knowledge Industry Publications, 1981, 232-234.

Kerr, E. and Hiltz, S.R. Computer-Mediated Communication Systems. New York: Academic Press, 1982.

Kiesler, S.; Siegel, J. and McGuire, T. "Does It Matter If You're Not All There? Social Psychology of Computer-Mediated Groups." Pittsburgh, PA: Carnegie-Mellon University School of Social Sciences, 1982.

Kiesler, S.; Sproull, L. and Eccles, J. "Second-Class Citizens?" Psychology Today, 1983, 17, 3, 40-48.

Killworth, P. and Bernard, H. "CATIJ: A New Sociometric and Its Application to a Prison Living Unit." Human Organization, 1974, 33, 335-350.

King, D. "Pricing Policies in Academic Libraries." The Economics of Academic Libraries: Library Trends, 1979, Summer, 47-61.

King, D. Energy Information Data Resources Directory Project. Final Report to Department of Energy. Rockville, MD: King Research, 1982, July.

King, J. and Kraemer, K. "Cost as a Social Impact of Information Technology," in Moss, M. (ed.) Telecommunications and Productivity. Reading, MA: Addison-Wesley, 1981, 93-130.

Kingston, J.; Taylor, J.; Rice, R.; Case, D.; Porteus, A. and others. Evaluation of the Terminals for Managers Program. Stanford, CA: Center for Information Technology, 1981.

Kirste, K. and Monge, P. Proximity: Location, Time and Opportunity to Communicate. Technical Report #3 (Contract #N00014-73-A-0476-0001). Arlington, VA: Office of Naval Research, 1974.

Klemmer, E., and Snyder, F. "Measurement of Time Spent Communicating." Journal of Communication, 1972, 22, 142-158.

Kling, R. "Social Analyses of Computing: Theoretical Perspectives in Recent Empirical Research." Computing Surveys, 1980, 12, 1, 61-110.

Knowledge Industry Publications. News Release. White Plains, NY: Knowledge Industry Publications, 1983, February 25.

Koomen, W. and Sagel, P. "The Prediction of Participation in Two-Person Groups." Sociometry, 1977, 40, 369-373.

Kotter, J. "What Effective General Managers Really Do." Harvard Business Review, 1982, 60, 6, 156-167.

Krueger, G. and Chapanis, A. "Conferencing and Teleconferencing in Three Communication Modes as a Function of the Number of Conferees." Ergonomics, 1980, 23, 2, 103-122.

Lancaster, F. and Fayen, E. Information Retrieval On-Line. Los Angeles, CA: Melville, 1973.

Landau, R. "Office Automation in the U.S. and Japan." ASIS Bulletin, 1983, 9, 5, 6-11.

LaRose, R. "Future Demand for Teleconferencing and Teleconferencing Suppliers." East Lansing, MI: ELRA Group, 1983.

Lawler, E., III; Porter, L. and Tennenbaum, A. "Managers' Attitudes Toward Interaction Episodes." Journal of Applied Psychology, 1968, 52, 432-439.

Lawrence, P. and Lorsch, J. Organizations and Environment. Boston, MA: Harvard University, Graduate School of Business Administration, School of Research, 1967.

Lazarsfeld, P. Radio and the Printed Page. NY: Duell, Sloan and Pearce, 1940.

Lazarsfeld, P. and Stanton, F. Radio Research, 1941. NY: Duell, Sloan and Pearce, 1942.

Leavitt, H. "Some Effects of Certain Communication Patterns on Group Performance." Journal of Abnormal and Social Behavior, 1951, 46, 38-50.

Leduc, N. "Communicating through Computers." Telecommunications Policy, 1979, September, 235-244.

Lee, R. The Flow of Information to Disadvantaged Farmers. Unpublished Ph.D. Dissertation. University of Iowa, 1968.

Leffingwill, W. The Office Appliance Manual. Office Equipment Catalogue, Inc., 1926. (Cited by Whalen.)

Lenk, R. "Mappings of Fields Based on Nominations." Journal of the American Society for Information Science, 1983, 34, 2, 115-122.

Lepper, M. "Microcomputers in Education: Motivational and Social Issues." Stanford, CA: Stanford University School of Psychology, 1982.

Lerner, D. The Passing of Traditional Society. NY: Free Press, 1958.

Lerner, R.; Metaxas, T.; Scott, J.; Adams, P. and Judd, R. "Primary Publication Systems and Scientific Data Processing." in Williams, M. (ed.) Annual Review of Information Science and Technology. Vol. 18. White Plains, NY: Knowledge Industries, 1983, 127-150.

Lerner, R.; Mick, C. and Callahan, D. "Database Searching and Document Delivery via Communications Satellite." AIP80-81, PB81-153314. NY: AIP, 1980, June.

Lesser, G.S. Children and Television: Lessons from Sesame Street. New York: Random House, 1974.

Levin, J.; Boruta, M. and Vasconcellos, M. "Microcomputer-Based Environments for Writing: A Writer's Assistant," in Wilkinson, A. (ed.) Classroom Computers and Cognitive Science. New York: Academic Press, 1983.

Levin, J. and Kareev, A. "Personal Computers and Education: the Challenge to Schools." La Jolla, CA: University of California at San Diego Center for Human Information Processing, 1980.

Levins, R. Evolution in Changing Environments. Princeton, NJ: Princeton University Press, 1968.

Levy, M. "Watching TV News as a Para-Social Interaction." Journal of Broadcasting 1979, 23, 69-80.

Lewin, R. "Santa Rosalia Was a Goat." Science, 1983, 221, 636-639.

Libs, S. "News and Speculation About Personal Computing." Byte, 1982, July, 426.

Lichenstein, A. and Rosenfeld, L. "Uses and Misuses of Gratifications Research: An Explication of Media Functions." Communication Research, 1983, 10, 1, 97-109.

Liebert, R.; Sprafkin, J. and Davidson, E. The Early Window: Effects of Television on Children and Youth, 2nd edition. New York: Pergamon, 1982.

Lincoln, J. "Organizational Dominance and Community Structure," in Liebert, R. and Imershein, A. (eds.) Power, Paradigm, and Community Research. Beverly Hills, CA: Sage Publications, 1977.

Lindquist, M. "An Explanation of the Coming Stagnation of Information Search Services." Online Review, 1977, 1, 2, 109-116.

Line, M. "Libraries and Information Services in a Post-Technology Society." Journal of Library Automation, 1981, 14, 4, 252-267.

Lipinski, H.; Spang, S. and Tydeman, J. "Supporting Task-Focussed Communication." Menlo Park, CA: Institute for the Future, 1980.

Lippitt, M.; Miller, J. and Halamaj. J. "Patterns of Use and Correlates of Adoption of An Electronic Mail System," in the American Decision Sciences Proceedings, Las Vegas, 1980, 1, 195-197.

Lodahl, T. "Cost-Benefit Concepts and Applications for Office Automation." Ithaca, NY: Cornell University/Diebold Group, 1980.

Lodahl, T. and Meyer, N.D. "Six Pathways to Office Automation." Administrative Management, 1980, March, 32ff.

Logan, R. "A Playful Alternative for Newspapers." Paper presented to the Mass Communication and Society Spring Meeting, Association for Education in Journalism, Atlanta, February 27, 1982.

Lometti, G.; Reeves, B. and Bybee, C. "Investigating the Assumptions of Uses and Gratifications Research." Communication Research, 1977, 4, 3, 321-338.

Lovins, A. and Lovins, H. "The Writing on the Wall," in Haigh, R. et al. (eds.) Communications in the 21st Century. New York: Wiley, 1981.

Lowenstein, R. "Office System Studies." White Plains, NY: IBM, 1979. (also Guide, 1978, 47, 93-106)

Lowenstein, R. et al. "Videotex and the University: Making the Journalism Connection." Paper presented to the Mass Communication and Society Division Spring Meeting, Atlanta, February 27, 1982.

Lucas, H. Implementation: The Key to Successful Information Systems. New York: Columbia University Press, 1981.

Lyle, J. and Hoffman, H. "Children's Use of Television and Other Media," in Comstock, G.; Rubenstein, A. and Murray, J. (eds.) Television and Social

Behavior. Vol. 5. Washington DC: U.S. Government Printing Office, 1972, 129-153.

Macarov, D. Worker Productivity: Myths and Reality. Beverly Hills, CA: Sage, 1982.

Machlup, F. The Production and Distribution of Knowledge in the United States. Princeton, NJ: Princeton University Press, 1962.

Maddox, B. Beyond Babel: New Directions in Communications. Boston: Beacon Press, 1972.

Madeo, L. and Schriber, T. "Algorithmic Search in Management Decision Systems." International Journal of Man-Machine Studies, 1980, 13, 423-435.

Malone, T. "What Makes Things Fun to Learn? A Study of Intrinsically Motivating Computer Games." Palo Alto, CA: Xerox Palo Alto Research Center, 1980.

Maloney, E. "Green Thumb Farm Info Project Takes Root in State of Kentucky." Microcomputing, 1982, 25, January, 341.

Mankin, D. "Innovation in Information System Impact Measurement." Santa Monica, CA: Rand Corporation. Presented to National Computer Conference, Anaheim, CA, 1983.

Mann, F. "Psychological and Organizational Impacts," in Dunlop, J. (ed.) Automation and Technological Change. Englewood Cliffs, NJ: Prentice-Hall, 1962, 43-65.

March, J. "Bounded Rationality, Ambiguity, and the Engineering of Choice." Bell Journal of Economics, 1978, 9, 587-608.

March, J. "Footnotes to Organizational Change." Administrative Science Quarterly, 1981, 26, 563-577.

March, J. and Simon, H. Organizations. New York: Wiley, 1958.

Marcum, D. and Boss, R. "Information Technology." Wilson Library Bulletin, 1981, November, 206-207.

Marketing News. "Most Consumers Find Videotext Services Useful: Half Would Pay, Survey Reveals." Marketing News, 1982, 16, 11, November 26, 8, 12.

Markey, K. Analytical Review of Catalog Use Studies. OCLC/OPR/RR-80/2, ERIC ED 186041. Dublin, OH: OCLC, 1980.

Markey, K. Online Catalog Use: Results of Surveys and Focus Group Interviews in Several Libraries. Final Report to the Council on Library Resources, Vol. II. OCLC/OPR/RR-83/3. Dublin, OH: OCLC, 1983.

Markoff, J. "ATandT: Only 7% of U.S. Homes Will Use Videotex in 1990." InfoWorld, 1982, 4, 15, April 19, 9.

Markoff, J. "Company Launches Satellite for Linking Up Microcomputers." Infoworld, 1983, 5, 3, January 17.

Markus, M. "Implementation Politics: Top Management Support and User Involvement." System, Objectives, Solutions, 1981, 1, 4, 203-216.

Markus, M. and Yates, J. "Historical Lessons for the Automated Office." Computer Decisions, 1982, June, 116 ff.

Marples, D. "Studies of Managers—A Fresh Start?" Journal of Management Studies, 1967, 4, 282-299.

Martin, J. The Wired Society. Englewood Cliffs, NJ: Prentice-Hall, 1978.

Marvin, C. "Telecommunications Policy and the Pleasure Principle." Telecommunications Policy, 1983, 7, 1, 43-52.

Marvin, C. and Schultze, Q. "The First Thirty Years: CB in Perspective." Journal of Communication, 1977, 27, 104-117.

Mason, G. "Computerized Reading Instruction: A Review." Educational Technology, 1980, 20, 18-22.

Mason, R. and Mitroff, I. "A Program for Research in Management Information Systems." Management Science, 1973, 19, 475-487.

May, R. "Some Notes on Estimating the Competition Matrix." Ecology, 1975, 56, 737-741.

Mayr, E. The Growth of Biological Thought: Diversity, Evolution, and Inheritance. Cambridge, MA: Belknap Press of Harvard University, 1982.

McCombs, M. "Mass Media in the Marketplace." Journalism Monographs, 1972, 24, 1-104.

McCombs, M. and Eyal, C. "Spending on Mass Media." Journal of Communication, 1980, 30, 1, 153-158.

McCombs, M. and Shaw, D. The Emergence of American Political Issues: The Agenda-Setting Function of the Press. St. Paul, MN: West Publishing, 1977.

McEwen, W. "Bridging the Information Gap." Journal of Consumer Research, 1978, 4, 247-251.

McEwen, W. and Hempel, D. "How Information Needs and Effort Affect Channel Choice." Journalism Quarterly, 1977, 54, 149-153.

McFarlan, F. and McKenney, J. Corporate Information Systems Management. Homewood, IL: Irwin, 1983.

McGuire, M. and Stanley, J. "Dyadic Communication, Verbal Behavior, Thinking and Understanding." Journal of Nervous and Mental Disease, 1972, 152, 242-259.

McGuire, W. "Theoretical Foundations of Campaigns," in Rice, R. and Paisley, W. (eds.) Public Communication Campaigns. Beverly Hills, CA: Sage, 1981, 41-70.

McKelvey, B. Organizational Systematics. Berkeley, CA: University of California Press, 1982.

McKelvey, B. and Aldrich, H. "Populations, Natural Selection and Applied Organizational Science." Administrative Science Quarterly, 1983, 28, 101-128.

McKenzie, R. The Metropolitan Community. New York: McGraw-Hill, 1933.

McKenzie, R. Roderick D. McKenzie on Human Ecology: Selected Writings (Hawley, A., ed.). Chicago, IL: University of Chicago Press, 1968.

McLeod, J. and Chaffee, S. "Interpersonal Approaches to Communication Research." American Behavioral Scientist, 1973, March/April, 469-499.

McLuhan, M. Understanding Media. New York: McGraw-Hill, 1964.

McLuhan, M. and Fiore, Q. The Medium is the Massage: An Inventory of Effects. New York: Bantam, 1967.

McQuillan, J. and Walden, D. "Designing Electronic Mail Systems that People Will Use." ACM SIGOA, 1980, 1, 2, 5-6.

Meadow, C. and Cochrane, P. A. Basics of Online Searching. New York: Wiley, 1981.

Meadow, C. and Tedesco, A. (eds.) Telecommunications for Management. New York: McGraw-Hill, 1984.

Media Science. "National Family Opinion/New Electronic Media Science Study Reveals Hidden Structure in the Home/Computer Hardware Market." New York: Media Science Newsletter, 1983, 4, 18, January, 1-15.

Melcher, A. and Beller, R. "Toward a Theory of Organizational Communication: Consideration in Channel Selection." Academy of Management Journal, 1967, 10, 39-52.

Meline, C. "Does the Medium Matter?" Journal of Communication, 1976, 26, 3, 81-89.

Melton, M. "Office Automation at Lincoln National Life Insurance Company." Auerbach Publishers, Inc. Electronic Office: Management and Technology. 005.0001.016, 1981, 1-11.

Mendelsohn, H. Mass Entertainment. New Haven, CT: College and University Press, 1966.

Mertes, L.H. "Doing Your Office over Electronically." Harvard Business Review, 1981, March-April, 127-135.

Meyer, D. "The Office Automation Cookbook: Management Strategies for Getting Office Automation Moving." Sloan Management Review, 1983a, Winter, 51-60.

Meyer, D. "Don't Plan." Computerworld Office Automation Supplement, 1983b, 17, 8A, February 23.

Meyer, M. "Automation and Bureaucratic Structure." American Journal of Sociology, 1968, 74, 3, 256-264.

Meyer, T. and Hexamer, A. "The Use and Abuse of Media Effects Research in the Development of Telecommunications Social Policy," in Schement, J.; Gutierrez, F. and Sirbu, M. Jr (eds.) Telecommunications Policy Handbook. New York: Praeger, 1982, 222-235.

Miller, G. "The Magical Number Seven Plus or Minus Two: Some Limits on Our Capacity for Processing Information." Psychological Review, 1956, 63, 81-97.

Miller, G.R. (ed.) Explorations in Interpersonal Communication. Beverly Hills, CA: Sage, 1976.

Miller, G.R. "The Current Status of Theory and Research in Interpersonal Communication." Human Communication Research, 1978, 14, 164-178.

Miller, G.R. and Steinberg, M. Between People: A New Analysis of Interpersonal Communication. Chicago: SRA, 1975.

Miller, J. and Nichols, M. "An Update in a Longitudinal Study of the Adoption of an Electronic Mail System," in Reeves, G. and Sweigart, J. (eds.) thirteenth Annual Proceedings of the American Institute for Decision Sciences, Boston, 1981, 1, 218-200.

Mills, M. "A Study of the Human Response to Pictorial Representations on Telidon." Canadian Department of Communications Contract 09SU.36001-0-3165. Montreal: University of Montreal. 1982.

Mintzberg, H. The Nature of Managerial Work. New York: Harper & Row, 1973.

Mohr, L. "Organizational Technology and Organizational Structure." Administrative Science Quarterly, 1971, 16, 444-459.

Mohr, L. Explaining Organizational Behavior: The Limits and Possibilities of Theory and Research. San Francisco: Jossey-Bass, 1982.

Mohrman, A., Jr. and Novelli, L. "Adaptively Researching the Impacts of Information Processing Technologies in the Office." University of Southern California Center for Effective Organizations, 1983. Previous version presented at Academy of Management conference, New York, 1982.

Molnar, J. "Tomorrow." Bell Laboratories Record, 1969, 47, 186-187.

Monge, P. "Systems Theory and Research in the Study of Organizational Communication: The Correspondence Problem." Human Communication Research, 1982, 3, 245-261.

Monge, P. and Cappella, J. (eds.) Multivariate Techniques in Human Communication Research. New York: Academic Press, 1980.

Monge, P.; Edwards, J. and Kirste, K. "The Determinants of Communication and Communication Structure in Large Organizations: A Review of Research," in B. Rubin (ed.) Communication Yearbook, Vol. 2. New Brunswick, NJ: Transaction Books, 1978, 311-331.

Montgomery, I. and Benbasat, I. "Cost/Benefit Analysis of Computer-Based Message Systems." MIS Quarterly, 1983, March, 1-14.

Mosco, V. Pushbutton Fantasies: Critical Perspectives on Videotex and Information Technology. Norwood, NJ: Ablex, 1982.

Mosco, V. and Herman, A. "Radical Social Theory and the Communications Revolution," in Schement, J.; Gutierrez, F. and Sirbu, M., Jr. (eds.) Telecommunications Policy Research Conference Proceedings. New York: Praeger, 1982, 58-84.

Moshowitz, A. The Conquest of Will: Information Processing in Human Affairs. Reading, MA: Addison-Wesley, 1976.

Mumford, E. and Banks, O. The Computer and the Clerk. London: Routledge and Kegan Paul, 1967.

Murdock, G. and Golding, P. "Capitalism, Communication and Class Relations," in Curran, J., Gurevitch, M. and Woolacott. H. (eds.) Mass Communication and Society. London: Arnold, 1977, 12-43.

Murray, J. Television and Youth: 25 Years of Research and Controversy. Boys Town, NE: Boys Town Center for Youth Development, 1981.

Murrel, S. "Computer Communication Systems Design Affects Group Decision-Making." Murray Hill, NJ: Bell Laboratories, 1983.

Muson, H. "Getting the Phone's Number." Psychology Today, 1982, April, 42-49.

Naisbitt, J. The Trend Report. Washington, DC: Naisbitt Group, 1980.

Naisbitt, J. Megatrends: Ten New Directions Transforming Our Lives. New York: Warner Books, 1982.

National Archives and Records Service. Office Automation in the Federal Government: A Status Report. Washington, DC: U. S. Government Printing Office, 1981.

National Bureau of Standards. National Bureau of Standards Special Analysis for Office Automation Systems. Special Publication 500-72. C#80-600179. Washington, DC: Superintendent of Documents, U.S. Government Printing Office, 1980.

National Institute of Mental Health. Television and Behavior: Ten Years of Scientific Progress and Implications for the 80s. Vol. 10., Summary Report. Washington, DC: U.S. Department of Health and Human Services, 1983.

Nau, D. "Expert Computer Systems." Computer, 1983, 16, 2, 63-85.

Needham, N. "The Impact of Videogames on American Youth." Today's Education, 1982, 71, 3, 52-55. Condensed version in Education Digest, 1983, February, 40-42.

Neustadt, R. The Birth of Electronic Publishing. Legal and Economic Issues in Telephone, Cable and Over-The-Air Teletext and Videotext. White Plains, NY: Knowledge Industry Publications, 1982.

Newell, A. and Sproull, R. "Computer Networks: Prospects for Scientists." Science, 1982, 215, 12,842-851.

Newman, J. "Understanding the Organization Structure: Job Attitude Relationships Through Perceptions of the Work Environment. Organizational Behavior and Human Performance, 1975, 14, 371-397.

Newman, J. "Human Factors Requirements for Managerial Use of Computer Message Systems," in Uhlig, R. (ed.) Computer Message Systems, New York: North-Holland, 1981, 453-465.

Nielsen, A.C. "The Outlook for Electronic Forms of Message Delivery." Nielsen Newscast, 1982a, 4.

Nielsen, A.C. "1982 Nielsen Report on Television." New York: A.C. Nielsen Co., 1982b.

Nilles, J.; Carlson, F.; Gray, P. and Hanneman, G. The Telecommunication-Transportation Tradeoff. New York: Wiley, 1976.

Nisbett, R. and Wilson, T. "Telling More Than We Can Know: Verbal Reports on Mental Processes." Psychological Review, 1977, 84, 231-259.

Noble, D. America by Design: Science, Technology and the Rise of Corporate Capitalism. Oxford: Oxford University Press, 1977.

Noll, M. "Teleconferencing Communication Activities." Proceedings of IEEE, 1977, 8-14.

OCLC. Channel 2000: Description and Findings of a Viewdata Test. Dublin, OH: OCLC, 1981, April.

Office of Technology Assessment. Implications of Electronic Mail and Message Systems for the U.S. Postal Service. Washington, DC: U.S. Government Printing Office, 1982.

Olgren, C. and Parker, L. Teleconferencing Technology and Applications. Dedham, MA: Artech House, 1983.

Olshavasky, R. "Time and the Rate of Adoption of Innovations." Journal of Consumer Research, 1980, 6, 425-428.

Olson, M. "New Information Technology and Organizational Culture." MIS Quarterly, 1982, 71-92.

O'Reilly, C. "Supervisors and Peers as Information Sources, Group Supportiveness, and Individual Decision Making Performance." Journal of Applied Psychology, 1977, 62, 632-635.

O'Reilly, C. III. "Variation in Decision Makers' Use of Information Sources: The Impact of Quality and Accessibility of Information." Academy of Management Journal, 1982, 25, 4, 756-771.

O'Reilly, C. III and Roberts, K. "Task Group Structure, Communication and Effectiveness in Three Organizations." Journal of Applied Psychology, 1977, 62, 674-681.

Packer, M. "Measuring the Intangible in Productivity." Technology Review, 1983, February/March, 48-57.

Page, J. "Economics and Politics of Information Technology: Some Trends in its Applications to Information for the Professional." Munich: IFLA, 1983.

Paisley, W. "Information and Work," in Dervin, B. and Voigt, M. (eds.) Progress in Communication Sciences, Vol. 2. Norwood, NJ: Ablex, 1980, 113-166.

Paisley, W. "Computerizing Information: Lessons of a Videotext Trial." Journal of Communication, 1983, 33, 1, 153-161.

Paisley, W. "Communication in the Communication Sciences," in Dervin, B. and Voigt, M. (eds.) Progress in Communication Sciences, Vol. 5. Norwood, NJ: Ablex, 1984.

Paisley, W. and Chen, M. "Children and Electronic Text: Challenges and Opportunities of the 'New Literacy." Stanford, CA: Stanford University Institute for Communication Research, 1982.

Palme, J. "Experience with the Use of the COM Computerized Conferencing System." Stockholm: Swedish National Defense Research Institute, 1981, December.

Palmer, A. and Beishon, R. "How the Day Goes." Personnel Management, 1970, 2, 36-40.

Palmer, E. "Formative Research in the Production of Television for Children," in Olson, D. (ed.) Media and Symbols: The Forms of Expression, Communication and Education. Chicago: University of Chicago Press, 1974.

Palmer, E. "Shaping Persuasive Messages with Formative Research," in Rice, R. and Paisley, W. (eds.) Mass Communication Campaigns. Beverly Hills, CA: Sage, 1981, 227-238.

Panko, R. "The EMS Revolution." Computerworld, 1980, August 25, 19, 34,45-56.

Panko, R. "Standards for Electronic Message Systems." Telecommunications Policy, 1981a, 5, 3, 181-197.

Panko, R. "The Cost of EMS." Computer Networks, 1981b, 5, 35-46.

Panko, R. "Office Automation Needs—Studying Managerial Work." Telecommunications Policy, 1981c, December, 265-272.

Panko, R. "Serving Managers and Professionals," in Sutton, J. (ed.) 1982 Office Automation Conference Digest. San Francisco: American Federation of Information Processing Societies, 1982, 97-103.

Panko, R. "The Costs and Benefits of Interpersonal Message Systems." Honolulu: College of Business Administration, University of Hawaii, 1983.

Panko, R. "Electronic Mail," in Tackle-Quinn, K. (ed.) Advances in Office Automation. New York: Wiley, 1984.

Panko, R. and Panko, R. "A Survey of EMS Users at DARCOM." Computer Networks, 1981, 5, 19-34.

Panko, R. and Sprague, R. "Toward a New Framework for Office Support," in Limb, J. (ed.) Conference on Office Information Systems. New York: Association for Computing Machinery, 1982, 82-92.

Papert, S. Mindstorms: Children, Computers and Powerful Ideas. New York: Basic Books, 1980.

Park, R. "Human Ecology." American Journal of Sociology, 1936, 42, 1-15.

Parker, E. "The New Communication Media," in Wallia, C. S. (ed.) Toward Century 21: Technology, Society and Human Values. New York: Basic Books, 1970a, 97-106.

Parker, E. "Behavioral Research in the Development of Computer-Based Information System," in Nelson, C. and Bollock, D. (eds.) Communication Among Scientists and Engineers. Lexington, MA: D.C. Heath, 1970b, 281-292.

Parker, E. "Information Utilities and Mass Communication," in Sackman, H. and Nie, N. The Information Utility and Social Choice. Montvale, NJ: AFIPS Press, 1970c, 51-70.

Parker, E. "Technology Assessment or Institutional Change?" in Gerbner, G.; Gross, L.P. and Melody, W.H. (eds.) Communications Technology and Social Policy: Understanding the New "Cultural Revolution." New York: Wiley, 1973a, 533-544.

Parker, E. "Information and Society," in Cuadra, C. A. (ed.) Annual Review of Information Science and Technology, Vol. 8. Washington, DC: American Society for Information Science, 1973b, 345-373.

Parker, E. "Technological Change and the Mass Media," in Pool, I.; Schramm, W.; Frey, F.; Maccoby, N. and Parker, E. (eds.) Handbook of Communication. Chicago: Rand McNally, 1973c, 619-645.

Parker, E. "Implications of New Information Technology." Public Opinion Quarterly, 1973d, 37, 4, 590-600.

Parker, E. "Social Implications of Computer/Telecoms Systems." Telecommunications Policy, 1976, 1, 1, 3-20.

Parker, E. "An Information-Based Hypothesis." Journal of Communication, 1978a, 28, 1, 81-83.

Parker, E. "Communication Satellites for Rural Development." Telecommunications Policy, 1978b, 2, 4, 309-315.

Parker, E. "Telecommunications Needs in Rural Areas of Developing Countries." Intel Trade, 1979, February 15, 2, 3, 3-5.

Parker, E. "Micro Earth Stations Make Business Satcom Affordable." Microwave Systems News, 1982, 12, 11, 71 ff.

Parker, E. "Satellite Micro Earth Stations—A Small Investment With Big Returns." Data Communications, 1983, January, 97 ff.

Parker, E. and Dunn, D. "Information Technology: Its Social Potential." Science, 1972, 176, 1392-1399.

Parker, E. and Hudson, H. "Medical Communication in Alaska by Satellite." New England Journal of Medicine, 1973, 289, 1351-1356.

Parker, E. and Hudson, H. "Telecommunication Planning for Rural Development." IEEE Transactions on Communications, 1975, 23, 10, 1177-1185.

Parker, E. and Lusignan, B. "Technical and Economic Considerations in Planning Radio Services," in Spain, P.; Jamison, D. and McAnany, E. (eds.) Radio for Education and Development: Case Studies, Vol. 2. Washington, DC: World Bank, 1977, 443-459.

Parker, E. and Mohammdi, A. "National Development Support Communication," in Teheranian, M.; Hakiszadeh, F. and Vidale, M. (eds.) Communications Policy for National Development: A Comparative Perspective. London: Routledge and Kegan Paul, 1977, 167-201.

Parker, E. and Paisley, W. "Research for Psychologists at the Interface of the Scientist and His Information System." American Psychologist, 1966, 21, 1061-1071.

Patrick, R. "Probing Productivity." Datamation, 1980, September, 207-210.

Pattison, R. On Literacy. Oxford: Oxford University Press, 1982.

Pea, R. "LOGO Programming and Problem-Solving," in Chameleon in the Classroom: Developing Roles for Computers. Symposium presented to the American Educational Research Association, Montreal, 1983.

Peled, T. and Katz, E. "Media Functions in Wartime: The Israel Home Front in October 1973," in Blumler, J. and Katz, E. (eds.) The Uses of Mass Communication. Beverly Hills, CA: Sage, 1974, 49-70.

Pelz, D. and Andrews, F. Scientists in Organizations: Productive Climates for Research and Development, revised edition. Ann Arbor, MI: Institute for Social Research, 1976.

Penniman, W. Rhythms of Dialogue in Human-Computer Conversation. Unpublished Ph.D. dissertation, Ohio State University, 1975.

Penniman, W. and Dominick, W. "Monitoring and Evaluation of On-Line Information System Usage." Information Processing and Management, 1980, 116, 17-35.

Perrow, C. Organizational Analysis: A Sociological View. Belmont, CA: Brooks/Cole, 1970.

Peters, T. "The Mythology of Innovation or a Skunkworks Tale. Part I." Stanford Magazine, 1983a, Summer, 13-21.

Peters, T. "The Mythology of Innovation or A Skunkworks Tale. Part II." Stanford Magazine, 1983b, Fall, 11-19.

Phillips, A. Attitude Correlates of Selected Media Technologies: A Pilot Study. Los Angeles, CA: Annenberg School of Communications, 1982.

Pianka, E. Evolutionary Ecology, 3rd edition, New York: Harper & Row, 1983.

Picot, A.; Klingenberg, H. and Kranzle, H-P. "Organizational Communication Between Technological Development and Socio-Economic Needs: Report from Field Studies in Germany," in Burgoon, M. (ed.) Communication Yearbook 6. Beverly Hills, CA: Sage, 1982, 674-693.

Picot, A. and Reichwald, R. Untersuchungen der Auswirkungen neuer Kommunikationstechnologien im Buro auf Organisationsstruktur und

Arbeitsinhalte, Phase 1: Entwicklung einer Untersuchung Konzeption. Eggenstein-Leopoldshafen, Germany: Fachinformationsssszentrum Energie, Physik, Mathematik, 1979.

Pool, I. de Sola (ed.) Talking Back: Citizen Feedback and Cable Technology. Cambridge, MA: MIT Press, 1973.

Pool, I. de Sola. (ed.) The Social Impacts of the Telephone. Cambridge: MIT Press, 1977.

Pool, I. de Sola. Forecasting the Telephone: A Retrospective Technology Assessment. Norwood, NJ: Ablex, 1982a.

Pool, I. de Sola. "The Culture of Electronic Print." Daedalus, 1982b, 3, 4, 17-32.

Pool, I. de Sola. Technologies of Freedom. Cambridge, MA: Harvard University Press, 1983.

Poppel, H. "Who Needs the Office of the Future?" Harvard Business Review, 1982, 60, 6, 146-155.

Porat, M. The Information Economy: Definition and Measurement. Washington, DC: U.S. Government Printing Office, 1977.

Porat, M. "Communication Policy in an Information Society," in Robinson, G. (ed.) Communications for Tomorrow: Policy Perspectives for the 1980s New York: Praeger, 1978, 3-60.

Porter, L. and Roberts, K. "Communication in Organizations," in M. Dunnette (ed.) Handbook of Industrial and Organizational Psychology. Chicago: Rand McNally, 1976.

Posa, J. "A Fax in Every Office?" High Technology, 1983, August, 24, 28, 29.

Putman, L. and Pacanowsky, M. (eds.) Communication and Organizations: An Interpretive Approach. Beverly Hills, CA: Sage, 1983.

Pye, R. Communications within the Scottish Office. Report No. W/74174/PY. London: University College, Communications Studies Group, 1974.

Pye, R. "Information Retrieval Services." Telecommunications Policy, 1978, 2, 1, 73-78.

Pye, R. and Williams, E. "Teleconferencing: Is Video Valuable or Is Audio Adequate?" Telecommunications Policy, 1977, June, 230-241.

Pye, R. and Young, I. "Do Current Electronic Office Systems Designers Meet User Needs?" In Landau, R.; Bair, J. and Siegman, J. (eds.) Emerging Office Systems. Norwood, NJ: Ablex, 1982, 73-94.

Quinn, J. "Topical Summary of Current Literature on Human Ecology." American Journal of sociology, 1940, 46, 191-226.

Quantum Science Corporation. "Report on Teleconferencing Market." New York: Quantum Science Corporation, 1981.

Radnor, M.; Rubenstein, A. and Tansik, D. "Implementation in Operations Research and R&D in Government and Business Organizations." Operations Research, 1970, 18, 967-991.

Ragland, J. and Warner, P. "Green Thumb National Pilot Test." EDUCOM Bulletin, 1981, Fall, 16-19.

Ramsey, H. and Atwood, M. Human Factors in Computer Systems: A Review of the Literature. Office of Naval Research Contract NOOOI4-76-C-0866; Technical Report SAI 79 111 DEN, 1979. Englewood Cliffs, NJ: Science Applications, Inc. A shorter and more focused version appears as: Ramsey, H. and Grimes, J. "Human Factors in Interactive Computer Dialog," in Williams, M. (ed.) Annual Review of Information Science and Technology, Vol. 18, White Plains, NY: Knowledge Industry Publications, 1983, 29-60.

Ramsing, K. and Wish, J. "What Do Library Users Want? A Conjoint Measurement Technique May Yield the Answer." Information Processing and Management, 1982, 18, 5, 237-242.

Randolph, W. and Finch, F. "The Relationship Between Organizational Technology and the Direction and Frequency Dimensions of Task Communications." Human Relations, 1977, 30, 1131-1145.

Rayburn, J. and Palmgreen, P. "Dimensions of Gratifications Sought and Gratifications Obtained: A Study of *Good Morning America* and *Today*." Paper presented to the Theory and Methodology Division, Association for Education in Journalism Annual Convention, East Lansing, MI, August 1982.

Rees, A. et al. (Panel to Review Productivity Statistics.) Measurement and Interpretation of Productivity. Washington, DC: National Academy of Sciences, 1979.

Reeves, B. and Wartella, E. " 'For Some Children Under Some Conditions': A History of Research on Children and Media." Madison, WI: University of Wisconsin Mass Communication Research Center. Presented to International Communication Association, Boston, May 1982.

Reid, A. "Comparing Telephone with Face-to-Face Contact," in Pool, I. de Sola (ed.) The Social Impact of the Telephone. Cambridge, MA: MIT Press, 1977, 386-415.

Remp, R. "The Efficacy of Electronic Group Meetings." Policy Sciences, 1978, 5, 101-115.

Rhee, H. Office Automation in Social Perspective: The Progress and Social Implications of Electronic Data Processing. Oxford: Basil Blackwell, 1968.

Rice, R.E. "Impacts of Organizational and Interpersonal Computer-Mediated Communication," in Williams, M. (ed.) Annual Review of Information Science and Technology, Vol. 15, White Plains, NY: Knowledge Industry Publications, 1980a, 221-249.

Rice, R.E. "Computer Conferencing," in Dervin, B. and Voigt, M. (eds.) Progress in Communication Sciences, Vol. 2. Norwood, NJ: Ablex, 1980b, 215-240.

Rice, R.E. "Communication Networking in Computer Conferencing Systems: A Longitudinal Study of Group Roles and System Structure," in Burgoon, M. (ed.) Communication Yearbook 6. Beverly Hills, CA: Sage, 1982, 925-944.

Rice, R.E. and Borgman, C. "The Use of Computer-Monitored Data in Information Science and Communication Research." Journal of The American Society for Information Science, 1983, 34, 247-256.

Rice, R. and Case, D. "Electronic Messaging in the University Organization," in Lunin, L.; Henderson, M. and Wooster, H. (eds.) 1981 Proceedings of the American Society for Information Science: The Information Community, Alliance for Progress. White Plains, NY: Knowledge Industry Publications, 1981, 228-230.

Rice, R. and Case, D. "Computer-Based Messaging in the University: A Description of Use and Utility." Journal of Communication, 1983, 33, 1, 131-152.

Rice, R.; Johnson, B.; Feltman, C. and Kowal, D. "Survival of the Fittest: Design of Organizational Word Processing." Paper presented to the Academy of Management, Dallas, August 1983.

Rice, R.E.; Johnson, B. and Rogers, E.M. "The Introduction of New Office Technology," in 1982 Office Automation Conference Proceedings. San Francisco: American Federation of Information Processing Societies, 1982, 653-660.

Rice, R.E. and Paisley, W. "The Green Thumb Videotext Experiment: Evaluation and Policy Implications." Telecommunications Policy, 1982, 6, 3, 223-236.

Rice, R. and Parker, E. "Telecommunications Alternatives for Developing Countries." Journal of Communication, 1979, 29, 4, 125-136.

Rice, R.E. and Richards, W. "An Overview of Network Analysis Methods," in Dervin, B. and Voigt, M. (eds.) Progress in Communication Sciences, Vol. 6. Norwood, NJ: Ablex, 1984.

Rice, R. and Rogers, E.M. "Reinvention in the Innovation Process." Knowledge, 1980, 1, 4, 499-514.

Richards, W., Jr. and Rice, R.E. "NEGOPY Network Analysis Program." Social Networks, 1981, 3, 3, 215-333.

Ricklefs, R. Ecology. New York: Chiron Press, 1979.

Ricord, L. "Computer Assistance in Hospital Information Systems," in Petrarca, A.; Taylor, C. and Kohn, R. (eds.) Information Interaction: ASIS Proceedings. White Plains, NY: Knowledge Industries Publications, 1982, 374.

Roberts, D. and Bachen, C. "Mass Communication Effects." Annual Review of Psychology, 1981, 32, 307-356.

Roberts, K.; Hulin, C. and Rousseau, D. Developing an Interdisciplinary Science of Organizations. San Francisco: Jossey-Bass, 1978.

Roberts, K. and O'Reilly, C., III. "Measuring Organizational communication." Journal of Applied Psychology, 1974, 59, 321-326.

Roberts, L. "The Evolution of Packet Switching." IEEE Proceedings, 1978, 66, 11, 1307-1314.

Roberts, S. and Crawford, S. "American Medical Association Medical Electronic Information Network," in Petrarca, A.; Taylor, C. and Kohn, R. (eds.) Information Interaction: ASIS Proceedings. White Plains, NY: Knowledge Industries Publications, 1982, 245-246.

Robinson, G. O. (ed.) Communications for Tomorrow: Policy Perspectives for the 1980s. New York: Praeger, 1978.

Rogers, E.M. "Communication and Development: The Passing of the Dominant Paradigm." Communication Research, 1976, 3, 2, 213-240.

Rogers, E.M. Diffusion of Innovations, 3rd edition, New York: Free Press, 1983.

Rogers, E.M. "Foreword," in Williams, F. and Williams, V. Microcomputers in Elementary Education. Belmont, CA: Wadsworth, 1984.

Rogers, E.M. and Agarwala-Rogers, R. Communication and Organizations. New York: Free Press, 1976.

Rogers, E.M.; Daley, H. and Wu, T. The Diffusion of Home Computers: An Exploratory Study. Stanford, CA: Stanford University, Institute for Communication Research, 1982.

Rogers, E.M. and Kincaid, L. Communication Networks: A New Paradigm for Research. New York: Free Press, 1981.

Rogers, E.M. and Larsen, J. Silicon Valley Fever. New York: Basic Books, 1984.

Rogers, E.M. and Picot, A. "The Impacts of New Communication Technologies." in Rogers, E.M. and Balle, F. (eds.) The Media Revolution in America and in Western Europe. Norwood, NJ: Ablex, 1983.

Rosenberg, V. The Application of Psychometric Techniques to Determine the Attitudes of Individuals toward Information Seeking. Unpublished manuscript, Lehigh University, 1966.

Rosenbloom, R. and Wolek, F. Technology and Information Transfer: A Survey of Practice in Industrial Organizations. Boston, MA: Harvard University Press, 1970.

Rothman, J. "Video Information Systems." Presented to KCET Teletext Conference, Los Angeles, March 1980.

Rouse, W. "Design of Man-Computer Interfaces for On-Line Interactive Systems." Proceedings of the IEEE, 1975, 63, 6, 847-857.

Rouse, W. "Human-Computer Interaction in the Control of Dynamic Systems." Computing Surveys, 1981, 13, 1, 71-99.

Rubin, A. "The Interactions of TV Uses and Gratifications." Paper presented to the Theory and Methodology Division, Association for Education in Journalism Annual Convention, East Lansing, MI, August 1981a.

Rubin, A. "What 'Watching 60 Minutes' Means." Paper presented to the Mass Communication and Society Division, Association for Education in Journalism Annual Convention, East Lansing, MI, August 1981b.

Ruch, W. and Ruch, J. White Collar Productivity. Work in America Institute Studies in Productivity: Highlights of the Literature, No. 23. New York: Pergamon Press, 1982.

Ruchinskas, J. "The Consumer in the Electronic Marketplace: How People Use Entertainment and Information Services." Research Report #79-2. Los Angeles: University of Southern California Center for Communications Policy, 1980.

Ruchinskas, J. Communicating in Organizations: The Influence of Context, Job, Task, and Channel. Unpublished Ph.D. dissertation, University of Southern California, Annenberg School of Communications, 1982.

Ruchinskas, J. "Predictors of Media Utility." Paper presented at Thirty-third Annual Conference of the International Communications Association, May 31, 1983, Dallas, TX.

Ruchinskas, J. and Svenning, L. Atlantic Richfield Video Teleconferencing Project. Technical Report #2. Los Angeles: University of Southern California Annenberg School of Communications, 1981.

Russell, J. "All the Info, All the Time—Online." Data Management, 1983, 21, 2, 41-42.

Saffady, W. "Facsimile Transmission for Libraries: Technology and Application Design." Library Technical Reports, 1978, 14, 5, 445-531.

Salomon, G. Interaction of Media, Cognition and Learning. San Francisco: Jossey-Bass, 1979.

Salomon, G. "Television Watching and Mental Effort: A Social Psychological View," in Bryant, J. and Anderson, D. (eds.) Children's Understanding of Television: Research on Attention and Comprehension. New York: Academic Press, 1983.

Sandler, C. "Electronic Mail: The Paperless Revolution." PC: The Independent Guide to IBM Personal Computers, 1983, 1, 9, 52-58.

San Francisco Chronicle, 1983, May 12, pp. 1, 18.

Schabas, A. and Tompa, F. "Trees and Forests: User Reactions to Two Page Access Structures," in Videotex '83 Proceedings. New York: London Online, 1983, 197-209.

Schiller, H. Who Knows? Information in the Age of the Fortune 500. Norwood, NJ: Ablex, 1982.

Schoener, T.W. "Some Methods for Calculating Competition Coefficients from Resource Utilization Spectra." American Naturalist, 1974, 108, 332-340.

Schramm, W. "The Nature of News." Journalism Quarterly, 1949, 26, 3, 259-269.

Schramm, W. Mass Media and National Development. Stanford, CA: Stanford University Press, 1964.

Schramm, W.; Lyle, J. and Parker, E. Television in the Lives of Our Children. Stanford, CA: Stanford University Press, 1961.

Schwartz, B. "Queues, Priorities, and Social Process." Social Psychology, 1978, 41, 3-12.

Schwartz, B. "PacMan Eats L.A." Los Angeles: University of Southern California Annenberg School of Communications, 1982.

Scott, J. "The Mechanization of Women's Work." Scientific American, 1982, 274, 3, 166-187.

Scriven, M. "Explanation and Prediction in Evolutionary Theory." Science, 1959, 130, 477-482.

Seashore, S. and Mirvis, P. (eds.) Assessment of Organizations: A Guide to Practice. New York: Wiley Interscience, 1980.

Seeger, J. "No Innate Phases in Group Problem Solving." Academy of Management Review, 1983, 8, 4, 683-689.

Shane, B. "Open and Rigid Communication Networks: A Reevaluation by Simulation." Small Group Behavior, 1979, 10, 2, 242-262.

Shannon, C. and Weaver, W. The Mathematical Theory of Communication. Urbana, IL: University of Illinois Press, 1949.

Shaw, D. "Communication Networks," in Berkowitz, L. (ed.) Advances in Experimental Social Psychology. New York: Academic Press, 1964, 111-147.

Shaw, D. "Page 1 News: Press Rarely in Agreement," and "It All Goes Together at the News Conference." Los Angeles Times, 1977, June 24.

Sheingold, K. "Issues Related to the Implementation of Computer Technology in Schools: A Cross-Sectional Study." New York: Bank Street College of Education. Presented to the National Institute of Education Conference, Washington, DC, 1981.

Sheposh, J.; Holton, V. and Knudsen, G. Implementation of Planned Change: A Review of Major Issues. San Diego, CA: Navy Personnel Research and Development Center, 1982.

Short, J.; Williams, E. and Christie, B. The Social Psychology of Telecommunications. New York: Wiley, 1976.

Shulman, A. and Steinman, J. "Interpersonal Teleconferencing In an Organizational Context." in Elton, M.; Lucasa, W. and Conrath, D. (eds.) Evaluating New Telecommunication Services. New York: Plenum Press, 1978, 399-424.

Shultz, G. and Whisler, T. (eds.) Management Organization and the Computer. Glencoe, IL: The Free Press, 1960.

Shweder, R. (ed.) New Directions for Methodology of Behavioral Science: Fallible Judgement in Behavioral Research. San Francisco, CA: Jossey-Bass, 1980.

Siegel, I. Company Productivity: Measurement for Improvement. Kalamazoo, MI: W.E. Upjohn Institute for Employment Research, 1980.

Siegel, J.; Kiesler, S. and McGuire, T. "Participation, Affect and Decision in Computer-Mediated Groups." Pittsburgh, PA: Carnegie-Mellon University School of Social Sciences, 1982.

Simmons Market Research Bureau, Inc. Patterns of Media Consumption Intermedia Analysis, Vol. 9. New York: Simmons, 1979.

Simmons Market Research Bureau, Inc. Patterns of Media Consumption Intermedia Analysis, Vol. 13. New York: Simmons, 1983.

Simon, H. Models of Man. New York: Wiley, 1957.

Simon, H. The Shape of Automation. Englewood Cliffs, NJ: Prentice-Hall, 1960.

Simon, H. "Applying Information Technology to Organizational Design." Public Administration Review, 1973, 33, 3, 268-278.

Simon, H. "How Big Is a Chunk?" Science, 1974, 183, 482-488.

Sims, H. "Commentary on Kiesler, Siegel and McGuire." Stanford, CA: Stanford University Department of Psychology, 1982.

Singer, B. "Incommunicado Social Machines." Social Policy, 1977, 8, 3, 88-94.

Singer, B. "Crazy Systems and Kafka Circuits." Social Policy, 1980, 11, 2, 46-54.

Singer, B. "Organizational Communication and Social Disassembly: An Essay on Electronic Anomie," in Thayer, L. (ed.) Understanding Organizations, in press.

Skinner, H. and Allen B. "Does the Computer Make a Difference? Computerized Versus Face-to-Face versus Self-Report Assessment of Alcohol, Drug and Tobacco Use." Journal of Consulting and Clinical Psychology, 1983, 51, 2, 267-275.

Slack, J. "Surveying the Impacts of Communication Technologies," in Dervin, B. and Voigt, M. (eds.) Progress in Communication Sciences, Vol. 5. Norwood, NJ: Ablex, 1984.

Slack, J. and Fejes, F. (eds.) The Ideology of the Information Society. Norwood, NJ: Ablex, 1984.

Small, D. "An Experimental Comparison of Natural and Structured Query Languages." Human Factors, 1983, 25, 3, 253-263.

Smith, A. Goodbye Gutenberg: The Newspaper Revolution of the 1980's. New York: Oxford University Press, 1980.

Smith, M. "Health Issues in VDT Work," in Bennett, J.; Case, D.; Sandelin, J. and Smith, M. (eds.) Visual Display Terminals: Health Concerns and Usability Concepts. New York: Prentice-Hall, 1984.

Smith, R. The Wired Nation: Cable TV: The Electronic Communications Highway. New York: Harper & Row, 1972.

Sony. Press Release Materials—Video Communications. Park Ridge, NJ: Sony, 1982/1983.

Sproull, L. Managerial Attention in New Education Programs: A Micro-Behavioral Study of Program Implementation. Unpublished Ph.D. dissertation, Stanford, CA: Stanford University, 1977.

SRI. SRI Values and Lifestyle Program. Menlo Park, CA: Stanford Research International, 1982.

Steinfield, C. Explaining Managers' Use of Communication Channels for Performance Monitoring: Implications for New Office Services." Paper presented at the International Communication Association, Minneapolis, May 1981.

Steinfield, C. Communicating Via Electronic Mail: Patterns and Predictors of Use in Organizations. Unpublished Ph.D. dissertation, University of Southern California, Annenberg School of Communications, 1983.

Stephenson, W. The Play Theory of Mass Communication. Chicago: University of Chicago Press, 1967.

Sterling, T. "Consumer Difficulties with Computerized Transactions: An Empirical Investigation." Communications of the ACM, 1979, 22, 5, 283-289.

Steward, J.G. "Office Automation—Amoco Production Company." AFIPS Office Automation Conference Digest. Arlington, VA: AFIPS Press, 1982, 581-593.

Stewart, R. Managers and their Jobs. London: Macmillan, 1967.

Stewart, R. How Computers Affect Management. London: Macmillan, 1971.

Stewart, R. Contrasts in Management. London: Macmillan, 1976.

Stodolsky, D. "Automatic Mediation in Group Problem-Solving." Behavioral Research Methods and Instrumentation, 1981, 13, 235-242.

Stogdill, R. and Shortle, C. Methods in the Study of Administrative Leadership. Research Monograph No. 80, Bureau of Business Research. Columbus, OH: Ohio State University, 1955, 44-53.

Stone, G. and Wetherington, R., Jr. "Confirming the Newspaper Reading Habit." Journalism Quarterly, 1979, 56, 3, 554-561.

Strassman, P. "Managing the Costs of Information." Harvard Business Review, 1976, September/October, 133-142.

Strassman, P. "Office of the Future." Technology Review, 1980, 54-65.

Strategic Inc. "Electronic Conferencing Impact and Opportunities." Report #37, San Jose, CA: Strategic, Inc., 1981.

Strickland, L.; Guild, P.; Barefoot, J. and Patterson, S. "Teleconferencing and Leadership Emergence." Human Relations, 1978, 31, 583-596.

Surgeon General's Scientific Advisory Committee on Television and Social Behavior. Television and Growing Up: The Impact of Televised Violence. Washington, DC: National Institute of Mental Health, 1972.

Sutherland, S. "PRESTEL and the User: A Survey of Psychological and Ergonomic Research." A Report for the (British) Central Office of Information, May 1980.

Svenning, L. Predispositions Toward a Telecommunications Innovation: The Influence of Individual, Contextual, and Innovation Factors on Attitudes, Intentions, and Projections Toward Video-Conferencing. Unpublished Ph.D. dissertation, University of Southern California, Annenberg School of Communications, 1982.

Svenning, L. "Individual Response to an Organizationally Adopted Telecommunications Innovation: The Difference Among Attitudes, Intentions and Projections." Presented to the International Communication Association Conference, Dallas, TX, 1983, May.

Svenning, L., and Ruchinskas, J. Predicting the Use of Video-Conferencing: Variations by Levels and Jobs. Paper presented at the International Communication Association, Minneapolis, May 1981.

Svenning, L. and Ruchinskas, J. "Teleconferencing—Making a Good Decision." Interface '82 Proceedings. New York: McGraw-Hill, 1982, 106-111.

Talbott, E.G. "Position on Office Productivity." AFIPS Office Automation Conference Digest. Arlington, VA: AFIPS Press, 1982, 401.

Talbott, E.; Savage, T. and Borko, H. "Office Automation Research at TRW Using a Local Area Network." Torrance, CA: TRW, 1982.

Tannenbaum, P. (Ed.) The Entertainment Function of Television. Hillsdale, NJ: Erlbaum, 1980.

Tapscott, D. Office Automation: A User-Driven Method. New York: Plenum Press, 1982.

Taviss, I. (ed.) The Computer Impact. Englewood Cliffs, NJ: Prentice-Hall, 1970.

Taylor, J. "A Day in the Life of a WP Operator." Words, 1980, October, 26-32.

Taylor, R. "Value-added Processes in the Information Life Cycle." Journal of the American Society for Information Science, 1982, 33, 5, 341-346.

Taylor, S. and Thompson, S. "Stalking the Elusive 'Vividness' Effect." Psychological Review, 1982, 89, 155-181.

Telephony. "French Market Trial Yields Usage Statistics." Telephony, 1983, 204, 4, January 24, 44-52.

Terborg, J.; Howard, G. and Maxwell, S. "Evaluating Planned Organizational Change: A Method for Assessing Alpha Beta and Gamma Change." Academy of Management Review, 1980, 5, 1, 109-121.

Tersine, R. and Price, R. "Productivity Improvement Strategies: Technological Transfer and Updating." Journal of Systems Management, 1982, November, 15-23.

Thiessen, E. "Communication Media Used and Difficulties Experienced by Selected Kansas Business Firms." Journal of Business Communication, 1978, 14, 2, 43-48.

Thomason, G. "Managerial Work Roles and Relationships, Part I." Journal of Management Studies, 1966, 3, 270-284.

Thomlinson, T. "Communication Training Needs for Business Organizations." University of Evansville. Presented to International Communication Association, Boston, 1982.

Thompson, J. Organizations in Action. Chicago: McGraw-Hill, 1967.

Thorngren, B. "Silent Actors: Communication Networks for Development," in Pool, I. de Sola (ed.) The Social Impact of the Telephone. Cambridge, MA: MIT Press, 1977, 374-385.

Threlkeld, R. and Pease, P. "Northern Network: Audio Teleconferencing in Northern New England," in Parker, L. and Olgren, C. (eds.) Teleconferencing and Electronic Communications, Madison, WI: University of Wisconsin-Extension, 1982.

Tichy, N. "A Social Network Perspective to Organization Development," in Cummings, T. (ed.) Systems Theory for Organization Development. New York: Wiley Interscience, 1980.

Tichy, N. "Networks in Organizations," in Starbuck, W. and Nystrom, P. (eds.) Handbook of Organization Design, Vol. 2. Oxford: Oxford University Press, 1981, 229-249.

Tichy, N. and Fombrun, C. "Network Analysis in Organizational Settings." Human Relations, 1979, 32, 923-965.

Tichy, N.; Tushman, M. and Fombrun, C. "Social Network Analysis for Organizations." Academy of Management Review, 1979, 4, 507-519.

Time. "The Computer Moves In." Time, 1983a, January 3.

Time. "Video Games Go Crunch!" Time, 1983b, October 17.

Time. "Donkey Kong Goes to Harvard." Time, 1983c, June 6, 77.

Times-Mirror. "Summary of Results from GATEWAY Test." Los Angeles: Times-Mirror News Release, 1983.

Toffler, A. The Third Wave. New York: Bantam Books, 1981.

Towers, W. "Newspaper Research and a Simplified Approach to some Uses-and-Gratifications Statements." Paper presented to the Speech Communication Association Annual Convention, Mass Communication Division, Louisville, KY, November 1982.

Treu, S. "Uniformity in User-Computer Interaction Languages: A Compromise Solution." International Journal of Man-Machine Studies, 1982, 16, 183-210.

Tucker, J.H. "Implementing Office Automation: Principles and an Electronic Mail Sample," in Limb, J. (ed.). SIGOA Conference on Office Information Systems, 1982, 93-100.

Turoff, M. and Hiltz, S.R. "The Electronic Journal: A Progress Report." Journal of the American Society for Information Science, 1982a, 33, 4, 195-202.

Turoff, M. and Hiltz, S.R. "Author's Reply." Journal of the American Society for Information Science, 1982b, 33, 5, 298.

Tushman, M. Organizational Change: An Exploratory Study and Case History. Ithaca, NY: Cornell University, 1974.

Tushman, M. "Work Characteristics and Subunit Communication Structure: A Contingency Analysis." Administrative Science Quarterly, 1979, 24, 82-97.

Tuttle, H. "Bringing Your Productivity Improvement Efforts into Focus." Productivity, 1982, 89, 2, 68-75.

Tversky, A. and Kahneman, D. "Judgment Under Uncertainty: Heuristics and Biases." Science, 1974, 185, 1124-1131.

Tydeman, J.; Lipinski, H.; Adler, R.; Nyhan, M. and Zwimpfer, L. Teletext and Videotex in the United States. New York: McGraw-Hill, 1982.

Tydeman, J.; Lipinski, H. and Spang, S. "An Interactive Computer-Based Approach to Aid Group Problem Formulation." Technological Forecasting and Social Change, 1980, 16, 311-320.

Tyler, M. "Videotext, Prestel and Teletext: The Economics and Politics of Some Electronic Publishing Media." Telecommunications Policy, 1979, 3, 1, 37-51.

Tyler, M. "Telecommunications and Productivity: The Need and the Opportunity," in Moss, M. (ed.) Telecommunications and Productivity. Reading, MA: Addison-Wesley, 1981.

Tyler, M.; Katsoulis, M. and Cook, A. "Telecommunications and Energy Policy." Telecommunications Policy 1976, 1, 21-32.

Uhlig, R.; Farber, D. and Bair, J. The Office of the Future: Communications and Computers. New York: North-Holland, 1979.

Utterback, J. "Innovation in Industry and the Diffusion of Technology." Science, 1974, 183, 620-626.

Vallee, J.; Johansen, R.; Randolph, R. and Hastings, A. Group Communication Through Computers, Vol. 2: A Study of Social Effects. Menlo Park, CA: Institute for the Future, 1974.

Vallee, J.; Johansen, R.; Randolph, R. and Hastings, A. Group Communication Through Computers, Vols. 4 and 5. Menlo Park, CA: Institute for the Future, 1978.

Van de Ven, A.; Delbecq, A. and Koenig, R. "Determinants of Coordination Modes Within Organizations." American Sociological Review, 1976, 41, 332-338.

Van de Ven, A. and Ferry, D. Measuring and Assessing Organizations. New York: Wiley, 1980.

Veith, R. Talk-Back TV: Two-Way Cable Television. Blue Ridge Summit, PA: Tab Books, 1976.

Volard, S. and Davies, M. "Communication Patterns of Managers." Journal of Business Communication, 1982, 19, 1, 41-54.

Wade, S. Discussant to the Theory and Methodology Division's Special Session on Uses and Gratifications Research. Association for education in Journalism Annual Convention, East Lansing, MI, August 1981.

Wade, S. and Schramm, W. "The Mass Media as Sources of Public Affairs Science and Health Knowledge." Public Opinion Quarterly, 1969, 33, 197-209.

Walker, C. and Guest R. The Man on The Assembly Line. Cambridge, MA: Harvard University Press, 1952.

Wall Street Journal. "Many Schools Buying Computers Find Problems Using Them." Wall Street Journal, 1983, April 7.

Wartella, E. "Children and Television: The Development of a Child's Understanding of the Medium," in Wilhoit, G. and deBock, H. (eds.) Mass Communication Review Yearbook, Vol. 1. Beverly Hills, CA: Sage, 1980.

Waters, R. "Telefacsimile: An Effective Document Transfer Tool?" The Serials Librarian, 1979, 4, 2, 215-218.

Watson, B. (trans.) Chuang Tzu: Basic Writings. New York: Columbia University Press, 1964.

Webb, E.; Campbell, D.; Schwartz, R.; Sechrest, L. and Grove, J. Nonreactive Research in the Social Sciences. Boston: Houghton-Mifflin, 1981.

Webster, F. and Robins, K. "Mass Communications and Information Technology." The Socialist Register, 1979, 285-316.

Weeks, G. and Chapanis, A. "Cooperative Versus Conflictive Problem-Solving in Three Telecommunication Modes." Perceptual and Motor Skills, 1976, 42, 879-917.

Weick, K. The Social Psychology of Organizing. Reading, MA: Addison-Wesley, 1969.

Weick, K. "Organization and Design: Organizations as Self-Designing Systems." Organizational Dynamics, 1977, Autumn, 31-46.

Weinberg, B. "The Kurzweil Machine: Half a Miracle." American Libraries, 1980, 11, 10, 603-604, 627.

Weiss, R. and Jacobson, E. "A Method for the Analysis of the Structure of Complex Organizations," in Moreno, J. (ed.) The Sociometry Reader. Glencoe, IL: Free Press, 1960, 522-533.

Weizenbaum, J. Computer Power and Human Reason: From Judgment to Calculation. San Francisco: Freeman, 1976.

Werner, D. A Study of the Information-Seeking Behavior of Research Scientists. Unpublished master's thesis, Northwestern University, 1965.

Wessel, M. Freedom's Edge: The Computer Threat to Society. Reading, MA: Addison-Wesley, 1976.

Westrum, R. Communication Systems and Social Change. Unpublished Ph.D. dissertation, University of Chicago, 1972.

Whalen, T. "Office Technology and Socio-Economic Change: 1870-1955." Atlanta, GA: Georgia State University Decision Sciences Lab, 1983.

Whisler, T. The Impact of Computers on Organizations. New York: Praeger, 1970.

Whittaker, R. and Levin, S. Niche Theory and Application. Stroudsberg, PA: Dawden, Hutchinson and Ross, 1975.

Wicklein, J. Electronic Nightmare: The New Communications and Freedom. New York: Viking, 1981.

Wiener, N. Cybernetics, 2nd edition. New York: MIT Press and Wiley, 1961.

Wigand, R. "The Direct Satellite Connection: Definitions and Prospects." Journal of Communication, 1980, 30, 2, 140-146.

Wigand, R. "Direct Satellite Broadcasting: Selected Social Implications," in Burgoon, M. (ed.) Communication Yearbook 6. Beverly Hills, CA: Sage, 1982, 250-288.

Wiio, O. "Information Society and Communication Research." Paper presented at the Nordic Conference on Mass Communication Research, Reykjavik, Iceland, 1981.

Wiio, O.; Goldhaber, G. and Yates, M. "Organizational Communication Research: Time for Reflection?" in Nimmo, D. (ed.) Communication Yearbook 4. New Brunswick, NJ: Transaction Books, 1980, 83-97.

Wilkens, H. and Plenge, G. "Teleconference Design: A Technological Approach to Satisfaction." Telecommunications Policy, 1981, September, 216-227.

Willard, D. and Strodtbeck, F. "Latency of Verbal Response and Participation in Small Groups." Sociometry, 1972, 35, 1, 161-175.

Williams, D.; Paul, J. and Ogilvie, J. "Mass Media, Learning and Retention." Canadian Journal of Psychology, 1957, 11, 157-163.

Williams, E. "Medium or Message: Communications Medium as a Determinant of Interpersonal Evaluation." Sociometry, 1975, 38, 1, 119-130.

Williams, E. "Teleconferencing: Social and Psychological Factors." Journal of Communication, 1978, 28, 125-131.

Williams, F. The Communications Revolution. Beverly Hills, CA: Sage, 1982. (Revised version; New York: New American Library, 1983).

Williams, F.; LaRose, R. and Frost, F. Children, Television and Sex-Role Stereotyping. New York: Praeger, 1981.

Williams, F.; Phillips, A. and Lum, P. Some Extensions of Uses and Gratifications Research. Los Angeles: University of Southern California, Annenberg School of Communications, 1982.

Williams, F. and Rice, R.E. "Communication Research and the New Media Technologies," in Bostrom, R. (ed.) Communication Yearbook 7. Beverly Hills, CA: Sage, 1983, 200-224.

Williams, F.; Rice, R.E. and Dordick, H. "Behavioral Loci of the Information Society," in Ruben, B. (ed.) Information and Behavior, Vol. 1. New Brunswick, NJ: Transaction Books, 1984.

Williams, F. and Williams, V. Microcomputers in Elementary Education. Belmont, CA: Wadsworth, 1984.

Williams, L. and Lodahl, T. "Comparing WP and Computers." Journal of Systems Management, 1978, February, 9-11.

Williams, M.E.; Lannom, L. and Robins, C.G. Computer-Readable Databases: A Directory and Data Sourcebook. White Plains, NY: Knowledge Industry Publications, Inc., 1982.

Wilson, J. "Innovation: Notes Toward a Theory," in J. Thompson (ed.) Approaches to Organizational Design. Pittsburgh, PA: University of Pittsburgh Press, 1966.

Winner, L. Autonomous Technology. Cambridge, MA: MIT Press, 1977.

Woelfel, J. and Fink, E. The Measurement of Communication Processes. New York: Academic Press, 1980.

Wofford, J.; Gerloff, E. and Cummins, R. Organizational Communications: The Keystone to Effective Management. New York: McGraw-Hill, 1977.

Woolfe, R. Videotex: The New Television-Telephone Information Services. Philadelphia: Heyden and Son, 1980.

Word Processing and Information Systems. "WP/IS Survey Indicates Growth, Greater Systems Integration." Word Processing and Information Systems, 1981, 8, 1, 25-30.

Wright, P. "The Harrassed Decision-Maker: Time Pressures, Distractions, and the Use of Evidence." Journal of Applied Psychology, 1974, 59, 555-561.

Wynn, E. Office Conversation as an Information Medium. Unpublished PhD. dissertation. University of California, 1979.

Yankelovich, Skelly and White, Inc. The Yankelovich Monitor. New York: Yankelovich, Skelly and White, Inc., 1979, June, p. 19.

Yates, J. "From Press Book and Pigeonhole to Vertical Filing: Revolution in Storage and Access Systems for Correspondence." Journal of Business Communication, 1982, 19, 3, 5-26.

Zaltman, G.; Duncan, R. and Holbeck, J. Innovations and Organizations. New York: Wiley, 1973.

Zimmerman, J. (ed.) Technological Woman: Interfacing. New York: Praeger, 1982.

Zisman, M. "Office Automation: Revolution of Evolution?" Sloan Management Review, 1978, 19, 3, 1-16.

Zuboff, S. "New Worlds of Computer-Mediated Work." Harvard Business Review, 1982, 60, 5, 142-152.

Subject Index

About the Contributors

James H. Bair (B.S., Utah State, 1965; M.A., Pennsylvania State University, 1972) was at Stanford Research Institute as a Senior Information Scientist and Leader of the Office Automation Consulting and Research Program, from 1973 to 1979. Prior to 1973, he was a Behavioral Scientist for the Air Force. His industry- and government-sponsored research interests include productivity measurement, evaluation of automated offices, implementation strategies, and impacts of office automation. He is co-author of *The Office of the Future: Communication and Computers* (North-Holland, Amsterdam, 1979), co-editor of *Emerging Office Systems* (Ablex, 1982), associate editor of *Transactions on Office Systems (ACM)*, and on the editorial board of *Behavior and Information Technology.*

Milton Chen (B.A., Harvard College, 1974; M.A., 1983 and Ph.D., 1984, Stanford University) focuses his research on the educational potential of communication technologies, especially television and microcomputers. His doctoral dissertation analyzed high school students' computer attitudes and experiences, based on a survey of five Bay Area high schools in 1983. Since 1972 he has been a researcher and consultant at the Children's Television Workshop, where he served as director of research for 3-2-1 CONTACT, a children's science series. During the spring of 1982, he was a guest lecturer at the Beijing Broadcasting Institute in the People's Republic of China. His co-authored paper with Professor William Paisley on "Children and The New Computer Technologies" received the Top Paper Award in Human Communication Technology in 1983 from the International Communication Association.

John Dimmick (Ph.D., University of Michigan, 1973) is Associate Professor in the Department of Communication and a member of the graduate faculty of the School of Journalism at The Ohio State University. His research interests include decision making in media organizations and in media audiences.

David M. Dozier (Ph.D., Stanford University, 1978) is on the faculty of the Department of Journalism at San Diego State University. He is a member of the steering committee of the Communication Technology and Policy Committee of the Association for Education in Journalism and Mass Communication. His primary research interests include diffusion of emerging communication technologies and public relations research. Dr. Dozier is a member of the editorial board of *Public Relations Research and Education.*

Mary Ellen Jacob (M.S., Library Sciences; M.S., Engineering Sciences) is currently Director of Library Planning, Online Computer Library Center in Dublin, Ohio. She is responsible for planning activities at OCLC in regard to libraries and library services. She also functions as a liaison between OCLC and a number of national programs including CONSER, the U.S. Newspaper Project, Association of Research Libraries Major Microforms Project, the Library of Congress Network Advisory Committee, and American National Standards Institute Committee Z39 for bibliographic and information services. Mrs. Jacob has worked in public, special, and academic libraries over the last twenty years. She joined OCLC in 1977 to establish the user support and marketing functions at OCLC and in 1982 became Director of Library Planning. She has participated in a variety of continuing education programs and the Columbia Executive Program in Business Administration. She is the author of numerous papers and journal articles.

Robert Johansen (B.S., 1967, Ph.D., Northwestern University) is Senior Research Fellow at the Institute for the Future (IFTF) in Menlo Park, California. His primary interests are in applied research on the integration of communication and personal computing. His work at IFTF is with both user organizations and providers of new information systems. Dr. Johansen's books include *Electronic Meetings* (with J. Vallee and K. Spangler; Addison-Wesley, 1979) and *Teleconferencing and Beyond* (McGraw-Hill, 1984).

Bonnie McDaniel Johnson (M.A., Ph.D., State University of New York) has been a faculty member in the Communication Departments of Pennsylvania State University and the University of Oklahoma. Dr. Johnson spent a year at Stanford University as a Visiting Scholar, where she administered the project on Innovation and Word Processing sponsored by the National Science Foundation reported in this book. She is currently Director of Office Automation in the Corporate Strategic Planning Division of Intel Corporation. Her books include *Communication: The Process of Organizing* (second edition, American Press, 1983) and *Getting the Job Done* (Scott Foresman, 1983).

W. David Penniman (B.S., 1960 and M.S., 1962, University of Illinois; Ph.D., Ohio State University, 1975) is currently Director of Libraries and Information Systems, Bell Laboratories. In his previous position as Vice President, Planning and Research for Online Computer Library Center, Inc., he was responsible for coordinating the planning and research functions at OCLC. He established the Research Department at OCLC in 1978 and directed it until 1980, when he became director of the Development Division. In 1977 Dr. Penniman was selected as a U.S. delegate for the International Institute for Applied Systems Analysis in

Laxenburg, Austria. Awards and honors include: Technical Person of the Year (1982), Columbus Technical Council; Columbus Area Leadership Program, selected participant 1978/1979; U.S. Scientific Representative to IIASA, 1977; Phi Eta Sigma (Scholastic Honorary); Pi Tau Sigma (Mechanical Engineering Scholastic Honorary).

Ronald E. Rice (B.A., Columbia University, 1971; M.A., 1978 and Ph.D., 1982, Stanford University) is Assistant Professor at the Annenberg School of Communications, University of Southern California. His research interests include the social impacts of telecommunications, human communication network analysis, media campaigns, and the diffusion of innovations. His dissertation on how groups communicate over time while using a computer conferencing system, won a 1982 American Society for Information Science Best Dissertation award. He has co-edited (with William Paisley) *Public Communication Campaigns* (Sage, 1981), and published in the fields of communication, telecommunications policy, and information science.

Everett M. Rogers is Professor of International Communication in the Institute for Communication Research at Stanford University. His most recent books are *Network Analysis: A New Paradigm for Communication Research* (with Larry Kincaid; Free Press, 1981); *Silicon Valley Fever: High Technology Culture* (with Judith K. Larson; Basic Books, 1984), and *Diffusion of Innovations* (Free Press, 1983). His central interests are in the social impacts of the new communication technologies, the diffusion of innovations, and communication network analysis. Dr. Rogers is a past president of the International Communication Association.

Eric W. Rothenbuhler (M.A., Ohio State University, 1982) is a member of the doctoral program in Communication Theory and Research at the Annenberg School of Communications, University of Southern California. His research interests include communication systems in social structures and the commercial production of culture.

John E. Ruchinskas (B.A., Rutgers College, 1977; M.A., 1980 and Ph.D., 1982, University of Southern California) is Associate Director of Research Development at the Annenberg School of Communications. He is co-founder and director of the Telecommunications Research Group, which has conducted design, implementation, and evaluation research on Atlantic Richfield's ARCOvision video-conferencing system over the past three years. His research interests include the design, implementation, and evaluation of telecommunication systems; information seeking; organizational communication; and communications planning. He has written numerous articles on teleconferencing, communication technology design and impacts, and is co-author, with Richard B. Byrne, of "Telecommunications and Value Systems: Policy Issues for the Information Society" (in M. Boaz, ed., *Strategies for Meeting the Information Needs of Society in the Year 2000* [Libraries Unlimited, 1982]).

Lynne L. Svenning (B.A., Emerson College, 1960; M.A., Emerson College, 1964; A.B.D., Michigan State University, 1969; M.A., University of Southern California, 1980; Ph.D., University of Southern California, 1982) is Associate Co-Director of research development for the Annenberg School of Communications at USC. She also co-directs the Telecommunications Research Group, a consulting firm specializing in the design, implementation, and evaluation of new communication and computer systems. Research interests in the diffusion of innovations, organizational and societal impacts of telecommunication and computer technologies, organizational and community communication needs assessments, and health communications are reflected in numerous conference presentations, published articles, and reports. Her publications range from *Modernization Among Peasants: The Impact of Communications* (co-authored with Everett Rogers; Holt, Rinehart and Winston, 1969) to "Teleconferencing: Making A Good Decision" (co-authored with John Ruchinskas; Interface Proceedings—McGraw-Hill, 1982).

Frederick Williams (M.A. and Ph.D., University of Southern California, 1962) is a communications professor, author, and consultant. He is on the faculty of the Annenberg School of Communications at the University of Southern California, where from 1972 to 1980 he served as the founding dean. He has written over 75 articles on various facets of human communications, as well as thirteen books. From 1978 through 1982 he served as a consultant to WED Enterprises in the design of the "Spaceship Earth" pavilion at Walt Disney World's new EPCOT Center. In 1978-1979, Dr. Williams served as president of the International Communication Association. His most recent books include *Executive Communication Power* (Prentice-Hall, 1983), *The Communications Revolution* (New American Library, 1983), *Managing The New Information Technologies* (with Herbert Dordick; Wiley, 1983); and *Kids and Computers* (with Victoria Williams; Morrow, 1983).